Art and
Psychoanalysis

Art and Psychoanalysis

LAURIE SCHNEIDER ADAMS

IconEditions

An Imprint of HarperCollinsPublishers

HarperCollins books may be purchased for educational, business, or sales promotional use. For information, please write: Special Markets Department, HarperCollins Publishers, Inc., 10 East 53rd Street, New York, NY 10022.

FIRST EDITION

Designed by Abigail Sturges

Library of Congress Cataloging-in-Publication Data

Adams, Laurie Schneider
    Art and psychoanalysis / Laurie Schneider Adams.
      p. cm.
    Includes bibliographical references and index.
    ISBN 0-06-430297-0
    1. Psychoanalysis and art. I. Title.
N72.P74A32   1993
701'.05—dc20   92-56205

93 94 95 96 97 CC/CW 10 9 8 7 6 5 4 3 2 1

Contents

List of Illustrations

1. Leonardo da Vinci, *La Gioconda (Mona Lisa)*, 1503–6. Oil on panel, 30 1/4″ × 21″. Louvre, Paris.
2. Leonardo da Vinci, *Madonna and Christ with Saint Anne*, 1501–13 (?). Panel, 66 1/2″ × 51 1/4″. Louvre, Paris. Giraudon/Art Resource, New York.
3. Leonardo da Vinci, *Saint John the Baptist*, 1506–13. Panel, 69 × 57 cm. Louvre, Paris. Photo courtesy of James Beck.
4. Leonardo da Vinci, *Madonna and Christ with Saint Anne*, 1498 (?). Charcoal with white on brown paper, c. 54″ × 39″. National Gallery, London.
5. Duane Hanson, *Artist with Ladder*, 1972. Polyester and fiberglass, life size. Photo courtesy of O. K. Harris, New York.
6. George Segal, *Chance Meeting*, 1989. Plaster, paint, aluminum post and metal sign, 123″ × 41″ × 55″. Photo courtesy of Sidney Janis Gallery, New York.
7. Pablo Picasso, *Girl Before a Mirror*, 1932. Oil on canvas, 64″ × 51 1/4″. Museum of Modern Art, New York. Gift of Mrs. Simon Guggenheim.
8. Robert Smithson, *Second Mirror Displacement*, from *Incidents of Travel in the Yucatán*, 1969. Estate of Robert Smithson. Courtesy of John Weber Gallery, New York.
9. René Magritte, *The False Mirror (Le Faux Miroir)*, 1928. Oil on canvas, 21 1/4″ × 31 7/8″. Museum of Modern Art, New York. Purchase.
10. Andrea del Castagno, *David*, c. 1450. Leather, 45 1/2″ × 30 1/4″ to 15 1/8″. National Gallery of Art, Washington, D.C. Widener Collection.
11. Michelangelo da Caravaggio, *David with the Head of Goliath*, c. 1605–10. Oil on canvas, 125 × 100 cm. Galleria Borghese, Rome. Alinari/Art Resource, New York.
12. Vincent van Gogh, *Skull with a Cigarette*, 1885–86. Oil on canvas, 32.5 × 24 cm. Stedelijk Museum, Amsterdam. Vincent van Gogh Foundation/Vincent van Gogh Museum, Amsterdam.
13. René Magritte, *The Betrayal of Images (This Is Not a Pipe)*, 1926. Oil on canvas, 23 5/8″ × 37″. Los Angeles County Museum. Purchased with funds provided by the Mr. and Mrs. William Preston Harrison Collection.
14. Lucas Furtenagel, *Portrait of Hans Burgkmair and His Wife*. Kunsthistorisches Museum, Vienna.
15. Masaccio, *The Trinity*, c. 1428. Fresco. Santa Maria Novella, Florence. Photo courtesy of James Beck.

Preface

The purpose of this book is to present an overview of the interdisciplinary potential of art and psychoanalysis, and to demonstrate that each field can enrich and enlarge the other. This is not intended to be a definitive study, but rather a series of related essays exploring some of the ways in which psychoanalytic insights elucidate creativity and its products. I survey a few of the "quarrels" between art historians and psychoanalysts over methodology and also apply psychoanalytic readings to works of art and artists from iconographic, textual, biographical, and aesthetic points of view. Clinical and other asides that are explanatory or that illustrate theoretical material are set apart from the main text and printed in italics. Unless otherwise indicated, clinical examples are taken from my own psychoanalytic practice.

My focus is historical as well as methodological and therefore emphasizes the contributions of Freud as the foundation of most psychoanalytic thinking. Readers will also note numerous references to classical antiquity and observations on the relationship between child development and creativity. This is because psychoanalysis at its best—whether as a clinical procedure or a method of cultural interpretation—highlights the relevance of past to present. Classical psychoanalysis subscribes to the principle that knowing history helps to prevent repeating the worst of it and offers the hope of a better-informed future.

Wisdom, according to Socrates, is knowing that you don't know what you don't know. Imagine how different history might have been if Oedipus had *known* that he did not know the identity of his real parents.

* * *

Friends and colleagues have contributed to this effort, and I am extremely grateful to them for their generosity. Bradley Collins and Mary Wiseman reviewed the entire manuscript with a fine-tooth comb and offered many valuable suggestions. Leo Steinberg lent his expertise to the Michelangelo chapter, and, although we do not agree on every particular, he has saved me from several egregious errors. Other parts of the manuscript were read by John Adams, Paul Barolsky, James Beck, Larissa Bonfante, Sidney Geist, Wendy Lehman, Carla Lord, Ildiko Mohacsy, Muriel Oxenberg Murphy, and Maria Grazia Pernis. I thank them all for their observations. The enthusiasm of the students in my 1990 and 1991 City University of New York seminars on art and psychoanalysis, as well as on artists' biographies and autobiographies, helped to fertilize the research for this book.

Assistance with photographs was generously provided by James Beck, Sidney Geist, Duane Hanson, Carroll Janis, George Segal, and the museums and galleries that allowed their works to be illustrated. Finally, without the support and encouragement of my editor, Cass Canfield, Jr. and his assistant Bronwen Crothers, this book would not have seen the light of day.

Art and Psychoanalysis

ONE

Beginnings

A rt history and psychoanalysis have been married and divorced several times in the past hundred years. On the face of it, these are two fields that ought to get along. Both are concerned with creativity—art history rather more with the products of creativity, psychoanalysis with its process. Both are concerned with imagery—psychoanalysis with the imagery of dreams and fantasies, art history with imagery as a material product of the artist. Finally, both fields require a historical approach—art history to chronologies of culture, documentation, and style, and psychoanalysis to the developmental history of the individual.

The first marriage of these two fields took place in the late nineteenth century, when Sigmund Freud began the work that culminated in the formulation of psychoanalysis. Even before Freud, however, nineteenth-century artists—Goya, Fuseli, and the Symbolists, for example—had depicted states of mind and dreams as internal rather than external phenomena, and Walter Pater's[1] descriptions of Renaissance art reflected a new awareness of the psychology of the artist and the personal link between artists and their work.

Also antedating psychoanalysis was archaeology. The ruins of Herculaneum had been discovered in 1738 and those of Pompeii ten years later. In 1821, Jean-François Champollion revealed the meaning of Egyptian hieroglyphs by deciphering the text of the Rosetta Stone. Heinrich Schliemann's study of Homer led to the excavation of Troy and Mycenae in the 1870s. And in the early twentieth century, Sir Arthur Evans discovered the ruins of Minoan Crete. Historical research and discovery were thus very much in the air as Freud began his exploration of the human mind

1

toward the end of the nineteenth century. He had been eminently well prepared for this endeavor by a classical education, which included a knowledge of Greek and Latin. Like Socrates, Freud devoted his life to the pursuit of self-knowledge. The command "Gnothi seauton" ("Know thyself"), inscribed in stone at the site of the Delphic oracle, became Freud's guiding principle, just as it had been that of Socrates.

In the course of the 1890s, Freud embarked on the landmark adventure of his own self-analysis,[2] which was a personal archaeological excavation. The very term "archaeology" literally means the "study of the beginning," from *archaios* (meaning "from the beginning" or "ancient"), and *logos* (meaning "word," in the sense of "knowledge" or "lore"). In returning to his childhood, Freud searched for his own beginnings and their significance. He derived the same excitement from exploring his childhood as Keats had experienced on first reading Chapman's *Homer.* In a letter of December 21, 1892, Freud wrote the following about his discoveries: "I hardly dare to believe it yet. It is as if Schliemann had again dug up Troy, which before him was a myth."[3] Later he was quoted as saying that "Only a good-for-nothing is not interested in his past."[4]

Freud's "archaeological" self-analysis laid the foundations for his subsequent work, and his knowledge of Greek and Roman mythology fortified him in these labyrinthine byways. "Mythology," he wrote in 1926,[5] "may give you the courage to believe psychoanalysis." By the process of association, Freud followed his thoughts back in time to his childhood. There he located three cornerstones of psychoanalysis: infantile sexuality, the power of the unconscious, and the Oedipus complex. Like the great humanists of the Renaissance, Freud had recourse to classical examples to illustrate and validate his ideas. He recognized the expression of the Oedipus complex in the work of Sophocles, narcissism in the myth of Narcissus, and Eros, or the life force of the libido (a Latin term), in the Greek god of love.

Freud used the process of "free association" to search through his childhood, as he instructed patients to do in his clinical work. By the same process, both Freud and his patients explored the meaning of dreams. When he unearthed the mechanisms of dreaming, he recognized the revolutionary significance of his discovery. "Insight such as this," he wrote, "falls to one's lot but once in a lifetime" (preface to the third English edition of *The Interpretation of Dreams*). In a letter to his friend Wilhelm Fliess, he suggested that a memorial plaque be installed outside his home, stating that on July 24, 1895, "The Secret of the Dream was revealed to Sigmund Freud."

FREUD'S ARCHAEOLOGICAL METAPHOR

In the following year, 1896, Freud gave a lecture entitled "The Aetiology of Hysteria,"[6] in which he introduced archaeology as a metaphor for the *process* of psychoanalysis. Like the archaeologist, the psychoanalyst begins with visible remains (such as symptoms), clears away the rubbish collected over time, and searches for buried material. "Saxa loquuntur!" ("The rocks speak!"), Freud declared, meaning that physical ruins are the archaeologist's primary sources. Just as the archaeologist tries to reconstruct (or read) ancient civilizations from architectural ruins, sculptural remains, traces of mural paintings, pottery shards, and other artifacts, so the psychoanalyst reconstructs the patient's buried childhood history from phenomena such as dreams, jokes, memories, symptoms, fantasies, mistakes, slips of the tongue (parapraxes), and so forth.

In 1900, Freud[7] took daydreams as artifacts of the mind and compared their wish-fulfilling function to architectural revision. Just as Renaissance and Baroque architecture assimilate elements of ancient Greek and Roman buildings, he wrote, so the daydream assimilates elements of childhood and creates a wish-fulfilling narrative. Extending the architectural metaphor even further, Freud called the daydream the "facade of the dream."[8]

Freud conceived of personal history not only in terms of archaeological layers, but also in terms of individual artifacts. Nevertheless, he drew two important distinctions between archaeology and psychoanalysis. First, for the archaeologist, reconstruction is the end result of the search, whereas for the psychoanalyst it is preliminary. And second, the analysand, in contrast to the buried civilization, is alive and working with memories, free association, dreams, and other means of access to the unconscious.

Freud's archaeological metaphor recurs in his writings from 1896 on. Its relevance to psychoanalysis and the influence it exerted on Freud was continuous.

RECONSTRUCTION AND THE HISTORY OF ART

The art historian, like the archaeologist, faces a task of reconstruction. He may not always have to deal with a buried civilization, but any examination of the past, even the most recent past, requires historical reconstruction. Whether creating a catalogue raisonné of an artist's work, making an attribution, or sequencing style, the art historian is engaged in a process of reconstruction. In contrast to other historians, art historians deal primarily with images. The archaeologist's task is facilitated by knowing how to read the language of a buried culture, and the art historian benefits from being able to "read" images.

In addition to the traditional formal and iconographic readings of the visual arts, psychoanalysis offers the potential for dynamic readings. The term "dynamic" in psychoanalysis refers to the determination of human psychology by conflicting forces—instinctual unconscious drives and wishes in conflict with reality; ego, id, and superego in conflict with one another; sadism in conflict with masochism; and so forth. In contrast to the dynamic view, the traditional reading of history tends to interpret human behavior in a literal, static manner. By taking into account the dynamics of internal conflict, psychoanalysis can make connections between an artist's life and work, revealing meanings in both that might not otherwise be apparent.

There are different approaches to imagery among art historians, and there is no single, definitive psychoanalytic approach. Each analyst writing about art brings to bear on the subject a particular training, experience, intellectual bias, and aesthetic response. Because good works of art synthesize numerous sources, they are sturdier than any one bias and outlast the critical quarrels of history.

ART AND PSYCHOANALYSIS

Of the categories of psychoanalytic thinking that have been applied to the visual arts since the late nineteenth and early twentieth centuries, four can be readily identified. They are symbolism, sublimation, creativity, and biography and autobiography.

Symbolism

From the beginning, symbolism has played a prominent role in psychoanalysis. Whether in symptom formation, dreams, myths, folklore, or religion, Freud recognized the importance of symbolization as a mental operation. Reading symbols is also an essential aspect of interpretation in the arts. The term "symbol" derives from the Greek word *sumbolon*, which, in antiquity, designated a coin, medal, or other object that could be broken in half and fitted back together for purposes of identification. In other words, the two parts "added up" to a whole that identified someone or something, and came to mean a "token" or "symbol" in their present sense.

Freud proposed that symbols are related to what is symbolized by analogical criteria such as shape, size, or usage; small animals can symbolize children, long thin objects a phallus, and windows and doors the orifices of the body. Both Freud and his English follower Ernest Jones[9] insisted that, although there is an enormous number of symbols, the objects or ideas symbolized are limited in number. Psychoanalytic symbols are restricted to the body and its functions (particularly the sexual ones), family members, birth, and death. Because of these limitations, symbolic interpretations of artistic imagery are often criticized for "reducing" the many and varied to the few, or for "reducing" the creative artist to the status of an ordinary mortal.

An important subsequent contribution to the theory of symbolization came from D. W. Winnicott,[10] a leading member of the English Object Relations school of psychoanalysis (see Chapter 7). Winnicott identified the so-called transitional object as the infant's first symbol. Whether a teddy bear or a piece of cloth, the transitional object is selected by the child before he reaches one year of age; it permits the child to separate from the mother, especially before going to sleep, and creates a transitional, symbolic space. The transitional object constitutes the child's first created symbol, which, according to Winnicott, forms the basis for adult creativity.

The French analyst Jacques Lacan[11] addressed symbolism in the context of linguistics. Lacan worked in the tradition of Ferdinand de Saussure, the French linguist who objected to the notion of a "linguistic symbol." For Saussure,[12] the word (or "linguistic signifier") was not naturally related to the object or idea it "signified"; a psychoanalytic symbol, on the other hand, *is* related in some articulable way to what it symbolizes. The linguistic model is clearly in contrast to the original Greek derivation of "symbol" as one half of the split "token." Instead, according to Saussure, signifier and signified are related by virtue of structural, linguistic requirements rather than by analogy.

Lacan tried to integrate the structural-linguistic approach to symbolism with psychoanalysis, claiming that the unconscious is structured like a language. He envisioned the structure of language as contained within a symbolic order, whose laws are those of a "symbolic father." He called this symbolic lawgiver "the Name of the Father," which may be considered a linguistic equivalent of the superego. In French, "le Nom du Père" sounds like "le Non du Père" (the "No of the Father"), the latter being the verbal

expression of the father's function as a disciplinarian and psychic structural-
ist. Such punning has its own artistic quality and is well within the tradition
of Duchamp, Dada, and the French taste for wordplay.

Lacan's work on the symbolic power of the gaze has also entered the
literature on art and psychoanalysis. He related the gaze to desire and to
the complex, often contradictory, functions of the eye. Power, evil, benevo-
lence, envy, and love are among the motivating forces of the gaze (that is,
the psychological impact of the eye). The visual operation of these forces
has been related to painting in several ways. They can operate within the
iconographic or narrative content of a picture, between picture and artist,
and between picture and observer.

Sublimation

Sublimation, a term first proposed by Freud, is the process that facilitates
creative and intellectual activity. Although creativity and intellect appear
to be distinct from sexuality, they are nonetheless thought to be fueled by
libidinal energy. According to classical psychoanalytic drive theory, a
sublimated instinct is one that is redirected away from its sexual aim and
object on to a "higher" cultural level, such as art, science, sports, and other
socially valued pursuits. The sublimatory activity is thus a transformation
of an instinctual activity. For example, the baby's instinct to play with feces
might be sublimated into making mud pies, molding clay, kneading dough,
finger-painting, and eventually creating art.

From 1914, Freud[13] modified his view of sublimation to take into
account the role of the ego. In the ego, the libido is desexualized, integrated, and only then redirected into cultural endeavors. This attachment
of sublimated energy to the ego is consistent with the ego's narcissism. In
the context of the structural theory, formulated in 1923,[14] Freud's description of the ego includes its synthetic, or integrative, function. The ego's job
is to mediate between the instinctual wishes of the id (for example, playing
with feces) and the demands of reality (for example, society's admiration
for works of art). In this function, the ego is the unifying life force of libido
and the ego's narcissism can be seen as "reflected" in the creative product.
The particular shape that such a "reflection" takes is the work of art and
depends on a confluence of factors, most notably on the expressive talents
of the artist.

The concept of sublimation is one of the most elusive in classical
psychoanalysis. Although Freud discussed sublimation throughout his

writings, he did not arrive at a satisfactory theoretical formulation of it. Most of his focus on sublimation involved the role of the libido (Eros); but he also considered that the aggressive, or death, instinct could undergo sublimation.

Creativity

Sublimation may be thought of as a necessary route to creativity, to which it is closely related but not identical. In this book, the focus is mainly on creativity in the visual arts, whereas Freud's earliest studies of the subject dealt with writers. In 1908,[15] Freud related the child at play to the creative writer. Both, according to Freud, create a fantasy world that they take seriously and invest with a great deal of emotion. Freud compares the daydream to a "castle in the air," or fantasy narrative whose purpose is to gratify a wish; the wish is gratified by the story line of the fantasy which "corrects" a piece of reality. Daydreams are set in motion when a memory trace from childhood attaches itself to an unsatisfactory present-day situation. The wish-fulfilling aspect of the daydream belongs to the future and is usually erotic and/or ambitious in nature.

This temporal condensation of the daydream is made explicit by the comparison with pictorial juxtaposition. Freud wrote that "Just as, in many altar-pieces, the portrait of the donor is to be seen in a corner of the picture, so, in the majority of ambitious phantasies, we can discover in some corner or other the lady for whom the creator of the phantasy performs all his heroic deeds and at whose feet all his triumphs are laid."[16] This passage highlights the pictorial character of both the fantasy and the painted image; the latter juxtaposes past (the Christian event depicted), present (the donor), and future (the donor's wish for salvation), just as the daydream does.

Creative writing, in Freud's view, is "like a day-dream." It is "a continuation of, and a substitute for, what was once the play of childhood."[17] The author turns the fantasy into a written narrative that satisfies both his own narcissism and the reader's pleasure. He creates a central hero who, like the hero of the daydream, "reflects" the author's narcissism.

In the briefest way, Freud related the mechanisms of creative writing and daydreaming to the development of myth. All three phenomena derive from an early period, whether childhood or an early historical era, and fulfill wishes. All therefore combine different periods of time and are motivated by an unsatisfactory reality. Whereas a single daydream or creative work is the product of an individual, myths are projections of entire cultures and therefore operate on a grander scale. Myths, according to Freud, are "the secular dreams of a youthful humanity."[18]

So far Freud had addressed the dynamics and content of the creative product that derive mainly from unconscious and conscious wishes. The ego transforms such wishes into the product by taking account of the reality demands of technique, material, and audience response. This aspect of creativity is less completely formulated by Freud than its dynamic and narrative content, although he notes that the writer alters the daydream through the medium of a formal, or aesthetic, framework. The creative writer, in effect, "sublimates" his wish by transforming libido into aesthetic form.

In his studies of Leonardo da Vinci (Chapter 2) and Michelangelo's *Moses* (Chapter 6), Freud turned to the visual arts. Nevertheless, despite his attention to the formal necessities of creativity, he did not consider them analyzable. In 1928, he declared that "Before the problem of the creative artist analysis must, alas, lay down its arms."[19] It was left to later psychoanalytic writers to refine further the description of the creative process, particularly the transition from id impulse to aesthetic form.

In 1950, Daniel E. Schneider[20] discussed creativity in terms of psychic economy. In his view, ego mastery is necessary as the "transformer" of the endless source material in the unconscious. The artist must thus be in continual contact with his unconscious. Dreams are a special source of unconscious material; a work of art, according to Schneider, may be considered as a kind of "dream turned inside out." By that he means that the analysis of a dream is the reverse of creating art; when a dream is analyzed, its hidden structure is opened up and *de*constructed, whereas a work of art assembles or *con*structs the creative material.

Ernst Kris,[21] an art historian as well as a psychoanalyst, described the creative process as "regression in the service of the ego" in 1952. In other words, the artist must be able to "regress" to early instinctual impulses in such a way that they are controlled and formed by the ego. This controlled regression is somewhat akin to the technique of method actors, who call on experiences from their own past as source material for emotions required by a particular role. In 1957, Phyllis Greenacre[22] referred to this process as "access to childhood." All such descriptions of creativity assume the artist's internal psychic flexibility, which permits identification with, and portrayal of, a wide range of characters and themes. The emphasis on "regression" and childhood "access" derives from the relatively flexible psychic structures and identifications of children as compared with adults.

Even more elusive than the creative, or sublimatory, process is aesthetic form. In clinical practice, aesthetics is extremely difficult, if not impossible, to analyze. And yet one's aesthetic response is definitely influenced by psychological factors. Among the analysts who have addressed the issue of aesthetics and creativity, readers are referred to Anton Ehrenzweig,[23] Pinchas Noy,[24] William G. Niederland,[25] and Gilbert Rose.[26]

With some variation, most analytic writers on creativity view aesthetic form as the solution to, or reconciliation of, internal impulses or states of being in opposition to requirements of the outside world. By virtue of its aesthetic quality, the work of art permits conscious pleasure in forbidden wishes and impulses that reside in the unconscious. For example, a young child may express anger at a mother by drawing a witch with long fingernails or at a father by drawing an ogre. Puns and jokes permit the release of hostility by translating it into a humorous form (for example, the frequency of mother-in-law jokes). Similarly, the oedipal crimes of incest and parricide become art in the plays of Sophocles and Shakespeare.

Psychobiography of the Artist

Freud's 1910 study of Leonardo (Chapter 2) was the first psychobiographical study of an artist. As a genre, psychobiography borrows from the clinical case study, differing from traditional biography in its emphasis on certain kinds of data. As in clinical psychoanalysis, the psychobiographer pays close attention to dreams, memories, symptoms, and behavior patterns. Such material is analyzed, in addition to being presented and described. In order to effect such an analysis, the writer needs some psychodynamic insight, and ideally some training in psychoanalysis. The psychobiographer relates the subject's biography to aspects of his work and reasons from the work to an analysis of the subject.

Since the publication of Freud's *Leonardo,* many psychobiographies of artists have appeared, with those of van Gogh being by far the most numerous. Artists' letters, journals, autobiographies, and casual statements given in interviews have been psychoanalyzed. The ideal psychobiography of an artist combines the available literary documentation with visual evidence. Biographers of artists, following Freud's lead, have begun to call on childhood events, memories, and dreams, to understand not only the course of the subject's life, but also the form and content of his or her work. As interest in the contemporary artist as a psychobiographical subject increases, a new technique for gathering information has developed—namely, the "interview." If the artist is recently deceased and his contemporaries are still alive, the researcher can interview those who knew him; such has been the case with Picasso. When the artist is still living, however, interviewers have access to the proverbial horse's mouth, which raises new issues.

If the interview is recorded and the interpretation left up to the reader, then the potential for controversy is kept to a minimum. But if a psychological reading, beyond the literal value of the artist's statements, is attempted, potential problems arise. First, it becomes necessary to consider the status of a statement knowingly made for publication. What image, for example, does the artist wish to project? Is he or she trying to cover up something? Does a financial, philosophical, or psychological motive in making a particular statement render that statement self-serving? Is the artist's hidden agenda conscious or unconscious? Is there a hidden agenda at all? Second, the analytic interpreter may be constrained by the laws of libel from printing what he or she really believes.

Other psychobiographical approaches to art history focus on iconography and cultural context. Iconographic choices can be determined by convention or the wishes of a patron, while the cultural context of a work of art influences its style and content. We would assume, for example, that a picture created in 1650 in Holland would be in the Baroque style. We would expect a work commissioned by a medieval church to depict a Christian subject. We would not be surprised if a ruler commissioned his own portrait, nor if the artist idealized the subject and emphasized the ruler's political power. But no matter how rigorous the convention or how demanding the patron, the artist also makes choices. When it is possible to isolate the various iconographic sources of a work of art, one necessarily learns something of the artist's character and talent by distinguishing between what in the work was dictated by convention and patronage and what was chosen by the artist.

Even within the boundaries of convention and style, the artist can make significant choices. But the range of these choices is affected by their time and place. An Early Christian, Byzantine, Romanesque, or Gothic artist would have had a more limited range than a Renaissance or Baroque artist. The cultural factors accounting for this differentiation are many and varied. In the Renaissance, the increased range of patronage, as well as an educational system that encouraged classical studies and a renewed sense of history, contributed to the artistic expansion of that period. Likewise, industrial development in the nineteenth century inspired an entirely new iconography of factories, machinery, and urban tension, as well as peaceful landscapes providing an escape from urban pressures into leisure and relaxation. In the late nineteenth and twentieth centuries the development of psychoanalysis is reflected in artistic styles such as Surrealism and Abstract Expressionism. But, while the insights of psychoanalysis have consciously informed the arts of the past hundred years, the validity of the psychoanalytic method of art criticism extends to ancient as well as to recent history.

The application of psychoanalysis to works of art and culture that historically precede the development of psychoanalysis itself has been a controversial issue. One aspect of the controversy revolves around the nature and readability of evidence. Art historians have traditionally preferred dealing with written documents such as contracts, archival records, and other contemporary texts that can reasonably be related to the artist or work being studied. While a reliable psychoanalytic researcher would have to take such documentary evidence into account, he would also give serious attention to other types of data—for example, dreams and memories. He would still, however, be relying on the *report* of a dream or memory, most likely to have been recorded in written form. The main documentary source is the work of art itself, which, in the case of the visual arts, is an image or a building, rather than a written text.

Biographical significance adds another dimension to the iconography of a work. Whether one reasons from the work to the artist or vice versa, both imagery and documentation are read by the psychoanalytic critic in a way that takes into account the psychology of the artist. The difficulty of this task is increased by the very transformation that the artist makes from the original impulse and the unconscious source material to the final aesthetic product. One must "see through" all the conscious layers of reworking, including convention, style, context, and often the requirements of a patron. In order to do so, one must "read" psychologically, which, like the interpretation of an interview, depends on the reader's ability and insight.

In the final analysis, one important principle emerges from the introduction of the psychoanalytic method into art history: the traditional notion of documentation has been enlarged.

In this book, I begin with the foundations of art and psychoanalysis as established by Freud. Chapters 2 and 6 consider Freud's two major studies of art, *Leonardo* (Chapter 2) and Michelangelo's *Moses* (Chapter 6), and some of the most significant responses to them. Chapters 3 through 5 attempt to relate works of art to the general nature of imagery (Chapter 3), the Oedipus complex (Chapter 4), and the dynamics of dreaming (Chapter 5).

The second half of the book deals with different methods of reading art from a psychoanalytic perspective. In Chapter 7, Winnicott's transitional object is discussed in relation to creativity and symbolization. Chapter 8 considers the mother-child relationship in Western art in the light of Freud and later psychoanalysts; it concludes with a discussion of the gaze as formulated by Lacan. In Chapter 9, the work of art is read as a text independently of the artist's biography; the example taken is the primal scene, which contains implications for the gaze as well as for classical psychoanalysis. Chapters 10 and 11 review different approaches to psychobiography. Chapter 12 analyzes the libel trial between Whistler and Ruskin as an example of the psychological meaning of aesthetic response.

To date, most psychoanalytic studies of art have focused on the twentieth century. One rationale for this has been the notion that the Oedipus complex cannot be documented earlier, as Freud had not yet formulated it. That, of course, reflects the static view of history, for if the psychoanalytic method is valid, it must apply to all periods of human history. Partly for that reason, and partly because of my own areas of specialization, I have, in addition to some twentieth-century material, concentrated on earlier periods of Western history.

NOTES

1. Walter Pater, *The Renaissance*, Berkeley and Los Angeles, 1980.
2. Cf. Didier Anzieu, *Freud's Self-Analysis*, Madison, Conn., 1986.
3. Suzanne Cassirer Bernfeld, "Freud and Archeology," *American Imago* 8 (1951): 111.
4. Ibid.
5. Freud, "The Question of Lay Analysis," S. E. XX, 1926, p. 211. Here and elsewhere, S. E. refers to *The Complete Psychological Works of Sigmund Freud* (24 vols.), London, 1953–73.
6. Freud, "The Aetiology of Hysteria," S. E. III, 1896, pp. 191–221.
7. Freud, *The Interpretation of Dreams*, S. E. V, 1900, p. 492.
8. Ibid., p. 493.
9. Ernest Jones, "The Theory of Symbolism," in his *Papers on Psychoanalysis*, London, 1950.
10. D. W. Winnicott, "Transitional Objects and Transitional Phenomena," in his *Playing and Reality*, New York, 1971.

11. Jacques Lacan, *Ecrits*, Paris, 1949; *Speech and Language in Psychoanalysis*, Baltimore, 1968; and *The Four Fundamental Concepts of Psychoanalysis*, New York, 1978.
12. Ferdinand de Saussure, *Course in General Linguistics*, trans. Wade Baskin, New York, 1966.
13. Freud, "On Narcissism: An Introduction," S. E. XIV, 1914, pp. 67–102.
14. Freud, *The Ego and the Id*, S. E. XIX, 1923, pp. 12–66.
15. Freud, "Creative Writers and Day-Dreaming," S. E. IX, 1908, pp. 141–53.
16. Ibid., p. 147.
17. Ibid., p. 152.
18. Ibid.
19. Freud, "Dostoevsky and Parricide," S. E. XXI, 1928, p. 177.
20. Daniel E. Schneider, *The Psychoanalyst and the Artist*, New York, 1950.
21. Ernst Kris, *Psychoanalytic Explorations in Art*, New York, 1952.
22. Phyllis Greenacre, "The Childhood of the Artist" (1957), in her *Emotional Growth*, vol. 2, New York, 1971, pp. 505–32; and "The Family Romance of the Artist" (1958), ibid., pp. 479–504.
23. Anton Ehrenzweig, *The Hidden Order of Art*, Berkeley and Los Angeles, 1967.
24. Pinchas Noy, "A Theory of Art and Aesthetic Experience," *Psychoanalytic Review* 55 (1968): 623–45, and "About Art and Artistic Talent," *International Journal of Psychoanalysis* 53 (1972): 243–48.
25. William G. Niederland, "Clinical Aspects of Creativity," *American Imago* 24 (1967): 6–34, and "Psychoanalytic Approaches to Artistic Creativity," *Psychoanalytic Quarterly* 45 (1976): 185–212.
26. Gilbert Rose, *The Power of Form*, New York, 1980.

TWO

Freud's Leonardo: The Controversy

F reud's psychobiographical study of Leonardo da Vinci was published in 1910,[1] and reflects the development of psychoanalysis up to that point. This includes the discovery of the Oedipus complex (although not its final formulation); infantile sexuality with the oral, anal, and phallic developmental stages; and the nature of dreams and childhood memories. The point of departure for Freud's *Leonardo* was the artist's recorded memory of a bird alighting on his crib and beating its tail feathers against the inside of his mouth. Taking this account as a psychic artifact, Freud proceeded to reconstruct Leonardo's childhood.

Responses to Freud's reconstruction have generated a remarkable amount of controversy, some of which rages still. Like the citizens of a small town taking sides in a bitter divorce case, art historians and psychoanalysts have reacted strongly either for or against Freud. Even today, the position of Freud's *Leonardo* in the art-historical and psychoanalytic literature is ambiguous. Part of Freud's study has been discovered to be invalid; some was invalid from the start. But it introduced a revolutionary, dynamic way of thinking about art and artists that has changed the course of intellectual history.

FREUD'S LEONARDO

Freud's motivation for writing *Leonardo*, his only full-length biography of a creative artist, can be traced to a confluence of factors.[2] In 1909, Freud wrote to Jung about a patient whose character was similar to Leonardo's, but who lacked the artist's genius. Freud had been reading about Leonardo and, in 1907, he listed *The Romance of Leonardo da Vinci* by the Russian writer Dimitri Merejkowski[3] as one of his favorite books. Freud's general interest in psychobiography appears in comments made during the December 11, 1907, meeting of the Vienna Psychoanalytical Society,[4] when he listed the propositions on which psychobiographies of poets and artists are based. These included the assumption of connections between the poet or artist and his creation. In reworking autobiography into art, according to Freud, artists reorder their material along thematic, rather than chronological, lines. This view of the creative process conforms to the absence of time in the unconscious.

Freud also endorsed the comments of Max Graf (1875–1958), a writer and musicologist, who recommended analyzing the greatest artists first, because their high level of productivity reveals their basic mental health. Pathology, Graf asserted, inhibits or destroys creativity. A good study of the artist must therefore focus on the creative process; "the ultimate goal of the analyses of artists," Graf said, "is finally to reach a 'theory of artistic creation.'"[5] Interestingly, Freud has been repeatedly accused of writing pathography (a formulation of creative productions in terms of neurosis), even though he made a special point of cautioning against such a practice. He said, "Every poet who shows abnormal tendencies can be the object of a pathography. But the pathography cannot show anything new. Psychoanalysis, on the other hand, provides information about the creative process. Psychoanalysis deserves to rank above pathography."[6]

Freud divided his psychobiography of Leonardo da Vinci into six sections. Part I reviews the evidence of Leonardo's personality and working methods culled from the artist's extensive notebook entries, his drawings and paintings, and from Vasari's sixteenth-century biography. Having studied these sources, Freud focused on details that highlight Leonardo's enigmatic character. A summary of Freud's account follows.

Born in 1452 in the little village of Vinci outside Florence, Leonardo was the illegitimate son of a notary, Ser Piero, and a peasant girl, Caterina. Leonardo lived with Caterina for approximately five years before entering the house of his father, who had in the meantime married Donna Albiera. Later—at what age is not known—Leonardo was apprenticed to Andrea del Verrocchio, a leading Florentine artist.

The enigma of Leonardo is partly a function of his contradictory nature. He combined the talents of a natural scientist and engineer with artistic genius; but his artistic creativity was inhibited by compulsive investigation. His attention to science—dissecting corpses, designing machines, researching nature, pursuing alchemy, and so forth—took time away from art. His obsessive slowness was proverbial; he left some works unfinished and spent years on others. On this point, Vasari and Freud agree. Vasari says that on receiving a commission, Leonardo prepared his varnish (which is applied when a painting is finished) before beginning the work. At this, according to Vasari, Pope Leo X exclaimed, "Alas! this man will never do anything, for he begins by thinking of the end of the work, before the beginning."[7]

Leonardo was handsome, charming, and kind. He was a vegetarian, opposed to killing animals for their meat, and was in the habit of freeing caged birds purchased in the marketplace. Despite his kindness, however, Leonardo accompanied condemned criminals to the scaffold to study and draw their reactions to their impending executions. His own reaction was apparently aloof and indifferent. Although opposing war, Leonardo worked as Cesare Borgia's military engineer and designed offensive weapons of an unusually sadistic kind. The fact that those weapons were used against his fellow Florentines does not seem to have concerned him in the least.

Freud turns to Leonardo's sexual life as a means of understanding his mental life. His conclusion that Leonardo became a homosexual was reinforced by several documented facts, notably that Leonardo was charged with, and acquitted of, sodomy while apprenticed to Verrocchio. As a master himself, Leonardo engaged attractive rather than talented students. In contrast to Michelangelo, who had an intimate intellectual friendship with Vittoria Colonna (see Chapter 6), Leonardo had no meaningful adult relationships with women.

Freud explains Leonardo's psychology in terms of classical drive theory as follows. His instinct for loving was transformed first into insatiable research, which later substituted for creating art. What had begun, in Leonardo's case, as investigation in the service of art took over and became the master. Freud's discovery of infantile sexuality[8] led him to connect adult research with childhood sexual curiosity. In Leonardo's case, Freud concludes, the artist renounced passion and emotion by redirecting affective energy into intellectual investigation.

The Fate of Infantile Sexuality

In human development, childhood sexual investigation undergoes a powerful wave of repression. But what then happens to the repressed instinct for research? Freud offers three possibilities:

> 1) Both research and sexuality remain inhibited; this circumstance also inhibits intelligence and is likely to produce neurosis.
>
> 2) The intellect is strong enough to evade the repression that sexuality undergoes and emerges as compulsive brooding. The persistent brooding replaces the repetitive questioning of childhood.
>
> 3) The libido is not repressed, but rather is sublimated into curiosity. Neurotic brooding and inhibition are minimal or absent.

Of these three variations, Freud believed that the third applied to Leonardo—that the artist sublimated his childhood curiosity into scientific research and that his sexual life became limited to "ideal" or "sublimated" homosexuality. Such was Freud's assessment of Leonardo's instinctual life and its relation to his intellect. However, the hypothetical character of this view was clear to Freud, who admitted being limited by the available biographical material.

The Screen Memory

In Parts II and III, Freud turns to Leonardo's memory, which is the only notebook reference to the artist's childhood: "It seems that I was always destined to be so deeply concerned with vultures," Leonardo wrote, "for I recall as one of my very earliest memories that while I was in my cradle a vulture came down to me, and opened my mouth with its tail, and struck me many times with its tail against [in Italian "dentro," meaning "inside"] my lips."[9] A mental artifact of this kind would not, prior to 1910, have been susceptible to a psychoanalytic reading, nor would it have been possible to propose a historical reconstruction based upon it.

Through his self-analysis, Freud had discovered that such memories cannot be taken literally. In a letter of October 15, 1897,[10] Freud described a memory of his own from the age of two and a half:

> He was looking for his mother in a cupboard and cried because he saw that she was not there. When she came in by the door, she looked beautiful.

By the process of free association, Freud arrived at the memory's latent meaning as the fear that his mother, like the nurse who had been fired,

would leave him. He related the cupboard as an unconscious symbol of the
womb to his mother's recent confinement with his baby sister. The discrepancy between the conscious memory and its latent meaning led Freud to
recognize a kind of historical distortion created by the human mind—that
is, the later memory was a distortion of the earlier event. He called such
recollections "screen memories."

In two subsequent papers, of 1899[11] and 1901,[12] Freud provided the
following formal account of screen memories. Childhood recollections that
refer to a time before the age of seven can be vivid, even though their
content seems uninteresting. In such cases, the adult looks back on himself
as a child from the distance of an outside observer. The fact that, as a child,
he had participated in the original event prevents the memory from being
an exact one. He experienced it as an actor might experience his role in a
play, whereas in the later memory he has become distanced from the event,
like the audience. Recognizing this change, Freud concluded that the ego
must have revised the original event.

As is true of hysterical symptoms, screen memories compromise the
wish to remember with the resistance against remembering. This occurs
when an image associated with the event is remembered instead of the
event itself, whose content was most likely sexual. "The essential elements
of an experience," Freud writes, "are represented in memory by the inessential elements of the same experience."[13] Because the ego has replaced
essential with inessential, the original event is disguised. By virtue of its
disguise, the memory can be vivid without seeming to betray the truth of
its source.

In screen memories, time is affected in three possible ways. The most
usual way, according to Freud, is illustrated in his own memory of the
cupboard, in which a later memory "screens" an earlier event. But an earlier
memory can equally well screen a later event; that is, the later event is
remembered *as if* it had happened earlier. Freud called this type a "retroac-
tive" screen memory, one which has been displaced backward in time. A
screen memory can also be contemporaneous with the actual event, in
which case displacement occurs without temporal change.

Leonardo's memory is a screen of the first type; it was remembered
and written down many years after the event to which it referred. Freud
justified treating this mental artifact of Leonardo's childhood with seriousness by a comparison with writing history. When Western man began to
write history, according to Freud, he satisfied two motives. One was to
produce an ongoing record of the present and the other, to recapture the

past. In the latter, the historian recorded contemporary views of the past. Seen in retrospect, the past typically became an age of heroes, legends, and myths, all of which contained elements of truth, but which had been distorted by the passage of time and the bias of the present. "If it were possible," Freud wrote, "by a knowledge of all the forces at work, to undo these distortions, there would be no difficulty in disclosing the historical truth lying behind the legendary material. The same holds good for the childhood memories or phantasies of an individual. What someone thinks he remembers from his childhood is not a matter of indifference; as a rule the residual memories—which he himself does not understand—cloak priceless pieces of evidence about the most important features in his mental development."[14]

This being said, Freud proceeded to translate Leonardo's memory and thereby to uncover its disguise. Tail, or *coda*, in Italian is slang for penis, and its action in the memory corresponds to a fellatio fantasy. Because of its oral nature, Freud situated the original event in the period of nursing, which is also consistent with Leonardo's passivity in contrast to the active vulture. The fellatio fantasy, in turn, is superimposed over the earlier recollection of being breast-fed.

The facts of Leonardo's life, as Freud knew them, included the absence of the artist's father for the first few years of his life. In the memory, therefore, Leonardo is alone with the vulture, which Freud identified as a symbolic disguise for his mother. As a bird, the mother is phallic, and here again Freud arrives at the bird's phallic nature by verbal association. The Italian word *uccello*, meaning "bird," is also slang for penis, and the German *vögeln* means "to bird" or "to have sexual intercourse with a woman." (Compare the English term "to goose.")

For confirmation that the vulture was a maternal image, Freud turned to Egyptian mythology. The vulture-headed Egyptian goddess Mut was associated with Isis and Hathor, who were mother goddesses. In Egyptian representations Mut had an erect phallus and female breasts. From the standpoint of human development, the myth of the mother goddess who possesses a phallus corresponds to the child's fantasy of the phallic mother.

Freud concluded that Leonardo had sublimated his infantile sexuality into a type of "ideal" homosexuality. He arrived at this conclusion by the passivity of the artist's relation to the active vulture. Bringing to bear his clinical experience, Freud noted that women and passive male homosexuals tend to fantasize and dream of passive participation in fellatio. He also had recourse to the absence of Leonardo's father during his early childhood; as

1. *Leonardo da Vinci,* La Gioconda (Mona Lisa), *1503–6. Louvre, Paris.*

a result, Leonardo's closeness to his mother would have been intensified in both fact and fantasy. Furthermore, the father's absence would, in Freud's view, have increased Leonardo's curiosity about the origin of babies and the father's part in making them. Finally, Freud links the childhood preoccupation with the riddle of birth to Leonardo's adult passion for discovering how birds fly. It was, in fact, Leonardo himself who provided Freud with this connection, for he claimed to know that he was destined to study the flight of birds precisely because a bird had alighted on his cradle.

For Freud, the father's absence was a crucial factor in the development of Leonardo's homosexuality. He elaborated its aetiology by combining what he knew of the Oedipus complex and narcissism, the latter a topic he had only recently mentioned in print.[15] Rather than identify primarily with his father, a boy whose father is absent (either literally or emotionally) is apt to enhance his identification with his mother; he may emulate his mother in choosing a male love object. In this way, the boy "finds the objects of his love along the path of narcissism"[16] just as the mythological Narcissus preferred his self-image to Echo, the nymph who loved him. According to this view of the aetiology of homosexuality, boys who are the love objects of homosexual men are substitutes, via regression to a stage of auto-erotism, for the men as children. Leonardo would thus have satisfied his feminine identification with his mother and loved boys as he felt loved, or imagined himself loved, or wished himself loved, by her. Freud also observed that, as an adult, Leonardo treated his pupils as children, and kept detailed accounts of their expenses. Such obsessional behavior reveals the artist's repressed anal erotism and a partial identification with his notary father.

In Part IV of *Leonardo*, Freud addressed aspects of the artist's paintings. The vulture fantasy, according to Freud, disguises a memory of Leonardo's mother kissing him on the mouth. With the stated reservation that works of art are elaborate transformations of the artist's mental and emotional life, Freud focused on the Mona Lisa's smile. Its hold on the artist is evident in its persistence in subsequent paintings. Freud linked the smile to Vasari's account of Leonardo's first works as "smiling women" and children. He also hypothesized that the woman who posed for Mona Lisa [1] smiled in a way that reawakened the artist's repressed memory of his mother's smile. Leonardo's conscious attraction to Mona Lisa's smile is suggested by Vasari's account—possibly apocryphal—of the artist's attempts to sustain her good humor while she posed. He reportedly hired musicians, singers, and jesters for this purpose.[17]

The same smile appears on the two women in Leonardo's *Madonna and Christ with Saint Anne* [2]. Freud connected the repetition of the smile in this painting to the unusual youthfulness of Saint Anne, Mary's mother. According to the apocryphal account of her life, Saint Anne was very old at the time of Christ's birth. Consequently, nearly all the previous paintings of this subject depict Saint Anne as an elderly woman. Leonardo, however, has made her youthful, which Freud interpreted as expressing the artist's memory of two young mothers, his real mother, Caterina, and his stepmother, Donna Albiera.

The nineteenth-century critic Walter Pater described Mona Lisa's

2. *Leonardo da Vinci*, Madonna and Christ with
Saint Anne, *1501–13 (?). Louvre, Paris.*

smile as "unfathomable . . . with a touch of something sinister" and Mona Lisa herself as Leonardo's "ideal lady . . . the animation of Greece, the lust of Rome, the mysticism of the middle age. . . . She is older than the rocks among which she sits; like the vampire, she has been dead many times, and learned the secrets of the grave . . . as Leda, was the mother of Helen of Troy, and, as St. Anne, the mother of Mary."[18] For Pater, Mona Lisa fulfilled the nineteenth-century image of the seductive, but deadly, woman that Mario Praz has identified as the embodiment of the "Medusean aesthetic."[19]

Freud took a psychodynamic view of Pater's characterization. He recognized that Mona Lisa is a mythic image of Leonardo's ambivalent relationship to his mother, who overstimulated and feminized him. Freud saw Leonardo's sexual ambivalence even more clearly in certain unmistakably androgynous figures, such as *Saint John the Baptist*, now in the Louvre [3]. Freud attributed the mysterious smile in that picture to having found the secret of love, which he keeps from the observer. "It is possible," Freud concluded this section, "that . . . Leonardo has denied the unhappiness of his erotic life and has triumphed over it in his art, by representing the wishes of the boy, infatuated with his mother, as fulfilled in this blissful union of the male and female natures."[20] If Freud is correct, then Leonardo sublimated his childhood experience of a "sinister," ambivalent, and seductive mother, and a distant father, and created an "ideal," alchemical androgyne (see Chapter 9), who seemed to merge the creative force of male and female in a bisexual union.

In Part V of *Leonardo*, Freud analyzed an error made by the artist in recording the time of his father's death. Like the screen memory, this is a detail on which a psychoanalyst is trained to focus, because it reveals an inner psychic state. Leonardo repeated the hour, seven o'clock, twice in his notation, indicating a suppression of emotion that threatened to erupt. From this fact Freud elaborated aspects of Leonardo's identification with his father.

Although Leonardo's homosexuality prevented his heterosexual identification with his father, he nevertheless identified with him in other ways. In Leonardo's love of material magnificence, for example, Freud recognizes an attempt to surpass his father, who had impressed the peasant girl Caterina and her illegitimate son with his gentlemanly airs. Freud also reports that once Leonardo completed a painting, he ceased to care about it—a repetition of his father's early absences, which Leonardo experienced as lack of interest in him, or abandonment. When the duke of Milan,

3. *Leonardo da Vinci,*
Saint John the
Baptist, *1506–13.*
Louvre, Paris.

Lodovico Sforza (for whom Leonardo created the *Last Supper* and the equestrian statue of Francesco Sforza), fell from power, Leonardo noted that the duke had left all his projects unfinished or abandoned. In this way Lodovico became a father image for Leonardo, paralleling Ser Piero's abandonment of his son. According to Freud, Leonardo's identification with Ser Piero also led him to leave works of his own unfinished.

With regard to scientific research, in contrast to art, Leonardo's "rebellion against his father was the infantile determinant of what was perhaps an equally sublime achievement."[21] Here Freud echoed Leonardo himself, who wrote, "He who appeals to authority when there is a difference of opinion works with his memory rather than with his reason."[22] In other words, the absence of Leonardo's father during the period of infantile sexual research prolonged the drive to investigate into a lifetime pursuit.

Leonardo's instinctual sexual curiosity had been sublimated into science. Freud further attributed Leonardo's indifference to religion to the absence of a strong father figure in early childhood. Whereas Leonardo accepted the notion of a creative force and the existence of natural law, nowhere did he refer to his own belief in a Christian view of God and the saints.

At the end of Part V, Freud resumed his consideration of Leonardo's interest in flight and related it to his childlike nature. He interpreted both the infantile and the dream wish to fly as a wish for sexual potency. In Leonardo's case, the artist himself had identified his interest in flight as deriving from childhood; his adult preoccupation with birds and flying machines is well known. The continuum from Leonardo's youthful sexual curiosity to later scientific research, according to Freud, indicates that, in contrast to sexuality, the impulse to investigate escaped repression.

Freud's assertion that Leonardo "remained like a child for the whole of his life"[23] is consistent with Vasari's accounts of his pranks. On one occasion in Rome, the artist made inflatable animals and blew them up so they would fly; as the air escaped, they fell back down. In these particular tricks, Leonardo's childlike activity is directly related to flight, illustrating another thematic continuum in the artist's life.

Leonardo concludes (Part VI) with comments on the nature of biography. Freud noted that most biographers idealize their subjects, an observation that places him in a contradictory position vis-à-vis Leonardo. For, far from glossing over the artist's neurosis, Freud delved into it. At the same time, however, he invoked Leonardo's "love of truth and thirst for knowledge"[24] as a justification and a model for his own method of inquiry.

In 1939, Kenneth Clark[25] accepted Freud's reading of Leonardo's youthful Saint Anne with Mary as a reflection of the artist's two young mothers. Apart from Clark, the reaction of prominent art historians to Freud's psychobiography was, at first, critical. The most outspoken critic, although not entirely opposed to Freud's discoveries or methods, was Meyer Schapiro.

SCHAPIRO'S LEONARDO

In two articles published in 1955[26] and 1956,[27] Meyer Schapiro challenged Freud's discussion of Leonardo's "slip" in repeating the hour of his father's death and Freud's methodology in using Leonardo's screen memory to reconstruct the artist's childhood. A curious feature of Schapiro's arguments is his literal approach to Leonardo documents, in contrast to occasional flirtations with psychoanalytic method when describing Freud's interpretations. Schapiro's main objection was that Freud "assigned to the sparse documents an extraordinary significance"[28] in reconstructing Leonardo's early life from the screen memory.

In "Leonardo and Freud: An Art-Historical Study," Schapiro proposed an art-historical assessment of Freud's psychobiography, based primarily on documentary information. The first piece of information is that the Italian word *nibbio* actually means kite, whereas Freud had relied on a German text which incorrectly translated *nibbio* into the German word for vulture—hence the "vulture" in Leonardo's screen memory. Schapiro's point is well taken here—a caution to biographers to know the language of their subject or, next best, to be sure that secondary sources and translations are accurate.

As Schapiro pointed out, the kite, which is the real bird in question, is the most frequently cited bird in Leonardo's notebooks, since it offered the best means of observing how birds fly. Inspired by the observations of the Roman author Pliny the Elder, whose *Natural History* Leonardo owned, he compared the motion of a ship's rudder to the tail movements of a kite. According to Pliny, the kite was the very symbol of steering a boat, and the sixteenth-century Italian author Piero Valeriano identified the kite as the emblem of pilots.

Schapiro next considered why Leonardo located the screen memory in his childhood. He cited a number of texts available to the artist in which small animals enter the mouth of a sleeping infant destined for greatness. Ants, for example, filled the mouth of the future King Midas with wheat; bees alighted on Plato's lips, placed beeswax on Pindar's lips, and swarmed into the mouth of Saint Ambrose. Each of these tales was a prediction, recognized in hindsight, of the infant's future. From these accounts, Schapiro identified the tradition, known to Leonardo, associating the visit by a small animal to the mouth of a sleeping infant with future greatness. In the very content of the tales there is a logical connection with the future of the individual. Thus, Midas's wealth is prefigured by hard-working ants that store wheat as an image of economic foresight. Likewise, the sweetness of honey prefigures great powers of speech, poetry, and song.

Schapiro related these conventions to Leonardo's memory, noting that a bird may have expressed the artist's wish to invent a flying machine and solve the riddle of flight. Coincidentally, the upward motion of birds in flight is a traditional metaphor for success. A "high flyer" is someone who is considered successful, and being "up" denotes greater good fortune than being "down." Inspiration and genius, as Schapiro pointed out, are also traditionally related to birds.

With regard to the actual character of the kite, Schapiro noted that it is the opposite of the vulture's. Whereas the vulture is a good mother, the kite is not. This fact was as familiar to Leonardo as to Schapiro. In a fable composed by Leonardo, Envy is exemplified as a kite; he wrote that kites peck at the sides of their children and keep food from them when they are too fat. The true identity of Leonardo's bird thus alters the character of his memory. Schapiro suggested that in this light a psychologist might "infer . . . that Leonardo did not forgive Caterina his illegitimacy and her willingness to abandon him to a step-mother."[29]

When Schapiro considered the problem of the two young mothers in *Madonna and Christ with Saint Anne,* he addressed both form and iconography. He rightly called on the psychoanalyst to review the relevant art-historical data before applying the methods of his own discipline. Cultural and iconographic patterns must be identified in order to isolate a particular artist's individual contribution in any work. Since the cult of Saint Anne was developing in the late fifteenth century, including the tradition that she had conceived Mary immaculately, discussion of her role was very much in the air. This new interest in Saint Anne, according to Schapiro, lay behind Leonardo's painting. Furthermore, Schapiro argued that Freud was mistaken about the representation of the two female saints as youthful being unusual. Nor did he accept Freud's assertion that Leonardo invented the pyramidal form of the figural arrangement in the painting. What *was* new, Schapiro said, was the complexity of the figures' poses and interactions. Strongly implied in Schapiro's conclusions is a failure on Freud's part to do his art-historical homework.

Schapiro also called into question Freud's explanation of Mona Lisa's smile, which is similar to the smiles in *Madonna and Christ with Saint Anne, Saint John the Baptist,* and other late paintings. Since the London cartoon of *Madonna and Christ with Saint Anne* [4] predates Mona Lisa, Freud's assertion that meeting the real Mona Lisa had reawakened Leonardo's memory of his mother's smile seems to be on thin ice. Other drawings for *Madonna and Christ with Saint Anne* indicate that Leonardo experimented with Saint Anne's age; in some she is old and in others young. This, in Schapiro's view, "recalls the uncertainty of the doctrine of the Immaculate Conception during this time."[30]

As for the smile, Schapiro noted that Verrocchio, with whom Leo-

4. *Leonardo da Vinci,* Madonna and Christ with
Saint Anne, *1498 (?). National Gallery, London.*

nardo served his apprenticeship, also created smiling women and children. Even Verrocchio's bronze David smiles as if in inward triumph, in a way that reminded Schapiro of Leonardo's Saint Anne. In the matter of the smile, therefore, Schapiro objected to Freud on the grounds of reductionism. He accused Freud of linking a late work (Mona Lisa) with the artist's "infantile impressions,"[31] reducing the one to the other, as if no intervening transformations had occurred.

Although neither the pyramidal form nor the youth of Saint Anne was an invention of Leonardo, according to Schapiro, the presence of John the Baptist was. To explain this new iconographic motif, Schapiro took a leaf from Freud's methodology. The essence of Schapiro's interpretation turns on the fact that in the London cartoon both John the Baptist and Christ are present, whereas in the final painting a lamb takes John's place. The lamb, for theological reasons, is an attribute of John as well as an image of Christ—the "Lamb of God." In being an ascetic, John the Baptist can also be taken as an image of Leonardo; as such, Schapiro proposed that the lamb projects and conceals the artist's "narcissistic and homosexual wish,"[32] and thus contains both theological and psychological ambiguity.

Schapiro feared that reading Freud would create the impression that Leonardo painted mainly soft women and effeminate young men. This, he thought, skewed the issue of Leonardo's identification with his father. He noted that the now-destroyed *Battle of Anghiari* (1504–5) was striking for its savagely fighting horsemen. He further took Freud to task for omitting *Leda* (which Freud, in fact, mentioned) and *Saint Jerome* (because of his ascetic character) as evidence that Leonardo did not avoid erotic subjects. The former painting, now lost, depicts a mythological seduction, and the latter, according to Schapiro, is "a powerful image of masculine ascetic feeling."[33] In general, Schapiro does not credit Freud's discussion of Leonardo's identification with his father, especially the argument that Leonardo abandoned his pictures because he felt abandoned by his father.

Freud interpreted Leonardo's refusal to eat meat and his habit of releasing caged birds as defensive reaction formations against sadism. Here again Schapiro had recourse to cultural patterns and texts. He mustered justifications from folklore to philosophy for Leonardo's behavior. Freeing birds, for example, was believed to bring good luck; vegetarianism had been advocated by ancient authors and revived in the Neoplatonic circles of Renaissance Florence. In Schapiro's view, Leonardo's aggression would have been better illustrated by his drawings of deformed people and his painting (according to Vasari) of a monster intended to have the effect on his father of a Medusa head.

Schapiro summed up his general response to Freud's *Leonardo* as follows: "I believe this study of Freud's book points to weaknesses which will be found in other works by psychoanalysts in the cultural fields: the habit of building explanations of complex phenomena on a single datum and the too little attention given to history and the social situation in dealing with individuals and even with the origin of customs, beliefs, and institutions."[34]

Although Schapiro was not alone in his criticism of Freud's *Leonardo*, his observations are among the most scholarly. As a result, when Kurt Eissler, a distinguished Freudian psychoanalyst, set out to reevaluate Freud's study and some of the reactions to it, he primarily addressed Schapiro's arguments. In presenting a brief view of Eissler's rebuttal of Schapiro, I concentrate on Part I ("Polemics") of his book *Leonardo da Vinci: Psychoanalytic Notes on the Enigma*, published in 1961.[35] Part II contains a wealth of interpretation to which the interested reader is referred.

EISSLER'S LEONARDO

Methodologically, the main bone of contention between art history and psychoanalysis over Freud's study is whether the screen memory is a valid historical artifact. Eissler agreed with Schapiro that the change from vulture to kite discredited the mythological associations to the Egyptian goddess Mut, but disagreed that the dynamic principles were thereby altered. He objected to Schapiro's selection of historical conventions in which a small animal enters the mouth of a future genius, on the grounds that it reduced Leonardo to a mere imitator.

There are other grounds than Eissler's, however, on which to oppose Schapiro's literal reading of the conventional stories. Aside from King Midas, the childhood conventions that Schapiro cited as prefiguring great futures for their subjects applied to writers only. Since the medium of writers is words, the mouth would be the appropriate place for insects to direct their attention. Leonardo, on the other hand, was a visual artist and therefore subject to the conventions indicating future artistic, as opposed to literary, greatness. In Schapiro's own terms, therefore, apples are being compared to oranges when Ambrose, Stesichorus, and Cicero are offered as prototypes for Leonardo. Schapiro seems to have overlooked the fact that the content of the literary conventions is not parallel to Leonardo's memory.

A further discrepancy between these stories and Leonardo's memory is in the action of the little animal. In the ancient accounts, the animal enters the mouth, or alights on or drops something sweet on the lips. In Leonardo's memory, the bird's tail feathers beat or flapped against the inside of the lips. It was in that specific action that Freud identified the fellatio fantasy and its associations to the earlier breast-feeding situation.

In his accounts of infant augury, Schapiro also disregarded the motif of sleep. Since the child in question is asleep at the time of the "visitation," he cannot claim to have remembered or fantasized the event; rather, he is the subject of someone else's story, which has become a convention by virtue of its persistence in the cultural memory. In this way, conventions have a mythic, or legendary, character, which distinguishes them from individual fantasies.

Eissler accepted that the artist's adult study of the kite's method of flying precipitated the screen memory. Precipitating factors, however, are never the whole story, although they can, if properly analyzed, provide an avenue to unconscious meanings. Here again we are dealing with time and therefore with history. For stored in the unconscious mind are all the impressions of childhood; they are only occasionally accessible and then often in disguise. In Leonardo's case, the study of kites was the adult factor that, in stimulating the memory, evoked his childhood past.

Having entered the realm of childhood, we confront the content of the memory and try to decipher it. On this count, Eissler agreed with Schapiro that the kite represents an envious mother who sadistically deprives her children of food. He did not, however, agree that Leonardo's homosexuality was called into question as a result. A hostile mother, as well as a seductive one, is consistent with homosexual development; and in either case, the father's absence is a powerful contributing factor.

Eissler took up the question of psychoanalytic reconstruction and history, whereas Schapiro preferred that psychoanalysts stick to psychological phenomena and not try to reconstruct history from them. In the clinical practice of psychoanalysis, the patient usually provides the external history, and the analyst, by virtue of living in the same time and place as the patient, automatically shares certain cultural information with him. It is quite often the case, however, that an analyst can reconstruct forgotten external circumstances that are hidden in a memory, fantasy, dream, symptom, or repeated behavior pattern. Eissler's disagreement with Schapiro is nowhere more evident than when he states: "In its application to history the potential of psychoanalysis as a tool of reconstructing external reality is destined to play a major role."[36]

Eissler related the ambiguity of Mona Lisa's smile to the artist's ambivalence toward his mother. Homosexuality in men is, in fact, consistent with the experience of the mother as both hostile and seductive and also with the ambivalent quality of *Mona Lisa*. Eissler took the same dim view of Schapiro's connection between Verrocchio's smiling women and the *Mona Lisa* as he did of the childhood omens of greatness. Rather than interpret Leonardo as having consciously imitated his teacher in depicting the smile, Eissler believed that, if there was a connection, it was that Verrocchio's figures evoked a tendency already present in Leonardo.

In his discussion of *Madonna and Christ with Saint Anne*, Eissler agreed that the two young mothers recall Leonardo's real mother and stepmother. He also proposed that an illegitimate artist would have a particular interest in the genealogical clarity contained in the traditional iconography of this image. He interpreted the two merged mothers in the London cartoon as an earlier, and primitive, fusion of these women. Meeting the real woman called Mona Lisa, according to Eissler's reconstruction, freed the artist to separate, or *de*-fuse, the merged figures and represent them individually in the final painting.

On the basis of his own research, Eissler concluded that Freud, and not Schapiro, had been right in two essential points: first, that the subject of *Madonna and Christ with Saint Anne was* rare in Italian art (he noted fifteen examples of it) and second, that there was only one example of a youthful Saint Anne (with Mary and Christ) in Italy at the time of Leonardo's painting. But, even if Freud had been wrong and Schapiro correct, Eissler believed that the psychoanalyst could validly still assign an internal dynamic meaning to Leonardo's choices.

Finally, Eissler's chapter "The Historian vs. the Psychoanalyst's Conception of Man" sums up the two methodological approaches epitomized by Freud and Schapiro. "For Freud," Eissler[37] wrote, "man is a system in conflict."

The psychoanalyst approaches the individual primarily in terms of internal forces, the historian primarily in terms of external forces. If Leonardo refused to eat meat, for example, the analyst suspects that the defense of reaction formation against sadism is operating. Schapiro, in contrast, attributes it to the influence of current medical and philosophical ideas. Nor is

Leonardo's aversion to sexuality, which is reported by the artist himself, taken at face value by the psychoanalyst; it is inconsistent with Freud's reconstruction of Leonardo's passionate childhood sexual curiosity. Leonardo, however, is a particularly complex case because of his high level of genius inhibited by powerful forces. Eissler left open the question whether Leonardo's abstinence was linked with inhibition, as Freud thought, or whether it was a necessary condition for the supreme achievements of those works that Leonardo did complete.

Eissler cited the law of overdetermination to distinguish the psychoanalytic from the pre-psychoanalytic (which he called historical) view of art. Every mental product is overdetermined; that is, a multiplicity of factors contributes to any single thought or action.[38] The determinants are internal as well as external, and they can be opposites. Factors such as sadism and masochism, which cannot be simultaneous in external reality, coexist in the unconscious. This state of affairs is possible because the unconscious has no sense of time, and therefore no temporal sequence. In the creation of a work of art, which is surely one of the most complex human activities, the dynamics of overdetermination cannot be overlooked if the work is to be understood. This is particularly true if the work is of the highest quality and originality, as in Leonardo's case, because the artist relies less on tradition and more on his own creative capacity than does a mediocre artist.

Iconographers such as Erwin Panofsky take overdetermination into account, though textually rather than psychoanalytically. A traditional art-historical iconographic study of the representation of a Christian event—the Nativity, for example—might consider the image as an illustration of a biblical or Apocryphal account. If there are unusual details in the scene, the researcher would try to decipher their meaning in the context of Christian symbolism, or their sense as secular, possibly genre, elements. If a contemporary donor appears in the picture, his or her relationship to the Christian figures might be considered. The location of the picture in a particular chapel, its connections to other scenes in the same chapel, and the ecclesiastic order (for example, Franciscan, Dominican, Carmelite) may have influenced the picture's iconography.

Cultural, textual, theological, and economic influences are thus within the bounds of traditional art-historical inquiry. But considerations of the artist's personal dynamic connection to the content of a scene are relatively recent. Because the subject of the Nativity includes the Holy Family, the psychoanalyst would look for resonance with the artist's own family and childhood. The psychoanalyst might wonder whether the Nativity evoked the artist's childhood fantasies about birth, or whether his relationship with his parents influenced the depiction of Mary and Joseph. Whether such a personal relationship can be recognized and explained would depend on the image, the artist, the available documents, and the skill of the analyst.

These, then, are some of the arguments engendered by Freud's study of Leonardo. Eissler's polemics highlight the contrast between the intellectual styles of the traditional historian and the psychoanalyst. Despite the divergent methodologies, however, the art-historical literature has reflected a progressive influx of psychological thinking in the more than three decades since the publication of Eissler's book.

FURTHER CONSIDERATIONS
IN THE LIGHT OF FREUD'S LEONARDO

In 1963, the art historians Rudolf and Margot Wittkower published *Born Under Saturn* to explore, as stated in the subtitle, "The Character and Conduct of Artists." In the section "Leonardo's Aloofness," the Wittkowers cited a passage from the artist's letter to a half-brother that well illustrates an adult derivative of the Oedipus complex. Leonardo wrote:

> I learned that you have an heir, which circumstance I understand has afforded you a great deal of pleasure. Now in so far as I had judged you to be possessed of prudence I am now entirely convinced that I am as far removed from having an accurate judgment as you are from prudence, seeing that you have been congratulating yourself on having created a watchful enemy, who will strive with all his energies after liberty, which can only come into being at your death.[39]

The aggression in Leonardo's letter is unmistakable and it cuts several ways. On the manifest level, Leonardo criticizes his half-brother's love for his child as imprudent and attacks the new father's narcissism by scoffing at his pride in having produced a son. Possibly the artist unconsciously envied his half-brother his new heir, even though he criticized him for being pleased. Leonardo expressed these conflicts in plastic form when he inflated toy animals and then enjoyed letting the air out of them. In the letter to his half-brother, Leonardo does likewise; he deflates the ego of the proud father with a reminder of his son's inevitable hostility toward him.

Only barely latent are the oedipal implications in Leonardo's remarks.

Their paranoid flavor emerges in the designation of the son as "watchful," implying danger from the father. The thought that the son's freedom depends on his father's death signals their ambivalent relationship. As long as the father is alive, Leonardo suggests, the son is an emotional prisoner. In all this, one must assume that Leonardo is talking about himself and his hostility toward his own father.

A counter view, which is more consistent with the traditional art-historical approach, appeared in a short article of 1985 by James Beck.[40] Beck argued that Leonardo and his father "had a long, cordial rapport . . . notwithstanding the illegitimacy of the artist's birth."[41] He cited the working relationship between Leonardo and Ser Piero and attributed the apprenticeship to Verrocchio to Ser Piero's wise choice of an "influential teacher" for his son. Later, according to Beck, Ser Piero helped Leonardo secure important commissions, thereby taking an active interest in promoting his son's career. Nevertheless Beck admitted that Leonardo would have been excluded from his father's guild (the Arte dei Guidici e Notari) because of his illegitimate birth. He also argued that the prominent references to Leonardo as illegitimate in his grandfather's tax statement of 1457 and his father's and uncle's statements of 1469 were for the purpose of taking Leonardo as a tax deduction. In Beck's view, neither instance would have caused hostility between Leonardo and Ser Piero.

In another instance cited by Beck, however, there can be no doubt of Ser Piero's latent hostility toward Leonardo. Ser Piero died intestate in his late seventies; this, Beck agreed, was an especially glaring lapse for a notary who regularly wrote wills for other people. As a direct result of his father's lapse, Leonardo received no inheritance from him, and his legitimate half-brothers shared the entire estate. Had Ser Piero made a will, he could have left something to Leonardo. "Was this," Beck wrote, "Ser Piero's intention or merely a monumental oversight?"[42] This formulation of the problem, in fact, begs the question of whether the omission was unconsciously motivated.

Could one ask for a more telling illustration of the ambivalent relation between father and son, not to say abandonment by the father, that Freud described? Reviewing just a few indications of the financial dealings between Leonardo and Ser Piero, one wonders whether the father did not take advantage of his son in other ways. He used Leonardo's illegitimate status for tax deductions, but favored his legitimate children over Leonardo at his death. The absence of a will, to which Beck refers as an "oversight," is evaluated differently by psychoanalytic methodology.

The psychoanalyst looks beneath the surface of an event or document and inevitably comes to a place where ambivalence operates. At this point, shifts between love and hate, concern and hostility, come into play; when such feelings are between father and son, derivatives of the Oedipus complex are at work. To dismiss the matter of Ser Piero's will as an "oversight," therefore, is rather like ignoring Leonardo's screen memory. These are mental artifacts that the psychoanalyst takes as raw material. Just as the archaeologist reconstructs the profile of a pot from a fragment, or the art-historical restorer fills in the lost part of an image, so the psychoanalyst draws psychological conclusions from the available artifacts of his discipline.

VASARI ON TWO PRANKS BY LEONARDO

The popular assertion "Many a true word is spoken in jest" hints at the underlying hostility in humor. By disguising hostility in the form of a joke, the teller makes it more socially acceptable. Freud first described the mechanisms of jokes and humor in 1905 in *Jokes and Their Relation to the Unconscious*, which he followed with "On Humor" in 1927.[43] As in works of art, it is the formal quality of the joke, more than the content, that determines its success or failure. But the analysis of a joke's content reveals something of the teller's psychology, just as analyzing the far more complex work of art can elucidate the artist.

One of Leonardo's characteristics that struck his contemporaries as odd was his predilection for jokes, which often took the form of pranks. He made fantastic constructions and played games with them. In such activities, the games themselves assume an artistic form and multiply the layers of disguise; they are like daydreams given concrete form and disguised as play.

An analysis of two pranks described by Vasari will serve to illustrate several fundamental concepts of Freud's *Leonardo*. One, briefly noted by Schapiro, disguises the artist's hostility to his father, and the other, his fantasy of the dangerous, phallic mother.

Medusa's Arrow

Vasari's account:

> A peasant working for Ser Piero asked him to have a wooden buckler painted for him in Florence. Ser Piero asked Leonardo to do the work, but

without saying for whom. Leonardo reworked the buckler, prepared its ground, and decided to paint on it a creature that would have the same effect as Medusa's head. In order to do so, Leonardo retired in isolation and assembled pieces of various animals—"lizards, . . . crickets, serpents, butter-flies, grasshoppers, bats. . . ."

When Ser Piero went to pick up the buckler, Leonardo arranged it on an easel, which was lit from a window. His father was startled and stepped back. Leonardo said that the work had had the desired effect and told his father to take it away. Ser Piero was so impressed that he kept the buckler for himself. For the peasant he bought another one that was painted with "a heart transfixed by an arrow."

Later Ser Piero sold Leonardo's painted buckler for one hundred ducats.[44]

In his account of this illusionistic prank, Vasari expresses the ambiva-lent, oedipal relation between Leonardo and his father, and provides an insight into Ser Piero's behavior with money. The decision to paint a "Medusa" head on the buckler is consistent with its appearance on Athena's shield and its subsequent popularity as a shield and armor device in Western Europe. Even more than creating the image itself, however, Leonardo wanted to replicate the *effect* of the image—namely, turning to stone any man who looked on it.

The determinedly sadistic character of Leonardo's preparations is also evident; he dismembered animals with the concentration of the very young child who tears the wings off insects, unaware that he is inflicting pain. The unconscious wish to kill his father appears in symbolically turning him to stone with the "Medusa" head. That Leonardo's father understood his son's intent, at least unconsciously, is clear from his substitution of the "heart transfixed by an arrow." Ser Piero then behaved toward Leonardo with hostility of his own by secretly profiting from his genius. In this relation-ship, as described by Vasari, the ambivalence between father and son is only barely disguised by the "games" they played.

In another detail of Vasari's account we may discern Leonardo's homosexual fear of women, here taking the form of a particularly horrify-ing *vagina dentata* fantasy. His painted creature emerges from a "dark and jagged rock,"[45] emitting fire and venom. Its fiery eyes, open throat, and smoking nostrils are traditional features of Medusa iconography in her most phallic and dangerous persona.[46] The dark, jagged rocks are a recur-ring motif in Leonardo's paintings; *Madonna of the Rocks, Madonna and Christ with Saint Anne,* and Mona Lisa represent maternal figures against a background of such rocks, which clearly had personal meaning for the artist.[47]

The Lizard in the Box

The fantasy of the phallic mother recurs in the pranks involving the "lizard in the box." Leonardo made wings out of lizards' scales, which he attached, along with eyes, horns, and a beard, to a living lizard. He kept the creature in a box and, when he showed it to his friends, they ran in fear.

The lizard combines phallic quality with a traditional reputation for cold aloofness, because it was believed incapable of falling in love.[48] Identical qualities have been applied to Leonardo himself and raise the possibility that his lizard is a self-image. Leonardo's additions—eyes, horns, wings, beard—served to multiply the lizard's phallic character. By keeping this creature in a box (itself a dream symbol of the female genital or womb), Leonardo reconstructed the fantasied hidden phallus of the mother, which he retained while also keeping it out of sight. The action of showing the lizard, whose wings quivered as it moved, was similar to showing his father the illusionistic monster that had the effect of a Medusa head. Its unexpected quality combines the young child's surprise that his mother is without a phallus with his simultaneous denial of that fact. Likewise, the exhibitionistic quality of "showing" one's creation, especially when it is so obviously sexual, echoes the child's narcissistic wish to be admired and the artist's wish to win recognition and fame.

In these and other pranks described by Vasari, Leonardo repeated, and tried to master, the traumas of his childhood. His infantile sexual curiosity, which Freud saw as the forerunner of scientific investigation, was replayed, with a sadistic component, in the dismemberment of the animals. In reassembling the parts, Leonardo seems to have been experimenting with a confused body image, as if trying to solve a problem of identity. When he inflated toy animals until they filled up a room—in essence, a large "box"—he replicated sexual intercourse in symbolic form. This action, followed by deflating the animals and watching them fall to the ground, was an attempt at sexual control. This game is particularly significant in the light of Leonardo's complaint that a man cannot always control his phallus, which acts independently of his conscious will.[49] In opening the lizard's box and exposing the frightening creature, Leonardo revised the myth of Pandora's box to suit his private fantasy; it was he, rather than the woman, who controlled the terrors of the earth.

NOTES

1. Freud, "Leonardo da Vinci and a Memory of His Childhood," S. E. IX, 1910, pp. 63–137.
2. Cf. Editor's Note to Freud's Leonardo, ibid., pp. 59–60.
3. Dimitri Merejkowski, The Romance of Leonardo da Vinci, 1903; Reprint, New York, 1928.
4. Nunberg, Herman and Federn, eds., Minutes of the Vienna Psychoanalytic Society, vol. 1, 1906–8, New York, 1962.
5. Ibid., p. 264.
6. Ibid., p. 265.
7. Giorgio Vasari, Lives of the Most Eminent Painters, Sculptors, and Architects, trans. Gaston du Vere, vol. 2, New York, 1979, p. 792.
8. Freud, "Analysis of a Phobia in a Five-Year-Old Boy," S. E. X, 1909, pp. 5–149.
9. Freud, Leonardo, p. 82.
10. Freud, "Letter 71," S. E. I, 1897, p. 265.
11. Freud, "Screen Memories," S. E. III, 1899, pp. 303–22.
12. Freud, "Child Memories and Screen Memories," S. E. VI, 1901, pp. 43–52.
13. Freud, "Screen Memories," S. E. III, 1899, p. 307.
14. Freud, Leonardo, p. 84.
15. Freud, "Three Essays on the Theory of Sexuality," (1905) S. E. VII, p. 145. Footnote added 1910.
16. Freud, Leonardo, p. 100.
17. Cf. Paul Barolsky, Why Mona Lisa Smiles and Other Tales by Vasari, University Park and London, 1991.
18. Walter Pater, op. cit., pp. 97–99.
19. Cf. Mario Praz, The Romantic Agony, Oxford and New York, 1983, Chapter 1.
20. Freud, Leonardo, pp. 117–18.
21. Ibid., p. 122.
22. Ibid., from Leonardo, Codex Atlanticus, F. 76r. a.
23. Ibid., p. 127.
24. Ibid., p. 130.
25. Kenneth Clark, Leonardo da Vinci, Harmondsworth, 1963, pp. 137–38.
26. Meyer Schapiro, "Two Slips of Leonardo and a Slip of Freud," Psychoanalysis 2 (1955): 3–8.
27. Meyer Schapiro, "Leonardo and Freud: An Art-Historical Study," Journal of the History of Ideas XVII, no. 2 (April 1956): 147–78.
28. Schapiro, 1955, p. 7.
29. Schapiro, 1956, p. 157.
30. Ibid., p. 165.
31. Ibid., p. 167.
32. Ibid., p. 170.
33. Ibid., p. 176.
34. Ibid., p. 177.
35. Kurt Eissler, Leonardo da Vinci: Psychoanalytic Notes on the Enigma, New York, 1961.
36. Ibid., p. 21.
37. Ibid., p. 58.
38. See Robert Waelder, "The Principle of Multiple Function: Observations on Overdetermination," Psychoanalytic Quarterly 5 (1936): 45–62.

39. Cited in Rudolf and Margot Wittkower, *Born Under Saturn*, New York, 1963, p. 76.
40. James Beck, "Ser Piero da Vinci and His Son Leonardo," *Source: Notes in the History of Art* V, no. 1 (Fall 1985): 29–32.
41. Ibid., p. 29.
42. Ibid., p. 31.
43. Freud, *Jokes and Their Relation to the Unconscious*, S. E. VIII, 1905, pp. 9–238, and "On Humor," S. E. XXI, 1927, pp. 159–66.
44. Vasari, *Lives*, vol. 2, p. 782.
45. Ibid., p. 781.
46. On Medusa iconography, see Laurie Schneider, "Ms. Medusa: Transformations of a Bisexual Image," *Psychoanalytic Study of Society* 9 (1981): 105–53.
47. On the dangers of the mother's body, castration anxiety, and *vagina dentata* fear, cf. Maurice N. Walsh, M.D., "Notes on the Neurosis of Leonardo da Vinci," *Psychoanalytic Quarterly* 30 (1961): 232–42.
48. Donald Posner, "Caravaggio's Homo-Erotic Early Works," *Art Quarterly*, 34 (Autumn 1971) p. 305.
49. E. MacCurdy, ed., *The Notebooks of Leonardo da Vinci*, New York, 1956, p. 120; Fogli B 13r.

THREE

The Psychological Impact
of Imagery

The power of imagery[1] is proverbial and is attested by the familiar adages that "a picture is worth a thousand words" and "seeing is believing." However, people are still inclined to attribute greater intellectual complexity to words than to pictures. One reason for this paradox lies in child development; since children understand pictures before words, pictures seem "easier," more infantile, than the written word. Average children can make paintings, drawings, and clay sculptures, and can build elaborate structures with blocks before learning to read and write.

Developmentally, images also precede language. Dreams, fantasies, and memories are pictorial and, as such, create a regressive path from words to pictures. This is not to suggest that a good picture, sculpture, or building is not as well thought out as a work of literature. In psychoanalysis, the term "regression" denotes going back in time or space—for example, from adult to child or from conscious to unconscious thinking. Pictures and pictorial phenomena, such as dreams, fantasies, and visual hallucinations, depend upon various degrees of regression from words to pictures.

Art historians have tended to prefer psychoanalytic interpretations of art based on literary sources to those based on images alone. Herein lies another psychological paradox, for another popular adage, "Don't believe everything you read," gets short shrift when a literary source contends with an image for interpretive primacy.

A review of some of the ways in which imagery exerts power over our minds may help to explain why psychoanalysis of art is possible, even fruitful, in providing new insights into familiar works.

IMAGERY AND ILLUSIONISM

First and foremost, images can create illusion. At one extreme of the illusory spectrum are psychotics who believe in the reality of visual hallucinations. At the other extreme, that of creative art, viewers suspend reality and consciously enter an illusory world. Between these extremes are innumerable variations that reveal the power of images.

The Greek myths of the sculptors Daedalus and Pygmalion deal with illusions. When encountered unexpectedly in antiquity, Daedalus's statues evoked reactions of fear or aggression. Because of his illusionistic skill, Daedalus was believed to have created automata, figures that could walk and talk. For this ability, Daedalus was credited by the Greeks with having been the first artist.[2]

Pygmalion used his illusionistic skill to satisfy a private fantasy of the ideal woman. Disappointed by the imperfections of the opposite sex, Pygmalion created Galatea out of marble and acted toward her as if she were real. He dressed her, gave her presents, and took her to bed. Finally, during a festival in honor of Venus, Pygmalion prayed for a woman as perfect as his statue. Venus answered his prayer by bringing his statue to life and effectively eliminated the boundary between reality and illusion. The Pygmalion myth fulfills the fantasy that illusion can be made real by means of a visual image. The fact that the intervention of Venus—descended from Near Eastern fertility goddesses—is required evokes the magical, pre-oedipal mother.

In the first century A.D., Pliny (23–79) recorded several examples of the significance attributed to illusionistic painting and sculpture in antiquity. In the early Olympiads, according to Pliny (NH 34, ix, 16–21),[3] athletes who won three Olympic victories were rewarded with portraits that were exact likenesses of themselves. Pliny also records that, in the third century B.C., artists began making public wall paintings of battles filled with convincing details (NH 34, vii, 23) and that, later still, at the turn of the first century B.C., a stage set illustrating roof tiles fooled crows into trying to land on it.

Pliny places a high value on the illusionistic skill of the Greek artist Zeuxis, who painted grapes so convincingly that birds tried to eat them (NH 34, xxxvi, 65–66). But when Zeuxis painted a child carrying grapes, which birds again tried to eat, the artist considered his effort a failure. Had his illusionism really succeeded, he said, the painted child would have scared the birds away.

A competing artist, Parrhasios of Ephesos, painted a curtain that fooled Zeuxis, who consequently awarded his rival the prize for illusionism. Parrhasios also painted two armed runners, who, Pliny asserts (NH 35, xxxvi, 71), seemed to be literally sweating and panting. The Greek painter Apelles, who worked for Alexander the Great in the fourth century B.C., was known for depicting horses at which live horses neighed (NH 35, xxxvi, 95). Likewise, his portraits were so convincing that the "physiogno-mists" could predict his subjects' futures—literally "read their foreheads" (NH 35, xxxvi, 88).

During the Italian Renaissance, the revival of antiquity fueled a new interest in naturalism and the illusion of three-dimensional space on a flat surface. Consequently, Classical anecdotes about illusionism were also revived and applied to certain contemporary artists. Giotto, for example, was said to have painted such a realistic fly on the nose of a painted figure that Cimabue tried to brush it off. The essential, if not literal, truth of this anecdote is illustrated by several illusionistic details in Giotto's Arena Chapel frescoes. Running through the entire history of Renaissance art, in fact, is the anecdotal tradition of an artist's ability to deceive observers by creating trompe l'oeil (meaning "fool the eye") illusionism.

By the second half of the fifteenth century, artists such as Andrea Mantegna were capable of creating entire illusionistic environments. His frescoes in the ducal palace in Mantua blend so convincingly with the actual architecture that it is difficult to distinguish reality from illusion. One's response to Mantegna's frescoes, and to later, more dramatic illu-sionistic environments, such as Giulio Romano's Palazzo del Te in Mantua, is ambivalent. On the one hand, the viewer experiences delight in having been fooled and, like the ancients, admires the evidence of skill and tech-nique. But the visual trickery of illusion evokes an uncanny sense of uncertainty and a fear of potential boundary loss.

The Photorealist American sculptor Duane Hanson creates sculptures that are frequently mistaken for real people [5]. By taking as his subjects everyday, middle-class people, Hanson combines illusionism with witty social commentary. The viewer can identify with Hanson's figures, often with amusement, while simultaneously admiring his technical skill. The uncanniness of Hanson's sculptures is only briefly experienced, and it occurs at the observer's moment of uncertainty, at the transition between believing the sculpture to be a real person and recognizing that it is not. The potential for a sense of loss of self in viewing Hanson's work is mitigated by its humor.

5. *Duane Hanson,* Artist with Ladder, *1972.*

BOUNDARY LOSS: EGO AND IMAGE

Interestingly, the absence of any recognizable form can be as provocative as illusionism. When such twentieth-century styles as Abstract Expressionism and Minimalism appeared, viewers' responses by and large suggested that their ego boundaries were even more threatened than they were by illusionism. Rather than evoking a sense of the uncanny, however, nonobjective art aroused anger. The artist's skill was denied rather than admired. Such responses had previously appeared in the nineteenth-century view of Impressionism as technically inferior to the clear edges and precise textures of Neoclassical painting (see Chapter 12). Likewise, when the Cubists "deconstructed" pictorial space in solid geometric terms, popular reception was negative.

Psychologically, it would seem, those who respond negatively to nonobjective imagery do so because there is no recognizable figure or object with which to identify. The objections to Impressionist works, which generally *do* contain recognizable forms, may have resulted from the spectacle of edges dissolving into increasingly prominent brush strokes. In Cubism, the planes are dislocated, thereby disrupting viewers' natural experience of three-dimensional space and confronting them with unfamiliar arrangements. The Abstract Expressionist and Minimalist artists present viewers with the formal elements of art—lines, shapes, colors, light, dark, and so forth—but do not "form" them into depictions of objects from the viewer's environment. Instead, the reverse takes place and forms are abstracted *from* the environment.

In all these styles, the viewers are, in a sense, "deprived" of the security engendered by recognition and familiarity. They are, instead, presented with the *un*familiar, which can have a jarring effect. As time passes, however, people begin to accept what once seemed outrageous.

FREUD AND THE UNCANNY

The psychological significance of the uncanny inspired one of Freud's rare discussions of aesthetics, "The Uncanny."[4] Though Freud takes his examples from literature, the psychic principles apply equally well to images and explain aspects of their power. Freud reviews the dictionary meanings of the German word *heimlich*, ranging from "familiar," or "homely," to "secret and hidden" to "dangerous and dreaded"; the latter is virtually equivalent to "*un*heimlich," or "uncanny," the opposite of the original meaning. The ambivalence of the word coincides with the psychological ambivalence of the feeling. In Freud's view of child development, the uncanny denotes regression to a stage of infantile helplessness long since repressed and superseded. When revived, this state of being is alien, as well as familiar, and carries with it a sense of dread.

Freud explores the psychology of the uncanny on two levels of child development: the pre-oedipal stage of primary narcissism and oedipal-level castration fear. Both can be related to the power of visual imagery as well as to certain kinds of literary impressions. In the uncanny experience, whether derived from primary narcissism or from castration fear, what was originally experienced as friendly and pleasurable reemerges as terrifying. The childhood conviction that dolls are alive, or can come alive, is experienced with dread when reencountered later in adulthood. Hence the uncanniness of automata, Daedalus's "living sculptures"; Hanson's Photorealism; and waxworks, such as Madame Tussaud's in London.

An important connection between primary narcissism and the uncanny is the image of the "double" in the child's mind. A frequent theme in folklore, literature, and the arts, which has been extensively analyzed by Otto Rank,[5] the double reinforces self-love as a denial of death. Shadows and reflections are natural doubles, and create positive as well as negative impressions. The anxiety experienced by the loss of one's shadow is evident, for example, in the determined attempts of Peter Pan to recover his. The positive, even delightful quality of shadows is conveyed by Robert Louis Stevenson's poem for children "My Shadow":

> I have a little shadow that goes in and out with me,
> And what can be the use of him is more than I can see.
> He is very, very like me from the heels up to the head;
> And I see him jump before me, when I jump into my bed.

The cavalier attitude of Stevenson's child poet notwithstanding, the belief that the shadow ensures against the death of the ego is found in many superstitions about shadows, reflections, and the soul. The absence of a shadow or a reflection may signify death or sexual impotence; its length also has significance in certain cultures.

In the visual arts and in literature, doubles are created. The psychological power of the double has inspired innumerable artistic transformations of the childhood belief in the animation of inanimate objects. In cultures as diverse as Neolithic Jordan and the modern Sepik River people of New Guinea, skulls have been reconstituted by modeling around them with plaster. Shells are inserted into the eye sockets and hair is sometimes attached to the head. The result is an uncanny image that seems to waver on the borderline of life and death.

The importance of ancestor cults in the ancient world led to the development of death masks. Gold death masks found in Mycenaean tholos tombs have preserved the features of their kings. In Rome, portrait busts (sculptures as well as paintings) of deceased individuals were kept in private houses. The sculptures were carved from death masks and served

6. *George Segal,* Chance Meeting, *1989.*

a genealogical purpose consistent with the ancient Roman interest in lineage.

A related technique is found in the sculpture of the contemporary American artist George Segal, who makes "life masks" by "mummifying" the living. He dips gauze bandages in wet plaster and wraps the subject's body. When the plaster hardens, Segal cuts it off in sections and reassembles it. The finished work is an effigy, usually in white, unpainted plaster but sometimes in gray or colored plaster, of an entire body or a section of a body. In *Chance Meeting* [6], three plaster figures come upon one another under a One Way street sign. Because they are essentially plaster "impressions" of real people, each conveys an individual character. At the same time, however, they are ghostly and seem to belong to another plane of existence. Segal's juxtaposition of living and not-living, of alien and familiar, arouses a feeling of uncanniness in the viewer.

In painting, portraits can play a "double" role. When we speak of the eyes in a painted portrait seeming to follow us as we move around a room, we are referring to its uncanny, lifelike quality. In that case, the feeling derives from the childhood conviction that parents can see, hear, and know what their children are doing. When that conviction persists consciously in the adult, it constitutes paranoid thinking and is a narcissistic perversion of the parent's gaze. It is a tribute to the power of imagery that a picture can evoke such infantile responses.

A classic literary portrait "doubling" for a person is Oscar Wilde's *Picture of Dorian Gray.*[6] The relationship of the picture to Dorian is an example of defensive splitting.

"Splitting of the ego" is used by Freud[7] to denote a psychological phenomenon in which two psychical attitudes co-exist unconsciously in the ego. One is in touch with, and functions in relation to, reality and the other functions as a wish. In Dorian Gray, the portrait is Dorian's split off, realistically aging and morally corrupt self. This allows him to preserve the wishful delusion that his real self remains youthful and virtuous. Whereas the mythological Narcissus is rivetted to his reflection and continues to gaze on it, Dorian can leave the picture because its significance is split off from his consciousness.

When Dorian's defense breaks down, he "kills" his portrait, whereupon his real self ages and dies, and the image in the picture regains its youth.

The image in Dorian's portrait *mis*reflects him, because the mechanism of splitting is rendered literally for the book's narrative purpose. Insofar as a portrait is a likeness, it "mirrors" its subject. With Dorian's misreflection, Wilde creates an uncanny effect. In Surrealist art, too, the unexpected character of misreflection is often uncanny. In Picasso's *Girl Before a Mirror* [7], the mirror reflects a different girl from the one we see looking at herself. A clue to the meaning of Picasso's surreal image is suggested by the French word *psyche* and the Spanish *psiquis*, both meaning "soul" and referring to the type of mirror in the painting.[8] Possibly the reflection is the girl's soul, or "double," her inner psychological self—which would correspond to traditional mirror superstitions.

7. *Pablo Picasso,* Girl Before a Mirror, *1932.
Museum of Modern Art, New York. Gift of
Mrs. Simon Guggenheim.*

CLINICAL CONSIDERATIONS

Clinical experience has shown that children of some six to eighteen months learn that their mirror reflections are really themselves and not another child—what Lacan calls the "stade du miroir," or "mirror stage."[9] This recognition marks an important developmental step in the sense of self.

Prior to the age of six to eighteen months, from the very moment of birth and to some extent into adulthood, the mother's gaze has a reflective function. At first it is the literal gaze of the mother (or her substitute), looking at the nursing infant. Later, the gaze becomes a general watchfulness motivated by the instinct to protect the child. The ideal maternal gaze takes into account the child's needs and "reflects" them in a metaphorical as well as a literal sense, with approval or disapproval as internal and external reality require. Eventually, in normal development, the mother's gaze is transformed into the community at large, and the adult seeks recognition from peers in the outside world.

In extreme cases, the mother's failure to reflect adequately her child's needs can result in borderline character disorders or even psychosis. The bizarre case of Mr. Q. illustrates both parents' failure to protect their child and his uncanny torture by older twin sisters.

When Q. was born, his sisters Betsy and Jill were sixteen years old. They vented their rage at being identical twins—doubles of each other—on Q., who was unique. Betsy and Jill invented a game that they called "Broken Betsy and Broken Jill." As soon as Q. was mobile, Betsy and Jill would jump out at him from behind doors and shout "Beware! Broken Betsy!" or "Beware! Broken Jill!" Little Q. was unable to tell his sisters apart; they were mirror images of each other. Even worse, they played the game with mirrors, thereby re-doubling themselves. When Q. howled with fear, his parents laughed along with his sisters. As a result of this constant barrage of uncanny doubling, and of whatever additional misguided child-rearing practices accompanied it, Q. had only the barest experience of having a self within his control. By the time he entered therapy, his ego boundaries had been quite literally shattered.

THE MATERNAL MIRROR

The maternal aspect of mirroring can be related to the ambivalent nature of mirror iconography in art and superstition. The Virgin Mary, for exam-

8. *Robert Smithson,* Second Mirror Displacement,
from Incidents of Travel in the Yucatán, *1969.*
Estate of Robert Smithson.

ple, is the idealized Christian mother and, as such, is conceived of as a
spotless mirror. A cracked mirror, on the other hand, can refer to a woman's
fall from innocence.[10]

Just as the maternal mirror can be both virginal and sexual, so it can
be dangerous as well as beneficent. The dangers of the maternal mirror are
contained in Robert Smithson's earth works entitled *Mirror Displacements*
[8]. Smithson's conscious awareness of the earth as a dangerous maternal
image is clear when he refers, however satirically, to "the ecological Oedipus complex." He describes the earth beneath his *Overturned Rock #1* as
"nameless slime . . . raw roots . . . abyss, a damp cosmos of fungus and mold
. . . clammy solitude,"[11] leaving no doubt about the perceived threat posed
by falling victim to the earth's dangers. Such remarks evoke Freud's finding

that for certain neurotic men the female genital is uncanny because it combines danger with familiarity (the womb). But Smithson is not the earth's victim; instead, he places mirrors on the earth's surface. In contrast to the pool of Narcissus, one cannot fall into a mirror. Smithson the artist directs the placement; by thus taking control, he sublimates narcissistic passivity into art.

The ambivalent nature of the mirror and its consequent ability to arouse feelings of uncanniness is given visual form in Magritte's *The False Mirror* [9]. Its "falseness" derives from the ambiguity of its double view; the observer does not know if he sees a reflection of the sky or if he is looking through the eye *at* the sky. This calls into question the observer's own point of view, and he is momentarily thrown off balance. Nor is it clear whether the eye in the painting looks at *us* or at the sky. A persistent equivalent ambiguity in the parental gaze (or attention) would very likely result in the child's development of a "false self."[12] The so-called false-self character is typically as "off balance" and unsure of his identity on a continual basis as the observer of an ambiguous image is on a momentary basis.

9. René Magritte, The False Mirror
(Le Faux Miroir), *1928. Museum of Modern Art,
New York. Purchase.*

THE UNCANNY AND CASTRATION FEAR

Freud has shown that, on the oedipal level of development, the uncanny derives not so much from the loss of self as from the dread of castration. In literature and the visual arts, castration fear can be evoked by images of severed limbs or other detached body parts, such as an eye or a head, which have unconscious phallic meaning.

Detached shadows, which also create uncanny effects, are the subject of Robert Louis Stevenson's "North-West Passage," the child's nighttime journey along the corridor to his bedroom. Unlike the reassuring doubling shadow that "goes in and out" with the child poet of "My Shadow," these shadows have a will of their own and thus evoke dread:

> Now my little heart goes a-beating like a drum,
>   With the breath of the Bogie in my hair;
> And all round the candle the crooked shadows come,
>   And go marching along up the stair.

The sense of the uncanny is particularly strong if, like Daedalus's automata and Stevenson's hallway shadows, the inanimate figures or detached body parts can move independently.

Taking the example of Offenbach's *Tales of Hoffmann*, Freud relates the uncanny character of the Sandman to the fear of losing one's eyes. Although in his more popular form the Sandman induces sleep in children by sprinkling sand in their eyes, in another version he tears their eyes out. In the unconscious, he represents the castrating oedipal father feared by the child at night when darkness diminishes the eye's power. This circumstance recapitulates Oedipus' self-blinding as a castration metaphor (see Chapter 4).

A forty-year-old male patient slated to inherit ten million dollars on his ailing father's death dreamed that he was in love with the wife of an old friend. It struck the patient as odd that he had not seen the friend in years, had never met his wife, and had no idea what she looked like. He only knew that the friend's wife was a dancer as his own mother had been. At first he could not even remember his friend's last name.

When I suggested that perhaps the dream had oedipal implications, the patient recalled that his friend was Mr. Zandemann. The friend turned out to be his Sandman father in disguise, who would punish him for his reawakened death wishes towards him and his erotic interest in a disguised, youthful version of his mother.

The uncanniness of a detached eye is virtually inevitable and is a common motif in Surrealism. It is also familiar in Egyptian art, as an apotropaion against the dangers of the evil eye. The uncanny character of the detached and conventional frontal eye in Egyptian painted and relief profiles is nevertheless mitigated by stylization. The veristic Surrealism of Magritte, on the other hand, allows for more direct identification with the image than is possible with a stylized convention. The realism of the eye in *The False Mirror* [9] increases the uncanny effect of its juxtaposition with

10. *Andrea del Castagno,* David, *c. 1450. National Gallery of Art, Washington, D.C. Widener Collection.*

11. *Michelangelo da Caravaggio,* David with the Head of Goliath, *c. 1605–10. Galleria Borghese, Rome.*

the sky. Magritte's symbolic eye can represent the watchful father as well as the ambivalent ("false") mother. As one who watches, the father can also be ambivalent and therefore dangerous. These two dynamics operate on different levels of child development. The maternal eye has an earlier, reflective, "mirroring" function, while the paternal eye is the source of later superego retribution for real or imagined transgressions. (This is, of course, a construct; in actuality, parental functions overlap dynamically.)

The uncanny effect of detached or severed body parts that can move on their own is clear from a comparison of Castagno's *David* [10] with Caravaggio's *David with the Head of Goliath* [11]. Both paintings contain Goliath's decapitated head. In the Castagno, Goliath is dead; his eyes are closed and the stone is embedded in his forehead. Caravaggio's Goliath, on the other hand, is very much alive, despite having been beheaded. His eyes are wide open and the horrified expression on his face indicates that he is aware of his predicament. It is the lifelike quality of Goliath's head that

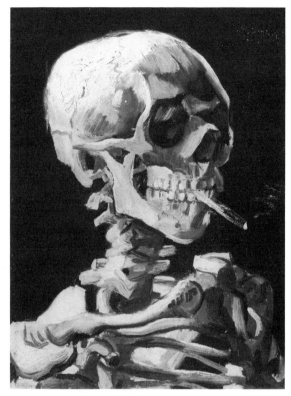

12. *Vincent van Gogh,* Skull with a Cigarette, *1885–86. Stedelijk Museum, Amsterdam. Vincent van Gogh Foundation/Vincent van Gogh Museum, Amsterdam.*

13. *René Magritte,* The Betrayal of Images (This Is Not a Pipe), *1926. Los Angeles County Museum. Purchased with funds provided by the Mr. and Mrs. William Preston Harrison Collection.*

Ceci n'est pas une pipe.

evokes the viewer's empathy and consequent dread of suffering a similar fate.

Caravaggio's Goliath is comparable to the Jericho skulls in being a transition between life and death. It literally represents the "living dead." Another example of the living dead rendered literally is van Gogh's *Skull with a Cigarette* [12]. There is no evidence in the van Gogh of decapitation or severed limbs; the reduction of the figure to a skeleton, however, bespeaks an extraordinary depressive content. Its uncanny quality derives from the impossibility of a skeleton with no lungs, muscle, or skin actually smoking a cigarette.

Because the early ego is a body ego, an integrated self requires an intact sense of one's body. The removal of skin, therefore, destroys the body ego and evokes a loss of self that threatens primary narcissism. In being a detached body part, the absent skin revives the oedipal fear of castration. By removing the skin from the bones of the skeleton, van Gogh has created an image that is transitional between the level of primary narcissism and the Oedipus complex, as well as between life and death.

Related to the uncanny double of oneself is the image that stands for someone else. Pygmalion's statue of Galatea is such an image; he reacted to it as if it were a real woman, even though he knew that it was not. Although viewers may not actually *believe* that images are real, they have been known to make important decisions based on them. In 1501 in Florence, a man got drunk and threw horse manure at an image of the Virgin Mary. He was hanged for defiling a sacred icon.[13] In sixteenth-century England, a wax effigy of Queen Elizabeth I stuck through with pins was discovered. The court astrologer John Dee was immediately summoned to counteract the effects of witchcraft. The uncertainty whether an image is real or only an image is a subject of Magritte's *Betrayal of Images* [13]. Magritte alerts viewers to their potential betrayal by his painted pipe by writing across the picture plane "Ceci n'est pas une pipe" (This is not a pipe). His image is also about the ambivalent response to illusionism.

IMAGES THAT WARN OF DEATH

The *vanitas* tradition in Western art was made possible by the power of imagery as a warning. Since warnings imply a future danger, such images contain references to the passage of time. Particularly popular in seventeenth-century Netherlandish painting, the *vanitas* theme derives from the

14. Lucas Furtenagel,
Portrait of Hans
Burgkmair and His
Wife.
*Kunsthistorisches
Museum, Vienna.*

notion that temporal possessions and pursuits are all empty (*vanus* in Latin) in the face of inevitable death. Certain motifs, such as the skull, hourglass, and candle, remind the viewer of the passage of time. Sometimes, as in the *Portrait of Hans Burgkmair and His Wife* by Lucas Furtenagel [14], a mirror reflection denotes the future. Burgkmair's wife holds up a mirror in which two reflected skulls uncannily signify the couple's inevitable future.

Giorgione's *Old Woman* conveys the same message without the use of a mirror. A haggard, toothless crone displays the inscription "Col Tempo," meaning "With Time [you too will be as I am]." Essentially the same message is conveyed in the medieval transi tombs with skeletal effigies on their lids. A painted version appears below Masaccio's *Trinity* fresco on the nave wall of Santa Maria Novella in Florence [15]. The illusionistic tomb with the effigy of a skeleton bears the inscription "I was once what you are, and what I am you will become." Such warnings carry

15. *Masaccio,* The
Trinity, *c. 1428.*
Santa Maria Novella,
Florence.

16. Giotto, The Last Judgment, *c. 1305.*
Arena Chapel, Padua.

a moral injunction against vain pleasures and are an implied call to the worship of God.

A related warning occurs in Last Judgment scenes located above entrances to churches and cathedrals. The Last Judgment warns of Christ's Second Coming, when the eternal fate of everyone's soul will be decided. As worshipers approach the church entrance, they confront the image of Christ welcoming the saved into heaven juxtaposed with the tortures of the damned.

In contrast to Last Judgments that visitors encounter before entering a church, Giotto's *Last Judgment* in the Arena Chapel in Padua is on the inside of the entrance wall [16]. As a result, it is the last image seen on the way out. In the Arena Chapel, therefore, the temporal relation of the Last Judgment to the worshiper corresponds to the Christian view of time in which Christ's Second Coming marks the end of the world.

The warning and the possible punishment contained in the iconography of the Last Judgment evoke the role of the superego in the unconscious. The conventional arrangement that associates up with heaven and the saved, and down with hell and the damned has a parallel in childhood and therefore in the adult unconscious. Children experience themselves as being at a disadvantage because they are "down" (that is, shorter) in comparison to adults.

The falling of the damned souls, an echo of the original Fall of Man, has a sexual character evident in the fact that throughout medieval art only the damned are nude. Likewise, falling in dreams denotes passive sexual seduction, reflected in the colloquial term "fallen woman." The abundance of hanged figures in Giotto's Hell illustrates the very punishment that requires the downward pull of gravity in order to bring about death.[14] The typically disordered depiction of the damned and the medieval emphasis on oral aggression in contrast to the order and dignity of the saved denote the regressive, or developmentally "downward," confusion and anxiety in the image of Hell.

It is even possible that there is an evolutionary aspect in these visual conventions, for before man developed an upright posture he was literally "lower down" and more primitive. This evolutionary development is recapitulated in every individual who crawls before he walks. If we judge by the triumphant delight when a child learns to walk, it is not surprising that, in imagery of all kinds, up connotes victory and down, defeat.

Another convention of Last Judgment scenes is the left-right disposition of saved and damned souls in relation to Christ—the saved on his

17. Ambrogio Lorenzetti, detail of Securitas *from the* Allegory of Good Government, *1338–40. Palazzo Pubblico, Siena.*

right and the damned on his left. This arrangement is consistent with the negative connotations of left; in Latin, left is *sinister*. In dreams, and in the unconscious, the left can be the evil or sexual side, and "to be left" is "to be abandoned." The term "right," on the other hand, denotes correctness and morality. The French word for right, *droit*, also means "law."

The right-left disposition of good and evil, respectively, also characterizes scenes of the Crucifixion. Mary, for example, is usually on Christ's right. In Giotto's Arena Chapel *Crucifixion*, Christ's family and friends are on his right and the Roman soldiers on his left. Likewise, in narrative fresco cycles in Christian chapels, it was usual for Old Testament scenes to be on the left wall and New Testament scenes on the right.

The antiquity of distinguishing left from right is highlighted by the interesting discovery of a Paleolithic settlement in Siberia. The interiors of houses had been consciously divided into right and left. The left half contained objects used only by women, and the right half, objects used by men.[15]

EXEMPLARY IMAGES

The exemplary character of the Last Judgment is contained in its power as a warning. Throughout Western history, exemplary images have been believed to have a real effect on viewers, and sometimes they do. During the fifteenth century in Italy, Alberti suggested the use of such imagery to reform wayward boys. "We may exhibit the life of other wicked men before him as a kind of mirror," he wrote. "There he may look at himself and recognize the ugliness and filth of his criminal ways."[16]

A corollary to Alberti's advice was the Italian practice, recorded from the twelfth century, of painting defaming pictures *(pitture infamanti)* in fresco on exterior walls of public buildings (see Chapter 7).[17] These included caricatures of those perpetrating commercial crimes, such as fraud, and images of hanged criminals—especially traitors. The originals no longer exist, but several drawing studies from the late fifteenth century by Andrea del Sarto of men hanging upside down have been preserved. Although the practice had declined in the rest of Italy by the quattrocento, its continued importance in Florence is evident in the stature of the artists commissioned to paint such pictures—for example, Andrea del Castagno, Sandro Botticelli, and del Sarto.[18]

Similar sentiments had inspired Ambrogio Lorenzetti's inclusion of a gallows held up by Securitas above the peaceful landscape in his *Allegory of Good Government* [17]. Located in the Palazzo Pubblico of Siena, Ambrogio's allegories of good and bad government reflected fourteenth-century humanism in Italy. The message of those pictures is that there is a cause-and-effect relationship between good government and peace and prosperity on the one hand, and bad government and crime, poverty, and disorder, on the other. Ambrogio's depiction of a hanged criminal is an example to those who would disrupt the law and order of good government by resorting to crime.

THE CORRUPTING POWER OF IMAGES

The belief in the power of images to corrupt is apparent in the aversion to exposing children to pornographic pictures, in the practice of rating movies, and in discussions of the impact of television violence on crime. Pliny (NH, 36 iv, 20–24) describes two statues by the fourth-century B.C. sculptor Praxiteles that incited observers to perverse sexual acts. According to

Pliny, a man fell in love with Praxiteles's Aphrodite of Cnidos and left a stain on it that betrayed his lust. The same thing happened when another man became enamored of the artist's sculpture of a nude Cupid.

During the Iconoclastic Controversy (A.D. 730–843), passions ran high over the question of making images of saints. Would the images incite the viewer to worship the image itself rather than what the image represented? Absolutely! declared the Iconoclasts. And furthermore, the Bible specifically warned against the worship of graven images. No! countered the Iconophiles; viewers could be trusted to distinguish between the representation and what was represented. The edict of A.D. 730 against images of saints adversely affected the production of sculpture in the Byzantine era; many artists left Byzantium, while others renounced religious subject matter.

In the sixteenth century, Michelangelo's severest critic, Pietro Aretino, objected to the artist's imagery on grounds of impropriety. Contrasting Michelangelo's figures with Raphael's, which he preferred, Aretino advised parents against exposing their children to Michelangelo's work. "If you've seen one Michelangelo," he wrote, "you've seen them all,"[19] meaning that men, women, and children were similarly and inappropriately represented. When he beheld the nudes of Michelangelo's *Last Judgment,* Aretino pronounced them fit for a bathroom, not for a papal chapel.

The Counter-Reformation was quite explicit about the corrupting power of imagery. Mythological subjects and nudity were considered heretical, as were certain other iconographic improprieties. Draperies were painted on the nude saints in Michelangelo's *Last Judgment.*

In 1573, the Inquisition brought up the northern Italian painter Veronese on charges of heresy for his *Last Supper.* The Inquisitors objected to dogs, dwarfs, Germans, and Saint Peter picking his teeth in Christ's presence. Veronese claimed artistic license and pointed out that a big dinner at the time probably would have included dogs and dwarfs, if not Germans, and that it was perfectly natural for Saint Peter to pick his teeth. The Inquisition was unimpressed and gave Veronese three months to make the necessary alterations. The real objection to the Germans, of course, was that they would remind viewers of Martin Luther, whose campaign against the corruption of the Catholic Church had set off the Protestant Reformation. Veronese changed only the painting's name—to *The Feast in the House of Levi*—and the Inquisitors were satisfied.

In nineteenth-century France, Honoré Daumier delighted in caricaturing various professions and social classes in the press. He depicted the corruption of lawyers and judges, the greed of businessmen, and the vanity of actors. When he turned his hand to the monarchy, however, he encountered trouble. In 1835, France enacted a law prohibiting anti-government pictures in the press. The fact that literary commentary containing similar anti-monarchist messages was permitted reflects the belief in the power of imagery to incite rebellion and confirms the adage that "a picture is worth a thousand words."

IMAGES THAT PROVOKE
THEIR OWN DESTRUCTION

Whether or not an image can incite a rebellion independently of other factors, once a rebellion is under way, images often fall victim to the rebels. During the French Revolution, many statues of biblical kings and queens were destroyed. In the 1990s, when communism began to fall in Eastern Europe, statues of Communist leaders were toppled or dismantled.

Images can evoke violent responses on the most unexpected occasions and for individual, as well as religious, cultural, or political motives. In the sixteenth century, someone, possibly an outraged pious Christian, scratched out the eyes of Saint James's executioner in Mantegna's fresco in the Eremitani Church in Padua. While such an action might not have been ordered by the Inquisition, it is not inconsistent with painting draperies on Michelangelo's saints or the sentiments of the Counter-Reformation.

Although such actions clearly qualify as vandalism, they have complex psychological meanings. In 1911, for example, a cook was fired from his job in the Dutch navy, and he later took revenge on Holland by slashing Rembrandt's *Night Watch*. On that occasion, the painting, which was highly valued by the state and located in a state museum, was punished as a proxy; in effect, it "doubled" for the Dutch government.

Three years later, in 1914, a British suffragette slashed Velázquez's *Rokeby Venus* [18] in London's National Gallery. She was protesting the imprisonment of the suffragette leader, Mrs. Pankhurst, by destroying the image of "the most beautiful woman in mythological history." Mrs. Pankhurst, the suffragette claimed in the March 11, 1914, edition of the London *Times*, was "the most beautiful character in modern history." It is difficult to believe that there was not also a sexual motive in the suffragette's crime, especially since she later admitted her objection to men "gaping" at the picture.

18. *Diego Velázquez,* Rokeby Venus, *1650s.*
National Gallery, London.

As was true of *The Night Watch,* the *Rokeby Venus* was in a national museum and could thus double for the state. At the same time, however, such vandalism bespeaks a paranoid regression on the part of the vandals that can be related to the *content* of the images. *The Night Watch* represents a shooting company, led by Captain Banning Cocq. A group of enthusiastic armed men, standard bearers, and a drummer stride forth from the city of Amsterdam. It is likely that the quasi-military character of the crowd evoked in the cook the naval setting in which he had been fired. The military authority empowered to fire him could have been taken by the unconscious as a metaphor for paternal authority. In that context, the vandal symbolically vented his rage at a perceived paternal injustice that had cost him his job, wounded his narcissism, and adversely affected his sense of self-worth.

In the second case, the suffragette was disturbed by men *looking* at a Venus depicted in rear view. Her own statement suggests that she identified with the image as well as with Mrs. Pankhurst. By slashing the figure, the vandal literally "tore her to shreds," as if to ward off the dangers of being sexually observed from behind. The mirror held by Cupid "doubles" the paranoid fear. On the one hand, Venus's mirror reflection "looks back" at the viewer as well as at the slasher. On the other hand, by identification with Venus, the slasher experiences being looked *at* by men. As iconoclasts, therefore, the sailor unconsciously attempted to destroy his father, and the suffragette, men who appear to dominate women by their gaze.

The vandalism committed by both the sailor and the suffragette had a public as well as a private motive. Both drew the attention of the press, which brought their grievances into a public forum. In contrast, John Ruskin's paranoia (see Chapter 12) led him to destroy works of art for personal reasons only. In 1857 Ruskin was in charge of several thousand drawings by the great English Romantic painter Joseph Mallord William Turner that were destined for the National Gallery in London after the artist's death. Among the works was a package of erotic drawings that Ruskin called "grossly obscene."[20] Together with the keeper of the National Gallery, Ruskin sanctioned burning the offending pictures, thereby destroying an important part of Turner's artistic and psychological legacy.

IMAGES THAT DAZZLE AND BLIND

According to Pliny (NH 36, iv, 32), the Greek sculptor Menestratos placed a statue of Hecate, the mythological witch, in the precinct behind the temple of Diana (the Roman equivalent of Artemis) at Ephesos. The priests warned visitors that the glare of the marble was so bright that it would harm their eyes. Such warnings concern the dangers of sexual observation, in this case observation of the witchlike aspect of the mother. Psychologically, it would appear, Hecate's role as a blinding force represents the split-off evil mother. Her opposite, at Ephesos, was embodied by the statue of the nurturing Diana, which was endowed with many breasts.

Looking on gods, goddesses, kings, and queens has been considered dangerous throughout history. In ancient Egypt, seeing the pharaoh could result in being burned by his radiance. In Greek myth, Semele, the mortal mother of Dionysos, looks at Zeus, who has impregnated her, and instantly burns up. Zeus then takes the unborn Dionysos and places him in his thigh, which acts as a substitute womb. The real dangers to vision from staring at the sun may be at the root of such accounts, but, if so, they have become attached to fantasies about gods and rulers and their images.

In the pantheons of ancient Mesopotamia, Egypt, Greece, and Rome, the chief male god is associated with the sun and the sky. In Christianity, God is light, Christ is related to the sun, and divinity is signified by a halo, or glow of light around a person's head. The divine right of kings can be traced to their association with the sun as a god. Louis XIV of France, for example, proclaimed himself "Le Roi Soleil" and decorated his palace at Versailles accordingly. And when a statue of George Washington was commissioned to project his image as the first American president, the sculptor, Horatio Greenough, chose the monumental statue of Zeus from the temple at Olympia as his model.

Western rulers, although symbolically "descended" from the sun, are no longer believed to have "blinding" power. Nevertheless, they, like their female counterparts, represent parents in the unconscious. Looking on gods and rulers stands in the unconscious for the sexual observation of parents. The dangers of this circumstance can be seen within the context of child development. Children who are overexposed to parental nudity or sexual activity, repeatedly molested, or otherwise overstimulated tend to develop learning problems that stem from an unconscious refusal to "see," or understand.

Reading, which requires the use of the eye to grasp and absorb meaning, can be inhibited by having "seen too much" in early childhood. This phenomenon—particularly frequent in the children of the sexually casual 1960s generation of parents and in those from economically deprived backgrounds where crowded living conditions encourage sexual precocity—can inhibit the ability to read. Such children internalize the dynamics embodied by the myths of blinding parental figures (for example, gods and rulers), which are cultural projections of the individual mind.

ARCHITECTURAL IMAGES

The psychological response to architecture, as well as to pictures and sculpture, appears in dream images, jokes, metaphors, and other mental productions. A house built on a firm foundation, for example, is assumed to be lasting, while one built on sand is not. That architecture can symbolize psychological as well as physical stability is expressed in the witticism that "neurotics build castles in the air and psychotics live in them."

To say that "people in glass houses should not throw stones" indicates the degree to which we identify with architectural enclosures. This is confirmed in dreams, where a building can stand for the human body, whose orifices are symbolized by windows, doors, and other openings. The traditional association of the woman with domestic interiors is reflected in the term "housewife," and to be "house proud" is to be concerned about the *appearance* of one's home. To say that "a man's home is his castle" indicates his metaphorical role as a king inside his own four walls.

The initial impact of a building is made by its exterior. Once inside, like the proverbial "man of the castle," we experience its interior in relation to ourselves. The effects of closed versus open space, inside and outside, up and down combine physical and psychological states of being. The fact that in places of worship the most interior space is usually also the most sacred reflects the psychological value of intimacy. Likewise, in everyday language, we speak of "being on the inside" and in the "inner circle" as more important than being an "outsider." Good political and social contacts are people who can "open doors" that admit us to advantageous situations.

Because buildings serve a particular purpose and are cultural as well as personal expressions, they are designed to project certain psychological images. These images are reflected in language. Cottages are apt to be "cozy," castles "imposing," palaces "sumptuous," and jails "forbidding." When Sigismondo Malatesta built his Castel Sismondo in Rimini in the fifteenth century with the most advanced defensive and offensive fortifications, he intended an image of power. Louis XIV's seventeenth-century palace at Versailles, one of the most sumptuous in the world, was designed to project the king's image as the sun, and therefore as a source of power and even life itself. The medieval Bargello in Florence expressed power in another way. It housed the *podestà*, or legal "power," of the city, notably the office of the chief police magistrate. The drab, plain dark gray exterior walls and small windows were reminders of interior jail cells and torture chambers. Reinforcing its forbidding image were the fortresslike crenelations around the roof and tower.

Gateways and other entrances create the architectural transition between outside and inside. Some entrances are welcoming, others are forbidding. Some are guarded by sentries or doormen; others are guarded symbolically by effigies of guardians, often in animal form.

The role of guardian animals, whether Chu dogs in China or lions in the West, has a particular significance. The animals confront the would-be visitor directly, as if challenging his approach. A colossal sphinx guarded the funerary complex at Giza; a pair of lions flanked the entrance to the

Hittite city of Hattusas and the column over the entrance to the Mycenaean citadel. On Fifth Avenue at Forty-second Street in New York City, another pair of lions flanks the entrance to the New York Public Library. The guardian function of lions derives from ancient superstitions that they are watchful—like attentive parents—and even sleep with their eyes open. A similar belief in the power of the guardian eye has led to the so-called electric eyes that protect the interior spaces of our technological era.

When Christian liturgy refers to the Virgin as the "house of God," it evokes her role as Christ's literal "house," the womb that housed him before birth. In this aspect, Mary appears in art as monumentally large so that she either fills an architectural space or functions architecturally as an independent support and enclosure. She can also be Christ's tomb, which, according to Saint Augustine, is the justification for having to die before being reborn into heaven.[21] Mary's association with architecture is reinforced in Annunciation scenes (see Chapter 9), where she is usually inside—and sometimes next to—a building. Just as Mary can be the church building itself, and is related iconographically to architectural enclosures, houses in dreams are representations of the dreamer's own body.

An important purpose of religious architecture is to create the transition between people and their gods. The ancient Mesopotamians built ziggurats, which were imitation mountains believed to be the natural dwellings of the gods. The presence of a ziggurat in a Mesopotamian city served to reassure the inhabitants that the gods were nearby. Greek temples, set in sacred landscape precincts, were conceived of as "houses" for statues of gods and goddesses. The domes of mosques and churches stood for the all-encompassing sky, or dome of heaven, and the vertical towers of Christian churches expressed in concrete terms the belief that heaven is up.

Funerary architectural images can serve as "doubles" for life and therefore as a denial of death. The pyramids of ancient Egypt expressed the pharaoh's power while on earth and his security in the afterlife. Seen from the exterior, each sloping triangular wall of the pyramid appears to rise toward the sun. Originally capped with gold, the top of the pyramid was an architectural metaphor of the sun, whose descending rays were signified by gold on the outer surface of the walls. This image reinforced the pharaoh's role as sun-on-earth, the representative in human form of the sun itself. Inside the pyramid, walls were decorated with scenes of the pharaoh's life, thereby re-creating his entire existence in effigy for his use in the next world.

Some cultures create *necropoleis*, or cities of the dead. These serve as a kind of large-scale urban, or civic, "double," as if the dead can, in fact, "take it with them." By building a familiar architectural environment for the afterlife, people attempt to deny the distinctions between life and death. The Etruscans (see Chapter 7), who built *necropoleis*, extended the doubling of life and death into large sarcophagi conceived of as houses; these contained pieces of furniture as well as the body of the deceased.

The continuing appeal of antiquity in Western art has led to various revivals of classical style. When Thomas Jefferson sought an architectural style to express the ideals of the young American republic, he turned to the republics of ancient Greece and Rome. He was an originator of the American Federal style, with its classical orders and triangular pediments, as an image of democratic rule. As a result, American government buildings, such as courthouses, post offices, and public libraries, are traditionally derived from the architecture of Greek and Roman antiquity.

The very term "classical" has come to mean "traditional," "long-lasting," and "of high quality." These associations have led to the frequent use of classical elements in American bank buildings. People like to think that their money is safe and will last, an impression enhanced by the traditional appearance of bank architecture. But when a much larger amount of money is involved, enough to symbolize the nation itself, it is housed in a building referred to as a "fort."

NOTES

1. For a lengthy study of this subject, see David Freedberg, *The Power of Images*, Chicago, 1989.
2. For references in antiquity, see Ernst Kris and Otto Kurz, *Legend, Myth, and Magic in the Image of the Artist*, New Haven and London, 1979, pp. 66–68.
3. Here and throughout, references to Pliny in the text are from *Natural History* (10 vols.), Loeb Library Editions, Books 33–35, Cambridge and London, 1984, and Books 36–37, Cambridge, Mass., and London, 1971.
4. Freud, "The Uncanny," S.E. XVII, 1919, pp. 218–56.
5. Cf. Otto Rank, *The Double*, Chapel Hill, 1971.
6. Cf. Karl Beckson, "Oscar Wilde and the Masks of Narcissus," *Psychoanalytic Study of Society* 10 (1984): 249–67.
7. Cf. Freud, *An Outline of Psychoanalysis*, S. E. XXIII, 1940, pp. 202–3.
8. Cf. Carla Gottlieb, "Picasso's *Girl Before a Mirror*," *Journal of Aesthetics and Art Criticism* 24 (1966): 509–18.
9. John Muller, "Lacan's Mirror Stage," *Psychoanalytic Inquiry* 5, no. 2 (1985): 233–52.
10. See U. Kulturmann, "William Holman Hunt's *The Lady of Shalott*," *Pantheon* 38 (1980):

386–92. In Hunt's painting *The Lady of Shalott* (Wadsworth Athenaeum, Hartford, Conn.), the lady allows her attention to the traditional female art of weaving to be distracted by the sight of Sir Lancelot and its sexual implications. As a result, the threads slip from the loom and entangle her. "The Mirror," writes Tennyson, whose poem Hunt's painting illustrates, "crack'd from side to side";

"The curse is come upon me," cried
The Lady of Shalott.

11. R. Hobbs, *Robert Smithson: Sculpture*, Ithaca and London, 1981, p. 161.
12. Cf. D. W. Winnicott, "True and False Self" (1960), in his *Maturational Processes and the Facilitating Environment*, New York, 1965, Chapter 12.
13. Samuel Y. Edgerton, Jr., *Pictures and Punishment*, Ithaca and London, 1985, p. 47.
14. Cf. Howard McP. Davis, "Gravity in the Paintings of Giotto" (1971) in Laurie Schneider, ed., *Giotto in Perspective*, Englewood Cliffs, 1974, pp. 142–59.
15. Mircea Eliade, *A History of Religious Ideas*, vol. 1, Chicago 1978, p. 20.
16. Leon Battista Alberti, *The Family in Renaissance Florence*, trans. Renée Neu Watkins, Columbia, S. C., 1969, p. 78.
17. Edgerton, *Pictures and Punishment*, pp. 50 ff.
18. Ibid., p. 70.
19. "Chi vede una sola figura di Michel'Agnolo, le vede tutte." Cited by Mark W. Roskill, *Dolce's "Aretino" and Venetian Art Theory of the Cinquecento*, New York, 1968.
20. Joan Abse, *John Ruskin, the Passionate Moralist*, London, 1980.
21. Augustine, *Sermon* 248, "De Sepultura Domini," *P.L.* xxxix, col. 2204.

FOUR

Art and
the Oedipus Complex

E vidence of the Oedipus complex appears not only in ideas and
myths about art, but also in the behavior of artists and in the images
they create. The pervasive theme of competition, its nature and
consequences, provides a window on the various and inevitable oedipal
transformations in the visual arts. The fact that art is seen to have a history
and a development, that artists learn from their predecessors, and that they
compete with one another creates a sense of lineage and family with which
artists identify and which is a prerequisite for oedipal dynamics. Pliny (NH
34, ix) describes a genealogy in the *subjects* of art as well; he says that
bronze was first used for statues of gods and only later for human figures.

FREUD AND THE OEDIPUS COMPLEX

The first recorded mention of the Oedipus complex is in Freud's letter of
October 15, 1897, to Fliess (Letter 71), in which he also referred to the
memory distortion resulting in screen memories. Freud described his own
early love for his mother and his awareness of his father's jealousy, recognizing that it accounted for "the rivetting power of *Oedipus Rex*" by
Sophocles. "Each member of the audience," wrote Freud, "was once, in
germ and in phantasy, just such an Oedipus, and each one recoils in horror
from the dream-fulfillment here transplanted into reality, with the whole
quota of repression which separates his infantile state from his present
one."[1]

Starting with this first reference in 1897, Freud embarked on a series
of new insights into what he considered the nucleus of every neurosis. His

delineation of the Oedipus complex was an ongoing process, lasting more than thirty years. The first insights came during his self-analysis by way of parallels with Sophocles' tragedy and Shakespeare's *Hamlet*. In the course of clinical analyses of men, women, and children, Freud learned more about the operation of the Oedipus complex—its appearance in dreams, symptoms, jokes, primitive cultures, religion, and literature.

By 1915–17,[2] Freud had formulated the relationship of pre-oedipal material to the complex itself. Pre-oedipal events—including loss of love or abandonment, the period of toilet training, and the sight of the female genitals—can contribute to oedipal castration fear. The child's first love object, the mother's breast, supplies food and erotic pleasure. From the attachment to the breast, the child progresses to the mother herself; both breast and mother are absorbed into the Oedipus complex and influence its development.

In the so-called positive oedipal constellation of a boy from two and a half years to six years, the child desires his mother and is hostile to his father as the obstacle to his wishes. He fears his father's retaliation in the form of castration, which corresponds to the talion law of the unconscious. The biblical "eye for an eye" expresses the literal character of the unconscious thinking that motivated Oedipus' self-blinding as upwardly displaced self-castration. In the so-called negative constellation,* the boy identifies with his mother and becomes, in fantasy, his father's passive love object.

By 1923, in *The Ego and the Id*,[3] Freud had recognized that the Oedipus complex operates bisexually—that is, the negative and positive constellations interact in every case. Although the boy is hostile to his father, he also loves him, which sets up an ambivalent relationship. In the 1928 essay "Dostoevsky and Parricide,"[4] Freud described the bisexuality of the Oedipus complex as heightened in neurosis and in certain creative individuals. Whether the positive or negative constellation predominates, however, the boy fears castration—in the former case as punishment and in the latter as a prerequisite for his feminine identification.

With the dissolution of the Oedipus complex,[5] the father's authority is introjected into the ego by the process of identification and forms the core of the superego. The superego, in turn, prohibits incest and murder, sublimating the libidinal and aggressive forces of the Oedipus complex.

---

*The terms "positive" and "negative" are used here, as they are by Freud, in the sense of reversal, as in negative film and positive print, and not in the sense of good and bad.

The aim of those forces is thereby inhibited and, in ideal circumstances, they are transformed into affection.

With regard to the Oedipus complex of the girl, Freud did not publish his final formulation until 1931.[6] Whereas he had originally considered male and female development to be parallel, he later realized that the girl's dynamics differed from the boy's. Continuing his archaeological metaphor, Freud compared this insight to unearthing the Minoan civilization, which had only been hinted at in myths and legends during the Greek era.

The girl, like the boy, takes her mother as her first love object; but there is less hostility in the girl's relationship to her father. In contrast to the boy, the girl's positive Oedipus complex requires a change in object from mother to father that corresponds to renouncing the clitoris as the primary genital zone in favor of the vagina. In girls, the fantasy that castration has already taken place precedes and paves the way for the Oedipus complex, whereas in boys, it is the fear of castration that destroys the Oedipus complex. These discoveries shed a new light on the importance of the girl's pre-oedipal stage and helped to explain her tendency to remain attached to her mother. They also clarified the complexity of female development, the likelihood of a prolonged Oedipus complex, and the greater flexibility of the superego as compared with males.

Freud was careful to point out that his formulation of the Oedipus complex is a construct and that all people are bisexual.[7] Nevertheless, the interplay of oedipal forces and their variations form a cornerstone of psychoanalytic theory. Because of the fantasy aspect of the complex, it carries with it a visual character that helps to explain the power of exemplary imagery. The sight of the nude female operates in the Oedipus configuration as just such an image, for it is taken by the little boy as the feared and future consequence of oedipal transgression (that is, incest and murder) and by the little girl as a punishment that has already been exacted. In considering the visual arts—whether subject matter, history and criticism, the creative process, the artists, viewers, or patrons—a recognition of oedipal derivatives can enrich the understanding of the material immeasurably.

THE SEARCH FOR ORIGINS:
SELF AND ART

The most persistent question of childhood, "Where did I come from?" (or "Where do babies come from?"), has a parallel in the history of art. Artists and writers on art have raised the same question about the origin of the first image and the first artist. Pliny's (NH 35, v) discussion of this question goes from the empirical to the mythical in much the same way that people deal with the origins of children. Although adults know perfectly well how babies are made, they have created explanations attributing their arrival to various mythic go-betweens, including cabbages and storks. For children, the question persists until answered; the longer they have to wait, the more time and inclination they have to weave fantasy explanations that can result in confusion, frustration, and neurosis.

According to Pliny, the Egyptians claimed to have originated painting six thousand years before his own era and to have taught it to the Greeks. Pliny dismisses the Egyptian version and reports the Greek belief that painting began either at Sicyon or Corinth. In any event, he asserts, all agree that painting began when someone drew a line around a man's shadow. At first, Pliny continues, pictures were of one color only and then others were added.

Various writers, including Quintilian,[8] Alberti,[9] and Leonardo,[10] repeated the account of the outlined shadow as the first painting. Alberti also reports the view that painting is the invention of Narcissus, "embracing with art of what is presented on the surface of the water in the fountain."[11] In most versions, the outline traced, whether belonging to a shadow or a reflection, is that of a human figure. The narcissistic character of such legends is a variation on the tendency to create gods in human form, which, in turn, reverses the belief that gods made people in their own image.

GODS, ARTISTS, AND FATHERS

In the unconscious, gods, artists, fathers, and such derivatives as patrons can be interchangeable. All are seen as controlling and powerful in some way, and all are related to creativity. Gods, artists, and fathers are creators, while patrons control the finances, or resources, of artistic production. The interchangeability of these paternal figures in the unconscious is reflected in myths and legends about the order, history, and genealogy of artists and their arts.

A genealogical approach to the visual arts raises the question of the first artist as well as the first image. The Greeks, as we have seen, credited Daedalus with being the original sculptor and also the original architect, who built the labyrinth on Crete. The Egyptians considered Imhotep, who designed the step pyramid of King Zoser at Saqqara [19], as the first to build monumental stone architecture. His legendary elevation to a god, worshiped at Heliopolis (City of the Sun), is consistent with the equation of artists with gods. Ancient Babylonian texts refer to God as a builder,[12] and in the Middle Ages God was depicted drawing the world with a compass. In the same period, Nicholas of Cusa (*De visione Dei*, Chapter 25) described God as a painter, mixing colors and preparing to paint his own likeness,[13] and in the sixteenth century Dosso Dossi depicted Zeus as the painter of the world.

Epic heroes who "found" cities are also seen as builders. In that sense, their function as symbolic "fathers of their country" is enhanced by an architectural metaphor. The first literary epic hero, Gilgamesh, was credited with having built the walls of Uruk, "Uruk of the Sheepfold," in ancient Mesopotamia. It is to Aeneas, who brought the household gods from Troy to Italy, that Virgil attributes the founding of Alba Longa, and the subsequent construction of Rome's "high walls." There is thus a genealogy of sorts, from gods as original creators, to epic heroes, to artists, and finally to the mortal father.

Although in a genealogical sense, gods precede artists as original creators, a reverse process exists in the tendency to elevate artists to divine

19. *Imhotep*, Step Pyramid, *c. 2750 B.C. Saqqâra, Egypt.*

20. Henry Moore, King
and Queen, 1952–53.

status (for example, Imhotep). A parallel dynamic operates when secular
kings who rule by divine right are deified after death, as the Roman
emperors were. Artists, too, have been "deified." Ingres called Raphael the
"god of painting," and Chaim Soutine called Rembrandt a "giant" and a
"god";[14] but, among Western visual artists, Michelangelo comes closest to
deification in the popular imagination. His designation as "divine" *(il divino)*
during his lifetime reveals the fine line between human and godly creators
in our minds. A similar mechanism is at work when children unconsciously
elevate their parents to royalty and they themselves implicitly become
heirs to the throne. Freud called this the "family romance,"[15] and pointed
out its correlation with kings and queens in fairy tales.

A good iconographic illustration of the family romance is Henry
Moore's bronze sculpture entitled *King and Queen* [20]. Its unusual character
puzzled even the artist,[16] who related it to reading his daughter fairy tales.
The King's head contains the key to the statue's meaning.

Moore described the head as "a combination of a crown, beard, and face symbolizing a mixture of primitive kingship and a kind of animal, Pan-like quality."[17] In reality, Moore's own father treated his chair, which occupied a corner of his small, coal-miner's house, as if it were a throne. No one was allowed to touch him while he sat in it, and Moore referred to the corner as "sacrosanct." That Henry Moore was the last of seven children is related to the "animal, Pan-like quality" of the King's head and is consistent with the artist's image of his father's active sexuality.

The otherwise elusive meaning of Moore's *King and Queen* can best be understood as a kind of "family romance" given visual form in bronze. The artist has elevated his father to kingship, while also referring to his lusty nature. His mother, more idealized and therefore seemingly less sexual, has become a queen. That the royal couple is set on top of a hill and presides over an open landscape is an attempt to "repair," by reversal, the confined and crowded space of Moore's childhood house (see Chapter 9).

DIVINE INSPIRATION
AND THE DREAM

Artistic inspiration is often thought of as "divine"; the very term "genius," in fact, originally referred to a divinity. The gods are seen as able to inspire, or speak through, artists and patrons, making them into divine "mouthpieces." Ernst Kris and Otto Kurz[18] cite the account of an angel appearing to Hagia Sophia's architect in a dream and describing the structure of the building. Pliny says that the ancient Greek architect Parrhasios claimed descent from Apollo and that his painting of Heracles was based on the hero's appearance to him in a dream. Reports such as these may derive from the fact that problems can be worked out in dreams when access to the unconscious is more available than in waking life.

About 2000 B.C., Gudea, king of Lagash, reported the following dream, which is recorded in fifty-four columns of text on two Mesopotamian cylinders:[19]

> A giant man, wearing a crown and winged with the wings of a lion-headed bird, appeared and spoke. The lower part of his body was a flood wave flanked by lions. Gudea did not understand the giant's words. When day came—still in the dream—a woman appeared; she held a gold stylus and studied a clay tablet on which a star-studded sky was depicted. A hero came with a lapis lazuli tablet and drew the plan of a house. He also

placed bricks in a mold, which, together with a basket, was set before Gudea. A male donkey pawed the ground.

Not understanding his dream, Gudea went to Nanshe, a dream interpreter. The giant, Nanshe said, was her brother, the god Ningirsu, instructing Gudea to build the Eninnu Temple. Daybreak came in the form of Ningishzida, who was Gudea's personal god, rising like the sun. The woman with the stylus was the goddess of writing and patron of the Sumerian school, an important literary educational center. The hero with the tablet was Nindub, the architecture god, and his drawing was a temple plan. The basket and brick mold were building materials, and the donkey was a symbol of Gudea's impatience to begin.

Gudea's dream and his report of its interpretation combine several traditional ingredients of the aetiological view of creativity in the visual arts. He receives instructions directly from the gods, while his personal god is equated with the rising sun. From the perspective of twentieth-century psychoanalytic methodology, it is possible to add another, more psychological level of meaning to the dream—for, although Gudea's associations are unavailable, his account of Nanshe's interpretation is. If we take her remarks as associations and combine them with the manifest content of the dream, the familial relationship between Gudea and his gods becomes clear.

The crowned giant with wings is a paternal figure; the repetition of lions recalls the leonine associations of kings in the ancient world. Lions, birds, and wings all have a phallic character in the unconscious. The flood wave, endowed like lions with roaring sound, denotes the power of male sexuality as expressed by the thunder and sea gods of antiquity. The association of daybreak with Gudea's patron god, and therefore with himself, evokes the traditional regal and paternal implications of the sun.

The woman with the gold stylus is the positive, magical aspect of the phallic mother, who encourages creativity. The hero, interpreted as the architect god by Nanshe, is Gudea himself, who will, in reality, effect the temple's construction. The detail of the tablet carried by the hero reinforces the celestial origin of Gudea's inspiration, since, in the ancient Near East, the blue color of lapis lazuli led to the belief that it came from the sky.

The dream's regressive (that is, childhood) character appears in the donkey pawing the ground, interpreted by Nanshe as Gudea himself. The accuracy of her interpretation is suggested by the totemism of childhood—or the readiness to identify with animals. The donkey's impatience is Gudea's dream persona as a child being instructed by "giant" gods, who, in turn, represent the child's view of parents as very large. That Gudea does not understand the giant's meaning conflates the time of the actual dream, when Gudea is an adult, with a time in early childhood when words spoken by adults are unintelligible.

On waking from a second and clearer dream, Gudea resumes his position as a benevolent king. He proclaims a general amnesty, intended to purify the city, and sacrifices to the gods. He thus establishes his genealogical position between gods and men, which is reflected in the statues of himself with his hands clasped in prayer. Gudea's image as a temple builder is preserved in the sculptures of him seated with a temple plan on his lap.

ARTISTS AS GIVERS OF LIFE

Equating artists with gods in the popular imagination is the belief that both endow their creations with life. Artists, as when tracing a line around a shadow or reflection, do so less directly than gods, or by a kind of substitution. Likewise, Daedalus created sculptures reportedly able to walk and talk rather than actual people. Pygmalion created a statue that he treated as if it were real; but it took a goddess to make it come alive.

In ancient Egypt, artists performed a symbolic "rebirth" on actual people, but only after they were dead. The ritual Opening of the Mouth ceremony consisted of "opening the mouth" of the deceased to "restore" the senses and the ability to breathe. That the Opening of the Mouth typically took place in a sculptor's workshop reflects the Egyptian designation of artists as "givers of life."

Artists generally think of their works as their children. In a fourteenth-century anecdote, Dante asked Giotto why his paintings were so beautiful and his children (of which he had six) so ugly. Giotto replied that he painted by the light of day and procreated at night. Michelangelo said that he had no children because his works were his children. The twentieth-century painter Josef Albers considered a mixed color the offspring of its component colors. Just as neighbors admiring a new baby remark on its likeness to its father or mother, so, said Albers, the mixed color contains characteristics of its component, or parent, colors.

Leonardo, according to Freud, behaved as if his works were his children, discarding them as he had felt discarded by his father. The notable exception would have been the Mona Lisa [1], which he treated like the mother of his childhood, remaining "true" to her and keeping her until his death. He continued to work on her image and took her to the court of France; as if following the precept of Rodgers and Hammerstein, once he had found her, he "never let her go."

James McNeill Whistler (see Chapter 12), in the nineteenth century, treated the portrait of his mother in much the same way as Leonardo treated the Mona Lisa. He was equally reluctant to give her up. With regard to his other pictures, Whistler's outrageous behavior can only be attributed to a conviction that they remained "his" even though they had been sold to others. On occasion, he removed his paintings from their owners' houses; but he ignored and disowned his two biological children.

The parental role of the artist recalls Freud's view of the artist's innate bisexuality.[20] Kris's "regression in the service of the ego"[21] and Greenacre's "access to childhood,"[22] which characterize the creative individual, are related to Freud's account of the developmental stages of childhood and the flexibility of early sexual identifications.[23] In having the ability to draw on childhood, therefore, artists derive energy from early psychosexual experience. This dynamic is fueled by the absence of time in the unconscious, which is also the basis of Proust's discussion of art in *Le Temps retrouvé*.[24] His view of the creative process, embodied in the déjà vu of the madeleine, is consistent with that of Freud, Kris, and Greenacre.

WHISTLER'S FIRST ARTIST

The notion of the artist's bisexuality is delineated in Whistler's account of the first artist. On the evening of February 20, 1885, he delivered the Ten O'Clock Lecture at London's Princes Hall.[25] He appeared, as he said, "in the character of The Preacher, to talk about Art." As such, he assumed the persona of the sermonizer who, like Gudea, purports to convey the word of God. In the course of that lecture, Whistler described his image of the first artist as follows:

> In the beginning, man went forth each day—some to do battle, some to the chase; others, again, to dig and to delve in the field—all that they might gain and live, or lose and die. Until there was found among them one, differing from the rest, whose pursuits attracted him not, and so he stayed by the tents with the women, and traced strange devices with a burnt stick upon a gourd.
> This man, who took no joy in the ways of his brethren—who cared not for conquest, and fretting in the field—this designer of quaint patterns—

this deviser of the beautiful—who perceived in Nature about him curious curvings, as faces are seen in the fire—this dreamer apart, was the first artist.

Whistler's first artist has a more pronounced feminine identification than the hunters and warriors. Rather than use nature for hunting or farming, Whistler's artist abstracts natural forms to use for his own creations. The artist's ability to reorganize the chance shapes of nature requires heightened perception and the talent to give them aesthetic form. In that procedure, Whistler's artist is like the creators of the legendary first image, who seized on the chance shadows and reflections of nature and preserved them by tracing their outlines and "fixing" them.

Also in keeping with traditional views of the artist as intermediary between gods and men is Whistler's assertion that artists are chosen by gods. As such, they improve on the very nature created by the gods:

> And presently there came to this man [the first artist] another—and, in time, others—of like nature, chosen by the Gods—and so they worked together; and soon they fashioned, from the moistened earth, forms resembling the gourd. And with the power of creation, the heirloom of the artist, presently they went beyond the slovenly suggestions of Nature, and the first vase was born, in beautiful proportion.

OEDIPAL CHALLENGE IN
THE VISUAL ARTS

The parental character of gods endows challenges to them with an oedipal cast. When those challenges are in the realm of creativity, a heightened narcissism of both gods and artists is called into play. Pliny (NH 35, xxxiii) cites the example of Nero, the Roman emperor (A.D. 54–68) who commissioned a colossal portrait of himself, painted on linen, one hundred twenty feet high. When completed, the painting was placed outdoors in a garden; but lightning struck, burning up both the portrait and the gardens.

Pliny's designation of Nero's commission as a "folly" *(insanium)* indicates his view that the emperor had taken leave of his senses. The manner of the picture's destruction recalls traditional punishments for hubris in the ancient world. From a psychoanalytic perspective, hubris denotes a grandiosity that is bound to fail because it is unreal. Nero's grandiosity derives from the early narcissistic childhood wish to be big and show oneself off—in this case as a likeness. The destruction of his image by lightning requires the hand, and implicitly the anger, of Jupiter.

Jupiter's response to Nero's portrait suggests that he experienced it as a threat, or challenge, to himself and his authority. He destroys his challenger in effigy, as it were, and to the extent that the colossal portrait stood for Nero's narcissistic self, it suffered the fate of grandiose ambition. In this case, size corresponds symbolically to would-be importance and recalls the vain attempts of children to be as big as their parents. At the same time, however, parents know that their children will eventually grow up, possibly even surpass their own accomplishments, and probably outlive them. While they may consciously desire their child's success, parents can unconsciously resent it and try to destroy it. The particular instance of Nero's picture prefigures the emperor's insane reaction to the burning of Rome. It furthermore creates a psychological continuum between Nero's childhood grandiosity as persisting in the unrealistic "folly" described by Pliny and his psychotic retaliation when he indifferently "fiddles while Rome burns."

The childhood fantasy that "big" and "tall" are related to "important" can be seen in derivative form throughout the history of art and architecture. The oedipal implications of architectural grandiosity, epitomized by the Tower of Babel, and the parental wish to inhibit it are apparent in its consequences. According to the Bible, God sees people working on the tower and fears that "nothing will be restrained from them, which they have imagined to do" (Gen. 11 : 6). As a result, he creates a "babel" of tongues and scatters the builders across the earth. They speak in different languages and lose their ability to communicate.

Another, Talmudic, version of the Tower of Babel[26] reinforces the view of God's punishment as causing symbolic regression in his challengers. God changes the builders into apes rather than confounding their human language, thereby "casting them down" to a lower position on the evolutionary scale. In Genesis, God causes disunity and geographic separation in people who had been unified in the pursuit of a common goal— namely, the building of a great city with a tower reaching to the heavens.

The sixteenth-century Dutch painter Pieter Brueghel the Elder painted two versions of the Tower of Babel. One, signed and dated 1563, is in the Kunsthistorisches Museum in Vienna [21] and the other, in Rotterdam's Museum Boymans–van Beuningen. Both depict the tower as an elaborate ziggurat in the process of construction. Interestingly, in both versions, the tower begins to crumble, as if disintegrating from within. In Genesis, however, the tower is not destroyed; instead, construction stops, the builders scatter, and the work remains incomplete. Brueghel's departure

21. *Pieter Brueghel the Elder,* The Tower of Babel,
1563. Kunsthistorisches Museum, Vienna.

from the biblical text is significant and insightful, for his pictures are architectural metaphors of a psychological state.

His crumbling towers recapitulate the disintegration of the self whose narcissism has undertaken a task of grandiose proportions that cannot succeed. The manifest reason for inevitable failure, here as in the case of Nero's portrait, is the deity's response. Both Jupiter and God, the latter made explicit in the text, regard the works as threats to their own power and authority. Instinctively, they are compelled to destroy them.

In Brueghel's image, however, the destruction is depicted as if the internal structure of the tower begins to collapse and crumble. The fall of Brueghel's building is an architectural parallel to developmental regression and failure. In a similar way, although chronologically in reverse, the picture of Dorian Gray as young and handsome disintegrates and becomes old. As with Nero's portrait and the Tower of Babel, Dorian's narcissistic grandiosity is destroyed by the demands of reality. But Dorian challenged the reality of time rather than an anthropomorphic god, as did Nero and the citizens of Babel. His challenge is rather more narcissistic than oedipal and thus operates on an earlier developmental level. In all three cases, however, the literal disintegration that occurs *de*-constructs, or *de*-synthesizes, and therefore destroys the ego's creative functioning.

MYTHS OF THE FALL: ICARUS AND PHAËTHON

Because myths contain psychological truth, they offer rich material for the visual artist. James Saslow[27] has shown that different artists, as well as different cultures, respond to a myth according to individual and social forces. The mythic "text" is a "context," which the artist invests with his own inclinations and talent rather than producing an objective, or literal, illustration of it.

Brueghel's Icarus

Although relatively little information on Brueghel's life is available, the fact that he painted two versions of the Tower of Babel suggests an affinity for themes of creative challenge. Brueghel was part of a humanist circle in the Netherlands and would have been familiar with classical myths and literature. *The Fall of Icarus* [22] of c. 1554–55, which is his only known mythological painting, is another instance of Brueghel's interest in the potential dangers of ambition.

According to Ovid (*Meta.* VIII, 217–222),[28] Icarus and his father, Daedalus, were prisoners of the Minotaur on Crete. Daedalus used his skill as a sculptor to fashion wings out of feathers and wax that would enable Icarus and himself to escape. Daedalus warned his son not to fly too close to the sun; but Icarus disobeyed, and the sun melted his wings. He fell into the Aegean Sea and drowned.

Brueghel's Icarus is barely noticeable at the lower right of the picture plane. He has fallen head first into the sea, and his legs flail in the air above the water. Brueghel's characteristic moralizing irony contrasts the expansive seascape, boat, and landscape with its stolid peasants to the more flimsy Icarus. The irony is enhanced by the single-minded concentration of the peasant plowing the earth and the viewer's knowledge that Icarus has tried to defy the reality of earth-bound work. The peasant's focus on the ground contrasts with the shepherd staring up at the sky, probably at what was originally an image of Daedalus flying over the sea.[29]

22. *Pieter Brueghel the Elder*, The Fall of Icarus,
c. 1554–55. Musées Royaux des Beaux-Arts, Brussels.

The laws of gravity disregarded by Icarus are almost literally rendered in the ponderous, serious character of the working peasant. Furthermore, the upside-down position of Icarus can be seen as an image of his defiant disobedience, his attempt to "overturn" symbolically the established order, in this case the order of authority—from Apollo to Daedalus to Icarus. For Brueghel, as is also evident in his painting *Netherlandish Proverbs*, the image of being turned upside down generally represented human folly.

Relating the iconography of oedipal themes in Brueghel's work to his life is hypothetical at best. However, the psychologically minded observer is assisted by the evidence of related themes elsewhere in Brueghel's oeuvre. Brueghel's profound belief in the exemplary power of imagery emerges in his many works in which vices and virtues are held up as a moral mirror of humanity. He clearly believed, with Socrates and Freud, that self-knowledge of the kind that Icarus lacked was the surest way to avoid folly.

The *Parable of the Blind* [23] of 1568 is perhaps Brueghel's masterpiece dealing with the theme of falling that results from the failure to "see."

Following Christ in Matthew (15 : 14)—"If the blind shall lead the blind, both shall fall into the ditch"—Brueghel creates a diagonal of blind men from left to right across the picture plane. They form a sequence of cautious, slow-motion movement, which abruptly shifts as one of them does indeed "fall" backward "into the ditch." That the next in line loses his balance and is about to topple forward leaves no doubt about the fate of all the blind men.

The psychological overdetermination of blindness is particularly telling in relation to the theme of falling. Its oedipal significance as upwardly displaced castration can be associated to Icarus's fall, for hubris requires a failure to "see" intelligently and in*sight*fully and is punished accordingly. It is, in Brueghel's iconography, as grandiose for a blind man to lead others as for Icarus to disobey Daedalus, and for the citizens of Babel to build a tower reaching to the heavens.

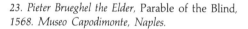

Michelangelo and Raphael:
Phaëthon and Icarus

The myth of Icarus has a cognate in the myth of Phaëthon. Both are inspired by oedipal dynamics in which a son disobeys a father and is

23. *Pieter Brueghel the Elder,* Parable of the Blind,
1568. Museo Capodimonte, Naples.

destroyed. Both children become grandiose and fall to their deaths by way of symbolic regression to a "feminizing" pre-oedipal passivity. References to these myths by Michelangelo and Raphael, respectively, reveal facets of the oedipal struggles in their lives. And because there is much more evidence available on Michelangelo and Raphael than on Brueghel, the attempt to read personal significance in their imagery is reinforced by other documentation.

Michelangelo's Phaëthon

In 1532 the fifty-seven-year-old Michelangelo met the twenty-three-year-old nobleman Tommaso de' Cavalieri and fell in love with him. The artist gave the young man several so-called presentation drawings. One of these illustrated the myth of Phaëthon, who held his father, Apollo, to his promise to let him drive the chariot of the sun. Phaëthon was unable to control Apollo's horses, which went too close to the earth and burned it. Responding to the pleas of Phaëthon's victims, Zeus hurled a lightning bolt at the youth and killed him.

In Michelangelo's drawing [24], Zeus is astride his eagle attribute and dominates the top of the picture. Phaëthon falls backward in a pose that recalls the traditional reclining nude—usually female—and is passive in nature. In the very arrangement of the drawing, Michelangelo's iconography corresponds to the dynamics of narcissistic grandiosity, which is bound to fail.[30] In literally going down, Phaëthon symbolically regresses to a pre-oedipal state and dies.

The regressive meaning of this particular fall is reinforced by certain iconographic details at the bottom of the drawing—namely, a reclining river god and Phaëthon's sisters. Phaëthon's descent toward the river god implicitly relates his death with water, which is explicit in the myth of Icarus. This connection evokes the role of water in dreams, and therefore in the unconscious, as an ambivalent image of birth and death. Because of its biological association with birth, water can have a maternal character, particularly when its function is a receptive one. In such a context, Phaëthon's fall is consistent with regression to dependence on a maternal figure. The homosexual sentiments that inspired Michelangelo to create this image are consistent with its latent meaning; Phaëthon's death represents the artist's wish—whether conscious or unconscious is not demonstrable—to be passively loved by Tommaso.

24. Michelangelo, The Fall of Phaëton, *1530s.*
Windsor Castle, Royal Library.

25. Michelangelo,
The Rape of
Ganymede, 1530s.
Harvard University
Art Museums,
Cambridge, Mass.
Gifts for Special
Uses Fund.

Negative Oedipal Dynamics:
Michelangelo's Ganymede *and* Tityos

Michelangelo's feminine identification is even clearer in two other presentation drawings for Tommaso—namely, *The Rape of Ganymede* [25] and *Tityos* [26]. They depict aspects of the negative oedipal constellation[31] as it emerges in Greek myth and legend. Zeus's abduction of Ganymede, a handsome Trojan shepherd, is well known in classical literature, beginning with Homer (*Iliad* V, 266, and XX, 352; Virgil, *Aeneid* V, 250–57; Ovid, *Meta.* X, 155–61). In Michelangelo's drawing,[32] Zeus (the Roman Jupiter), disguised as an eagle, swoops up Ganymede in his embrace. Ganymede represents the boy's wish to be passively loved by an idealized father, here in the form of Zeus's eagle. Michelangelo indicates the anal character of that wish in the eagle's position behind Ganymede, "depicting the boy

26. *Michelangelo,* Tityos, *1530s. Windsor Castle, Royal Library.*

frontally and as if the eagle were physically penetrating him" [from the rear].[33] In so arranging Ganymede, Michelangelo clearly had in mind the response of his intended viewer, thereby creating a visual homoerotic "dialogue" with young Tommaso.

Here, as in dreams, flying has a sexual connotation; but the passivity of Ganymede is also a kind of ecstatic, exhibitionistic death reminiscent of Michelangelo's *Dying Slave* in the Louvre. Once settled on Mount Olympos, Ganymede became Zeus's cupbearer and dislodged Hebe, Hera's daughter, from that role. Ovid's assertion that Ganymede remained Zeus's cupbearer against Hera's will reveals her objection to her husband's homosexual inclinations. As the goddess of marriage, Hera (Juno in Rome) is destined to oppose the implications of Ganymede as well as of Zeus's heterosexual infidelities.

Related dynamically to *Ganymede,* and apparently presented to Tommaso with it, is Michelangelo's *Tityos.* This, like the *Phaëthon,* is an image of regression from oedipal challenge to a negative oedipal position. But it is more sexually explicit. Tityos tried to seduce Latona, mother of Artemis and Apollo and consort of Zeus. The gods punished him by sending a vulture to nibble at his liver. In changing the vulture to an eagle, Michelangelo reinforces its reference to Zeus. Even more to the point, the eagle does not eat Tityos's liver in the drawing; he stands behind him in a position consistent with the act of anal penetration.

Raphael's Icarus

For an important part of Michelangelo's career, including the period of his work for Pope Julius II on the Sistine Ceiling, Raphael was his chief rival. Significant psychological differences between these two artists are apparent in a comparison of their respective responses to the myths of Phaëthon and Icarus.

Raphael's image of the Icarus myth occurred not in a picture, but in a letter to Baldassare Castiglione, author of *The Courtier* and an influential social figure in sixteenth-century Italy. Raphael had been appointed by the pope to succeed Bramante, who was in charge of the reconstruction of Saint Peter's and overseer of Roman antiquities. For a young artist—Raphael was then in his thirties—this was a position of the highest distinction. It also represented an intellectual and artistic synthesis for Raphael, who, as a humanist, was devoted to learning and assimilating the cultures of ancient Greece and Rome.

These considerations inspired his remarks to Castiglione; he wrote that he wished to recover the beautiful forms of ancient architecture ("Vorrei trovar le belle forme degli edifici antichi") and added that he hoped his ambition would not prove to be the flight of Icarus ("ne so se il sara d'Icaro").[34] In that comment, Raphael expressed his knowledge that he had indeed risen high and intended to rise higher still. At the same time, he extended a caution, more to himself than to Castiglione, against the dangers of grandiose hubris.

Although Raphael and Michelangelo are among the greatest artists of any age, neither escaped the psychodynamic laws of human development. Michelangelo's most private concerns are revealed in his presentation drawings, which were intimate personal communications. How conscious he was of the psychological meaning of a particular image may never be known, but the meaning is there nevertheless and, in some measure, accounts for the character of the work. Certainly the oedipal conflicts involving struggle with paternal authority can be seen throughout Michelangelo's life, especially in his impulsive, and sometimes paranoid, relations with the pope. Raphael, on the other hand, avoided the overt expression of such conflicts. His social and political skills combined with his genius to create good relationships that furthered his career with apparent ease. The cautionary note in his letter reflects both the force of his ambition and his recognition that thought must precede action.

Of particular significance as a reflection of the psychology of these artists is the very fact that of two myths dealing with the dangers of ambition, Michelangelo chose Phaëthon, and Brueghel and Raphael chose Icarus. Despite the similar dynamics, the Icarus myth has artistic content, which is absent in the Phaëthon myth. For whatever other reasons these artists selected as they did, there is unavoidable personal meaning in their choice, as there is in their iconography. In the case of Michelangelo and Raphael, at least one powerful motive can be identified in their fathers' response to having a creative son.

Fathers and Sons

Michelangelo's father, according to Vasari, was opposed to his son becoming a sculptor and beat him for his desire to do so. Finally, when Michelangelo was fourteen, his father apprenticed him not to a sculptor, but to the painter Ghirlandaio. By the age of sixteen, Michelangelo had been discovered by Lorenzo de' Medici, who took him into his household to study and work. Lorenzo recognized the mediocrity of Michelangelo's father, to whom he said disdainfully, "You will always be poor."[35]

Lorenzo assumed the role of a higher-level "father" for the artist, exposing him to the ancient art in his collection and to the intellectual humanist circles he frequented. Nevertheless, the destructive behavior of Michelangelo's biological father toward his son's exceptional genius reverberated in certain themes of Michelangelo's art and in his sadomasochistic behavior with patrons.

Raphael's father, Giovanni Santi, was the court poet and painter at the enlightened humanist court of Federico da Montefeltro in Urbino. Raphael grew up in a highly cultivated atmosphere, while Michelangelo spent his childhood first in the country and later in a lower-middle-class district of Florence. Michelangelo had to struggle against his environment, specifically against his father, before gaining access to prominent intellectual and artistic circles. In contrast to Michelangelo, Raphael had his father's encouragement from birth, and when his father died—at which time Raphael was eleven—two uncles continued to play a paternal role on his behalf. Although Raphael's life did not proceed without conflict, it appears from the available data that his relations with patrons benefited from the "blueprint" of his father's cultural and psychological enlightenment.

Vasari's report that Giovanni Santi insisted on Raphael's being nursed by his own mother in an era when wet nurses were the norm points to a particularly progressive attitude. It is probably also no accident that Santi worked at Urbino, whose library had a copy of Alberti's *Book of the Family*, for Santi's approach to Raphael's life and talent is remarkably consistent with the recommendations on child rearing advocated by Alberti. Alberti's observation most relevant to Raphael entails the benefits of a father recognizing and encouraging his son's abilities, just as an architect plans and oversees the development of a building.

Raphael's childhood also conforms to the psychoanalytic findings of Greenacre[36] on the ideal family circumstance for creative children. Her clinical experience, as well as her studies of creative individuals (primarily men), have indicated that having a parent (usually a father) who is less skilled than the child, but in the same field, is ideal. In addition, the father's attitude must minimize the child's anxiety and guilt for his innate superiority to his father. In other words, the father must be self-confident enough to allow his son to win realistically.

Giovanni Santi, it seems, satisfied these criteria and enhanced Raphael's success. Because Michelangelo's father behaved like the God of Genesis toward the tower builders, the artist continued to struggle with sadomasochistic themes of dominance and submission in iconography and in life. Raphael, aware of such themes, could control rather than be controlled by them. Brueghel's relations with his father are unknown. Nevertheless it is clear that in his moralizing rendition of oedipal themes, he, like Raphael, was consciously aware of the dangers of hubris. In choosing Icarus as his only known mythological work, Brueghel, like Raphael, identified with the creative, artistic aspects of oedipal struggle.

People who unconsciously associate success with transgressing the oedipal taboos of incest and murder are destined to fail. They typically arrange their own failure in order to elude the taboo. One young man, for example, refused to beat his father at chess even though he was a better player. A woman writer became anxious when her first book was in press because her mother would recognize unflattering references to the family. An otherwise successful businessman failed to receive a promotion because he could not get along with his superiors. His father had failed to gain a company presidency for the same reason.

In all cases, the inhibition could be traced to an unconscious fear of destroying the parents of the same sex by surpassing them. In some instances, the creative activity had unconscious sexual significance, which threatened the incest barrier and so had to be blocked. It is not until such fears are made conscious and worked through in analysis that the inhibitions can be over-come. Psychoanalysis, as Freud knew, cannot create talent; but it can free it from the chains of childhood conflict and the compulsion to repeat failure.

The father's traditional role in the Western family creates a transition between the nurturing environment of the home and the financial reality of work. Both Alberti in the fifteenth century and Greenacre in the twentieth are thus correct in their emphasis on the importance of a father's interest in, and encouragement of, talented children. It remains to be seen how much the recent influence of feminism and the increasing numbers of professional women alter these dynamics.

The well-known anecdote in which Cimabue comes upon the young Giotto drawing a sheep on a rock, recognizes his genius, and trains him to be a painter has been taken as an example of oedipal dynamics.[37] It can also be seen as a prefiguration of Giotto's introduction of a new humanist naturalism in the visual arts. Dante's verse referring to Cimabue and Giotto—

> O empty glory of human powers! How short the time
> its green endures at its peak, if it be not
> overtaken by crude ages! Cimabue thought to hold
> the field in painting, and now Giotto has the cry,
> so that the fame of the former is obscured.[38]

—not only highlights the transience of fame, but also the necessity of young artists superseding previous generations. It is a fact of creative progress and development that "children" push beyond the boundaries of the past and forge into new territory. This process can evoke more or less anxiety and inhibition, depending on a variety of factors, including the family, the cultural environment, and the strength of the individual's talent.[39]

That Giotto's talent, like that of Michelangelo, Raphael, and Brueghel, was prodigious is indisputable. Like Raphael, and in contrast to Michelangelo, however, Giotto is credited with a relatively smooth passage from childhood to fame. Both Ghiberti in the fifteenth century[40] and Vasari in the sixteenth[41] emphasized the role of Giotto's father in this circumstance by elaborating on his encouragement of a talent that revealed itself in childhood. To the account of Cimabue discovering Giotto drawing, Ghiberti and Vasari add that Giotto asked his father's permission to leave home and be trained by the older artist. His father willingly agreed.

At this point, a few methodological observations are called for. A skeptic's response to the reasoning proposed here might question Ghiberti's and Vasari's sources. Very likely the sources would be in the form of tradition; both biographers might, for example, have reasoned backward from Giotto's adult reputation and fame, in which case they would have made a historical reconstruction. In so doing, they would be operating much like the clinical psychoanalyst. They would also be enriching an already existing "myth," for anecdotes about Giotto, including his encounter with Cimabue, are recorded from the fourteenth century; and some of those were patterned on anecdotes about ancient Greek artists. In either case, however, the reports of Ghiberti and Vasari would have a ring of psychological truth; for nowhere in the record of Giotto's life is there even the slightest hint of what Harold Bloom calls the "anxiety of influence."[42] They would, in effect, be linking the enlightened character of Giotto's father with the artist's reputation for conflict-free expression of genius. In making such a connection, however implicit, the Renaissance biographers reach conclusions that are consistent with those of modern psychoanalysis.

The same connection could be made in regard to the early success of the Italian Baroque sculptor, Gianlorenzo Bernini. His identification with the victorious David, in contrast to Caravaggio's, whose beheaded Goliath (see Chapter 5) is a self-portrait, is consistent with the experience of a supportive and encouraging father. Whereas Michelangelo's sadomasochistic relationship with his father replicated itself with Julius II, Bernini's parallel relationships were less conflicted. The Roman cardinal, who was destined to become pope, reportedly visited Bernini's studio and held up a mirror to assist the artist in self-portraiture.[43] Psychologically, the meaning of holding up the mirror is its function as a "reflector." The cardinal—a future "papa"—places the mirror between himself and Bernini, thereby "reflecting" back to the artist/child his own image. In clinical psychoanalysis, this kind of interaction between analyst and analysand has been termed "mirror transference."[44] Its purpose is to repair a defective sense of self, resulting from parental failure to respond adequately to a child's experience of himself or herself.

The history of art is filled with variations on oedipal derivatives in the lives and work of artists. Ideal cases, such as Giotto's and Bernini's, are relatively rare. Even Raphael, if one considers his biography in depth, can be seen to have avoided marriage and children, as Giotto did not. In that area, at least, Raphael failed to identify with his father, and, in a letter to one of his uncles, explicitly noted that he would have achieved neither wealth nor fame had he married earlier.[45] Raphael's death at the age of thirty-seven precludes conclusions about what might have been.

The popular Renaissance comparison of Giotto with the Greek artist Apelles (for example, Boccaccio, *Genealogy of the Gods,* Book 14) recalls that Apelles was also an oedipal "winner," though in a different way. According to Pliny (NH 36, iv), Alexander the Great would allow himself to be painted only by Apelles. He commissioned Apelles to paint his mistress Pancaspe and, when Apelles fell in love with her, Alexander gave her to the artist. In that account, Alexander can be taken as a paternal derivative in being a patron controlling the artist's source of money. His unusual generosity toward Apelles hides an incestuous underpinning, a father as patron and a son as the one patronized sharing the same woman, which identifies its oedipal nature.

At the opposite extreme of such oedipal victory is the failure to compete at all when confronted with a superior adversary. Tradition has it, for example, that Verrocchio gave up painting and devoted himself entirely to sculpture after seeing work by the young Leonardo. The fact that Verrocchio was the master and Leonardo the apprentice is a symbolic instance of the father's renunciation in favor of the son. Verrocchio did not, of course, give up art altogether—only painting, which was not his forte in any case.

A more radical renunciation is evident in the tradition that Hugo van der Goes committed suicide on realizing that he could not produce a work as great as Jan van Eyck's Ghent Altarpiece. In such situations, the person's relationship to competition takes precedence over his relationship to work. Disappointment resulting from "seeing" that someone else is more accomplished can lead to depression, here expressed as withdrawal from the activity. The work is thus inhibited by the unconscious agenda. When the rage of depression is extreme, as with Hugo van der Goes, so is the renunciation.

A more constructive approach to one's artistic predecessors is to assume the posture of a student and learn. Through the learning process, the younger artist assimilates some of what the older artist has to offer. When such learning becomes infused with oedipal prohibitions—either aggressive or sexual—it can be conflicted or inhibited.

Freud's short paper "School Boy Psychology"[46] describes the boy's ambivalent relationship to teachers as a transformation of the earlier relationship with his father. At a certain age, according to Freud, sons grow dissatisfied with a formerly idealized father and become aware of his limitations. So it is with teachers; "we were from the very first," wrote Freud, "equally inclined to love them and to hate them, to criticize and respect them."[47]

The next transference that takes place is onto what Greenacre calls "collective alternates," or role models in the field of one's choice. The artistic predecessor is such a figure, and in the psyche of the young artist the predecessor assumes paternal significance. Hence the activation of oedipal dynamics. This circumstance is implied, for example, in the stylistic and iconographic relationship between Brueghel and Bosch, the two leading Dutch painters of the sixteenth century.

Brueghel's most significant artistic predecessor was Hieronymus Bosch. If we take only the evidence of Brueghel's works, it is clear that he struggled to achieve stylistic independence from Bosch and to find his own visual "voice." The influence of Bosch's fantastic forms can be seen throughout Brueghel's development, but more so at the start of his career. In order to arrive at an individual style, Brueghel had to steer a course between Bosch's impact from the past and his Italianate contemporaries in the north. During a trip through Italy, Brueghel absorbed a taste for the expanses of southern and Alpine landscapes, which helped to free him from Bosch's turbulence. Landscape also provides a strong contrast with the agitation often accompanying themes of human folly in Brueghel's pictures. Although Brueghel quoted poses, gestures, and even compositions from Botticelli, Raphael, and Michelangelo, he assimilated them into his own idiom and avoided the more obvious "Italianism" current among northern artists. In becoming known as "peasant Brueghel," despite his contact with humanists, Brueghel maintained a distinctive artistic persona.

Brueghel's continuing, or renewed, oedipal struggle with Bosch seems indicated by his painting *The Fall of the Rebel Angels* [27] of 1562. There is virtually no relief in landscape; instead, the picture plane is crowded with agitated, Bosch-like forms. The sun dominates the top of the picture like a giant eye staring down at the confusion below. Anthropomorphic angels, led by Saint Michael, frantically brandish swords against myriad sub-human creatures. Here, as in Bosch, rebels are cast down literally and symbolically. Like the builders of Babel, the grandiose angels are turned into lesser beings. Those angels who remain loyal to God retain their human form and character.

When Michelangelo, while in the Medici household, studied Masaccio's frescoes in the Brancacci Chapel, he was also learning from a predecessor. The power of Masaccio's influence on Renaissance painting

27. *Pieter Brueghel the Elder,* The Fall of the
Rebel Angels, *1562. Musées Royaux des
Beaux-Arts, Brussels.*

contributed to his "paternal" character in relation to the young Michelangelo. The main evidence of conflict at this period of Michelangelo's life has
an oedipal character, displaced from Masaccio to a fellow student. Indeed,
the learning atmosphere of the Brancacci Chapel, where artists of Michelangelo's generation gathered as in an academy to study Masaccio, was
shattered when Michelangelo's jealous rival, Pietro Torrigiani, hit Michelangelo and broke his nose. Torrigiani claimed to have been provoked
by Michelangelo's sneering, superior attitude—in other words, to have
acted with justification.[48] He had taken offense because Michelangelo
"looked down his nose" at him. Since the nose is a traditional sign of
virility, Torrigiani acted according to the principles of the oedipal talion
law—"an eye for an eye, and a nose for a nose." The two artists, vying for
domination, enacted the oedipal drama with Torrigiani playing the offended father and Michelangelo the upstart son. The irony of this episode

lies in the fact that Michelangelo, and not the outraged Torrigiani, was by far the greater artist.

In having been virtually "deified," Michelangelo stepped into Masaccio's shoes as a powerful and paternal figure for subsequent artists. Some responded positively and others did not. The twentieth-century Romanian sculptor Constantin Brancusi, for example, reacted to Michelangelo with an instinctive aversion. "Michelangelo is too strong," he said. "His *moi* overshadows everything."[49] That a sexual inhibition underlay Brancusi's aversion emerges in his rhetorical question "Who could imagine having a Michelangelo in his bedroom, having to get undressed in front of it?"[50] The paranoid character of Brancusi's query is revealed in the notion that the work by Michelangelo would be "watching" his state of undress.

The twentieth-century sculptor Henry Moore, on the other hand, overcame the inhibitory effect of Michelangelo's magnitude. Moore attributed his decision to become a sculptor to having heard the following anecdote about Michelangelo:

> A passer-by observed Michelangelo carving the head of an old faun. "An old faun," said the passer-by, "wouldn't have all its teeth in." Michelangelo promptly knocked out two of the teeth.[51]

For Henry Moore, this incident conveyed Michelangelo's membership in the human race rather than his deification. It was thus "safe" for Moore to throw his hat into the artistic "ring" and compete. It is also true that the symbolic content of knocking out the teeth—compare "a tooth for a tooth"—relates castration with old age. The sexual character of the faun, diminished by age, is mitigated by the loss of two teeth. This, in turn, renders Michelangelo less threatening to Henry Moore, as a young would-be artist. Furthermore, the implicit unconscious association between Michelangelo's old faun and Moore's father is contained in the "animal, Pan-like quality" of the bronze *King*.

The nineteenth-century artist Jean-Auguste-Dominique Ingres reported a similar dynamic, allowing him to break the inhibition that blocked the completion in 1833 of his *Portrait of Louis-François Bertin* (Louvre), one of the most influential journalists of his day. In this case, it was the living Bertin rather than an artistic "father" who became humanized in the painter's view. Wollheim[52] cites two versions of the episode, which can be summarized as follows:

> 1) Ingres had become so depressed at his difficulty with the portrait that he "burst into tears." When Bertin comforted him, Ingres could finish the picture.

2) Ingres overheard a political discussion between Bertin and his two sons. Although Bertin disagreed with his sons, he was tolerant of their opinions. After that, Ingres completed the portrait.

In the interchange with his sons, according to Wollheim, Bertin "did not have to claim divinity as the only alternative to accepting destruction."[53] As with Michelangelo, when Bertin seemed to descend from Mount Olympos and become human, he shed the forbidding aura of divine status. As a result, Ingres was able literally to "confront" him, and be confronted by him, on the realistic plane of artist and subject rather than on the fantasy plane of oedipal boy and idealized, godlike father.

Raphael's School of Athens

Raphael's *School of Athens* [28] combines oedipal with sibling dynamics in its subtext. The genius of this painting is its synthesis of High Renaissance style with humanism. In a single, unified space, Raphael has assembled the leading philosophers, mathematicians, and scientists of Greek antiquity. That he has done so in the apartment of the Christian pope—Julius II—confirms the unusual and progressive intelligence of his patron. The depiction of ancient Greek personages as portraits of Raphael's contemporaries synthesizes his own era with antiquity. Raphael also injects personal, autobiographical references into the iconography, which have oedipal as well as sibling significance.

At the center of the composition, on the top step, Plato and Aristotle are deep in conversation; Plato, a portrait of Leonardo, holds a copy of the *Timaeus.* His pointing gesture is a quotation from Leonardo, who was surely one of Raphael's most significant artistic predecessors. From Leonardo, Raphael assimilated the pyramidal composition and quoted the Mona Lisa's pose for his *Portrait of Maddalena Doni* (c. 1503–8, Pitti Palace, Florence). Raphael's architectural ideas were influenced by Donato Bramante as well as by Leonardo. The tradition that Bramante himself arranged for Raphael to succeed him just before his death is reinforced by Raphael's letter to his uncle describing himself as "in locho Bramante" ("in the place of Bramante").

In *The School of Athens,* Plato and Aristotle stroll before a domed space that corresponds to Bramante's architectural principles. Raphael thus pays homage to Leonardo as a philosopher and a painter, and to Bramante as an architect. Bramante's portrait in the figure of Euclid at the right acknowledges the geometric character of his architecture. In these visual "com-

28. Raphael, The School of Athens, *c. 1508–11.*
Stanza della Segnatura, Vatican Palace, Rome.

ments," Raphael has created a kind of pictorial "family romance," nearly deifying Leonardo, but also honoring Bramante and other contemporaries whose portraits he inserts into the great thinkers of antiquity.

Raphael's inclusion of Michelangelo, however, is of another order. In contrast to Leonardo's central placement at the top of the stairs, both Raphael and Michelangelo occupy the ground plane. Just as he endowed Leonardo with the artist's own gesture, so he painted Michelangelo in Michelangelo's style. Working alone on the Sistine Ceiling at the very time Raphael was decorating the pope's apartments, Michelangelo jealously guarded his solitude. No one was allowed in, at least in part because of Michelangelo's fear that someone would steal his style or plagiarize his ideas about painting. On one occasion, he accused Bramante of secretly arranging for Raphael's admission to the chapel. He also accused Raphael of having improved his style as a result: "Che cio aveva dell'arte, l'aveva da me"[54] ("What he had of art, he had from me"). Michelangelo could have been referring to his portrait by Raphael, synthesized with the brooding and solitary figure of Heraclitus, who resembles his own Prophet Jeremiah in the Sistine Chapel and was a late addition to *The School of Athens*.

Raphael's self-portrait, gazing at the viewer, is at the far right of the fresco. Next to Raphael is the painter Sodoma, whose style is remarkably close to Leonardo's. Sodoma's relation to Leonardo, in fact, could be described as Michelangelo described Raphael's to him. Sodoma virtually did get what he had of art from Leonardo, whereas, although some of Raphael's figures show the influence of Michelangelo, in the main they are quite distinct.

In placing himself within a group, Raphael identifies himself as the social and political animal that he was. The contrast between his sociability and Michelangelo's isolation was expressed in the popular anecdote of their chance meeting on the street: "Where are you going, surrounded like a provost?" Michelangelo asks Raphael. "And you?" replies Raphael. "All alone like an executioner?"

Bronzino's Allegory: *An Oedipal Reading*

One of the most elusive and intriguing images in Western painting is Bronzino's *Venus, Cupid, Folly, and Time*, also called *Allegory* [29]. Vasari[55] reported that the painting had been commissioned by Cosimo de' Medici and sent to Francis I of France. He described it as an image of Cupid kissing a nude Venus in the midst of Pleasure, Play, and other Cupids on one side, and Fraud and Jealousy and various passions of love on the other.

Erwin Panofsky, in his 1934 essay "Father Time,"[56] considered the iconography in greater detail. He called the picture "an image of Luxury rather than an ordinary group of Venus embracing Cupid, . . . corroborated by the fact that Cupid kneels on a pillow, a common symbol of idleness and lechery,"[57] and identified the figures as follows: the figure tearing her hair on the left is Jealousy (combining Envy and Despair). The putto strewing roses is Jest. The figure by the masks of young and old faces with a dragon tail, a fishlike body, and griffin claws is Fraud. Her right and left hands are reversed. In her right hand she holds out a honeycomb, and her left hides a poisonous animal.[58] Time is the old man with wings and an hourglass on the right; he unveils the embrace. Assisting him at the upper left is the female figure of Truth. Panofsky concludes that Bronzino's *Allegory* depicts the "exposure of luxury" and was a companion to an uncompleted tapestry, which illustrated the "Vindication of Innocence." In

29. *Bronzino,* Venus, Cupid, Folly, and Time,
c. 1546. National Gallery, London.

both, the "two-fold function of Time the Revealer" was "to unmask false-hood and bring truth to light."[59]

More recently (1991), Paul Barolsky and Andrew Ladis have proposed reading the *Allegory* in the context of courtly wit and playful irony.[60] They call attention to the intentional iconographic ambiguities in creating the witty spirit of the painting. They point out that Venus's pose conflates Michelangelo's *Doni Madonna* and his Eve of the Sistine Ceiling *Temptation*, which makes her both a virgin and a fallen woman. Such ambiguous play, in Barolsky's and Ladis's view, accounts for both the style and the elusive iconography that were typical of sixteenth-century courtly games.

To these and numerous other interpretations of the *Allegory*, I would add that an oedipal reading is also possible. Its message warns of the dangers of incest in a context of courtly eroticism and witty disguise. The central image is the embrace between Venus and her son Cupid, here rendered as an adolescent. Venus's ambiguity, as Barolsky and Ladis observe, is her dual role as Venus and Eve, emphasizing her maternal persona. Despite her elegant exterior, she is a cold, "castrating" figure, disguised in the playful, symbolic "unmanning" of her son by removing an arrow from his quiver. Cupid, in turn, is sexually ambivalent as he simultaneously flirts with his mother and tantalizes the viewer with anal provocation.

The juxtaposition of luxurious textures, cold porcelain skin, the playful putto, and the dark, enraged figure on the left compounds the ambiguity of the image. The reversed hands of the sphinxlike figure at the right echo the iconographic opposites—also evident in the two masks at the lower right. From a psychological standpoint, the reversal refers to the *dis*order created by mother-son incest and literally plays with the question of rightness and wrong, natural and unnatural.

At the upper right, the powerful figure of Father Time angrily enters the scene and exposes the incestuous couple. Hera defends the laws of marriage and family on Mount Olympos disrupted by the arrival of Ganymede, while Father Time objects to the "untimely" nature of incest. Cupid and Venus defy his paternal role as well as his role as a keeper of time (the hourglass)—for incest denies the reality of time, and the fact, in this case, that a mother belongs to a different generation than her son.

Contained in the anger of Father Time are various meanings of his role as a "watcher of time." Hourglasses were also called "watch glasses"—hence "watch" in the sense of "timepiece." To "be on watch," as "on patrol," means to be on the lookout for danger.[61] Chronos thus combines the order of time with being on the lookout for disruptions of his control. Further complicating the ambiguities of Bronzino's image is the fact that

Chronos himself was actually a Titan and therefore belonged to the generation before Venus. This highlights the biological reality that a young woman with an older man is more likely to produce children and therefore continue the temporal order of descent than a young man with an old woman. Nor is Chronos Venus's spouse; his anger is not oedipal in the sense of the nuclear family, but rather stems from his role as the cosmic temporal authority. And, although Cupid is Venus's mythological son, he has no father; he is derived from the Greek Eros, a primeval force in Hesiod. Since Cupid is "fatherless," his very nature is "out of time," which contributes to his playful manipulations as the love god, as well as to his lawless character in this painting.

The personal significance of the *Allegory* for Bronzino is unknown. The Counter-Reformation Council of Trent had forbidden, among other things, the portrayal of nudity in Christian art. In the portraits of men, women, and children that Bronzino painted for Cosimo for public display he observed these strictures. In the *Allegory*, however, which was commissioned by Cosimo as a private gift for the king of France, we see that courtly images could take on airs of lascivious conceit.

POSTSCRIPT:
THE OEDIPAL SUBTEXT OF PIERO DELLA FRANCESCA'S
FRESCOES ILLUSTRATING THE LEGEND OF THE
TRUE CROSS IN AREZZO'S CHURCH OF SAN FRANCESCO [62]

In 1452, Piero della Francesca, the leading painter from the Italian region of Umbria, was commissioned to decorate the Bacci Chapel in San Francesco in Arezzo with scenes from the popular medieval legend of the Cross. The Bacci family were apothecaries and thus probably interested in the healing powers of True Cross relics and the life-giving quality of the oil of mercy that figures in the legend. Piero's complex iconography and the unusual order of his scenes has been the subject of extensive scholarly discussion.[63] Indeed, his True Cross cycle synthesizes a new and monumental style with history, liturgy, and narrative in an unprecedented way. In the following brief summary of what will form the basis of a longer study, I try to show that Piero's expressive power derives in part from his psychological approach to the choice, order, and juxtaposition of figures and events.

The legend of the True Cross may be summarized as follows (number references in the text correspond to those in Figure 30):

As Adam lies dying (No. 1), he sends his son Seth to retrieve the oil of mercy promised by the Archangel Michael. Instead, Michael gives Seth a branch to plant on Adam's grave. The branch becomes a tree, which Solomon tries to use in building his temple. Unable to cut the wood to the desired length, Solomon has it thrown across a pond to serve as a bridge (No. 2). When Sheba visits him (Nos. 3 and 4), she recognizes that the wood is holy and warns Solomon that it will end the kingdom of the Jews. To thwart her prophecy, Solomon hides the wood; but it resurfaces later and is made into Christ's Cross.

In the fourth century A.D., Constantine wages war against Maxentius for control of Rome. An angel appears to Constantine (No. 5), telling him to carry the image of the Cross into battle. Constantine obeys and is victorious (No. 6). Impressed with his miraculous victory (No. 6), Constantine sends his mother Helena to Jerusalem to find the actual Cross. She is told that a certain Judas knows its location, but he refuses to divulge it. Helena has him thrown into a dry well for seven days until he agrees to tell her (No. 8). She digs up three crosses (No. 9), buried under a temple of Venus, which she destroys. Helena then "proves" the True Cross by its power to restore a dead youth to life (No. 10). Judas becomes Bishop of Jerusalem.

In 615 A.D., the Persian Emperor Chosroes steals the Cross and creates a false trinity with himself as God, the Cross as the Son, and a rooster as the Holy Ghost (No. 12). The Holy Roman Emperor Heraclius defeats Chosroes (No. 11), has him beheaded (No. 12A), and restores the Cross to Jerusalem (No. 13).

Comparing this account with the diagram, it is clear that Piero's scenes on the right wall are in chronological order, but those on the left are not. Nor is the Annunciation (No. 7) part of the legend. Piero departs from earlier True Cross cycles in the inclusion of Adam's Death (No. 1), the Dream (No. 5) and Victory (No. 6) of Constantine, Judas Drawn from the Well (No. 8), and the Meeting of Solomon and Sheba (No. 4). These additions and their arrangement create an oedipal subtext that resonates both with the legend itself and with the historical success of Christianity. When, for example, Christ says that he is greater than Solomon, he refers to the very competition necessary for progress and implies the oedipal struggle between established authority (whether construed as Freud's superego or Lacan's *"Non"/"Nom" du pere*) and the "son's" challenge to it. Such comparisons formed the basis of the typological system (see Chapter 5) in which personages and events of the Old Testament ("types") were

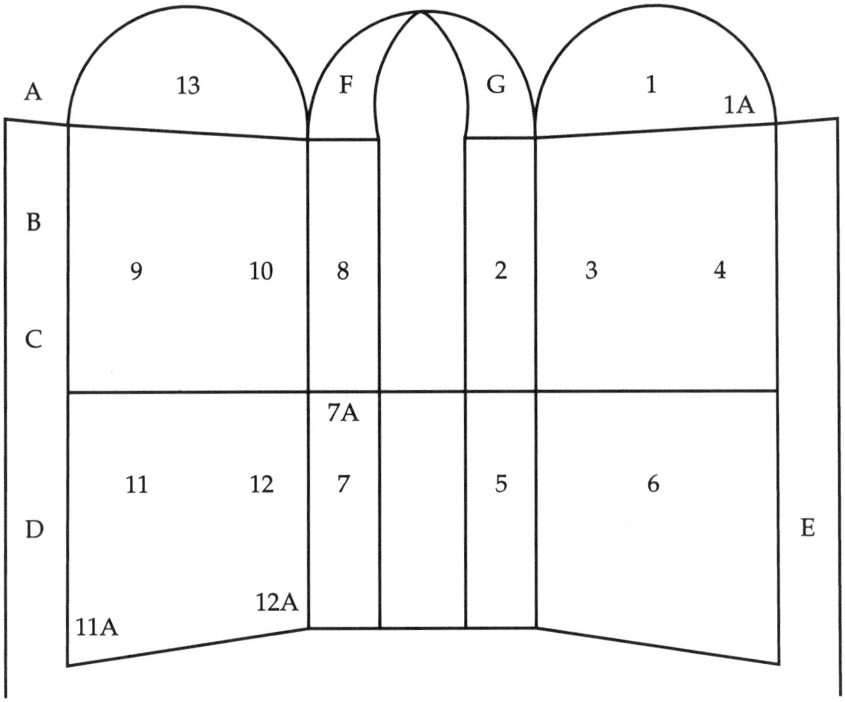

A	13	F	G	1 1A
B				
	9 10	8	2	3 4
C				
		7A		
	11 12	7	5	6
D				E
11A	12A			

A   St. Augustine
B   Cupid
C   St. Louis of Toulouse
D   St. Peter Martyr
E   Angel
F and G Two Prophets

1   Death of Adam
1A   Figure of Eve
2   Lifting the Wood
3   Sheba Adores the Wood
4   Meeting of Solomon and Sheba
5   Dream of Constantine
6   Battle of Constantine against Maxentius
7   Annunciation
7A   Figure of God
8   Judas is Drawn from the Well
9   Discovery of the Cross
10   Proof of the Cross
11   Heraclius Defeats Chosroes's Army
11A Severed figure
12   Execution of Chosroes
12A Kneeling Chosroes
13   Heraclius Returns the Cross to Jerusalem

30. Diagram of the Bacci Chapel, Church of San
Francesco, Arezzo.

31. *Piero della Francesca,* Discovery and Proof of
the Cross, *c. 1452. Bacci Chapel, Church of San
Francesco, Arezzo.*

paired with, and conceived of as having prefigured, those of the New. Christ does not appear in the legend of the True Cross, but Piero's frescoes contain hidden allusions to him which evoke the oedipal triumph of the New Dispensation over the Old.

Adam's Death (No. 1) faces the Exaltation of the Cross (No. 13) which Heraclius restores to Jerusalem. This juxtaposes the instrument of Christ's (the son's) death with the death of the primal father. In death, therefore, Christ re-enters (and reclaims) the earthly city typologically paired with the paradise, or heavenly city, lost by Adam. The unprecedented Meeting of Solomon and Sheba (No. 4) contains the conventional oedipal narrative in which one who has insight (Sheba) warns a reigning king that a descendant will destroy him. Such was the story of Herod and Christ, Chronos and the Olympians, Laios and Oedipus Rex. In the legend of the True Cross, Christ is displaced onto the holy wood and Sheba warns Solomon about the wood. Likewise, the Dream of Constantine (No. 5)—for the first time depicted as a nighttime sleep dream (see Chapter 5, Figure 44)—makes possible his Victory (No. 6), inspiring his conversion to Christianity, which triumphs over paganism in Rome. What changed the course of Western history—i.e., Constantine's relationship to the Christian religion—is attributed by Piero to the edict of a dream. In effect, Constantine achieves an oedipal synthesis, both obeying God (the father) and also overturning an old belief system in favor of a new one.

Piero's unprecedented additions to the visual narrative of the True Cross legend emphasize four sets of the mother-son dyad which, like the father-son conflict, vie for historical dominance. Eve and Seth are types for Mary and Christ, and their presence at Adam's death and burial relates Piero's opening scene with the Annunciation. Helena and Constantine locate the Cross and establish Christianity as the official religion of Rome. In so doing, they supersede Solomon and fulfill the prophecy of Sheba. Venus and Cupid refer to the pagan era; by destroying Venus's temple, Helena symbolically tears down the Old to make way for the New.

Piero alludes to this circumstance through Cupid's presence on the left

32. Piero della Francesca, Annunciation, c. 1452. Bacci Chapel, Church of San Francesco, Arezzo.

33. *Piero della Francesca,* The Defeat
of Chosroes, *c. 1452. Bacci Chapel,
Church of San Francesco, Arezzo.*

pilaster (B in the diagram) and the architectural motifs in the Helena scenes, *The Discovery and Proof of the Cross* [31]. The distant city—at once the Arezzo skyline and the walled Jerusalem—in the Discovery of the Cross (No. 9) is juxtaposed with the Albertian temple facade in the scene of the Proof (No. 10). The innovative character of Alberti's architecture, in contrast to the medieval skyline on the left and the contemporary street

34. *Detail of Figure 33.*

35. *Ramboux (after Piero della Francesca),* Victory of Constantine over Maxentius, *c. 1452. Bacci Chapel, Church of San Francesco, Arezzo.*

buildings to the right, allies it with the new Renaissance style as well as with the New Dispensation. The power of the New Order is expressed by the miracle taking place directly in front of the avant-garde facade.

By introducing both Eve (No. 1A) and Mary (via the *Annunciation* in Figure 32) into his Arezzo cycle, Piero at once splits and synthesizes two facets of the maternal image. Eve is both the primal mother and the fallen woman and Mary is the virgin who redeems the sins of Eve as Christ redeems Adam's. Since Adam's Death, the Annunciation, and Christ's Crucifixion are all celebrated on March 25 in the Church calendar, the split is symbolically repaired and reintegrated through liturgical coincidence. Liturgy thus recapitulates psychology.

More manifest is Piero's rendition of the paternal split into the good father (God) and the negative father (Chosroes). This drama unfolds in the lower tier of the cycle, in the two battle scenes (Nos. 6, 11, and 12 in Figure 30, and Figures 33 and 35), the Annunciation (No. 7 in Figure 30, and Figure 32) and Constantine's Dream (No. 5). In the corresponding physiognomy of God (No. 7A in Figure 30, and Figure 32) and Chosroes (No. 12A in Figure 30, and Figure 33), Piero identifies each with the other. But Chosroes, by his grandiose attempt to usurp God's position, suffers the fate of those who challenge the gods.

The sexual implications of Chosroes's challenge are contained in the substitution of a rooster for the Holy Ghost. For the rooster is a barnyard

Don Juan and "cock of the walk," sacred to Mars because of its willingness to kill. In deleting the scene of Chosroes *en*throned and substituting Chosroes *de*throned, Piero evokes his impending punishment, namely decapitation. Chosroes kneels passively in defeat, while God, his physiognomic "double," is elevated, active, and potent. The childish, mindless, and impulsive quality of Chosroes's presumption is revealed in the talion nature of his punishment. Chosroes's failed oedipal challenge contrasts with the triumph of Constantine, who obeys God's command by virtue of the insight of his dream. Unlike Chosroes, Constantine renounces the old, pagan beliefs and achieves victory.

The latent meaning of Chosroes's punishment and his challenge is the unconscious equation of decapitation with castration, which is given visual form in the violent battle [33]. One soldier kneels on the ground, blood dripping from the back of his neck. Another, in the fray of battle under the stolen Cross, is stabbed in the throat. At the far left, almost unnoticed, is a detail that confirms the association of decapitation with castration [34]. Half a man is visible from the waist down. Between his legs, lying in a pool of blood, is a severed head.

What in fact most distinguishes Piero's two battles—both waged as Crusades in the name of the Cross—is the pronounced opposition of violence and disorder with calm and order. In the *Defeat of Chosroes* [33], swords and armor clash, trumpets blare, and blood is spilled. In *Constantine's Victory* [35], quiet prevails. Despite the haste of the routed army of Maxentius on the right, the advancing army of Constantine is dignified and orderly. The Tiber is like glass, so undisturbed that a family of ducks glides serenely across its surface.

The opposition of order and disorder, calm and violence in the two battles corresponds to the disposition of the saved and damned respectively in traditional Last Judgment scenes. Disorder in Chosroes's battle mirrors the disordered character of his hubris—he is "out of order" in usurping the role of God the Father. His implicit damnation is opposed to the equally implicit salvation of Constantine, who succeeds while following God's command. Constantine literally and figuratively "keeps his head," whereas Chosroes loses his.

NOTES

1. Freud, S. E. I, 1897, p. 265.
2. Freud, "Introductory Lectures on Psychoanalysis," S. E. XV, 1915–17.
3. Freud, *The Ego and the Id*, S. E. XIX, 1923, pp. 12–66.
4. Freud, "Dostoevsky and Parricide," S. E. XXI, 1928, pp. 183–96.

5. Freud, "On the Dissolution of the Oedipus Complex," S. E. XIX, 1924, pp. 173–79.
6. Freud, "Female Sexuality," S. E. XXI, 1931, pp. 225–43.
7. Freud, "Some Psychical Consequences of the Anatomical Distinction Between the Sexes," S. E. XIX, 1925, pp. 251 ff.
8. Quintilian, *De institutione oratoriae* X, ii, 8, in Loeb Library Edition, vol. 4 of 4 vols., Cambridge, Mass., and London, 1979.
9. Leon Battista Alberti, *On Painting*, trans. John R. Spencer, New Haven and London, 1966, p. 64.
10. See, for citations, Robert Rosenblum, "The Origin of Painting: A Problem in the Iconography of Romantic Classicism," *Art Bulletin* 39, no. 4 (December 1957): 279–90.
11. Alberti, *On painting*, 64.
12. Ernst Kris and Otto Kurz, *Legend, Myth, and Magic in the Image of the Artist* (1934), New Haven and London, 1979, p. 53.
13. Ibid., p. 55.
14. Avigdor W. Poseq, "Soutine's Paraphrases of Rembrandt's *Slaughtered Ox*," *Konsthistorisk Tidskrift*, LX, Hafte 3–4, 1991, pp. 210–22.
15. Freud, "Family Romances," S. E. IX, 1909, pp. 235–41.
16. Cf. Laurie Schneider, "A Note on the Iconography of Henry Moore's King and Queen," *Source: Notes in the History of Art* II, no. 4 (Summer 1983): 29–32.
17. Robert Melville, *Henry Moore*, New York, n.d., p. 24.
18. Kris and Kurz, *Legend, Myth, and Magic*, p. 57.
19. Samuel Noah Kramer, *The Sumerians*, Chicago and London, 1963, pp. 138–39.
20. Freud, cf. "Dostoevsky and Parricide."
21. Ernst Kris, *Psychoanalytic Explorations in Art*, New York, 1952.
22. Phyllis Greenacre, "The Childhood of the Artist" (1957) and "The Family Romance of the Artist" (1958), in her *Emotional Growth*, New York, 1971.
23. Freud, "Three Essays . . . ," S. E. VII, 1905, pp. 135–245.
24. Marcel Proust, *What Art Is*, New York, 1991 (private publication commemorating the 20th anniversary of the Proust Group). I am indebted to Leola and Robert MacDonald for this reference.
25. James McNeill Whistler, "Whistler's Ten O'Clock," in Robin Spencer, ed., *Whistler: A Retrospective*, New York, 1989, pp. 212–27.
26. Kris and Kurz, *Legend, Myth, and Magic*, p. 86.
27. See James Saslow, *Ganymede in the Renaissance*, New Haven and London, 1986. The author takes the myth of Ganymede as a constant, and traces its appearance in art from the Italian Renaissance through the seventeenth century in northern Europe.
28. Here and elsewhere in the text, references to Ovid are from *Metamorphoses*, Loeb Library Edition (2 vols.), Cambridge, Mass., and London, 1984.
29. Wolfgang Stechow, *Brueghel*, New York, 1990, pp. 50–51, takes the evidence of a smaller version of this painting in a private collection, where the shepherd looks up at Daedalus.
30. For a discussion reaching related, but not identical, conclusions, see Saslow, *Ganymede in the Renaissance*, Chapter 1.
31. See Saslow, ibid., and Robert Liebert, *Michelangelo: A Psychoanalytic Study of His Life and Images*, New Haven and London, 1983, pp. 173–80.
32. The original presentation drawing is lost; but it is known from versions in the Fogg Art Museum (Cambridge, Mass.) and the Royal Library, Windsor Castle. The Fogg version illustrated here is the more complete and includes Ganymede's dog barking below; cf. Saslow, *Ganymede in the Renaissance*, p. 19.
33. Saslow, ibid., fn. 61, pp. 39 and 41; Liebert, *Michelangelo*, p. 173; and Eissler, *Leonardo da Vinci: Psychoanalytic Notes on the Enigma*, New York, 1961, pp. 111–12 and 130–31.

34. Vincenzo Golzio, *Raffaello nei documenti, nelle testimonianze dei contemporanei e nella letteratura del suo secolo*, Vatican, 1936, p. 30.
35. Cf. Liebert, *Michelangelo*, p. 29.
36. Phyllis Greenacre, "The Childhood of the Artist."
37. Kris and Kurz, *Legend, Myth, and Magic*, p. 32. Cf. also Paul Barolsky, *Giotto's Father and the Family of Vasari's Lives*, University Park and London, 1992.
38. Dante, *Purgatory* 11, 91–96, in Millard Meiss, *Painting in Florence and Siena after the Black Death*, Princeton, 1951, p. 5.
39. Cf. Harold Bloom on this phenomenon in literature, *The Anxiety of Influence*, New York and London, 1973.
40. Ghiberti, *Commentaries*, in Laurie Schneider, *Giotto in Perspective*, Englewood Cliffs, N.J., 1974, p. 39.
41. Giorgio Vasari, *Lives of the Most Eminent Painters, Sculptors, and Architects*, trans. Gaston du Vere, vol. 1, New York, 1979, p. 98.
42. Cf. note 39.
43. Avigdor W. Poseq, "Bernini's Self-Portraits as David," *Source: Notes in the History of Art* IX, no. 4 (Summer 1990): 14–22.
44. On "mirror transference" cf. Heinz Kohut, *The Restoration of the Self*, New York, 1977, pp. 25, 34, 50, 52, 213; and D. W. Winnicott, *Playing and Reality*, New York, 1971, pp. 111–18.
45. "I am sure you will agree," Raphael wrote to his uncle of his good fortune in not having married, "that I would never have got where I am, having three thousand gold ducats put aside in Rome." In Golzio, *Raffaello nei documenti*, p. 31.
46. Freud, S. E. XIII, 1914, pp. 241–44.
47. Ibid., p. 242.
48. See the discussion in Paul Barolsky, *Michelangelo's Nose*, University Park and London, 1990, pp. 7–10.
49. Sidney Geist, *Brancusi*, New York, 1975, p. 12.
50. Ibid.
51. Cf. note 16.
52. Richard Wollheim, *Painting as an Art*, Princeton, 1987, pp. 278–89.
53. Ibid., p. 279.
54. Golzio, *Raffaello nei documenti*, p. 289.
55. Vasari, *Lives*, vol. 3, p. 2073.
56. Erwin Panofsky, *Studies in Iconology*, New York, 1962, pp. 86–91.
57. Ibid., p. 88.
58. Cf. ibid., fn. 78.
59. Ibid., p. 91.
60. Paul Barolsky and Andrew Ladis, "The 'Pleasurable Deceits' of Bronzino's so-called London *Allegory*," *Source: Notes in the History of Art* X, no. 3 (Spring 1991): 32–36.
61. For these verbal connections, I am indebted to Muriel Oxenberg Murphy.
62. This postscript summarizes a talk entitled "Psychological Metaphors in the Iconography of Piero della Francesca," which I gave at the February 26–27, 1993, CUNY Symposium, *Facets of Piero della Francesca*.
63. Cf., for example, Laurie Schneider, "The Iconography of Piero della Francesca's Frescoes Illustrating the Legend of the True Cross in the Church of San Francesco in Arezzo," *Art Quarterly* 32, no. 1 (1969): 22–48; Eugenio Battisti, *Piero della Francesca*, London and New York, 1969; Marilyn Aronberg Lavin, *The Place of Narrative*, Chicago and London, 1990; Ronald Lightbown, *Piero della Francesca*, New York, 1992.

FIVE

Dreams, Delusions, and Art

This chapter reviews the similarities between the mechanisms of dreaming and artistic techniques. Because such similarities exist, the analysis of dreams and other pictorial productions of the mind can contribute to iconographic analysis. It must be said at the outset, however, that Freud was careful to distinguish between dreams and art,[1] which differ in important ways. The mechanisms by which dreams are formed are not creative in the artistic sense because they are not given aesthetic form. They make no judgments, and reach no conclusions. Themes and motifs may be repeated by an individual dreamer, but they do not address an audience, as do works of art. Memories and daydreams are pictorial, and screen memories of the kind Leonardo reported are composed of particularly vivid images. Delusions and hallucinations, although sometimes auditory, are more usually visual. Even certain symptoms are pictorial insofar as they are metaphors for conflicting ideas.

For example, a woman who was fired from her job without warning became convinced that she had developed an obstruction in her throat that disrupted her ability to swallow. Numerous medical examinations failed to identify any physical cause. In this case, the symptom proved to be nothing more than a "picture" of the woman's difficulty in "swallowing" her unjust treatment.

FREUD ON DREAMS

Because dreams are the most significant and universal psychic images, Freud called them the "royal road to the unconscious."[2] There have been no significant theories of the psychology of dreaming since Freud. His first publication, *The Interpretation of Dreams*, in 1900, was followed by a shorter summary, "On Dreams," in 1901. Aside from subsequent footnotes, Freud stuck to the principles of dreaming which he discovered early in his career. Dreams, he wrote, are "disguised fulfillments of repressed wishes."[3]

Freud identified three classes of dreams in 1901—wish fulfillments, anxiety dreams, and dreams in which the content is disturbing but the feeling is not. Despite these distinctions, all three types, according to Freud, are motivated by a wish. In the first category, the disguise is successful and the dream proceeds undisturbed. In the second, the disguise is absent or insufficient; the forbidden wish emerges, causes anxiety, and the dreamer wakes up. The third category accounts for a particular kind of dream in which the wish is particularly well disguised by a misalliance of content and feeling.

Freud's only significant addition to the principles of dreaming came in 1920 in *Beyond the Pleasure Principle*.[4] Having treated World War I shell-shock victims who psychically reexperienced their traumas in repeated nightmares, Freud could not sustain the view that all dreams have a wish-fulfilling motive. He amended his theory to include the newly discovered "repetition compulsion," which he related to the death instinct. In dreams, the compulsion to repeat is essentially an unsuccessful attempt to return to a previous trauma and try to "solve" it.

The Mechanisms of Dreaming

Dreams are primarily pictorial; they have been changed from ideas, thoughts, feelings, and impressions, which can be expressed verbally. According to Freud, a dream is triggered when a thought or impression of the previous twenty-four hours (the "dream-day") connects with an impression from the past. The memory and report of the dream are its "manifest content," and the underlying dream-thoughts, accessible by interpretive means, are the "latent content." The latent content is the result of what Freud called "primary process," or unconscious thinking. The manifest content is the conscious memory of the dream and its revision into logical thought; it reflects "secondary-process thinking," which determines "secondary revision," that is, the waking description of a dream.

With the formulation of the structural theory[5] dividing the mind into id, ego, and superego, latent content was assigned mainly to the id, the superego was the censoring agency, and the ego created the defenses. In the context of the structural system, the dream is a compromise among the latent, unconscious, wishes of the id, the requirements of the superego's censor, and the ego's defenses. The wishful latent content is thus transformed, remembered, and described.

Dreams obey the laws of visual rather than verbal representation, because the dreamer regresses from words to pictures. As a result, dreams, like primary-process thinking, are without logic—such as "if . . . then" and "either . . . or"; what is expressed in words in waking life is translated by the dream into concrete, visual form. Conflict, for example, which is abstract, can be represented pictorially in a dream by the inability to move. Likewise, many of the puns in dreams are the result of a concrete, visual representation of sound.

Puns in Dreams

An eighteen-year-old man, who was the youngest of ten children, dreamed that he killed his father by hitting him over the head with a rake. His dream expressed his anger at his father's "rakishness" and the wish that his father not have any more children (which he could not do if he were dead).

A businessman dreamed that his alarm clock said $6.30 instead of 6:30 A.M.—an illustration of the adage that "time is money."

A woman asking for an unreasonably high divorce settlement dreamed that her leg became weak and would not support her. Aside from many other meanings, the dream reflected her awareness that she "didn't have a leg to stand on."

A graduate student's dream of overeating while outlining his Ph.D. dissertation expressed the abstract idea of "food for thought."

A man dreamed of defecating on the floor after a lengthy phone call from his compulsively verbal mother, thereby depicting the notion of "verbal diarrhea."

A single mother who had been arguing with her son about repeatedly getting into trouble with the law dreamed that she was trying to boil crabs. The crabs kept jumping out of the pot and crawling around on the floor. The dreamer reported that her son had been particularly "crabby" the night before. In the dream, the boy had become the crabs, which "represented" the idea of in and out of trouble with the police, as in and out of "hot water." Another feature of unconscious thinking and dreaming illustrated by this dream is the absence of temporal sequence. Dreams depict repetition visually as multiples—in this case, several crabs and repeated action.

A sixty-year-old anthropologist doing fieldwork in Africa dreamed that he saw a distorted face appear through an opening in his tent as he slept. An arm reached over to the anthropologist and gently lifted off his watch. He awoke in terror. Three weeks later, the anthropologist had a serious heart attack and required double by-pass surgery. The dream was an internal warning that someone was trying to steal his "ticker," a reference to time and the dreamer's watch as well as being a slang term for the heart.

Each of these punning dream episodes could be shown to have multiple dynamic and symbolic meanings for the dreamer. As such, they, like Leonardo's screen memory and all artistic images, are overdetermined.

Freud identified four mechanisms of dreaming—the "dream work"—which effect the translation from verbal to pictorial. These are conditions of representability, condensation, displacement, and symbolization. The last three mechanisms satisfy the first and also create the disguise required to elude censorship. The physiological purpose of the dream is to preserve sleep; when the censor is disturbed because the wish is unmasked, as in anxiety dreams, the dreamer wakes up. Forbidden wishes are allowed some expression in dreams because the condition of sleep inhibits action. To counter the opposing views of dreaming, Freud pointed out the lengths to which a dream will go to keep the dreamer asleep; he cited the instance of a dreamer hearing a carpet being beaten. Instead of waking up, the dreamer turned the sound into the dream image of an audience clapping.[6]

In condensation, one or more images or ideas are superimposed or conflated. The businessman condensed $6.30 with 6:30 A.M., and the eighteen-year-old man conflated the two meanings of "rake"—a roué and a garden tool. Verbal "mistakes," whether in dreams, jokes, or slips of the tongue, can also be effected by condensation. For example, a female partner in a law firm, who was concerned about a power play by three male colleagues, dreamed that they had created a "triumpherate." The dreamer had condensed "triumph" with "triumvirate."

Displacement, which is a process of putting one element in the place of another, often facilitates condensation. In the crab dream, the unpleasant behavior of the dreamer's son was displaced onto the crabs. In the businessman's dream, a dollar sign had been placed before the number six, and a period had taken the place of the colon.

Symbolization works by pictorial analogy. Long, thin objects regularly represent the phallus, and concave objects, vessels, and containers represent the vagina. Although there are vast numbers of symbols, the things symbolized are small in number. By and large, they are restricted to people, body parts, and bodily functions.[7] In the crab dream, the crabs symbolized the boy as well as his crabbiness, and, since crabs move sideways, they also represented his inability to be "straight."

The pot symbolized the mother herself, and her action of dropping crabs in hot water was her attempt to control her son by keeping him home instead of allowing him to go out and get into trouble. Staying home, of course, meant staying home with her, which is "hot water" of another kind. Turning her son into a crab put him down on the evolutionary scale and symbolically infantilized him. In and out of the pot depicts the ambivalence of both mother and son individually, as well as their ambivalent relation to each other.

The capacity to symbolize assists not only representability, but also condensation and displacement. In the verbal-diarrhea dream, the verbal functions of the mouth were displaced downward, and the anal functions were simultaneously displaced upward. Here, therefore, the dreamer joined the symbolic connection of useless, rapidly flowing words and loose feces with the operations of upward and downward displacement by virtue of condensation. The space of the torso, between mouth and anus, was eliminated, or condensed, and the two orifices were superimposed to create the image of "verbal diarrhea."

In the "triumpherate" dream, the three letters "phe" were displaced onto the "vir" of "triumvirate," thereby condensing triumph and triumvirate. The substitution expressed the woman's sense that she had been excluded, and triumphed over, by three men. Having studied Latin, she knew that *vir* is the Latin word for "man"; the number three in dreams usually has phallic significance, because the male genital organ has three easily observable parts. By consonance of sound, "phe" equals "fe," the first two letters of "female," and depicts the dreamer's wish that women (phe) triumph over men (vir).

EXAMPLES OF "DREAM WORK" IN ART

Condensation

Castagno's *David* of c. 1450 [10] is a good illustration of condensation used consciously as a pictorial device. David is about to launch the stone that will slay Goliath; but Goliath's decapitated head indicates that he is already dead. Castagno has thus condensed time; he has depicted the before and after of Goliath's death simultaneously and within the same space.

Condensation of time is one of the most persistent, and conscious, pictorial techniques in Christian art. It permitted contemporary personages, often the picture's donor, to seem present at a past event. The reverse could also be true—that is, the donor or other contemporary figure could appear to have conjured up the past event as a devotional image. In Masaccio's *Trinity* [15], for example, the donors stand outside the barrel-vaulted sacred space. The ambiguous relation of the donors to the event—Are they meant actually to be there? Or is the scene "imagined" by them?—is served by temporal condensation.

Condensing time was particularly appropriate for typological images. By virtue of the typological system paralleling figures and events of the Old and New Testaments, Christian writers incorporated the Old Dispensation into the New. Everything that had preceded the era of Christ, including classical antiquity, could be shown to have "prefigured" Christ's coming as part of a grand cosmic plan. Christ was the new Adam and Mary, the new Eve; Adam and Eve were "types" for Christ and Mary. The story of Jonah and the whale "typified" Christ's death and resurrection, both requiring an interval of three days. Old Testament prophets and ancient sibyls were reinterpreted as having prophesied the coming of Christ. Eventually, later historical figures and events, often having contemporary political significance, were paralleled with biblical characters and events. The typological system was thus an elaborate revision of history, designed to demonstrate the all-embracing and universal nature of the Christian Church. This historical revision determined many iconographic programs, including the Sistine Chapel, where the left wall is decorated with Old Testament scenes and the right with New.

In individual paintings, typology is illustrated by temporal condensation. A work such as Fra Angelico's fifteenth-century *Annunciation with Expulsion* [36] refers to the "beginning of time" by including the Expulsion of Adam and Eve in the distance. This iconography parallels the Annunciation of Christ's birth with the Expulsion as the redemption of original sin. Although both scenes occupy the same picture plane, the Expulsion is smaller and in the background.

Perspectival developments in the Renaissance increased the range of condensation. Fra Angelico's Expulsion is small and distant, to denote temporal distance from the larger, foreground scene of the Annunciation. Viewers are reminded of the typological connection between the two

36. *Fra Angelico,* Annunciation with Expulsion,
*fifteenth century. Gabinetto Fotografico,
Soprintendenza Beni Artistici e Storici di Firenze,
Florence.*

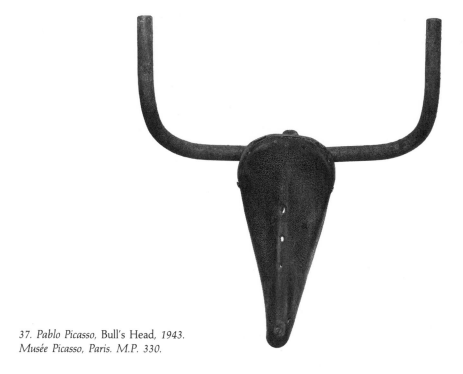

37. *Pablo Picasso, Bull's Head, 1943.*
Musée Picasso, Paris. M.P. 330.

events by the condensation of real time and spatial separation; past is pictorially distinguished from present by size and location. The Annunciation also refers to future time. Mary's gesture, crossing her arms as she leans toward Gabriel, is a visual reminder of Christ's Crucifixion and her foreknowledge of it.

With the development of new approaches to artistic media in the nineteenth and twentieth centuries, the possibilities for condensation expanded further. In collage and assemblage, for example, spaces between the literal components of the media are manipulated by the artist differently from more traditional paintings and sculptures. Picasso's *Bull's Head* of 1943 [37] is a case in point; it was made by "assembling" a bicycle seat and a pair of handlebars. The expected space between them was eliminated in the service of condensation. In contrast to the condensed elements of a dream, however, those in an artistic assemblage, such as the *Bull's Head*, are juxtaposed rather than superimposed.

That the metaphorical aspect of the *Bull's Head* requires condensation is clear if the logical steps preceding its creation are followed. They would presumably go something like this: "If the seat and handlebars of a bicycle are detached, the seat turned one hundred and eighty degrees and attached directly to the handlebars, and if the whole thing is cast in bronze, the resulting object will resemble the head of a bull." Picasso's metaphorical style of thinking has, in this instance, led him to assemble the parts of a modern mechanical object (the bicycle) in a way that formally suggests the traditional motif of the bull. The result is a witty and unlikely combination that "works"—like a good joke—because it carries intellectual and formal conviction.

Displacement and Symbolization

Displacement in the visual arts can reflect the unconscious symbolic relationships between parts of the body. Such displacements are familiar in popular language. The riddle that asks "Why do men think so much and women talk so much?" with the answer "Because men have two heads and women have four lips" expresses the respective upward and downward displacement of genitals and face.

Roman masks whose tongues are phalli [38] illustrate the unconscious equation of tongue and phallus. A related metaphorical expression of this equation informs the Christian characterization of Christ as "God's word made flesh." The fecundating power of the "word of God"—explicit in certain Annunciation scenes (see Chapter 9)—necessarily equates tongue and phallus.

38. Roman Drinking-Bowl Mask with Phallic Tongue, *first century* A.D.

The eye/phallus equation, which explains the self-blinding of Oedipus as upwardly displaced castration,[8] appears in a Greek vase painting fragment [39]. Two eyed phalli seem to peer over the edge of a pot and through a cloth, as if trying to see out. This equation was particularly significant in antiquity, as the phallus was believed to protect against the evil eye; herms (statues with erect phalli) guarded entrances and roadways. A curious first-century B.C. Roman terracotta statue shows a phallic figurine sawing through an eye, apparently to demonstrate the power of the phallus to counter the evil eye.[9]

The unconscious association of the entire body with the phallus appears in a tiny Roman bronze body/phallus now in the Boston Museum of Fine Arts [40]. The image corresponds to a fantasy that has been described by psychoanalysts[10] as usually found in vain, narcissistic characters with unresolved castration fear. In order to defend against that fear, men overcompensate by turning their whole bodies into what they unconsciously fear losing, and women, into what they fear they have already lost.

Works of art from antiquity elaborate the numerous symbols derived

39. Flying Angel Painter, Girl with Winged, Eyed Phalli, *500–475 B.C. Louvre, Paris.*

40. Bronze Body/Phallus, Roman. *Museum of Fine Arts, Boston. Donated by E. P. Warren, Res.08.320.*

41. Winged Phallic Tintinnabulum with Lion Feet, *from Herculaneum, first century B.C.–first century A.D. National Museum of Naples, Raccolta Pornografica no. 27835.*

from the human body. A widespread transformation of the phallus in art, as in popular language, is the bird—which determined Freud's interpretation of Leonardo's vulture/kite as the phallic mother. On the base of the large marble phallus at Delos, for example, is the relief sculpture of a bird whose neck and head are changed into a phallus. In the vase painting fragment in Figure 39, the girl holds a winged bird phallus. Many ancient Roman bronze tintinnabula are in the shape of winged phalli [41]; their purpose, like that of the herms, was to guard entrances against the evil eye.

The mechanism of displacement in art is most explicitly sexual in the ancient world and in Surrealism. Fra Angelico's *Annunciation with Expulsion* [36], on the other hand, could be said to have displaced the Expulsion forward into the time of the Annunciation. Raphael's *School of Athens* [28] displaces figures of antiquity into a Renaissance architectural setting. And Castagno's *David* [10] displaces Goliath's decapitated head backward in time to before his death. One result of all these displacements is temporal condensation; past and present coexist in the same space—as they do in the unconscious.

42. *René Magritte,* The
Rape (Le Viol), *1934.*
Menil Collection,
Houston.

43. *René Magritte,* The
Philosopher's Lamp,
1935. Private collection.

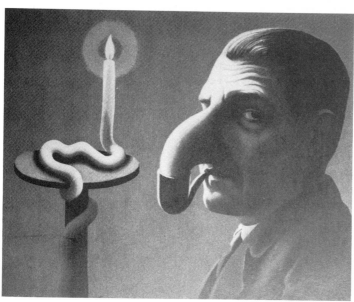

In Christian art, transformations of sexual symbols are rather more implicit than explicit. The most ubiquitous example of the bird/phallus association is the dove representing the Holy Ghost.[11] The dove's phallic role in the Annunciation scene is in its mission as the bearer of God's spirit. Its angelic counterpart is Gabriel, also winged, who delivers God's message verbally (see Chapter 9). Both figures have a phallic, impregnating character whose elaboration illustrates the artistic capacity for metaphorical transformation.

Many Surrealist artists consciously illustrated the unconscious dream mechanisms described by Freud. Magritte's *Rape* [42] is a witty example of the face/torso equation in the female body.[12] His *Philosopher's Lamp* of 1935 [43] relates the nose to phallic elements—pipe and candle—that are not part of the body. Both contain various implications, including the erotic significance of smoke and fire.

At the same time, however, the pipe is sexually ambivalent, because it combines a phallic stem with a concave (and receptive) bowl. The nose curving into the bowl is an image of upwardly displaced sexual intercourse. Echoing that image is the candle, which is at once an erect vertical rising toward a flame and also a limp, serpentine form slithering away. The candle's formal shift makes an erotic joke of the behavior of a phallus before and after the sexual activity symbolically taking place between the nose and the pipe bowl. In this painting, therefore, Magritte uses all the dream mechanisms described by Freud.

The Dream as a Subject of Art

As a subject of art, the depiction of dreams depends on the changing historical perception of their nature and significance as well as on the artist's style. Dreams, as in the Sumerian account of Gudea's dream (see Chapter 4), were first represented as external phenomena sent by God. Gradually the true character of dreams became better understood, especially in the nineteenth and twentieth centuries, and the depiction of dreams changed.

Piero della Francesca's fifteenth-century *Dream of Constantine* [44] takes place at night; Constantine is asleep in his tent, which is guarded by two soldiers. At the upper left an angel carries a tiny cross illuminated with holy light to alert Constantine to the power of the cross. The texts (for example, *The Golden Legend*) known to Piero describe this event as a waking, nocturnal vision; but Piero has changed it into a dream. The

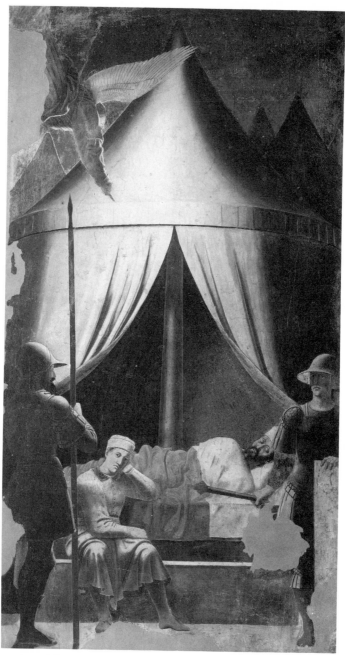

44. *Piero della Francesca*, The Dream of
Constantine, *c. 1450. Bacci Chapel, Church of San
Francesco, Arezzo.*

contrast between Constantine's sleeping state, typically associated with ignorance and sin in Christian art, and the cross's light heralds the en*light*-enment it brings. "In this sign, you conquer"—"In hoc signo vincis"—is God's explicit message. Constantine's subsequent victory suggests that dreams were believed to be truthful, because they were sent by a "higher power." Projecting the psychological "truth" of dreams onto a greater intelligence than the dreamer's is consistent with the greater power of the unconscious as compared with the conscious mind.[13]

In the course of the nineteenth century, as psychology developed into a distinct discipline, the representation of dreams in art changed accordingly. At the turn of the nineteenth century, in 1799, Goya created his famous etching and aquatint *The Sleep of Reason Produces Monsters* [45]. It shows the sleeping artist and reveals the contents of his dream images to be frightening nocturnal fliers—bats and owls. A wide-eyed lynx counters the artist's hidden face and state of sleep. The message of Goya's dream can be construed to convey political or social meaning—for example, monstrous things happen when reason loses control or goes to sleep.

But the dream also has an internal, psychological meaning. The bats and owls seem to come from a distance. As they alight around Goya's form, their wings flapping, they create an arc of staring faces. Their "monstrous" nature is at once regressive and sexual. Bats and owls, as flying creatures of the night, are phallic; in being small and less evolved than the adult human dreamer, they are childlike. The anxiety accompanying these figures is enhanced by their repetition, the motion of their wings, and their intent gaze. Although Goya remains asleep, his dream is clearly driven by an anxiety that crowds in on him—for if Goya's dream is read psychologically, its message defines the very nature of dreaming: when reason—the reality ego—sleeps, unconscious, primary process material—the "monsters"—emerges from the id.

Gauguin's *Reverie* of 1891 [46] leaves no doubt that the dream, which is in fact a *day*dream, is an internal phenomenon. The painting thus conforms to the aims of the Symbolist movement, with which the artist was associated. Gauguin's daydreamer reclines in a long diagonal, her pose a version of the traditional reclining nude Venus, implying that her daydream has an erotic cast. She holds a cloth over her vagina, which is a motif used elsewhere by Gauguin to denote a figure's symbolic reference to Eve's Temptation. This, in itself, suggests that the daydream is a sexual one; the dreamer, in effect, is "imagining" her own "Fall."[14]

Her abstracted gaze informs the viewer that her thoughts are else-

45. *Francisco José de Goya,*
The Sleep of Reason
Produces Monsters (Los
Caprichos, *plate 43: "El Sueño
de La Razon Produce
Monstruos"), 1799.
Metropolitan Museum of Art,
New York. Gift of M.
Knoedler and Co., 1918,
18.64(43).*

where, as happens in the construction of a daydream. The pictorial nature of her dream is reflected in the inclination of her head toward the painting in the upper left, which is like a "thought balloon." The picture within the picture is a metaphor for the pictorial daydream and reflects, in symbolic terms, its erotic content. Landscape, in sleep dreams, generally represents the female body, as does architecture. The daydreamer's sexual fantasy in Gauguin's painting is symbolized by both: the doors of the house and the landscape itself are "open," denoting the sexual availability of the dreamer.

Rousseau's *Dream* of 1910 [47] followed the publication of Freud's *Interpretation of Dreams* by a little over ten years and exemplifies the conscious use of dream work to depict the text of a dream. The nude dreamer participates in her own dream; she sits upright on a French bourgeois divan, pointing anxiously at the oddly tame wildlife surrounding her. It is clear that, by the mechanism of displacement, she has been transported from "civilization" to the jungle, thereby condensing time and

46. *Paul Gauguin,* Reverie
(Faaturuma *[Melancholic])*,
*1891. Nelson-Atkins
Museum of Art, Kansas
City, Missouri. Nelson
Fund, 38-5.*

space. Another temporal condensation is that of night (note the presence of the moon), which is the usual time for dreams, with the bright, daytime sky.

The curious, gray figure playing the pipe in the center is a composite of human and nonhuman, also created by condensation. In standing upright, wearing a tunic, and playing an instrument, he has a human quality. In his simian physiognomy and dark gray skin tone, he is not human. He is a variation on the mythological woodland creatures, such as satyrs, that populate forests and represent instinctual, or libidinal, forces. In being both human and subhuman, the musician creates an evolutionary link between the dreamer and the wildlife, and a psychic link between conscious and unconscious thinking.

The flowers, the birds, and the serpent can be read as fairly direct sexual symbols. Their abundance, together with the tame wild animals, is reminiscent of the Garden of Eden and its sexual consequences. The con-

47. *Henri Rousseau,* The Dream, *1910. Museum of
Modern Art, New York. Gift of Nelson A.
Rockefeller.*

trast between bright, clear wildlife and the dark, mysterious musician is
related to their functions as dream elements. The more vivid features—as
in screen memories—are also the most disguised. The darkness of the
musician makes him seem to emerge from the depths of the forest, as from
the depths of the dreamer's unconscious.

Rousseau's own comments on *The Dream* replicate the process of
secondary revision. In 1914, he described the painting as follows:

> In a beautiful dream
> Yadwigha gently sleeps
> Heard the sounds of a pipe
> Played by a sympathetic charmer
> While the moon reflects
> On the rivers and the verdant trees
> The serpents attend
> The gay tunes of the instrument.[15]

He accounted for the unusual juxtaposition by saying that the dreamer is sleeping on the sofa and has been transported to the jungle. Later he said that he put the sofa in the jungle because of its red color.

By the time Picasso had painted his *Dream* of 1932 [48], psychoanalysis was well on its way to becoming an international movement. Picasso's bright, unmodeled planes of color are typical of his early 1930s Surrealist style. His dreamer is represented in a more frontal version of the reclining nude than Gauguin's daydreamer and merges more formally with the shifting planes and colors of the chair. In the Picasso, the unlikely, surreal character of many dream images is reflected in the odd colors and spatial distortions of both figure and chair. Also unlikely, although humorous, is

48. *Pablo Picasso,*
The Dream, *1932.*
Private collection.

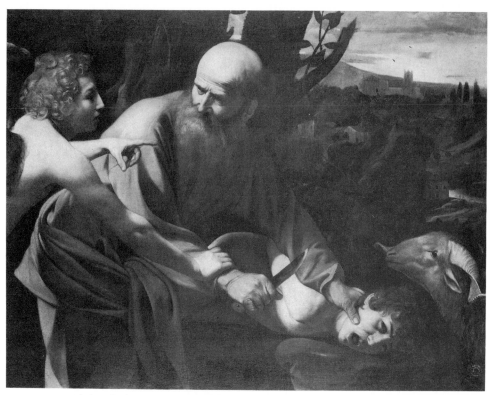

49. *Michelangelo da Caravaggio,* Sacrifice of Isaac,
1594–96. Uffizi, Florence.

the exaggerated hump of the woman's shoulder, creating a pillow for her head.

Ambivalence is represented pictorially in *The Dream* by a series of dual arrangements. Lavender interlocks with green, and red with yellow; part of the chair is flattened and part is volumetric. Picasso's characteristic facial duality, combining profile with front view, reinforces ambivalence. The dreamer's expression shifts; it is sober in profile and smiling in the front view. This shift can be read as a sequence of movement responding to an inner psychological state. That the dreamer's expression responds to an erotic dream wish is implied by her pose and gesture, as well as by the particular nature of her facial shift. A section of the face seems to become detached along the bridge of the nose, as if slowly floating upward. It cannot be a coincidence, in view of the dreamer's reclining pose and traditional erotic gesture, that the detached shape is unmistakably phallic.

Iconographic Choice and Dream Elements

The elements of a dream have to satisfy various requirements, including those of the dreamwork and the censor. The elements of a work of art have to satisfy formal and iconographic demands, but they may also have to comply with the wishes of a patron, the conscious bias of an artist, his general public, and possibly even critics and dealers. Regardless of these considerations, every original work of art contains unique choices made by the artist. These, in turn, reveal the artist's personal contribution to the image, just as dreams reveal the dreamer.

A comparison of the *Sacrifice of Isaac* by Caravaggio [49] and by Rembrandt [50] illustrates the psychological underpinning of iconographic

50. *Rembrandt,* Sacrifice of Isaac, *1635. Hermitage, Saint Petersburg.*

choice. Both artists worked in the Baroque style—the former in Italy early in the seventeenth century, and the latter, somewhat later in Holland. Both artists depict a biblical text that deals with a father's willingness to kill his son in obedience to a "higher" father—namely, God. God instructs Abraham to sacrifice his only son, Isaac, as proof of his faith. Abraham is distressed, but complies. As he is about to cut Isaac's throat, Abraham is interrupted by an angel who instructs him to substitute a ram.

An artist's response to this text is likely to reveal something of his emotional relationship to his own father and/or son, if he happens to have one. In Caravaggio's version, the tension between father and son is palpable; physical strain reflects anger and horror. Abraham grasps the knife firmly; Isaac's distorted face turns toward the viewer, emphasizing his anguish as a struggling victim. Caravaggio's Abraham is angry at the interruption; he glares fiercely at the angel and digs his fingers into his son's flesh.

Rembrandt's *Sacrifice of Isaac* is of an altogether different character. Isaac's face is not visible and therefore does not communicate his fear to the observer. One has the impression that Abraham hides his son's face from himself as well, as if to distance himself from the killing. The moment the angel arrives, Abraham drops the knife. From the same text, Rembrandt has created a father who kills with reluctance, while Caravaggio's kills with determination. Rembrandt's Isaac is passive and his face is hidden; Caravaggio's is anguished and rebellious. Neither of Caravaggio's figures obeys the rules of the text, whereas both of Rembrandt's do. In these rather striking differences are to be found clues to the artists' own characters as well as to broader considerations of their iconographic and thematic choices.

Self-Portraits and Self-Images

Freud first thought that dream personages were facets of the dreamer himself. Later, however, he amended that view. The identity and meaning of people in dreams can be as elusive as in works of art. Nevertheless, there are instances when artists quite literally displace their own self-portraits onto historical, biblical, or mythical characters. In such cases, their identifications are clear and direct rather than implicit, as in the *Sacrifice of Isaac* by Caravaggio and Rembrandt.

When Bernini created his self-portrait as David,[16] he portrayed an energetic and victorious fighter. Caravaggio's *David* [11], on the other hand, is the portrait of the artist's young lover, and the artist's self-portrait is in the severed but living head of Goliath.[17] The sadomasochistic relationship between David and Goliath in Caravaggio's image puts Goliath—and therefore the artist—in a passive, exhibitionistic role. He has been literally "bloodied" by his homosexual lover and exhibits himself as such.

David's gesture, in which he seems to offer Goliath's head to the observer, is a formal and psychological quotation from Michelangelo's Saint Bartholomew in the *Last Judgment* [51]. Both Caravaggio's David and Michelangelo's saint "exhibit" their respective artist's self-portrait in a depressive and masochistic way.

Caravaggio also borrowed the pose of Michelangelo's Saint Bartholomew for what is perhaps his most defiant and blatantly homosexual figure,

51. Michelangelo, Last Judgment, *detail of Saint Bartholomew, 1536. Sistine Chapel, Vatican, Rome.*

52. *Michelangelo da Caravaggio,* Victorious
Cupid, *1598–99. Staatliche Museen, Berlin.*

in *Amor vincit omnia,* or *Victorious Cupid* [52]. The Amor's pose resembles Saint Bartholomew's, although their manifest characters are entirely different. Caravaggio has, in effect, quoted visually from Michelangelo's saint for two paintings that are directly self-related and explicitly homosexual. Caravaggio thus adapted one of Michelangelo's self-related images to convey two facets of his own homosexual experience. The Amor exudes seductive confidence as he dominates the worldly and artistic pursuits represented by armor and the instruments of kingship and music. The *David* expresses the dangers of homosexual submission to a younger lover.

That Caravaggio chose to quote from Michelangelo in these two works has considerable psychological significance. Michelangelo had been Caravaggio's most illustrious artistic predecessor in Italy, which fact placed him in a paternal relation to the younger artist. Michelangelo also shared Caravaggio's homosexual orientation, even though its overt expression was quite different. Howard Hibbard, in fact, suggests that Caravaggio's visual quotations of Michelangelo include a desire to expose the homosexual impulse underlying his predecessor's attraction to the male nude in a direct and defiant way.[18]

The conflicts that Michelangelo had had with his father over his wish to become a sculptor would have been well known through Vasari. Caravaggio's violent conflicts with authority are evident from his *Sacrifice of Isaac* and his extensive criminal record (see Chapter 11). To the extent, however, that Caravaggio learned from Michelangelo and assimilated aspects of his work, he experienced him as a positive paternal influence. Nevertheless, Caravaggio's intensely conflicted relationship with Michelangelo is revealed in the split nature—one triumphant and the other submissive—of the two homosexual images derived from Saint Bartholomew.

Another kind of conflicted self is exemplified by Gauguin's *Self-Portrait with Halo* of late 1889 [53]. Like *Reverie,* the *Self-Portrait* belongs to the artist's Symbolist phase and consciously depicts a state of mind. The background is divided into two colors, red above and yellow below, a chromatic echo of Gauguin's inner self, caught between an identification with good and evil. The halo denotes sainthood, while the curved patterns of black outline the artist and evolve into a serpent. The apples, in such a context, must refer to original sin and the Fall. Gauguin's lifelong struggle with good and evil persists in the Christian themes integrated with Tahitian subjects. Although living in what seemed a "Paradise," Gauguin's Tahitian paintings continued to depict themes of loss of innocence, danger, and paranoia. Just as psychological conflict, or indecision, can be repre-

53. *Paul Gauguin,*
Self-Portrait with Halo,
1889. National Gallery of
Art, Washington, D.C.
Chester Dale Collection.

sented as immobility in a dream, so Gauguin seems caught between red and yellow, sainthood and Satan.

In van Gogh's *Resurrection of Lazarus* [54], inspired by a Rembrandt etching of the same subject, the artist displaced his own face onto the resurrected corpse. Van Gogh's recent discharge from a mental hospital reinforced his personal connection with Lazarus as one who has gained a new "lease on life." The two women, Mary and Martha, are Lazarus's sisters, who, in the Bible (John 11), plead with Christ to return their brother to life. In the painting, they are represented as opposites. One is expansive, frontal, illuminated, and brightly colored; the other is withdrawn, silhouetted, dark, and seen in a three-quarter rear view. The expansive woman stretches out her arms in the traditional gesture of Mary Magdalene at the Crucifixion. The gesture itself refers formally to the Cross, by echoing Christ's crucified pose.

In these figures, van Gogh has effected a series of conflations. Mary, who is Lazarus's sister, is related to the biblical prostitute through pose and gesture; as such, she is both saint and sinner (Mary Magdalene), a sexual object (the prostitute) and a taboo woman (sister). The two women can be read as van Gogh's split image of women—expansive (the prostitute) and depressive (the dark, withdrawn figure). Lazarus, in turn, is conflated with both Christ and the artist. Van Gogh himself intuits these meanings as he writes his brother Theo of "the personalities of whom I would have dreamed as characters."[19]

54. *Vincent van Gogh,* Resurrection of Lazarus, *1890. Stedelijk Museum, Amsterdam. Vincent van Gogh Foundation/Vincent van Gogh Museum, Amsterdam.*

The eerie white light pervading the picture suggests at once the glare of hospital light and the intensity of ordinary daylight when one wakes from a deep sleep. Dominating the sky and the natural light source of the painting is van Gogh's characteristic yellow sun. Here, the sun has replaced the figure of Christ in Rembrandt's Lazarus etching.[20] In addition to the traditional Christian association of Christ with the sun, the substitution in this painting has personal significance. Van Gogh's father was a minister, which had also been the artist's first calling. Only when he failed to be ordained, did van Gogh choose to be an artist.

The paternal implications of the sun and its role as the "eye of God" in Western iconography are an important feature of van Gogh's imagery. Albert J. Lubin has written extensively on the artist's relationship to the sun and its function as a symbolic halo in many of his pictures.[21] "Vincent," according to Lubin,[22] "worshiped the sun" and had no fear of confronting it directly.[23] These findings reveal van Gogh's sense of connection with, and idealization of, his father and his dreamlike conflation of him with Christ and God.

In most of his paintings containing a bright sun, the yellow circle is above the horizon and therefore *behind* a usually solitary figure, such as a sower or a reaper. These isolated workers, with whom van Gogh identified, do not actually "confront" the sun. But there is a paradoxical sense of intimacy between the sun and the figure—"so near and yet so far"—as if, in spite of its distance, the sun is connected to the figure's very existence. Likewise, the *Resurrection of Lazarus* is "warmed" by the paternal sun, whose light pervades the picture plane.

The Motif of the Sun

When Freud wrote *The Interpretation of Dreams,* he delineated, among other things, the iconography of the mind. If one considers an image such as van Gogh's sun, it is clear that a single manifest form can contain multiple layers of latent meaning. When a psychoanalyst interprets a dream, he follows the dreamer's associations until a theme emerges. A similar method defines the iconographic analysis of imagery in the visual arts. In the latter instance, however, free associations by the artist are usually unavailable.

The iconographer deals with specific artistic motifs by researching them. Associative links are made by knowing something of the culture in which the work was produced, the artist's milieu, the available texts, the tastes of a patron, and so forth. It is also helpful to know the artistic precedents of the work, if any, as well as the meanings of related images. Amassing such information and interpreting it is a form of historical reconstruction. For the same reason, it is useful for an analyst to have as much cultural information as possible about an analysand. Likewise, biographical information about an artist can sometimes enrich art-historical reconstruction and also elucidate the iconography of a work.

The meaning of the bright yellow sun in van Gogh's pictures can be understood by its association to his minister father, to his psychic relationship to his father, and to the sun's traditional significance in Western art, religion, and myth. The significance of the sun also informed the fifteenth-century personal emblem of Alberti, the winged eye, whose manifest character seems very far removed from van Gogh's sun. The sun is, of course, a broad subject; and what I am proposing here is a small example of the way in which probing the unconscious can contribute to iconographic exploration. I will begin with a brief consideration of Freud's landmark study of paranoia, in which the psychical meaning of the sun plays the central symbolic role. In this instance, it is a matter of looking into the meaning of delusions and hallucinations, which, like dreams, are visual phenomena and can be thought of as waking dreams. Both are believed at the time they occur; but dreamers wake up and resume a life based in reality, whereas those who hallucinate have lost touch with reality.

Freud on Schreber's Sun (1911)

In 1911, Freud published "Psycho-analytical Notes on an Autobiographical Account of a Case of Paranoia,"[24] generally referred to as the Schreber case. Freud analyzed the paranoid delusion of Daniel Paul Schreber, described by the patient himself in *Memoirs of a Nerve Patient (Denkwürdigkeiten eines Nervenkranken)*, published in 1903. Altogether Schreber suffered three breakdowns, was hospitalized, and attempted suicide. His most severe psychotic episode followed a promotion in 1893 to Presiding Judge of Dresden's Superior Court *(Senatspräsident)*. While in the hospital, Schreber kept detailed notes on his state of mind. Freud's analysis was undertaken from Schreber's writings rather than in a clinical situation, and it is thus, like his *Leonardo*, a psychobiography. The Schreber case became the classic study of paranoia, although subsequent revisions of it have contributed new perspectives on paranoia as well as on Schreber himself. In it Freud showed that, in contrast to the condensation, or compromise, necessary to create a hysterical symptom, paranoia is a process of *dis*integration. The analysis of hysteria—like the analysis of a dream—requires teasing out threads whose very entanglement has disguised the latent meaning. In the disintegration of paranoid delusions and hallucinations, the threads come apart of their own volition (compare "to come apart at the seams" and "to come unraveled") and expose the latent imagery.

The crux of Schreber's delusion was the belief that he had become a woman, because God had wished it. Convinced first that his doctor and then that God was persecuting him, Schreber appeased God by his transformation. As a result, God would impregnate Schreber through the sun's rays and create a superior race. The sun spoke to Schreber in human language, and Schreber shouted back at the sun. Schreber's delusion transformed his father into the sun, whose female counterpart was Mother Earth.

Freud analyzed the delusion in relation to the Oedipus complex as a defense against an outbreak of homosexual feeling. Instead of accepting that he loves another man, the paranoid of Schreber's type first changes the love to hate and then reverses the object relationship. In its final delusional form, the original homosexual love object—the father—becomes the persecutor.

The prototype, or first edition, of "the other man" is the oedipal father; in Schreber's case, this association was reinforced by the fact that his own father was a physician, whose treatment of him had been physically abusive.[25] William G. Niederland[26] has added to Freud's analysis the observation that Schreber was afraid to compete realistically with his father and consequently, when promoted, he suffered breakdowns. In so doing, he associated success with oedipal danger and regressed, like Phaëthon, to a passive, feminine position.

In his *Postscript* to the Schreber case,[27] Freud referred to myth to validate his view that the sun was a "sublimation" of the patient's father. Taking Schreber's delusion that he could safely gaze at the sun as his point of departure, Freud noted that in antiquity only eagles were believed to have such powers.[28] Since the eagle was associated with sky gods, notably Zeus and Jupiter in Greek and Roman mythology, it could stand specifically for the sun as well as for the heavens. That the sun also became the eagle's totemic ancestor is clear from the ancient belief that eagles subjected their young to a test of lineage. Before acknowledging its young as legitimate, the eagle forced them to look at the sun. If the young eagles blinked, they were thrown from the nest. Freud[29] explained such ordeals as expressions of totemic thinking, which assumes that the totem—or original ancestor—will not harm its legitimate descendants.[30]

Schreber's assertion that he, too, could stare at the sun without danger revealed the importance of establishing a divine lineage. In this way, wrote Freud, Schreber "rediscovered the mythological method of expressing his filial relation to the sun, and has confirmed us once again in our view that the sun is a symbol of the father."[31] Relating the iconography of Schreber's hallucinatory delusion to his biography was his obsession with his own biological lineage. He fabricated a delusional ancestry from the "Margraves of Tuscany and Tasmania";[32] in so doing, he created a version of the "family romance," by elevating his forebears to nobility. Elevating his father to the sun is an even loftier expression of the family romance, although in more symbolic guise.

Freud related the myth of the eagle's test for legitimacy to one of the key precipitating factors of Schreber's delusion—namely, his failure to have children. He had married a woman fifteen years his junior in 1878, one year after his older brother's suicide at the age of thirty-eight, and six years before his first breakdown. All six of his wife's pregnancies ended in miscarriage. Schreber solved his inability to produce descendants by the delusion that he was the woman, who, impregnated by the paternal sun, would continue the lineage of his family.

Alberti's Sun

In the fifteenth century, in Italy, the humanist author Leon Battista Alberti took as his personal emblem a winged eye.[33] It appears, together with Alberti's profile, in two reliefs; one is Matteo de' Pasti's medallion of c. 1446–50, in which the profile is on the obverse and the eye on the reverse [55]. At the top of the eye is a pair of eagle's wings, and emanating from each corner are rays. Below is the motto "Quid Tum," meaning "What then?" or "What next?" and surrounding it, a laurel wreath. In the other relief [56], a self-portrait plaque, the eye is placed under Alberti's chin.

The sun is part of the emblem's latent content in contrast to Schreber's sun, whose manifest character resulted from his delusional disintegration. The winged eye must be understood personally as well as in the context of fifteenth-century imagery. By pursuing the cultural, mythological, and biographical associative threads of the emblem's iconography, it is possible to arrive at an interpretation. Alberti himself connected the eye to God, because he is "all-seeing."[34] In this view, Alberti was sustained by the Egyptian hieroglyphic tradition, known in the Renaissance, in which God was represented by an eye. The eye, in turn, was associated with the sun and related as such to kings, mythological gods, the Christian God, and

55. *Matteo de' Pasti,* Medallion Portrait of
Alberti with Winged Eye, *1446/1450. National
Gallery of Art, Washington, D.C. Samuel H. Kress
Collection.*

56. *Leon Battista Alberti,*
Self-Portrait Plaque, *c. 1435.
National Gallery of Art,
Washington, D.C. Samuel H.
Kress Collection.*

Christ. The wings create the impression that Alberti's eye is in flight and evoke the eagle's role as Jupiter's attribute.

Since all of these features—eye, wings, rays of the sun—have phallic meaning in the unconscious, they can be related to the father's role in procreation. The biographical implications of Alberti's emblem, like Schreber's sun, derive from his conflicted identification with his father. Alberti's illegitimate birth contributed to his lifelong concern with lineage and to his adoption of the eagle's wings as part of his emblem. The myth of the eagle's totemic test for legitimacy was well known in fifteenth-century Italy through the works of Aelian (*On Animals* II, 26) and Saint Ambrose (*Patrilogia Latina* XIV, 231); since Alberti was a classical scholar and papal secretary, there can be little doubt of his acquaintance with these texts.

Alberti's preoccupation with the father's role in the family has many facets. In his *Book of the Family*, Alberti advises fathers to be watchful; if his son is wayward, according to Alberti, the father's blindness is to blame. In his book on architecture, Alberti refers to Janus, the Roman god of gateways, as "father Janus."[35] The significance of that image lies in the fact that Janus has two faces, with eyes in the front and the back of his head. As a result, he sees those who approach the gate and those who leave by it at the same time.

Alberti recognized his own father's failures in watching out for him. His father died when he was sixteen, and Alberti's illegitimate birth allowed unscrupulous relatives to interfere with his inheritance. It is also possible, though not documented, that Alberti held his father responsible for the family's exile from Florence. Alberti's birth, in Genoa rather than in the city with which he identified, created another broken link that he continually tried to repair.

The rays emanating from the corners of Alberti's emblematic eye can be related to a statement in his autobiography, the so-called *Vita anonima*, or *Anonymous Life*, which reveals his struggle to identify with his father. He claimed that a "ray" in his chest *(pectore radium)* facilitated his ability to see through other people and know their intentions.[36] In contrast to Schreber, who became the passive recipient of the sun's rays, Alberti reversed passive into active so that the rays originated with him. Despite the paranoid flavor of Alberti's "X-ray vision," he never succumbed to disintegration, as Schreber did.

One additional feature of Alberti's preoccupation with the watchful eye is apparent if the hair in his self-portrait plaque is compared with that

57. The Sun in Leo, *engraving. From* Rosarium philosophorum, *Frankfurt, 1550.*

in Matteo's medal. In the self-image, Alberti has leonine hair, thereby linking the motif of the lion with Janus as a watchful guardian (see Chapter 3). The phallic associations of the lion, like the features of the winged eye, are explicit in ancient art. The first-century B.C. Roman tintinnabulum in Figure 41, which also "guarded" an entrance, has the hindquarters and tail of a lion.

In the zodiac, known in antiquity and the Renaissance, the sign of Leo has solar associations. The sun is at its hottest point when approaching Leo, who is the "house of the sun." When so depicted in zodiac iconography, the sun entering Leo's mouth emits rays that resemble those of Alberti's winged eye [57]. The most convincing biographical connection of these motifs with Alberti is the fact that he himself adopted the name Leon—his given name was Battista. It is also suggestive in this regard that the Marzocco, or lion, was the symbol of Florence, the native city of the exiled Alberti family.

For Alberti, the emblem of the winged eye was a kind of totemic image, condensing motifs related to the sun in the intellectual, humanist context of fifteenth-century Italy. The specific selection and arrangement of motifs, however, also had biographical significance for Alberti. The eye on both the medal and the plaque is frontal, whereas Alberti's head is in profile. The viewer, therefore, confronts the detached eye directly—as Schreber confronted the sun.

There is a psychological continuum of sorts in the totemic relationship of

Alberti, van Gogh, and Schreber to the sun. All three men had elder brothers. Alberti's lived, and they were apparently on good terms. Van Gogh's died before he was born, which put him in the problematic role of a "replacement child," only somewhat relieved by the birth of his younger brother, Theo. Schreber's elder brother committed suicide at the age of thirty-eight. It is possible, in all three cases, that the older brother assumed a paternal role, whether in reality or fantasy. Van Gogh's distant sun could thus be seen as a conflation of his austere and emotionally distant father with his literally absent older brother.

Alberti never married; he was a rabid misogynist and probably homosexual. Van Gogh was heterosexual, but was drawn primarily to prostitutes, or debased women. Schreber married and tried to have children, but became convinced that he had turned into a woman. Even after his final discharge from the hospital and partial return to sanity, he continued to live with his wife, believing that he was a woman.

The role of the mother is, of course, a crucial one in such dynamics. Unfortunately, less is known of the mothers in question than of the fathers. Alberti's mother died when he was two. He mentions her only one time, and then indirectly, in his writings. Van Gogh's mother is more in evidence. At the time of his birth, she was probably still depressed from her first son's death. Derivatives of van Gogh's relationship with his mother are implied by his perpetually unsatisfied longing for maternal love from a woman. Of Schreber's mother,[37] it can be said that she failed to interfere with his father's physical abuse, which was a constant threat to his body image. To create a satisfactory mother, Schreber had to become one himself.

The psychological comparison of these three men for whom the mental image of the sun held such power is significant in terms of the ego. The synthetic quality of Alberti's genius fortified his ego. His humanist ability to assimilate antiquity with contemporary intellectual concerns and his personal life is reflected in the highly condensed character of his emblem. Van Gogh's genius sustained him only to the age of thirty-seven, when his final breakdown culminated in suicide. Schreber, despite his superior intelligence and legal training, tried but failed to kill himself. In his case, the synthetic function of the ego broke down completely, causing a hallucinatory regression.

Postscript: Brancusi's Sun

Brancusi repeated the motif of *Bird in Space* in nineteen marble and bronze sculptures [58]. In representing birds, these sculptures have a phallic quality;

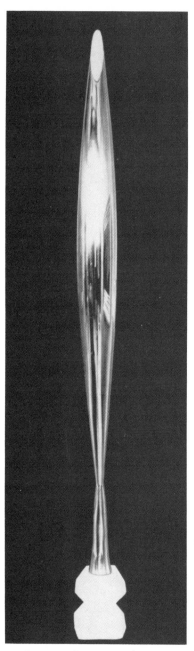

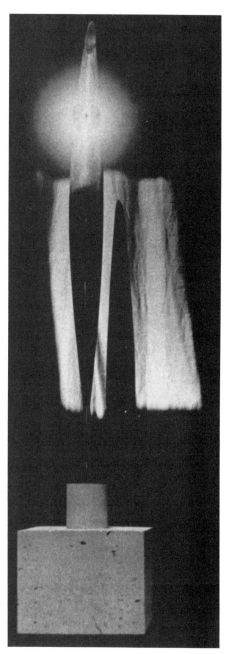

58. *Constantin Brancusi,* Bird in Space.
Peggy Guggenheim Foundation, Venice.

59. *Constantin Brancusi,* Studio Photograph of
Bird in Space.

they are erect and "in space," but not in flight. They are fictively airborne, but literally immobilized.

According to Sidney Geist,[38] Brancusi's *Birds* were self-images, and their highly polished bronze surfaces were a symbolic way of standing up to his father as the sun. The reflection of the bronze countered the sun's light, much as Schreber and van Gogh believed in their ability to confront the sun directly. That Brancusi was at least partly aware of these hidden meanings is suggested by a photograph he made about 1928 of a bronze *Bird* reflecting sunlight in his studio [59]. Geist believes that this photograph concretizes and confirms the artist's need to "outface his father." That he does so indirectly, or in effigy, indicates the role of his *Birds* not only as self-images, but also as apotropaic devices. They symbolically defend him from the power of his "solar father."

NOTES

1. Freud, "On Dreams," S. E. V, 1901, p. 667.
2. Freud, *The Interpretation of Dreams*, S. E. V, 1900, p. 608.
3. Freud, "On Dreams," S. E. V, 1901, p. 674.
4. Freud, *Beyond the Pleasure Principle*, S. E. XVIII, 1920, pp. 7–64.
5. Published in 1923, *The Ego and the Id*.
6. S. E. V, 1901, p. 681.
7. Ernest Jones, "The Theory of Symbolism," in his *Papers on Psycho-Analysis*, London, 1950.
8. George Devereux, "The Self-Blinding of Oidipous in Sophokles: *Oidipous Tyrannos*," *Journal of Hellenic Studies* XCIII (1973): 36–49.
9. In Catherine Johns, *Sex or Symbol*, Austin, 1982, figure 51.
10. Bertram D. Lewin, "The Body as Phallus," *Psychoanalytic Quarterly* II (1933): 24–47.
11. See Ernest Jones, "The Madonna's Conception through the Ear," in vol. 2 of his *Essays in Applied Psychoanalysis* (2 vols.), New York, 1964, pp. 266–357.
12. For a discussion of the eye/breast equation in a series of idols from Tell Brak, see Renato Almansi, "The Breast-Face Equation," *Journal of the American Psychoanalytic Association* 8 (1951): 43–70.
13. For two studies of divination in Mesopotamia that consider the issue of the origins of dreams and omens, see Ann Guinan, "The Perils of High Living: Divinatory Rhetoric in Summa Alu," in Hermann Behrens, Darlene Loding, and Martha T. Roth, eds., *DUMU-E.-DUB-BA-A: Studies in Honor of Ake W. Sjöberg*, Occasional Publications of the Samuel Noah Kramer Fund, 11, Philadelphia, 1989, pp. 227–35, and Ann Kessler Guinan, "The Human Behavioral Omens: On the Threshold of Psychological Inquiry," *BCSMS (Bulletin of the Canadian Society of Mesopotamian Studies)* 19, Toronto, 1990, pp. 9–13.
14. For this observation, I am indebted to Bradley Collins.
15. Herschel B. Chipp, *Theories of Modern Art*, Berkeley, Los Angeles, and London, 1968, p. 129.

16. Cf. Avigdor W. Poseq, "Bernini's Self-Portraits as David," *Source: Notes in the History of Art* IX, no. 4 (Summer 1990): 14–22.
17. Hibbard, *Caravaggio*, New York, 1983, p. 262.
18. Ibid., p. 159.
19. For a discussion of the maternal subtext of this painting, see H. R. Graetz, *The Symbolic Language of Vincent Van Gogh*, London, 1963, p. 165.
20. Ibid., p. 231.
21. Albert J. Lubin, *Stranger on the Earth*, New York, 1972, especially Chapter 12.
22. Ibid., p. 221.
23. Ibid., p. 207.
24. Freud, S. E. XII, 1911, pp. 9–82.
25. William G. Niederland, *The Schreber Case*, New York, 1974.
26. Ibid., p. 41.
27. Freud, "Notes on a Case of Paranoia," S. E. XII, 1911, pp. 80–82.
28. Ibid., p. 80, fn. 4, and S. Reinach, *Cultes, mythes et réligions*, vol. 3, p. 80, Paris, 1905–12, 4 vols.
29. Ibid., p. 81.
30. For references to other examples, see ibid., p. 81 and fn. 2.
31. Ibid., pp. 81–82.
32. Niederland, *The Schreber Case*, p. 87.
33. Cf. Renée Neu Watkins, "L. B. Alberti's Emblem, the Winged Eye, and His Name, Leo," *Mitteilungen des kunsthistorischen Instituts in Florenz* IX (1960): 256–58; and Laurie Schneider, "Leon Battista Alberti: Some Biographical Implications of the Winged Eye," *Art Bulletin* LXXII, no. 2 (June 1990): 261–70.
34. Watkins, "L. B. Alberti's Emblem," pp. 256–58.
35. Leon Battista Alberti, *On the Art of Building in Ten Books*, trans. J. Rykwert, N. Leach, and R. Tavernor, Cambridge, Mass., and London, 1988, vol. VII, p. 2.
36. Leon Battista Alberti, in R. Fubini and A. M. Gallorini, eds., "L'autobiografia de Leon Battista Alberti. Studio e edizione," *Rinascimento* XXII (December 1971): 76.
37. Cf. Robert B. White in Niederland, *The Schreber Case*.
38. Sidney Geist, "Brancusi's *Bird in Space*: A Psychological Reading," *Source: Notes in the History of Art* III, no. 3 (Spring 1984): 24–32.

SIX

Michelangelo's Moses
and Other Michelangelo Problems

I n 1914, four years after his *Leonardo*, Freud published an essay entitled
"The *Moses* of Michelangelo."[1] In the earlier work, Freud reasons from
a mental artifact—namely, the screen memory—to Leonardo's art and
character. In the essay on *Moses*, he begins with the work of art and reasons
from it to the artist and his patron. Both studies are built on the observation
and interpretation of details that had previously been overlooked or disregarded. The *Moses* essay, however, seems to be a study in aesthetic
response, in contrast to *Leonardo*, which lays greater emphasis on drive
theory and the unconscious motivations of the artist.

Michelangelo probably began work on his *Moses* [60] c. 1515, completing it by 1544. Originally intended for the second story of the tomb
of Pope Julius II, the figure would have been seen from below rather than
at eye level, as it is today. In 1505, Michelangelo contracted to produce
a freestanding tomb; the contract has been lost, but the pope is known to
have accepted Michelangelo's design, which included over forty figures.
He gave Michelangelo five years to finish the project, for which he paid
ten thousand ducats. Michelangelo got as far as quarrying the marble for
the tomb when the pope, to Michelangelo's despair, suspended the project
indefinitely. Julius was determined to have Michelangelo paint the Sistine
Ceiling in honor of his uncle, Pope Sixtus IV.

The contract for the ceiling was signed in May 1508; but the pope
died in February 1513, leaving money in his will for the still-unfinished
tomb. His heirs contracted with Michelangelo for a tomb of more than
forty sculptures, an additional payment of thirteen thousand ducats, and a
new, seven-year deadline. The original project was never carried out.

60. *Michelangelo,* Moses,
*c. 1513–15. San Pietro in
Vincoli, Rome.*

Today, *Moses* and other statues belonging to the original project are
located in the Church of Peter in Chains (San Pietro in Vincoli) in Rome.

Freud approaches Michelangelo's *Moses* as a frequent visitor to the
church and a longtime admirer of both the statue and its subject. Despite
his assertion that he was drawn more to the content of works of art than
to their "formal and technical qualities,"[2] Freud admired art and literature
of the highest quality. In the *Moses* essay, he reviews the art-historical
literature on the statue, noting that descriptions by various authorities are
"curiously inept."[3] He finds that, since the descriptions of *Moses* differ, their
authors arrive at contradictory interpretations.

FREUD ON MICHELANGELO'S *MOSES*

Freud summarizes the two main views of Michelangelo's *Moses* as follows.

1) God entrusted Moses with the Tablets of the Law on Mount Sinai. When Moses came down from the mountain, he saw the Hebrews worshiping a golden calf. Their pagan sentiments aroused his anger, and, at the moment represented in the statue, Moses is about to rise up and smash the Tablets.

2) Moses is not about to rise up at all. Rather, to preserve a higher purpose, he has overcome his rage, which is both *expressed* and *suppressed* through muscle tension. Intellect and civilization thus triumph over primitive impulse.

According to the former reading, Michelangelo follows the biblical text and depicts a specific narrative moment in the life of Moses. According to the latter, *Moses* is a study of character, which is timeless.

Freud observes that the gesture of Moses' right hand and the position of the Tablets have been misread. A section in Vasari is a good example of the traditional misreading; it says that Moses "rests one arm on the Tablets, which he holds with one hand, and with the other he holds his beard."[4] Freud counters that Moses holds neither the Tablets nor his beard. Instead, according to Freud, he conceals the thumb of his right hand and presses his index finger on his beard while bending the other three fingers against his chest.

Freud reads the arrangement of the right hand as a gesture of retreat, which he diagrams in four stages.[5] He relates the retreating gesture to his observation that the Tablets of the Law are upside down and resting on one corner. Remarking that sacred objects are not usually represented in such a position, Freud explores the significance of this curious arrangement. He concludes that both the retreating motion of the hand and the position of the Tablets are the result of something that has just happened.

Here, as with Leonardo's screen memory, Freud reconstructs a piece of history. In this case, it is the recent history of Moses' reaction to an event described in the Bible. According to Freud's reconstruction, however, Michelangelo's *Moses* does not behave as he does in the Bible, even though Freud assumes the same precipitating circumstances: the Moses of Michelangelo had been sitting quietly with the Tablets held under his right arm; their inverse position is accounted for by an indentation of the top that makes them easier to hold upside down. Moses' calm was interrupted when he saw his followers worshiping the golden calf; in the statue, he turns his head and prepares to rise in anger. Momentarily letting go of the Tablets, he puts his hand against his beard, as if turning his anger on himself. To prevent the Tablets from falling, Moses presses his arm against them; but they continue to slip and, in tilting, land on a corner. In another instant, Freud writes, "the Tablets would have pivoted upon their new point of support, have hit the ground with the upper edge foremost, and been shattered to pieces. It is *to prevent this* that the right hand retreated, let go the beard, a part of which was drawn back with it unintentionally, came against the upper edge of the Tablets in time and held them near the hind corner, which had now come uppermost."[6]

Reviewing the statue with this reconstruction in mind, Freud identifies three layers of emotion. In the foot he detects the residue of impulsive anger. The relation of the right hand to the beard and the torso indicates the suppression of the anger, which is further counteracted by the calm of the left hand. Finally, the face expresses the will to control. The power of Moses' mind over his impulse is thus given visual form.

By the combination of these emotional layers, Michelangelo creates a Moses who stands for intellectual control over the physical expression of rage. As such, Michelangelo's *Moses* departs from the biblical Moses in narrative detail, but conforms to his significance in the history of Western civilization. He is, writes Freud, "a concrete expression of the highest mental achievement that is possible in a man, that of struggling successfully against an inward passion for the sake of a cause to which he has devoted himself."[7] In this analysis, Freud synthesizes the two main views of Moses—a "timeless character study" and a specific moment in time.

From his discussion of the sculpture, which takes account of the biblical text, Freud relates form and iconography to psychology. He attempts to reconstruct Michelangelo's motives for the *Moses* iconography, considering the artist's patron, Julius II, and the fact that the pope commissioned the statue for his own tomb. Pope Julius, Freud points out, was a man of enormous ambition whose grand purpose was the unity of Italy under papal authority. He was impatient and, like the biblical Moses, willing to resort to violence to achieve his ends. Likewise, Michelangelo was aware of his own violent streak, which often erupted in impulsive behavior. According to Freud, therefore, Michelangelo created a new kind of Moses as a reproach to Julius and as a warning to himself. Read as a personal revision of history, Michelangelo's *Moses* is an exemplary image.

Freud's essay on Michelangelo's *Moses* has not created nearly as much controversy as has his psychobiography of Leonardo. No Meyer Schapiro or his equivalent has risen up in indignation from the ranks of art history to demolish Freud's *Moses*. It would seem that, despite no small disagreement with Freud's essay, the absence of a scholarly, frontal attack has allowed a freer pursuit of Michelangelo's psychology than of Leonardo's. Since 1914, many psychological studies of Michelangelo have appeared (for example, by R. and E. Sterba, Jerome Oremland, Ildiko Mohacsy, Robert Liebert, and Leo Steinberg).

LIEBERT ON "MOSES" AND *MOSES*

The most recent significant psychoanalytic work on Michelangelo is the 1983 study by Robert Liebert. This study contains interesting and provocative material, as well as much that is questionable and even demonstrably erroneous. In regard to Freud's *Moses* essay, however, Liebert's assessment is actually rather ambivalent. Citing Freud's biographer Ernest Jones, Liebert[8] recalls that Freud, like Moses, had to deal with "defections" among close followers; the implication is that Freud's fascination with Moses resulted from an identification with him as an admired predecessor and "ego ideal."[9]

Liebert[10] credits Freud with having captured the essence of Michelangelo's *Moses* as expressing "the highest ideal of mental and spiritual achievement through the controlled tension between potential action and restraint, portrayed on a monumental physical level." But Liebert questions Freud's reconstruction of Moses' action; he prefers instead the reading of *Moses* by the art historians Howard Hibbard,[11] Erwin Panofsky,[12] and Charles de Tolnay,[13] as well as Michelangelo's sixteenth-century biographer Ascanio Condivi,[14] as an "idealized character portrait." Liebert most closely follows Hibbard,[15] who rejects the view of *Moses* as referring to a historical moment in any sense. Both Liebert and Hibbard agree that *Moses* and a Saint Paul were originally planned as a pair to represent two aspects of Neoplatonic thought—"action and vision."[16] "To interpret the figure ... as about to reproach the Israelites for worshiping the Golden Calf," writes Hibbard,[17] "would destroy the meaning of the tomb as a whole."

What tends to be left out, or muted, by scholars who opt for the interpretation of *Moses* as a timeless character is the historical context and biblical sequence of events in which Moses participated. De Tolnay[18] provides a more complete account of the statue's forceful impact on viewers. He describes the figure as "trembling with indignation," and notes "the overriding force of passion" unleashing "elemental powers" and the "strength of the rugged knee which breaks through the flowing cloak as through boiling lava, . . . emanations of an internal agitation set up by anger and indignation."

Surely such extremes of emotion require a deeper and more specific interpretation than Neoplatonic spirituality[19] or the satisfaction of "a dynamic spatial-compositional demand."[20] Despite the psychoanalytic approach which Liebert uses to probe the psychology of Michelangelo and his statue, and his recourse to an ancient source, he nevertheless sticks to "timelessness," which denies, or obscures, a personal significance. Whether a portrait—which is, in fact, a likeness in time—can ever be "timeless" is debatable; de Tolnay's "character image outside time"[21] is, strictly speaking, a more accurate description.

One of the most interesting and potentially fruitful methodological aspects of Liebert's *Michelangelo* is the thesis that psychological significance can be assigned to an artist's choice of iconographic sources. Unfortunately, however, when Liebert applies this method to the *Moses* by reference to the Hellenistic marble sculpture *Laocoön*, his conclusions are not persuasive. Liebert identifies two *Slaves*, now in the Louvre, as intended to be below and on either side of *Moses*. He relates the slaves to Laocoön's sons, and Moses to the paternal Laocoön. Both Moses and Laocoön, Liebert points out, are bearded, as was Julius II, in defiance of papal convention.[22]

Liebert takes the connection between Moses and the pope further; he concludes that "by transforming the dying father in the *Laocoön* group into Moses, the artist was able to resolve the destructive aspect of his ambivalence toward the pope."[23] The problem with Liebert's comparison, despite the undeniable impact that *Laocoön* had on Michelangelo, is that, although the Louvre *Slaves* were planned for the tomb, their exact placement cannot be determined. Even more problematic are the unconvincing visual parallels between *Moses* and *Laocoön*. The similarity consists only of the fact that they are two powerful, bearded men caught in a dramatic moment. Liebert's reading of *Moses* as a transformed, dying Laocoön is not substantiated by formal evidence.

FREUD'S IDENTIFICATION WITH
MICHELANGELO'S *MOSES*

Both critics and admirers of Freud have commented on his identifications with the heroes of his studies. Peter Fuller,[24] for example, finds parallels of both theme and physiognomy between *Moses* and Freud's teacher Ernst Wilhelm von Brücke, whose "terrible gaze" (Fuller quoting Freud) Fuller relates to the piercing quality of Moses's angry glare. Fuller argues that Freud's *Moses* essay is not particularly psychoanalytic, but rather scientific in its approach. He says that Freud aligned himself with the systematic methodology of Giovanni Morelli, who authenticated works of art by noting similarities in anatomical details, such as the profile of an ear. This, according to Fuller,[25] reveals Freud's wish to present psychoanalysis as a traditional science and thereby make it acceptable to "disbelievers." "The cause whose Tablets seemed in danger of slipping," writes Fuller,[26] "was none other than that of psychoanalysis itself."

For Brücke, who was surely a significant teacher in Freud's medical career, one can read all the other "ideals" of Freud's life. These idealized figures correspond to Greenacre's "collective alternates" that combine the child's family romance with accomplished role models in the real world. Freud's wide range of ego ideals, which included Bismarck, Hannibal, Moses, Joseph (the biblical dream interpreter), Shakespeare, and Goethe, reflects his own versatile and synthetic genius.

The sport of turning Freud's *Moses* essay into a reflection on Freud himself has engaged many scholars and analysts. Even though Freud's study of *Moses* takes a more formalist approach than his *Leonardo*, it is nonetheless undeniable that Freud found the statue emotionally compelling. Freud responded—as one does to significant works of art—to the formal quality of Michelangelo's *Moses* as well as to its content. With regard to specific identifications reflected by the statue, whether those of Freud or of Michelangelo, the very fact of such identification illustrates the relevance of psychoanalysis to art criticism. The notion that Freud identified with Moses as one who is given insight is, by now, fairly well accepted. That he suffered from defections among his followers—for example, Carl Jung and Alfred Adler—is also common currency.

The manifest content of Freud's identification with Moses includes the reception of special knowledge which is disregarded by those whom it is intended to benefit. The latent content, however, plays on themes of an oedipal nature, which are reflected in the transgressions of Moses against the patriarchal Hebrew God. It is likely that the commission to design the pope's tomb also evoked Michelangelo's ambivalence toward paternal figures. On the one hand, he exalts his patron and pope by the monumentality of the project; as the artist who undertakes such a project, Michelangelo also exalts himself and proclaims his own greatness as a sculptor. On the other hand, a tomb is still a tomb, inevitably imbued with funerary associations. Michelangelo's sculptures for the tomb are, in effect, about the death and memory of Julius II—by definition, an ambivalent message. It would not therefore be surprising if the very nature of the tomb evoked the already charged relationship between artist and pope. The implication and likelihood (and the subsequent reality) that Michelangelo would outlive the pope is consistent with latent oedipal dynamics.

Freud's aesthetic response to *Moses* cannot have failed to absorb these implications. It is obvious that Freud, who formulated the Oedipus complex, would understand those features underlying the iconography and character of the work. It is also likely that, having effected the only known successful self-analysis in history, he would sense their presence in his own response. To the degree that Freud's overwhelming response to Michelangelo's *Moses* was oedipal, it can be read as an elaboration of the family romance.

Freud became aware of his ambivalence toward his own father during his self-analysis; he loved and admired him, but reported an incident that made him ashamed of his father for not standing up to an anti-Semitic Christian, who threw his father's hat into the street.[27] Insofar as Moses in particular, but also Julius II and Michelangelo, were paternal figures for Freud, they could represent the exalted father of his own family romance, thereby repairing his father's humiliation. As ego ideals, these figures stand for Freud's identification with great Western leaders.

THE LIEBERT-STEINBERG ENCOUNTER

Battle lines between art historians and psychoanalysts have not been as emphatically drawn over Freud's *Moses* essay as over his *Leonardo*. Nevertheless, the publication of Liebert's book in 1983, attempting a "psychoanalytic study of Michelangelo's life and images," set off a minor skirmish. The counterattack, in the form of a review by the art historian Leo Steinberg in the *New York Review of Books* (June 28, 1984, pp. 41–46), proved that the controversy was not yet dead.

The views of Freud, Liebert, and Steinberg are not as opposed methodologically as Freud's, Schapiro's, and Eissler's, a fact that mitigates the rancor of the engagement considerably. There are several reasons for the softer tone of the later encounter, not the least of which is that some of the earlier pitfalls were avoided. Liebert consulted with art historians, and

Steinberg is sophisticated in matters of psychoanalysis. In contrast to Schapiro and Eissler on the *Leonardo* study, Liebert and Steinberg are not at odds over a piece of writing by Freud *about* Michelangelo, but over the personality of Michelangelo himself.

Liebert sets out to demonstrate that the psychoanalytic method can elucidate Michelangelo's life and iconography. He links aspects of Michelangelo's childhood with his adult life and art—a perfectly reasonable endeavor from a psychoanalytic point of view. He also explores Michelangelo's antique sources as associations, and explicates his iconography by the psychological implications of the ancient model.

Steinberg objects to what he considers the "reductionist" character of Liebert's analysis, on the grounds that it does not satisfactorily distinguish between the artist's genius and his neurotic inhibition. Liebert's tendency to emphasize Michelangelo's fantasy life strikes Steinberg as minimizing the artist's success in reality. For example, when Liebert accepts a previous psychoanalytic reading of Saint Bartholomew in the *Last Judgment* [51] as brandishing his knife at the Virgin because Michelangelo's mother neglected him, and of the Virgin cowering by Christ as Michelangelo's rageful projection of his mother's guilt,[28] Steinberg waves the flag of anti-reductionism. He calls Liebert's reading "an unconscious resistance to Christian subject matter" that "estranges the author from the content of Michelangelo's art."[29] What of Michelangelo's anxiety about salvation? Questions of faith? Thoughts about the Christian mysteries? Steinberg asks. Since one of the chief rallying cries of psychoanalysis is the principle of overdetermination, it is indeed curious that Liebert does not elaborate the multiple layers of meaning in the imagery he considers.

Steinberg demonstrates that reductionist thinking led Liebert to misread visual evidence. In general, Liebert takes the position, based on modern clinical experience, that Michelangelo felt abandoned by his mother when he was sent to a wet nurse. On returning home and encountering the arrival of siblings, according to Liebert, Michelangelo's sense of abandonment was compounded by envious rage. Upon his mother's death when he was six and three-quarters years of age, Michelangelo would believe that she had been the victim of his own "rageful thoughts." This sequence of events, part documented and part reconstruction, is the basis for Liebert's view of Michelangelo's psychology.

Consistent with his focus on Michelangelo's oral rage, Liebert identifies a running child on a Medea sarcophagus as the inspiration for Michelangelo's Christ in the *Taddei Madonna*. Reasoning from the artist's iconographic source to the artist himself, Liebert posits Michelangelo's experience of a Medea-like mother, who murdered her children. The artist later, according to Liebert, projected that experience onto the aloof Madonna of the Taddei tondo. Psychoanalytically the sequence might be as follows: Michelangelo's rage at being sent away, compounded by sibling envy and the belief that his rage had killed his mother, is projected onto his mother. He then fears *her* rage and the envy of other men (as derivatives of sibling rivalry), both of which are actually *his* projection.

The trouble with this reading, Steinberg argues, is that, although the Medea sarcophagus might have been known to Michelangelo, its subject matter was not. On the sarcophagus, the two children who we now know to be Medea's are playing ball; there is no "fleeing," no visible threat.[30] Michelangelo, therefore, could not have identified the "fleeing" child with Medea's intended victim, because the sarcophagus was not associated with the Medea legend until the second half of the eighteenth century.

Steinberg objects not only to the specifics of Liebert's iconographic conclusions, but to the very premise on which they are based. Brimming with facetious gravity, Steinberg proposes a counter hypothesis. He notes the absence of evidence indicating that Michelangelo felt abandoned. "The boy, for all we know," writes Steinberg, "may have had a good time at the dugs of his foster mother."[31] On returning to his mother, Michelangelo may have found that she doted on him; and when she died and her place was taken by a grandmother and an aunt, they too may have doted on him. Furthermore, Steinberg reminds psychoanalytically minded readers, Signora Buonarroti did not die until her son was nearly seven years old, by which time his character had been formed—signifying, to those of us who believe in it, that Michelangelo's Oedipus complex had already run its childhood course. In opposition to Liebert's abandonment and envy, Steinberg attributes Michelangelo's victorious feelings of confidence to his having been the "undisputed darling of his mother." Such boys, according to Freud (and including Freud himself), have a sense that they are destined for great accomplishments.

Liebert follows Michelangelo's oral rage right into the quarry, where the artist searched for perfect blocks of marble. Steinberg takes Liebert to task for equating the marble with Michelangelo's image of a "cold breast." The implication of the equation is that working the marble substituted for the artist's "sadistic retaliation"[32] against his "obdurate and intransigent" mother.[33] In this approach, Liebert addresses the actual *process* of Michelangelo's work, rather than his iconography or style. And while it is true that an artist's process has psychological meaning, it is also true that a stone carver has to carve stone, which demands the use of sharp tools and hammers. To equate the reality of stone carving with aggression toward one's mother is problematic and not particularly psychoanalytic, because of its literal character. Even if Michelangelo had had the warmest and most loving relationship possible with his mother, he would still have had to chisel and hammer the marble, and he might have been just as fussy about selecting his block.

It is possible, nevertheless, to consider an artist's process psychologically. Freud, for example, discussed Leonardo's slow, obsessive-compulsive working procedure, which inhibited his production. Likewise, the efficient speed of Raphael's process can be understood in terms of his genius for assimilation and synthesis. It is not in being particular about the marble that Michelangelo reveals inhibition or rage, for a good block of marble facilitates the work. More to the point is Michelangelo's well-known *non finito*, or tendency to leave works *un*finished.

A possible psychological connection of the *non finito* with Michelangelo's childhood is the fact that it affected his sculptures more often than his paintings; the artist had no difficulty in completing his major paintings in the Sistine and Pauline chapels. This circumstance is more clearly explained by Michelangelo's relationship to his father than to his mother—for his father, having abusively opposed Michelangelo's wish to be a sculptor, did apprentice him to a painter. In this, his father implicitly gave Michelangelo permission to paint, but not to carve. By not completing certain sculptures, therefore, Michelangelo effects a typical symptomatic compromise; he simultaneously yields to, and reenacts, his father's disapproval of sculpture and frustrates him symbolically, or in derivative form, by disappointing the patron.

Steinberg reads Michelangelo's non finito *differently. He notes that Michelangelo left more sculptures unfinished later in his career than at the beginning. Steinberg points to the artist's delight in the finish of certain works, which he polished to a high gloss, and attributes the increasing* non finito *to two circumstances. The first is that Michelangelo felt more harassed after the frustrating interruption of the Julius tomb, which the artist believed would have been the culmination of his career. The second factor depends on the artist's relationship to a delivery date. According to Steinberg, when Michelangelo had a deadline, he could finish a work; otherwise, he preferred to keep his options open until the last minute.*

As in the *Leonardo* controversy, the Liebert-Steinberg encounter has its mistranslation, which Liebert uses as evidence of Michelangelo's homosexual ideation. To that end, Liebert cites Michelangelo's report that Julius II had a wooden bridge constructed in order to make secret visits to the artist's quarters (or, according to Liebert, to his *bedroom*). Liebert believes that Michelangelo's account was unlikely and concludes instead that, at the age of seventy-eight, the artist's wishful homosexual fantasy had been revived. Steinberg, however, points out that Liebert translates *stanza* as "bedroom," which in Italian is a *camera da letto.* Since *stanza* generally refers to *any* room, it *could* be a bedroom, but not necessarily so. Steinberg takes the report of Julius's wooden bridge at face value, as an indication of the pope's interest in Michelangelo's progress and his wish to keep abreast of it. Although Liebert's translation is arbitrary, Michelangelo's active homosexual fantasy life is revealed in his poetry and iconography, and implied in his behavior and lifestyle. Nor is it Steinberg's intention to deny the artist's homosexuality; he simply sees no evidence of its operation in regard to Julius II.

Steinberg also objects to Liebert's assessment of Michelangelo's passive, Ganymede-like servility and his sibling envy as being triggered by a mother who abandoned him. Michelangelo, Steinberg argues, lived very much in the real world; he amassed a fortune and was an expert at manipulating people. If anything, writes Steinberg, the young Michelangelo felt victorious—hence his disdain of Ghirlandaio, and the attack on Torrigiani, who broke the artist's nose (see Chapter 4). Furthermore, Michelangelo had a reputation for being difficult, not servile, which Steinberg illustrates with a quotation from Pope Clement VII: "When Michelangelo calls, I always ask him to sit down, because I know he will anyway."[34] According to Steinberg, the artist's "tragic self-image" did not emerge until shortly before the age of forty, when work on the Julius tomb was interrupted.

This last aspect of the encounter between Liebert and Steinberg invites some additional consideration, for a psychoanalyst would ask why, around the age of forty, Michelangelo's self-image changed and why it was related to the Julius tomb. If the emergence of a tragic self-image is discernible at forty, it probably has deeper meaning than the suspension of work on the pope's tomb, despite the artist's conviction that it would be the crowning achievement of his career.

Steinberg believes that the shift from Michelangelo's victorious self-image to a tragic one resulted from intense frustration at having come up against Julius's will, which was as powerful as his own. A psychoanalytic response to Steinberg's insight would have to consider the oedipal character of the struggle between Michelangelo and Julius. At least one aspect of the struggle appears to be its repetition of the clash of wills between Michelangelo and his father over the art of sculpture itself. When Julius ordered Michelangelo to stop working on the tomb, he repeated the stance of Michelangelo's father in apprenticing him to the painter Ghirlandaio rather than to a sculptor. Coinciding with the pope's loss of interest in his tomb was his attention to Donato Bramante's work in rebuilding the new basilica of Saint Peter's. By this shift of attention on Julius's part, Michelangelo's rival was favored. A reading of these events in terms of Michelangelo's childhood inevitably evokes the issue of sibling rivalry.

To the question that Steinberg rightfully puts to the psychoanalyst—namely, how to explain Michelangelo's victorious sense of himself in the early part of his career—I would propose the following. As a young man (before the age of sixteen), Michelangelo's genius had been recognized by Lorenzo de' Medici. From that time, Michelangelo was in his element, as if his "family romance" had been fulfilled. He had found a new "father," politically and socially "noble," who "adopted" him into an environment where, for the first time, he was surrounded by the intellectual elite of Florence. Michelangelo responded to his new "family," as it were, with a feeling of triumph, created by the recognition and support of his genius. His sense of triumph would also have been fueled by relief from guilt, which his father's negative attitude to his genius would probably have aroused.

How this circumstance is related—if indeed it is—to Michelangelo's childhood is not demonstrable, given the available documentation. What is certain, however, is that children born with a genius such as Michelangelo's sense early on that they are different from their families. If the family, or a significant member of the family, reinforces and encourages the child—as Raphael's father did—the outcome is likely to be favorable. There is no record of encouragement by Michelangelo's nuclear family, only of his father's opposition. Nevertheless, according to Vasari, a childhood friend who was apprenticed to Ghirlandaio gave Michelangelo drawings that furthered his contact with the arts. By fourteen, Michelangelo too had joined Ghirlandaio's workshop and soon thereafter entered the Medici household. His victorious self-image before the age of forty seems to have been a combination of ego strength, the assistance of a friend in eluding his father's prohibition, and confirmation of his genius in adolescence by Lorenzo de' Medici.

In Michelangelo's iconography, the most obvious evidence of his later tragic self-image is the self-portrait in the flayed skin held by Saint Bartholomew in the *Last Judgment.* This image raises new questions. Does the skin belong to Saint Bartholomew, who was flayed alive? Or is it Michelangelo's "signature," as Steinberg believes? Steinberg identifies the skin as Michelangelo's and *not* the saint's; he reads the image as Saint Bartholomew interceding on behalf of the artist to prevent the latter's descent into hell.[35] It seems to me, however, that the skin is a conflation, referring simultaneously to the saint and the artist, and that the self-portrait is merged with the conflated image. Bartholomew's ambivalence, rendered in pictorial form as a kind of "double self" (alive and flayed), could be read as a reflection of Michelangelo's own inner conflicts. The depressive, masochistic exhibitionism of the limp skin containing Michelangelo's features is, in any case, contrasted with the muscular figure of Saint Bartholomew, showing the instrument of his martyrdom.

Without for a moment denying the multiple Christian implications of these images, on which Steinberg has written eloquently elsewhere,[36] I would read the flayed skin as an image of Michelangelo's sense of "defeat" as well as a reference to Bartholomew's martyrdom. But now another paradox appears—for, despite Michelangelo's manifest tragic self-image, he would have had to have an enormous amount of confidence and ambition to continue working as successfully as he did. The shifts that are evident in his life, as in Saint Bartholomew and the limp skin, express a deep-seated ambivalence that is not inconsistent with the abuses of Michelangelo's father toward his son's genius or with Michelangelo's drive toward self-expression.

Likewise, the iconography of the presentation drawings (Chapter 4) reveals Michelangelo's alternation between themes of upward flight *(Ganymede),* of being chained to the earth and victimized *(Tityos),* and of the grandiose attempt at flight followed by falling and death *(Phaëthon).* Clement VII's anecdotal comment also reflects Michelangelo's ambivalence between domination and submission. If Michelangelo stands in the presence of the pope, he is at once in a formal relation to him and literally above him. If he sits, the artist assumes a more relaxed, informal pose, but has lowered himself to the pope's level.[37] In becoming the pope's equal in a social situation, therefore, Michelangelo ceases to stand over him. The fact that Clement and Michelangelo grew up together would only deepen the significance of these dynamics.

For Steinberg, the paradox of Liebert's argument is his insistence that art is not neurotic, while continually finding evidence of Michelangelo's neurosis in his art. Steinberg's fundamental objection to Liebert's approach is the alleged discovery of "unsublimated" material in the art. It is, however, debatable whether any of Michelangelo's art can be called "unsublimated," for the very fact of its being art requires sublimation. Steinberg agrees that unconscious impulses "feed into works of art,"[38] but objects to Liebert's notion that "the defensive aspects of the sublimation are incomplete." Steinberg has a firm belief in Michelangelo's conscious control.

Although Michelangelo did not produce a screen memory in the manner of Leonardo, he left a great many letters and poems, and influenced the biographies written by Vasari and Condivi. These works contain a wealth of information about Michelangelo that will continue to provide psychoanalytically minded researchers with significant data.

THE "PURE AIR OF AREZZO"
AND MICHELANGELO'S "CHISELS AND HAMMER"

Vasari quotes Michelangelo as having said, "Giorgio, if I have anything of the good in my brain, it has come from my being born in the pure air of your country of Arezzo, even as I also sucked in with my nurse's milk the chisels and hammer with which I make my figures."[39] On the face of it, such a statement appears straightforward enough, though a little hyperbolic. If Michelangelo's assertion is considered psychoanalytically, however, it can be shown to condense two significant aspects of his fantasy life. It reveals, on the one hand, Michelangelo's self-created myth, which is related to his family romance and, on the other hand, his image of the phallic mother, which contributed to his ambivalent, bisexual identifications.

The complex nature of Michelangelo's family romance emerges at the very beginning of Vasari's biography of him. Vasari reports, incorrectly, that the artist's parents were descended from the "most noble and most ancient family of the Counts of Canossa,"[40] which reflects the Renaissance convention of claiming descent from antiquity. Vasari's account of Michelangelo's birth is clearly intended to evoke Christ's. It takes place "under a fateful and happy star . . . near where Saint Francis received the stigmata"; the artist's father names him Michelangelo (the angel Michael) "because, inspired by some influence from above, . . . [he] wished to suggest that he was something celestial and divine beyond the use of mortals."[41] This, in turn, according to Vasari, was indicated by the artist's horoscope (also standard in the Renaissance), "which showed that from the art of his brain and of his hand there would be seen to issue forth works marvellous and stupendous."[42] A few lines further on, Michelangelo makes the same connection between his brain and hand in the citation given in the preceding paragraph. Through Vasari, Michelangelo establishes the nobility of his parents, celestial inspiration in the selection of his name, a proximity to the stigmata of Saint Francis that denotes his identification with Christ, and an even more direct association with Christ by virtue of being born "under a star."

In his statement to Vasari, Michelangelo implicitly equates breathing "the pure air . . . of Arezzo" with the good quality of his nurse's milk. Breathing and sucking are related in Michelangelo's image, as they are in the real nursing situation. Furthermore, the goodness is also in the artist's brain, which developmentally relates having been literally well fed with milk to having been encouraged in his chosen profession. This has a basis in psychological reality, since the more emotionally secure children are, the better their intellectual performance is likely to be.

Michelangelo's image of breathing "the pure air . . . of Arezzo" omits, and tries to repair, his real father's abusive efforts to prevent his being a sculptor, and to sabotage his talent, which is inseparable from his brain. In effect, Michelangelo edits out his father, merges the stonemason's tools with the milk of the stonemason's wife, and creates an oral myth to account for his artistic genius. He also colludes with Vasari, who is going to use *his* hand and brain to write the artist's biography; Michelangelo's message here is that he and Vasari share a bond by having been born in the same region of Italy and having breathed the same healthy air as children.

Michelangelo credits his wet nurse, rather than his mother, with having "fed" him the tools of his trade. Since the nurse is not the stonemason, and since in reality it is the stonemason who uses the hammer and chisels, Michelangelo's remark delineates his sexual confusion. It is a metaphor of the phallic mother, who fulfills the paternal function of establishing the artistic line of descent by handing down the tools to the son.

Another "mythic" function of the "chisels and hammer" is their relation to the artist's family romance. As a sculptor himself, Michelangelo is more akin to a stonemason than to the low-level functionary that his father was. By the subtle shift from his real father to the stonemason, Michelangelo has, in a sense, revised his own history, as if to establish the creative ideal identified by Greenacre. The stonemason takes on the paternal role for purposes of the family romance, and his tools merge with his wife's milk to form the bisexual image of the phallic mother.

When Michelangelo elevates his origins even higher, by inventing a noble lineage, Liebert says "family romance" and Steinberg counters with "a mild case of status-seeking"[43] that was perfectly normal in the context of the Italian Renaissance. Both authors are, in fact, correct; but the *content* and *context* of the family romance are as significant as its operation.

AN ICONOGRAPHIC INSTANCE
OF THE PHALLIC MOTHER

Michelangelo's fantasy of the phallic mother, whose milk supplies him with hammer and chisels, explains an iconographic detail in the presentation drawing (also for Tommaso de' Cavalieri) entitled *Children's Bacchanal* [61]. In that drawing, groups of putti, or little nude boys, indulge in bacchanalian activities. Panofsky describes the scene as imbued with pagan spirit in an atmosphere of "hopeless dejection and lethargy."[44] He notes the emphasis

61. Michelangelo, Children's Bacchanal, *1530s.*
Windsor Castle, Royal Library.

on "primitive natural functions,"[45] which presumably refer to the boy urinating into the wine vat, and the fact that the figures are either animals, young, or undignified and therefore less than "fully human." Barolsky calls the drawing "macabre," but with "playful details."[46] Liebert reads it as an image of Michelangelo's fantasy of an all-male and eternally youthful world, which he would like to inhabit with Tommaso.[47]

The comments by Panofsky and Barolsky reflect the drawing's ambivalent character. The large central group consists of putti struggling to carry a dead deer. Another group is about to boil a pig. The revelers are contrasted with the depressive, even sadistic, quality of the two lower groups, which Liebert reads as references to Michelangelo's image of his parents. According to Liebert, the sleeping, nude man being uncovered in the right foreground refers to the artist's inadequate father and is also reminiscent of the drunken Noah on the Sistine Ceiling. This reading can be related to Barolsky's observation that the putto carrying logs at the upper left is a quotation from a similar figure in the Sistine *Sacrifice of Noah.*[48]

The old female satyr at the lower left, in Liebert's view, is a negative comment on Michelangelo's mothering. The satyr's breast is withered and empty; she turns away from the nursing boy toward another child. But she contains layers of psychological meaning for the artist besides oral disappointment. Like nearly all of Michelangelo's female figures, she is strikingly muscular; her arms could easily belong to a man. In being a satyr as well, she is given a masculine character—for, even though mythological female satyrs do exist, they are rarely depicted in art.[49] The satyr more usually represents male lust in Greek mythology and stands for the male libido. Michelangelo's female satyr, by her very nature, conflates male with female and corresponds to his mental picture of the phallic mother.

As a combination of human with animal form, the satyr mirrors an underlying theme of the drawing as a whole—for, as Panofsky observes, the scene is filled with children and animals. This iconography is a sophisticated elaboration of developmental regression because, aside from the sleeping man, everything refers to a subhuman, or child, state. The part-animal character of the satyr refers to childhood; but that the animal in question is a goat emphasizes the phallic quality of the maternal figure (compare the popular meaning of "an old goat").

In conclusion, it must be said that the phallic mother fantasy, like the family romance and the Oedipus complex, occurs at a certain developmental stage in the life of every normal child. The dynamics of such stages become relevant to the study of artists and their art when they are in some way illuminating. Michelangelo is known to have had only one female friend, Vittoria Colonna. His description of her as *un grand amico*, or "a great *male* friend" (italics mine), suggests that he admired her for her masculine qualities. Likewise, his admiration for powerful, maternal women is abundantly clear from his art. These expressions of Michelangelo's attraction to a kind of "superwoman" seem to confirm the persistent phallic mother fantasy.

The fact that Michelangelo's erotic interests appear to have been directed solely toward young men indicates a failure to identify with his father and a bisexual confusion. What is significant psychologically is not that Michelangelo believed in the phallic mother at the age of three, but that the fantasy continued and affected his erotic life. From the point of view of the art historian, such a fantasy is significant if it can explain aspects of his art.

From the point of view of the nature of creativity itself, the persistence of Michelangelo's childhood fantasy, whether or not it is a distortion of reality, has another significance. It illustrates the paradox of the creative person who derives energy from the very accessibility of unconscious and childhood material. Because such access is there, it would not be surprising to find expressions of it in the work. Nor do such expressions necessarily denote neurosis, although they might—and the psychologically minded observer might be able to decipher them. What distinguishes the creative person is not, therefore, the fact of neurosis but, rather, the greater visibility of the unconscious, because it is the business of creativity to be expressive.

NOTES

1. Freud, "The *Moses* of Michelangelo," S. E. XIII, 1914, pp. 211–36.
2. Ibid., p. 211.
3. Ibid., p. 214.
4. Vasari, *Lives of the Most Eminent Painters, Sculptors, and Architects*, trans. Gaston du Vere, vol. 2, New York, 1979, p. 1851.
5. Freud, "The *Moses* of Michelangelo," pp. 226–27.
6. Ibid., p. 228.
7. Ibid., p. 233.
8. Robert Liebert, *Michelangelo: A Psychoanalytic Study of His Life and Images*, New Haven and London, 1983, p. 208 and fn. 2, citing Ernest Jones, *The Life and Work of Sigmund Freud*, New York, 1953–57.
9. Cf. Jacques Szaluta, "Freud's Ego Ideals: A Study of Admired Historical and Political

Personages," *Journal of the American Psychoanalytic Association* 31, no. 1 (1983): 157–85.

10. Liebert, *Michelangelo*, p. 209.
11. Howard Hibbard, *Michelangelo*, New York, 1974.
12. Erwin Panofsky, *Studies in Iconology*, New York, 1962.
13. Charles de Tolnay, *Michelangelo*, 5 vols., Princeton, 1943–60.
14. Liebert, *Michelangelo*, p. 206.
15. Hibbard, *Michelangelo*, p. 157.
16. Liebert, *Michelangelo*, p. 209.
17. Hibbard, *Michelangelo*, p. 157.
18. De Tolnay, *Michelangelo*, vol. 4, p. 39.
19. Hibbard, *Michelangelo*, p. 157.
20. Liebert, *Michelangelo*, p. 209.
21. De Tolnay, *Michelangelo*, vol. 4, p. 40.
22. Cf. Mark Zucker, "Raphael and the Beard of Pope Julius II," *Art Bulletin* LIX (1977): 524–33.
23. Liebert, *Michelangelo*, p. 210.
24. Peter Fuller, *Art and Psychoanalysis*, London, 1980, Chapter 2.
25. Ibid., p. 54.
26. Ibid., p. 55.
27. Freud, *Interpretation of Dreams*, S. E. IV, 1900, p. 197.
28. R. and E. Sterba, "The Anxieties of Michelangelo Buonarroti," *International Journal of Psychoanalysis* 37 (1956): 7–11, and "The Personality of Michelangelo Buonarroti: Some Reflections," *American Imago* 35 (1978): 156–77.
29. Steinberg, *New York Review of Books*, as in text, p. 44.
30. Ibid., p. 43.
31. Ibid., p. 41.
32. Ibid., p. 41.
33. Ibid., quoting Liebert.
34. Ibid., p. 43.
35. Cf. Steinberg, "Michelangelo's *Last Judgment* as Merciful Heresy," *Art in America*, November–December 1975, pp. 48–63.
36. See, for example, Steinberg, "A Corner of the *Last Judgment*," *Daedalus* 109, no. 2 (Spring 1980): 207–73. Steinberg reads a diagonal from upper left to lower right, linking, among other motifs, the wound of Christ and the crown of thorns with the self-portrait. The association of Christ's blood with Michelangelo's "signature" can be read psychologically as revealing the artist's unconscious, passive feminine identification. That Steinberg's diagonal also links heaven with hell reflects the ambivalent aspect of Michelangelo's uncertainty about his own future. His self-image is, in effect, hovering on the diagonal between salvation and damnation. For more on Michelangelo's diagonals and self-images, see Steinberg, "The Line of Fate in Michelangelo's Painting," *Critical Inquiry* 6, no. 3 (Spring 1980): 411–54.
37. Steinberg observes, in "Michelangelo's *Last Judgment*," 1975, p. 50, that, in the *Last Judgment*, Christ's own pose is ambiguous. "The pose of the Christ," he writes, "is describable in four or five different ways, seated, standing, rising or springing up, or striding forward."
38. Steinberg, in *New York Review of Books*, p. 45.
39. Vasari, *Lives*, vol. 2, p. 1833.
40. Ibid., p. 1832.
41. Ibid., p. 1833.
42. Ibid.

43. Steinberg, in *New York Review of Books,* p. 41.
44. Erwin Panofsky, *Studies in Iconology,* p. 222.
45. Ibid., p. 223.
46. Paul Barolsky, *Infinite Jest,* Columbia, S.C., and London, 1978, p. 54.
47. Liebert, *Michelangelo,* p. 291.
48. Barolsky, *Infinite Jest,* pp. 54–55.
49. Cf. Panofsky, *Studies in Iconology,* on the satyr family in Piero di Cosimo's *Discovery of Honey,* where a completely different mood prevails.

SEVEN

The Transitional Object
and Its Implications for
Creativity and Symbolization

D W. Winnicott's concept of the transitional object is probably the
most useful one for thinking about certain aspects of art to have
come out of the English Object Relations school of psychoanalysis. In psychoanalysis, the term "object" denotes any person, animal, thing,
or idea in which energy is invested. Freud first mentions the object in this
way in 1895[1] in terms that he later refers to as "anaclitic" (from Greek
anaklitos, meaning "leaning back" and denoting helplessness or dependency). When a helpless child receives satisfaction from someone, a bond
is created; Freud calls the resulting energy investment of the child in the
someone a "cathexis," from Greek *kathexis*, meaning "a keeping hold of."

A more poetic version of this dynamic is described by Antoine de
Saint-Exupéry in *The Little Prince* when the fox teaches the prince how to
tame him. "Créer des liens," says the fox, or one must "create links"; this
is done by patiently and regularly being in the same place at the same time
every day. Eventually the fox feels secure enough to trust the prince and
gradually moves closer to him until he has been tamed. The taming of the
fox can, of course, be read as a metaphor for the structure of psychoanalysis, which has to establish a regular schedule and a basis in trust in order
to proceed.[2]

Another episode in *The Little Prince* describes cathexis, or creating
links, of a romantic kind. When the prince discovers that there are millions
of roses on Earth, he loses faith in the uniqueness of the rose on his tiny
planet. Again it is the fox who teaches him about the nature of relationships; and when the little prince gains insight, he recognizes the power of
his emotional investment in the rose. "C'est le temps que tu as perdu pour

ta rose, qui rend ta rose si importante," he says. (Loosely translated: "It's the time that you have spent on your rose that makes her so important.")

Freud's earliest systematic discussion of the object can be found in the 1905 "Three Essays on Infantile Sexuality." According to Freud, the child's first anaclitic object is the mother's breast. The second object is narcissistic (for example, the nourishing mother and the protective father),[3] because it reinforces the child's own ego, or self. Objects at later stages of development include anal objects, phallic objects, oedipal objects, and so forth. Freud distinguishes between the object and the aim of an instinct, or drive, and he locates the source of the instinct somatically (i.e., in a part of the body). During the oral stage, for example, everything goes into the baby's mouth (the source) in the attempt to satisfy the instinctual aim (which is incorporation). The object is whatever satisfies that instinctual aim. In the case of the breast-as-object, two circumstances are satisfied. First, the instinct for self-preservation, which requires the intake of food, leads to the related oral erotic instinct. Second, the breast-as-provider becomes a kind of "first edition," or primal object relationship, which is "reprinted" in later object choices, such as adult lovers.

In 1915, Freud illustrated the vagaries of the instincts in greater detail.[4] They can be transformed, displaced, reversed, or sublimated, depending on the operation of ego defenses.[5] If, for example, the instinct of oral incorporation is defensively turned around onto the self, the child fears *being* eaten, or devoured. Later derivatives of the oral instincts include the refusal to eat (of which anorexia is an extreme form), overeating, compulsive eating, food fads, and bulimia.

Discussions of the object pervade most of Freud's writing. But, from the 1930s, particularly in England, a new and less instinctual view of the object came to the fore. The concept of "object relationship" became emphasized over Freud's "object choice," which is instinctual, and therefore biologically driven. The English Object Relations School deemphasizes biological drives in favor of interpersonal relations. As a result, the aim is thought of less as a historical sexual satisfaction than as a "relationship" in the present.

WINNICOTT'S TRANSITIONAL OBJECT

Despite the relatively ahistorical character of Object Relations, Winnicott's transitional object has a basis in childhood history. Having observed the psychological range of the mother-child dyad, Winnicott recognized a piece of early, pre-oedipal behavior with implications for creativity. In 1951, he formulated the hypothesis that there is a connection between the newborn's attempt to satisfy the oral drive (for example, by thumb-sucking) and the attachment to some special object by an infant of a few months.[6] Although trained as a Freudian and thus in the biological basis of drives and developmental stages, Winnicott believes that the special object is important for reasons besides the instinctual need to achieve the aim of oral satisfaction.

This special object is the first possession that is not part of the infant's body; it follows chronologically the autoerotic attachment to what *is* part of the body, such as the thumb. The object can be anything from a teddy bear, to a pacifier, to the corner of a rag; it appears at some time between four and twelve months of age. In the popular comic strip *Peanuts*, Charles Schulz has depicted this phenomenon in the image of Linus's blanket; the blanket is Linus's transitional object. It designates a space, or transition, rather than the thing itself. It is, in Winnicott's words, "between the thumb and the teddy bear, between oral erotism and the true object relationship, between primary creative activity and projection of what has already been introjected."[7] Even though Winnicott believes that the transitional object is a symbol, most likely of the breast, for him its importance supersedes symbolization. It implies a process as well as an object, what Winnicott calls a "journey of progress toward experiencing."[8]

In addition to the objects themselves, Winnicott identifies "transitional phenomena," which occupy the same space and have the same meaning; these include babbling, singing, playing, and so forth. For Winnicott, what is important about the transitional space—whether occupied by an object or an action—is its illusory character. The capacity to create such an illusion defends the child against the anxiety of being alone, without the mother. Winnicott summarizes the qualities of the transitional object as follows.[9] The child is its sole owner and only he can alter it. It survives the child's aggression as well as his love and has its own tactile nature. The adult sees it as external to the child, but the child does not. Nor does the child experience it internally as a fantasy or hallucination. The object also presumes the presence of an "adequate" mother, who agrees to let it be; she does not wash it when it gets dirty or throw it away when it begins to disintegrate.

In terms of Linus's blanket, we recognize that Linus must be in complete control. When Lucy or Snoopy grabs the blanket away from him, Linus suffers an anxiety attack. When he misplaces it, his one and only aim is to recover it. And when his mother does decide to wash it, he trembles until its return. Linus likes the way his blanket feels and holds it against his face while sucking his thumb. We, the reader, see the blanket as an external object; but for Linus it is partly himself and partly outside himself. It can be taken away; but when that happens, it is as if his very self has been assaulted. The ultimate fate of the transitional object, according to Winnicott, is gradual decathexis and loss of meaning.[10] The child "forgets" about it, but its existence has established a basis for future creativity.

With the "normal" loss of interest in the transitional object over time, the child expands into a wider sphere of activity, which includes positive as well as destructive behavior. Winnicott lists the derivations of the transitional object as play, art, religion, dreaming, fetishism, lying, stealing, drug addiction, falling in and out of affectionate feelings, obsessional talismans, and so forth.[11] Like the original transitional object, Winnicott's derivations all involve issues of separation from, and re-attachment to, the original object, which is the mother.

Talismans and fetishes as transitional objects, like Linus's blanket, provide reassurance. For example, a female patient who went to court over her divorce settlement called me frantically during a recess in the hearing. She had misplaced her "good-luck charm," which she kept hidden in her pocket and stroked when anxious. Without it, she was certain that the judge would decide in favor of her husband. The fact that the charm was a small, silver giraffe revealed its quality as a "phallic object" and evoked the implication of "castration" in being divorced from a man—that is, separated from his phallus. The loss of the charm repeated an earlier, childhood sense of deprivation in having been born a girl; the woman's infantile fantasy of the lost phallus was revived by the divorce as well as by her adult fantasy that the judge would prefer the man. For this woman, the giraffe-as-talisman was also a fetish, whose psychological purpose constituted a denial of castration.

Overdetermination in the choice of the giraffe as a transitional object is abundantly clear. Its long neck represented the upwardly displaced, and wished-for, giant phallus. In being a "charm," the giraffe assumed the magic character with which children typically endow the phallus. Later derivations can be seen in magic wands wielded by good (and phallic) fairy godmothers and in broomsticks ridden by bad (and phallic) witches. At the same time, the small size of the charm symbolized the girl's "little phallus," or clitoris, and simultaneously expressed the woman's self-image as less than a man and wish to be more so.

The regressive nature of the woman's bisexual conflict was symbolized by another aspect of the giraffe. Because of their long necks, their heads—which are small—are a long way from the rest of their bodies. The literal distance between the head, or intelligence, and body in this case represented the essential "stupidity" or "childishness" of the fantasy that possessing a phallus denotes superiority, for the giraffe can be seen as a visual metaphor of precisely the opposite—that is, a long neck (phallus) and a small brain. Finally, in calling her analyst, the woman expressed her transferential relation to me as a maternal object. She attempted to repair the dangers of losing the giraffe by making a regressive umbilical attachment through the telephone cord.

A basic health in the mother-child dyad is necessary for the establishment of the transitional object and requires the presence of what Winnicott terms the "good-enough mother." One of the most important tasks of the good-enough mother is the creation of illusion, which convinces the infant that he controls her breast. This means that the mother senses the infant's needs as they arise and satisfies them accordingly. The infant then has the illusion that his wish has produced, or created, the milk, allowing him to trust in his "own capacity to create" and providing "a neutral area of experience that will not be challenged."[12] As a result, a creative space exists in early infancy and becomes an unquestioned basis for all future creative experience. Unlike the transitional object, the illusion fostered by the mother is not simply forgotten, nor is its meaning gradually lost. Instead, it is followed by *dis*illusion, which has to be reasonably paced so that the transition from illusion to reality is tolerable.

THE TRANSITIONAL OBJECT
AND THE VISUAL ARTS

In a general way, all art has a transitional quality; it literally occupies the space between illusion and reality. Religious architecture, which mediates between people and gods, is largely determined by the transitional nature of a particular religion. In this light, Mircea Eliade's discussion of the megalithic architecture in Western Europe is particularly suggestive.[13]

Megaliths as Transitional Objects in Transitional Space

The megaliths of the Neolithic period are informed by ideas about the permanence of stone as a product of the earth. Eliade believes that menhirs, or upright stones, were "substitute bodies" intended to last forever.[14] As such, they were a "transmutation" of the deceased into stone, which, in turn, became animated as a perpetual "reservoir of vitality and power."[15] "Megaliths," writes Eliade, "constitute the unrivaled connection between the living and the dead"; they create a transition between the states of life and death. They are also transitional in terms of space, because they are located at an "outstanding cult site," which is also a social center.[16]

Megaliths are outside the routine of daily life by virtue of their ritual function; but they become a place of meeting and cultural interaction on certain occasions. Like the child's transitional object, megalithic structures are simultaneously exterior and interior. The same can be said of most ritual sites—whether for religious purposes, theatrical performances, sports events, and so forth; they are architecturally separate and culturally inclusive at the same time.

The megaliths illustrate this function of ritual architecture well, not only because they are the first known monumental stone structures, but also because they are materially less elaborated than later Western buildings. The stones are roughly shaped and unpolished, having minimal, if any, surface decoration. Their natural source, the earth itself, is expressed in the finished architectural product.

The great Neolithic complex on Malta (c. 3000 B.C.) combines several important transitions in architectural and sculptural form. The entire island, according to some scholars, was a sacred space in the Neolithic era[17] and contained over seventeen temples. A necropolis at Hal Saflieni has yielded womb-shaped, rock-cut tombs and the skeletal remains of thousands of people. In contrast, there is no evidence of burial in the Maltese temples. But their plans are shaped like the womb, and in them archaeologists have found stone sculptures of reclining women and one of a monumental seated goddess. It would seem that at Malta the necropolis acted as a transitional space between the architecture of the living and dead, as well as between the mother's womb and the tomb. By being cut into the rock, the Hal Saflieni burials were literal transitions between the natural and the man-made; their womblike shape reinforced the association of death with rebirth. Furthermore, the presence of the huge goddess linked the dark temple sanctuaries with the chthonian aspect of the burials and the mother's womb.

Malta, like Delos in the ancient Greek period, was probably a sacred island. Both are geographically located in a natural transitional space, which may even have influenced their selection as sacred entities. But the mainland of Western Europe also has many megalithic structures that are imbued with associations similar to those on Malta.

The great cromlech, or circle of stones, at Stonehenge in southern England [62] was built in stages from c. 3000 to 1800 B.C. At its earliest stage, according to Eliade,[18] the site was chosen in "a field of funeral barrows," presumably in relation to an ancestor cult, thereby connecting the living with the dead. A circular, elevated mound marked out the site as both distinct from, and part of, the existing landscape. The final stage, which is the large circle of connected trilithons and the smaller inner circles of upright stones and individual trilithons, rises with unexpected suddenness from Salisbury Plain.

The arrangement of the stones marks additional spaces, and creates greater varieties of spatial shapes than the original circular mound. As a result, the interaction between the completely open space of the natural plain and the enclosed space of the structure creates multiple levels of transition. The outer wall is open and closed at the same time. It is made

62. *Stonehenge, Neolithic, c. 2000 B.C. Salisbury Plain, Wiltshire, England.*

of shaped but uncut and unpolished stones, combining the natural with the man-made, as in the rock-cut tombs of Malta. The inside of the cromlech communicates with the outside as a result of its layout in relation to the original mound and various banks and recesses in the surface of the immediate site. The central stone ring also communicates with the so-called Heel Stone and other individual uprights placed at distant intervals.

The Heel Stone stands to the side of the "Avenue," about seventy feet wide, which runs down a hill into a nearby field. At the summer solstice, the sun rising directly over the Heel Stone has become an annual international tourist attraction. This event is one of many examples of the way in which Stonehenge, and other megalithic monuments, creates a transition between earth and the heavens. The absence of a roof over the cromlech opens up its interior to the sky; at Stonehenge, at Carnac, at Malta, and elsewhere, evidence of astronomical relationships has been discovered.

If these monuments are read in terms of Winnicott's transitional object, they can be seen to satisfy similar requirements. They have a symbolic maternal object relationship by their connection to the earth and, in the case of the islands, to water. They combine inner space with outer space, celestial with chthonic space, open space with closed space. They combine a relation to the dead with an affirmation of rebirth and life. Insofar as they were a product of the cultural transition from a nomadic to an agricultural way of life, the megaliths probably had some connection with festivals celebrating seasonal death and rebirth. Like the infant's transitional object, megalithic architecture constitutes a stable, created space, distinct from, and related to, a changing environment.

Burial Art and Transitional Space

Because most religions include beliefs about life after death, it is in the nature of burial art to bridge the existential gap between life and death. Such had been a primary purpose of the elaborate Egyptian tomb decorations during the dynastic period. This particular aspect of funerary art has been discussed by Simon A. Grolnick and Alfonz Lengyel[19] in regard to Etruscan burial iconography (ninth century to first century B.C.). They posit a continuum "between the bedtime rituals of infants and children and the rituals and art of a culture's burial practices."[20] Based on the unconscious equation of sleep and death, represented as twins in Greek myth, Grolnick and Lengyel review the parallel between the child's transitional object and the familiar treasures placed in graves. These objects later evolve into bedtime stories, songs, prayers, even dreams, which become culturally elaborated into myth and art intended to allay the fear of death.

The authors compare human-headed Etruscan cinerary urns, and those in the shape of houses, to the transitional object and point out that the Etruscans regularly buried toys with their children.[21] Both the anthropomorphic and architectural forms of the urns serve a dual function; their shapes connect the formless ashes of the deceased with the familiar forms of their life, and they provide a literal space, or container, for what once was the living person.

Wealthy Etruscans were buried in marble sarcophagi, often with effigies of banqueting couples or sleeping couples locked in an embrace. The sarcophagus contained the body of the deceased, which was replicated in a sculpture engaging in an activity of life—eating or sleeping—on the lid. Because of the anxiety associated with separation—the child from the mother, the child from the transitional object, of which derivatives are evident in castration fear and its unconscious equivalents, fear of going to sleep, and so on—these effigies seem to bridge a temporal as well as a spatial gap. Like the original transitional object, they are reassuring; in contrast to the transitional object, however, they do not reassure those to whom they belong—namely, the deceased.

The dead have already "passed over," as it were, or made the transition to whatever is on "the other side" of the space between life and death. The tomb sculptures and the anthropomorphic and architectural urns reassure the living by example; they are transitional objects of a cultural kind, implying a continuation of the activities of life by the example of the effigy.

Images of Martyrdom as Transitional Objects

In Christian art, the image of martyrdom can be seen as a kind of iconographic "transitional object," also with the content of death. Christ's Crucifixion could be typologically paralleled to any subsequent martyrdom because of its position as the prototypical martyrdom of Christianity. The image of Saint Sebastian pierced through with arrows, for example, evoked the image of Christ nailed to the cross, and Saint Peter's crucifixion upside down expressed his humility in refusing to be crucified in the manner of Christ. The stigmata of Saint Francis reinforced that saint's literal identification with Christ. Such images mark the real temporal "space" between two events, and also bridge it by visual and iconographic association.

Martyrdom has a transitional quality resulting from the conscious decision to accept death in order to keep alive a belief system. Part of that belief system is the conviction that the martyr will be reborn in heaven and achieve eternal life. Consistent with that conviction is the frequent depiction of martyrs in heaven as if they are still alive. Martyrs such as Saint Bartholomew in Michelangelo's *Last Judgment* [51] are depicted as whole,[22] even though their bodies suffered the most violent physical tortures before death. The martyrs thus reinforce the role of martyrdom as a transition to rebirth and salvation.

The "bridge" between the Crucifixion and Christian martyrdoms became "objectified" (in the literal sense of being an object) in the Renaissance *tavolette* used to comfort condemned criminals.[23] The tavolette, or little pictures, are small wooden panels, typically depicting Christ's Crucifixion on one side and a saint's martyrdom on the other. In being two-sided, the tavolette are like coins, or medals, which have different but related images on each side. The image on one side refers by association to that on the opposite side, replicating the "transitional" idea of simultaneous separation and connection.

Members of the Archconfraternity of San Giovanni Decollato (Saint John the Beheaded), a lay order founded in Rome in 1488, held up the tavolette before the eyes of the condemned. In that function, the images approximate the child's original transitional object; they are not chosen or created by the prisoners, but they are accepted, or agreed to, by them. Their conscious, contemporary use was exemplary—specifically, to effect salvation for the condemned by his identification with the suffering of Christ and a martyr. They implied that penance evoked by the sight of physical torture, even at the last minute, could lead to redemption. But, as a derivation of the transitional object, the tavoletta had the quality of a reassuring "talisman," both as a literal object and because of the images on it. As an object, the tavoletta replicated the talisman in warding off the trauma of seeing the scaffold and the executioner, which were blocked from view by the picture as the condemned approached. The content, or iconography, of the pictures was a transitional *sight* because it mediated between the depicted martrydom and the forthcoming execution of the condemned.

The service to the condemned that was provided by the Archconfraternity members has a parallel in psychoanalytic technique. In the analytic process of "working through" (see Chapter 11), traumatic events of childhood are re-experienced psychoanalytically; but in order to be processed, or "digested," they are reconsidered from different points of view and their derivatives understood in a benign, clinical environment. When, as in the case of the condemned, a traumatic event is known in advance, one can "prepare for the worst." Because executions of various kinds have so much weight in the unconscious, whether related to fears of separation, castration, sleep, or death itself, they are rich in psychic associations. [24]

As society becomes more psychologically sophisticated, people attempt to ease the traumas of childhood. In certain enlightened hospitals, for example, children are prepared in advance for surgery in order to deal with natural fears of separation and death. In playing surgical games with dolls, children can begin to work through their fears in advance.

In these games, children play different roles; they can be the doctor and the nurse as well as the patient. In so doing, they take control of the situation—in effigy—and become director, author, and participant. In talking about the surgery, children are given the feeling of verbal and intellectual control, because they can name what is about to happen.

The overdetermined character of the principle behind the tavolette, as well as their usage, plays on themes of identification through seeing, the dangers and benefits of sight, and the relationship of seeing to trauma. In childhood, the unexpected sight of something—especially if sexual, violent, or both—creates anxiety. A child who is repeatedly exposed to such events becomes a "witness" to them. On a manifest level, the fact that the Greek word for "witness" is *martyr* makes the Christian martyr a witness to his or her faith. But the multiple latent meanings of martyr/witness include the psychic "martyrdom" of the child who is forced to witness what is inappropriate.

The condemned criminal is about to become the victim of a fatal trauma. Even though he knows that this will happen, he is comforted by the sight of a martyrdom, which literally blocks the sight of the scaffold. In acting to block vision by offering a substitute, the image serves to focus the criminal on an effigy, much as normal children play out their traumas with dolls. That the instruments of sight—the eyes—are unconscious equivalents of the phallus associates the sight of something traumatic with castration fear. The phallic relationship to the martyr-as-witness is contained in the etymological connections between "testicles," the French word for "head," or *tête* (from the Latin *testis*), and "testify," which implies "swearing to having witnessed."

Members of the Archconfraternity who accompanied the condemned wore hoods, through which they could see others; but their own faces were unseen except for their eyes. As such, they were a mirror of the hooded executioner while also using the tavolette to guard their charges against seeing him. The very name of the Archconfraternity, Saint John the Beheaded, evoked the fear of death and castration by its connection to decapitation.

The Artistic Medium as a Transitional Object

Many things can stand between an artistic idea and its execution; the most concrete intermediary is the medium. It is through the medium that artists create form and structure out of what is originally formless and unstructured. Liebert interprets the stone in the marble quarry as a "substitute for [Michelangelo's] absent mother."[25] The trouble with Liebert's argument is its implication that Michelangelo's relationship to marble was regressive. Liebert considers the marble masses "comforting companions," reminding the artist of his "repressed or unremembered early childhood with the stonecutter foster family and wet nurse."[26] Michelangelo's time with his foster family, however, was not exactly "repressed" or "unremembered," even though it was probably distorted and it certainly contributed to the artist's self-created myth. Furthermore, it is likely, given Renaissance custom, that Michelangelo stayed in touch with the family of his wet nurse for several years after returning home. His memory of them would change, but they would not fade totally from consciousness through repression. Liebert's suggestion that Michelangelo's perfectionism was a neurotic result of the marble's transitional nature seems at odds with the realistic advantages of using the best-quality stone and having to spend time finding it.

This being said, it is nonetheless true that every artist selects a medium, and it would be surprising if that choice did not have significant psychological meaning. To this very point, the sculptor and art critic Sidney Geist has written, "Love of material is a psychological, not a sculptural affair."[27] Michelangelo's preferred medium was marble, but he nevertheless agreed to paint what is arguably the best known group of frescoes in the Western world. A thorough inquiry into the role of marble and paint as media for Michelangelo remains to be undertaken. It would have to consider why he had difficulty finishing marble sculptures and not the paintings in the Sistine Chapel. In the previous chapter, I suggested a relationship with his father's abusive objection to sculpture and his apprenticeship to the painter Ghirlandaio. But if these media are to be regarded psychobiographically on the developmental level of the transitional object, more accurate information about Michelangelo's early relationship to his mother is needed.

The same could be said of Brancusi's relation to polishing, of van Gogh's to his unusually thick brush strokes, or of Jackson Pollock's drips. The father's influence on these dynamics is more apparent than the mother's for several reasons. First, the father is the traditional link between the family and the outside world of work. Second, the average child's relationship to his father developmentally follows his relationship to his mother. In being the first "object," the mother is at once the more powerful and the more forgotten, or repressed. As a result, the mother-child relationship is less accessible to the adult's conscious mind than the father-child relationship. Although, in psychoanalysis and psychobiography, both relationships can be reconstructed from later derivatives, the maternal layer of development, like human prehistory, remains the more obscure.

Some scholars have taken the view that the actual mother-child relationship of a particular artist can be reconstructed from his mother-child iconography. Liebert, as we have seen, arrived at a Medea-like image of Michelangelo's mother, to which Steinberg took strenuous exception. Julia Kristeva attempted to characterize the relation of Giovanni Bellini to his mother by reference to *his* Madonnas and their interaction with the infant Christ.[28] Neither Liebert's nor Kristeva's efforts are particularly convincing, although logically it seems that such a connection must exist. Were specific information on an artist's real infantile transitional object available, including details of his relationship to his mother, such connections would probably be demonstrable. Until such time as the relevant data become available, the relationship of a particular medium to a particular artist's actual transitional object is difficult to pin down.

Discussions of media in terms of the transitional object, such as Grolnick's and Lengyel's, are more convincing and more useful in general than in particular. Susan Deri,[29] for example, relates the child's transitional object to the "found objects" of the artist. In the case of the child, the mother's cooperation—by noninterference—is a prerequisite.[30] The child eventually internalizes the mother's accepting posture, which encourages creativity.

Duchamp, Dada, and the Primacy of the Object

The artist's found objects resemble the child's transitional object in that they exist in reality before being selected and endowed with meaning. The

Readymades and Readymades-aided of Marcel Duchamp are a related kind of transition. Whereas found objects are generally thought of as natural—that is, stones and wood having evocative shapes—Readymades are manufactured objects. These developments of the twentieth-century artistic avant-garde mark a primacy of the object that is significant art-historically, but that also highlights the transitional role of the "object" in the creative process.

In 1915, Duchamp bought a shovel from a hardware store. By "naming" it—he called it *In Advance of a Broken Arm*—he bridged the space between a practical, manufactured object and an art object. In so doing, he replicated the behavior of the infant, who makes an existing found object his own and names it. Likewise, Duchamp took the shovel from the environment (the hardware store) and brought it into a new, created space (the world of the artist).

In the instance of his most famous Readymade-aided, dated 1919, Duchamp added a beard and a mustache to a reproduction of the Mona Lisa and called it *L.H.O.O.Q.* [63]. In this work, Duchamp imbued the preexisting object with multiple levels of verbal and psychological significance. He turned Mona Lisa into a bearded lady, implying the bisexual character of Leonardo and himself, as well as the relation of Mona Lisa to Leonardo's unconscious fantasy of the phallic mother. Bilingual and verbal puns are contained in the title—incidentally, a good example of verbal condensation, whose letters, as pronounced in French, read "Elle a chaud au cul," or "She has a hot ass."

As a single word, the title reads "LOOK," which is an instruction to the viewer; and backward it reads "KOOL." The combination of bisexuality with bilingualisms evokes the unconscious equations of the mouth and tongue with the female and male genitals, respectively. It is also consistent with the mirror image of LOOK and KOOL in the title. *L.H.O.O.Q.* satisfied Duchamp's "craving for alliterations," which was one of his stated motives for inventing the Readymade-aided.[31]

More than any other artist, Duchamp can be credited with the importance assumed by the object in twentieth-century art. It would be interesting from a psychohistorical point of view to investigate whether there is a connection between post–World War I pessimism and the object's role in the Dada philosophy of regression. The paradox of Dada lies in its unique combination of pessimistic nihilism with remarkable playful creativity. As a movement, Dada demonstrates the psychoanalytic view of creativity, whether "regression in the service of the ego" (Kris), "access to

63. *Marcel Duchamp,*
L.H.O.O.Q., *1919.*

childhood" (Greenacre), or Winnicott's transitional space that allows for symbolization. That Dada grew out of the destruction of World War I suggests a new beginning, a kind of symbolic return to childhood play and a rejection of the forces of annihilation.

The focal point of the Dada movement in Europe was Zurich's Cabaret Voltaire, founded in 1916 by the German writer Hugo Ball. Poetry readings and various other multilingual literary and artistic entertainments were regularly performed. Switzerland was the eye of Europe's storm during World War I, and, in Zurich, the Cabaret Voltaire was frequented by refugees from all over Europe. The German artist Hans (Jean) Arp described their activities as follows: "Revolted by the butchery of the 1914 World War, we in Zurich devoted ourselves to the arts. While the guns rumbled in the distance, we sang, painted, made collages and wrote poems with all our might."[32] As a gathering place for artistic experimentation in a peaceful oasis of war-torn Europe, the Cabaret can be seen as a metaphor of childhood play space. It was a kind of transitional space, whose safety in the midst of destruction permitted the development of creativity. The Dada movement was over by 1924. Later, from the 1960s, especially in the United States, the heirs of Dada would appear in the object-oriented style of Pop Art, in Happenings, and more recently in Performance Art.

The origins of the term "Dada" are obscure. Various accounts have been proposed,[33] all of which are related to childhood or play. In French, *dada* is "rocking horse," in Romanian it means *yes yes*, in German it denotes an idiotic, naive quality, and in parts of Italy it can mean "mother." At least one report attributes the term to a random finding in a German-French dictionary. "Da da" are also the first words, or syllables, spoken by children.

As an aesthetic theory, Dada gave free rein to the psychological ambivalence expressed by opposites. The Romanian Dadaist Tristan Tzara listed the following examples: "Order = disorder, Self = not-self, and affirmation = negation."[34] Dada has been called "Anti-art," a repudiation of art, and an expression of nihilism evoked by the war. Among the New York Dadaists, Duchamp and Man Ray edited a single issue of a periodical entitled *Rongwrong*. According to Hans Richter, "the realization that reason and anti-reason, sense and nonsense, design and chance, consciousness and unconsciousness, belong together as necessary parts of the whole—this was the central message of Dada."[35]

Dada's message parallels the message of psychoanalysis and the creative process. Both recognize the coexistence of opposites in the unconscious, but Dada uses them consciously and playfully in constructing works of art. Also conscious was the attempt to gain access to the unconscious by spontaneous free association and word play that is reminiscent of puns in dreams. The notion of chance, or happenstance, as another means of unconscious access became a "trademark" of Dada.[36] "For us," wrote Richter, "chance was the 'unconscious mind' that Freud had discovered in 1900."[37] The "classic" Dada example of chance is Arp's collage of 1920 entitled *According to the Laws of Chance*. Arp reportedly tore up a drawing that had frustrated him and threw the pieces on the floor. The chance arrangement of the discarded pieces so interested him that he replicated it in the collage.

TRANSITIONAL SEEING
AND THE CREATIVE PROCESS

Visual talent includes the ability to see new ways to put order into disorder, and to shape the environment. The artist can make the leap, or transition, from an object to a symbol, to a formal echo, or to a visual metaphor. Picasso's *Bull's Head* of 1943 [37] constitutes a transition of this kind. Parts of a manufactured "object," the bicycle, reminded the artist of the skull and horns of a bull because of formal similarities. Likewise, when Picasso replaced the face of a mother baboon with a car [64], he made a witty visual connection between their shapes. Both sculptures relate manufactured objects with nature, expanding the layers of transition beyond purely formal considerations. The contemporary Pop artist Claes Olden-

64. Pablo Picasso, Baboon and Young, *1951. Museum of Modern Art, New York. Mrs. Simon Guggenheim Fund.*

65. *Claes Oldenburg,* Soft Typewriter, *1963.*

burg uses visual metaphor to evoke transitions between objects and feelings. This is particularly true of certain soft sculptures of manufactured objects that nevertheless suggest human emotions or states of being. Oldenburg's soft, black vinyl typewriter [65], for example, sags and seems to have collapsed after a long day at the office. That its keyboard resembles an open mouth with teeth and the circular ribbon reels suggest eyes turns its surface into the face of a slightly sinister insect. Oldenburg, like Duchamp, plays with transitions created by metaphorical connections between object and feeling, human and nonhuman, organic and mechanical. To these opposing characteristics, Oldenburg adds unexpected juxtapositions of hard and soft, large and small, inflated and deflated.

Metaphorical transitions in the visual arts are not restricted to the twentieth-century "object." Leonardo's notebooks contain examples of drawings that illustrate the very process of these transitions. When he draws leaping, running, playing, and fighting cats, they evolve into horses before the viewer's eyes. In his drawing of an old man contemplating the flow of water around a stake, the swirls of water resemble the design of a woman's long, flowing hair; and the accompanying text confirms the visual metaphor. Leonardo's range of metaphorical thinking is particularly broad; it includes an elaborated parallel between the human body and the earth. For Leonardo, rocks are the bones of the earth, the waterways are its circulatory system, and the earth is its flesh. This metaphor, in fact, has inspired interpretations of Mona Lisa as a woman-mountain, a formal echo of the landscape background.[38]

66. *Michelangelo da Caravaggio,* Boy with a
Basket of Fruit, *c. 1595. Galleria Borghese, Rome.*

A more specific visual metaphor can be seen in Caravaggio's *Boy with a Basket of Fruit* [66]. In this image of a seductive, homosexual boy, the bare shoulder echoes the form of the peach in the basket. Shoulder and peach are identically cleft and shaped. In the context of the image, both forms function as tactile and oral seductions aimed at a presumed homosexual observer. They are psychological, as well as visual, metaphors for each other, and thus enhance Caravaggio's homoerotic dialogue between boy and viewer.[39]

Such expressions of creative, visual thinking are ways of bridging gaps by perceiving relationships; and they often include chance. Legends ascribing the origins of art to drawing lines around reflections and shadows (discussed in Chapter 4) refer to the chance perception of one form that simultaneously evokes another. Leonardo describes the same process as the artist's ability to discern hidden but recognizable shapes in the unformed, chance textures of a wall.[40]

A similar phenomenon is the so-called doodle and the pleasure of discerning recognizable form in a random scribble. Winnicott turned this into a "squiggle game," which he used as a diagnostic tool in psychiatric consultations with children.[41] Both Winnicott and the child began with a pad of paper and a pencil. Winnicott drew a squiggle on his pad and invited the child to turn it into something by adding to it. Invariably the child's addition had a special meaning.

By continuing this procedure and participating in it, Winnicott engaged the child's interest. Eventually a theme emerged, revealing the child's preoccupations. In Case One, Winnicott was consulted about a nine-year-old Finnish boy born with webbed fingers and toes, which had been only partly corrected by surgery. The boy turned Winnicott's first squiggle into a duck's foot and the second into a duck swimming. This sequence revealed the boy's anxiety about his deformity as well as the satisfaction that webbed feet are an asset in water.

Subsequent squiggles were turned into a shoe and a deformed hand, thereby moving the imagery more directly toward the boy's conscious concerns. He drew an eel that Winnicott considered the boy's image of himself before his limbs had been formed. By the end of the meeting, the boy had turned a squiggle into a full duck, rather than the single webbed foot of the first drawing. This, according to Winnicott, was a kind of synthesis, indicating the boy's need to be loved as he was before surgery, "for himself" (the symbolic duck), and as he had been born.

I played the squiggle game with a four-year-old girl whose mother was eight months pregnant. The girl turned the first squiggle into a kangaroo with a baby in its pouch, the second into a baby carriage with a baby in it, and the third, into a mother pushing the carriage. Clearly the four-year-old knew what was coming and foresaw that a lot of her mother's attention would be taken up by the new arrival.

Winnicott's squiggles, which, from the child's point of view are chance lines, evoked responses akin to visual free associations. By pursuing the inquiry, Winnicott encouraged his young patients to "free associate" visually, as a traditional psychoanalyst evokes verbal associations. His squiggle game

*is inspired by the same view of unconscious access through line that character-
ized the Dada and Surrealist interest in "automatic writing."*

Pliny's (NH 35, xxxvi, 103) anecdote describing creative chance is
strikingly reminiscent of the circumstances leading to Arp's *According to the
Laws of Chance* and can also be related to Winnicott's clinical use of the
squiggle. Pliny reports that Protogenes tried to depict with his brush the
foam produced by a panting dog. He could not, however, get it right. In
frustration he threw his sponge, which had absorbed all his colors, at the
picture. By chance, the sponge hit the dog's mouth; the pattern left by its
impact perfectly conveyed the illusion of foam in the very colors that
Protogenes had been using. According to Pliny, another painter, Neacles,
also threw a sponge at his painting and produced the effect of foam coming
out of a horse's mouth. These operations involve seeing something "by
chance," recognizing its artistic possibilities, and using it accordingly. They
require transitional, metaphorical vision, which defines a crucial aspect of
the creative process.

NOTES

1. Freud, "Project for a Scientific Psychology," S. E. I, 1895, p. 318.
2. Cf. Ildiko Mohacsy, "The Many Faces of Love," *Contemporary Psychoanalysis* 2, no. 1 (1992): 89–96.
3. This concept is further elaborated in "On Narcissism: An Introduction," S. E. XIV, 1914, pp. 67–102.
4. Freud, "Instincts and their Vicissitudes," S. E. XIV, 1915, pp. 109–40.
5. On ego defenses see Anna Freud, *The Ego and the Mechanisms of Defense*, New York, 1966.
6. D. W. Winnicott, *Playing and Reality*, New York, 1971, Chapter 1.
7. Ibid., p. 2.
8. Ibid., p. 6.
9. Ibid., p. 5.
10. Ibid.
11. Ibid.
12. Ibid., p. 12.
13. Mircea Eliade, *A History of Religious Ideas*, vol. 1, Chicago, 1978, Chapter 2.
14. Ibid., p. 117.
15. Ibid., p. 118.
16. Ibid., p. 123.
17. Ibid., p. 119, fns. 11 and 12.
18. Ibid., p. 118.
19. Simon A. Grolnick and Alfonz Lengyel, "Etruscan Burial Symbols and the Transitional

Process," in Simon A. Grolnick and W. Muensterberger, eds., *Between Reality and Fantasy*, New York and London, 1978, Chapter 24.

20. Ibid., p. 381.
21. Ibid., p. 395.
22. On the theological meaning of this imagery, see the Steinberg reference in my Chapter 6, fn. 35.
23. Samuel Y. Edgerton, Jr., *Pictures and Punishment*, Ithaca and London, 1985, Chapter 5.
24. Cf. Laurie Adams, "Les Sanson: An Oedipal Footnote to the History of France, *The Psychoanalytic Study of Society* 10 (1984): 227–48.
25. Robert Liebert, *Michelangelo: A Psychoanalytic Study of His Life and Images*, New Haven and London, 1983, p. 222.
26. Ibid.
27. Sidney Geist, *Brancusi: A Study of the Sculpture*, New York, 1968, p. 158.
28. Julia Kristeva, *Desire in Language*, New York, 1980, Chapter 9.
29. Susan Deri, "Vicissitudes of Symbolization and Creativity," in *Between Reality and Fantasy*, Chapter 4.
30. Ibid., p. 56.
31. Hans Richter, *Dada*, New York and Toronto, 1978, p. 89.
32. From *Dadaland*, cited in Richter, *Dada*, p. 25.
33. Ibid., p. 32.
34. Ibid., p. 34.
35. Ibid., p. 64.
36. Ibid., p. 51.
37. Ibid., p. 57.
38. Cf. Laurie Schneider and Jack Flam, "Visual Convention, Simile and Metaphor in the *Mona Lisa*," *Storia dell'Arte*, no. 29 (1977): 15–24.
39. Howard Hibbard, *Caravaggio*, New York, 1983, p. 17, attributes the boy's "strained shoulder" to "crude technique and fumbling knowledge of the body."
40. In Martin Kemp, ed., *Leonardo on Painting*, New Haven and London, 1989, p. 222.
41. D. W. Winnicott, *Therapeutic Consultations in Child Psychiatry*, New York, 1971.

EIGHT

Some Psychological Aspects
of the Mother-Child Relationship
in Western Art

One of the most pervasive images in Western art is mother-and-child; it is also the primary relationship in human development and therefore has been extensively studied by psychoanalysts. The representation of mother and child in art combines style and convention with the psychological insight and experience of a particular artist. From the Early Christian period until the seventeenth century, the paradigm of mother and child was the image of Mary with the infant Christ; because of the metaphorical richness of Christian art, representations of Mary and Christ synthesize aspects of psychological and biological reality with multiple levels of Christian symbolism. The nonobjective styles that developed in the course of the twentieth century freed artists from strict adherence to clear edges and recognizable natural shapes or objects. Non-representational imagery emphasized formal elements over naturalism, narrative, and literary symbolism. These developments offered artists new ways to depict traditional subjects, including the mother-child relationship.

The first systematic discussion of early childhood sexuality is Freud's "Three Essays on the Theory of Sexuality."[1] In this historic work, Freud debunks the prevailing view that sexual instincts are absent in children and begin only at puberty. He describes the manifestations of infantile sexuality, such as sucking (whether on a thumb or a breast), which begin at birth. From these he traces the progress of infantile object choice through the oral, anal, phallic, and genital stages of development.

Between three and five years of age, roughly corresponding to the Oedipus complex, the child's sexual life, according to Freud, reaches its peak. At this point—as Freud would explicate further in *Leonardo* (1910)—

the instinct for knowledge goes into high gear. The question of where babies come from preoccupies the oedipal child, just as Oedipus confronted the riddle of the sphinx, which poses the same question in distorted form. And, although children generally know a great deal more about sex than adults give them credit for, there are two regular gaps in their information: the fertilizing function of semen and the role of the vagina. The more persistent the gaps, the more likely the child is to concoct "theories" to explain them.

As the Oedipus complex is resolved, the child enters a period of amnesia, lasting from about six until the onset of puberty. During that time, which Freud calls latency, the child's sexual energy is sublimated into intellectual activity. Sexual instincts undergo no significant development during latency; but they re-emerge in puberty. As in the formulation of the Oedipus complex, which continued to evolve for some thirty years, Freud added new data and conclusions to the "Three Essays" for many years after its original publication.

In "On Narcissism: An Introduction" of 1914,[2] Freud returned to the early character of infancy. In that extremely complex paper, he postulates a primary narcissism, based on the observation that the two original sexual objects are the self and the woman who nurses.[3] This notion, in turn, is related to the omnipotence of thoughts and magic thinking. The association of the child's primary narcissism with the illusion that his thoughts magically control the environment evolves into the psychoanalytic metaphor equating infancy with kingship.

Freud's reference to "His Majesty the Baby"[4] expresses the egocentric character of primary narcissism. The phrase appears in English in Freud's original German text of "On Narcissism," and is a corollary to "His Majesty the Ego," which Freud had discussed in 1908 as the hero of the creative writer's daydream.[5] Strachey, the translator of the Standard Edition, has proposed that Freud knew the Edwardian painting in the Royal Academy in London in which two policemen stop traffic for a nanny pushing a pram across the street. The title of the painting: *His Majesty the Baby*.[6]

In 1913, Freud's Hungarian colleague Sandor Ferenczi published a classic paper detailing the development of the child's sense of reality.[7] He calls primary narcissism the period of "unconditional wishful omnipotence," when the infant is convinced that his wish is the world's command. In Ferenczi's metaphor, the world, from the baby's point of view, is the "entourage," or whatever and whoever fulfills his wishes. The counterpart to the royal baby and equivalent of the "entourage" is Winnicott's "good-enough mother."[8]

The entourage, whether a literal good-enough mother or a substitute, comprises the royal courtiers in microcosm. She, he, or it tends his majesty's bottom, checks the temperature and consistency of his food, launders the sheets, and irons the royal wardrobe. The entourage also, on occasion, fills the position of royal troubadour, court jester, medical consultant, and all-around valet.

It is the task of both entourage and good-enough mother to oversee the child's transition from royal illusion to the commoner's reality. In Ferenczi's account of this transition, the stage of primary narcissism is followed by the development of gesture and language. Whereas, at the level of primary narcissism, "wishing made it so," in subsequent stages the child learns that gestures and later that speech ("the royal command") also produce results. When adults enjoy reading fairy tales to their children, according to Ferenczi, they return to their own infantile past and the pleasure they themselves once derived from magical occurrences.

The image of the baby king became a medieval convention in depictions of Mary with the infant Christ. Mary, typically enthroned, was represented in her aspect as Queen of Heaven, while Christ, enthroned on *her* lap, was the king. In some images, Mary and Christ are crowned; in others, only Mary is.

In an anonymous thirteenth-century Byzantine panel from an altarpiece in the Church of Santa Maria del Carmine in Florence [67], neither is crowned; but Mary is seated on a jeweled throne. Christ is portrayed, according to medieval convention, as a homunculus, or little man. He is babylike only in being small and held in his mother's arms. His unnaturally small head, long, thin proportions, erect posture, and dress are those of an adult. Although physically supported by his mother and dependent on her, he turns toward the viewer and raises his hand in a gesture of blessing. By thus conflating infancy and early childhood with qualities of adult royalty, the medieval artists gave visual form to the metaphor of the baby king.

Contributing to the power of the medieval images of Mary and the infant Christ as King and Queen of Heaven is the way in which the artists at once reveal and disguise the oedipal quality of their relationship. Christ's adult character, which belies his small size, reminds viewers that he is a man. He is also king to his mother's queen, just as Oedipus was to Jocasta. The medieval Christian believed that Christ and Mary would be reunited

67. Madonna and Christ, *Byzantine, thirteenth
century. Brancacci Chapel, Santa Maria del
Carmine, Florence.*

after death in a mystical marriage and rule as King and Queen of Heaven. In this belief, the oedipal aspect of the mother-son relationship is fulfilled; but its latent sexual nature is superseded by its manifest spirituality. All three psychic agencies are thus served; the id's incestuous impulse, the superego's idealization, and the ego's pleasure in artistic skill are simultaneously satisfied.

With the waning of the Middle Ages and the development of the Renaissance, artists became interested in naturalism. Mary and Christ retained certain royal qualities; but their relationship is increasingly intimate and their proportions more accurately depicted. In Masaccio's *Madonna and Christ* [68] from the Pisa Altarpiece of c. 1425, Mary is enthroned, but she is volumetric and wears massive draperies that define her as a three-dimensional figure in space. Christ is no longer a medieval homunculus. He is nude, and his chubby proportions are those of a baby. Unlike the little suspended man in the Byzantine panel, Masaccio's Christ obeys the laws of gravity and sits firmly on Mary's lap.

Although sitting upright and facing the viewer as a little enthroned king, Christ sucks his fingers, which is consistent with the autoerotic activity of the oral stage. Conflating oral erotism with Christian symbolism is the image of Christ eating grapes, which allude to the wine of the Eucharist. In addition to merging infantile sexuality with Christian spirituality, this particular image also condenses time—that is, Christ's infancy and future death—and is related to the painting's function as an altarpiece. Worshipers taking communion at the altar confront an iconographic echo of the very ritual in which they themselves participate. They are also reminded of Christ's combined human and divine natures.[9] They can identify with Christ's humanity insofar as Masaccio's image expresses physical and psychological reality; and they incorporate Christ's body and blood in the wafer and wine of communion, thereby echoing Christ's own oral incorporation of grapes.

To be eating grapes at all is, of course, inappropriate for a baby of this age. Nevertheless, Mary, whose good-enough mothering is not questioned, willingly gives her son a handful of them. This feature of Masaccio's iconography highlights another psychological aspect of the conflation making Christ an adult as well as an infant—namely, his grown-up, superior intelligence. Steinberg has discussed this conflation, particularly as it relates to the Christian tradition of Christ's (as well as Mary's) foreknowledge of the future.[10]

As in other Christian condensations of Christ's image, however, there

68. Masaccio, Madonna and Christ, *Pisa
Altarpiece, c. 1425. National Gallery, London.*

69. *Titian,* Madonna
Nursing Christ, *c. 1570.*
National Gallery, London.

is a psychological truth in the notion of the superior intelligence of children. Ferenczi's short note of 1923 entitled "The Dream of the Clever Baby,"[11] deals with this particular issue. He observes that adults frequently dream of infants and young children who can perform well beyond their years and that they are often depicted as such in fairy tales, myths, and paintings. He cites the example of the Virgin's Debate with the Scribes; the revelation of Christ's superior wisdom is likewise a purpose of his Dispute with the Temple Doctors at the age of twelve. Dreams of "clever babies," according to Ferenczi, combine the childhood *wish* to surpass adults with the fact that children are in possession of a great deal of sexual knowledge repressed during the period of infantile amnesia.

Freud's primary narcissism and Ferenczi's period of unconditional omnipotence correspond to the newborn state of symbiosis. In this period, which Deri refers to as "dual union,"[12] the infant experiences himself as still biologically unified with his mother.

The conventions of medieval art precluded the naturalistic portrayal of symbiosis. Titian's late Renaissance *Madonna Nursing Christ* [69] of c. 1570, however, depicts Christ's symbiotic dependency on Mary. The loose brushwork serves the combined psychological and biological sense of merger between mother and child by literally blurring their edges. Aside from the possible trinitarian allusion of their triangular shape, both Mary and Christ in this painting could be any mother and child.

A similar use of a medium to portray symbiosis characterizes Picasso's bronze *Baboon and Young* [64] of 1951. As in the Titian, Picasso's baby turns and clings to his mother. Picasso's sculpture is devoid of Christian metaphor, but contains the visual metaphor comparing the mother's face with a car. The back of the baby's head, like the car and the mother's body, is differentiated by virtue of the clear edges and polished surface. The relative lack of polish and rough surface in the rest of the baby correspond to the infant's undifferentiated, symbiotic attachment to the mother.

The twentieth-century British sculptor Henry Moore created many images that chronicle the mother-child relationship. Those that convey mother-child symbiosis do so by a literal merging of the two figures through form and medium. In an example of 1936 [70], the curvilinear

70. Henry Moore, Mother and Child, *1936. The British Council, London.*

71. Henry Moore, Suckling Child, 1930.

planes flow between mother and child so that only the heads are differentiated. In this sculpture, Moore simultaneously shows the point of view of
mother and infant; both feel merged if their response to the symbiotic
period is "good-enough."

Moore's *Suckling Child* of 1930 [71] is an image of the child's oral
experience of symbiosis. As far as the baby is concerned, the mother does
not exist as a total person, but rather as a "part object," in this case a breast;
providing that the services rendered are "good enough," the child's illusion
of omnipotence is maintained, and he trusts in the reliability of the environment. Compared with *Mother and Child* of 1936, the *Suckling Child* is more
differentiated, although the child's face and hands merge with the breast.
Even further differentiated, though the child is still nursing, are the figures
in a mother-child etching [72]. There mother and child are clearly distinct
from each other. Nevertheless, from the baby's point of view, at the
moment depicted the only relevant breast is the one providing him with

milk. In place of the other breast, Moore hollowed out a space, corresponding to the baby's experience. The humorous contrast of the enlarged breast with the concavity opposite subsumes naturalism to psychological reality.

Some of Moore's most abstract images of mother-child symbiosis are his *Helmet* sculptures [73]. In these, he evokes themes of maternal protection, by way of the helmet casing around the little, childlike interior figure. These sculptures illustrate the interior-exterior quality of the first six months of life when, protected by the motherly "helmet," the infant makes the transition from the internal and enclosed space of the womb to the open, external space of the environment.[13]

Freud's discussion of infancy and early childhood in the 1905 "Three Essays" is primarily in terms of instinctual drives and ego development; Ferenczi's is in terms of language and gesture symbolism. From the 1960s, Margaret Mahler observed the behavior of infants and toddlers, which she correlated to their internal experience of the maternal relationship. Mahler developed four main steps in the process called "separation-individuation,"

72. *Henry Moore,*
Mother and Child. *Private collection, New York.*

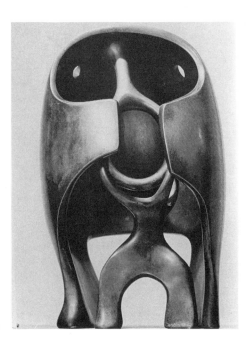

73. *Henry Moore,* Helmet, *1940.*

which she identified in the title of her book *The Psychological Birth of the Human Infant,* published in 1975.[14] This process includes the period from biological birth to approximately three years of age, and therefore comes to an end with the onset of the Oedipus complex as formulated by Freud.

Following the first symbiotic stage (ending at about six months), is differentiation, or "hatching," when the child gradually begins to sense his distinction from the mother, or from whoever functions as entourage. In this period, approximately from six to ten months, stranger anxiety takes effect as the child realizes that his mother is different from other people as well as from himself.

Mahler calls the third stage, which precedes object constancy, "practicing"; this lasts from about ten to eighteen months. In the practicing period, children typically begin to move around on their own. To the simultaneous delight and alarm of their entourage, they crawl, pull themselves upright, and begin to toddle.

At about three, the average child arrives at Mahler's fourth stage—"object constancy." The mother has now become internalized as a "constant object," which means that the child can retain a mental image of the mother even in her absence. As a result, three is a typical age for beginning nursery school, which requires that children relinquish the mother for an

74. *Henry Moore,* Rocking Chair
#1, 1950.

extended period of time. Prior to establishing object constancy, children correlate absence with nonexistence, or death.

Motion, like sucking and tactile experience, is an important aspect of child development. As early as 1905 in the "Three Essays," Freud notes the pleasure that babies and children derive from passive movement, such as rocking, riding, swinging, and being carried. In his *Leonardo,* he relates infantile pleasure in motion to the wish to fly and to the artist's interest in inventing a flying machine.

In the 1950s, Henry Moore cast a series of bronze rocking-chair sculptures that illustrate the child's enjoyment of motion. These were conceived as toys for his daughter and were designed to replicate the actual speed and motion of a rocking chair. In *Rocking Chair #1* [74], the mother rocks back and holds up the baby, who seems to clap his hands with delight. The thin proportions, open spaces, and curvilinear forms enhance the impression of movement, which corresponds to the baby's sensation of flight. The mother is literally the chair, rather than symbolically, as in Christian art, which concept conforms to the child's assumption that his mother's lap is his throne.

One of the most momentous events of childhood takes place during Mahler's practicing stage—namely, learning to walk. The psychological importance of this achievement is evident in the symbolic meanings of up and down that appear in art, religion, and myth, as well as in the unconscious (see Chapter 3). The image of the child's unsteady "first steps" was a popular subject in nineteenth-century academic art, especially sculpture. A comparison of this theme in three works—by van Gogh, Brancusi, and Picasso—illustrates some of the ways in which style and convention permit artists to express different psychological aspects of the same subject.

Van Gogh's *First Steps* [75], after Jean-François Millet, depicts a setting by a farmhouse. At the right, the girl who is about to walk reaches out to her father at the left. His arms are open and welcoming; he has left his cart and spade, and is caught up in the excitement of the moment. The girl's

75. *Vincent van Gogh,* First Steps. *Metropolitan Museum of Art, New York. Gift of George N. and Helen M. Richard, 1964, 64.165.2.*

76. *Constantin Brancusi,* Study for *The First Step, c. 1913. Museum of Modern Art, New York.*

mother, who towers over the child and partly envelops her, indicates her support by pose and gesture, although her face is blank.

Van Gogh emphasizes the ambivalent nature of a child's first steps by contrasting the connection between the girl and her mother with the open space separating her from her father. The artist evokes the child's developmental shift from the mother as a protective enclosure to the father, who is associated with work outside the house. Interior and exterior are thus among the psychodynamic implications of van Gogh's iconography, and they are highlighted by the sense of forthcoming triumph in the child's conquest of the space between her parents.

Brancusi's drawing *Study for the First Step* [76] is one of four sketches of c. 1913 for a sculpture that has been destroyed. In this work, the combined influence of Cubism and African art is evident in the geometric—especially cylindrical—shapes of the child. He proceeds somewhat un-

77. *Pablo Picasso,* First
Steps, *1943. Yale
University Art Gallery,
New Haven. Gift of
Stephen C. Clark, B. A.,
1903.*

steadily toward the viewer in the slightly wooden manner of a puppet. The
presence of his entourage is implied by the unseen figure assumed to be
holding his upraised hand. Because this child is depicted frontally and as
a close-up, and fills the picture plane, he seems to have nowhere to go
except forward—out of the picture. There is no welcoming father, as there
is in van Gogh's *First Steps.* That Brancusi's child registers fright at the
prospect of entering an unfamiliar and unprotected space is indicated by
the strong dark triangle representing his mouth. He seems to be crying out
as he approaches a viewer he does not know.

Picasso's *First Steps* of 1943 [77] also represents the child in front view
and as a close-up.[15] The mother, however, is very much in evidence, as a
looming, monumental figure, whose form is radically foreshortened to fit
within the picture space and yet surround the child. There is no doubt
about the mother's encouragement; she supports the child from behind to
prevent her from falling. The mother's intimacy and identification with the
child's efforts are reinforced by their synchronized steps. The right legs of

both mother and child act as vertical supports, while both left legs convey the sense of motion by their mutual diagonal planes.

Unlike Brancusi's child, Picasso's strides forward with a conviction upheld by the sense of maternal protection. In addition, Picasso takes advantage of the Cubist style, particularly the simultaneous viewpoint, to convey the wobbly, unsteady movement of even the most self-confident toddler. The child's left arm extends from the neck, rather than from the shoulder, as in nature, and creates a lopsided sense of unevenly distributed weight. The slightly disjointed quality of toddler motion—conveyed in the Brancusi by the puppetlike forms—is enhanced in the Picasso by the artist's characteristic facial distortions. The natural configuration of his child's face is disrupted; the left eye is higher than the right, the nose is to the left of the mouth, and the mouth is to the right of the chin. The resulting zigzag motion of the facial features, together with the forward motion of torso and legs, replicates the simultaneous forward and sideways gait of the toddler.

ARRESTED MOTION AND THE GAZE

Inspired by the French psychoanalyst Jacques Lacan, recent discussions of art, especially by those not trained as art historians, have given considerable attention to the "gaze."[16] In "What Is a Picture?"[17] Lacan situates the riveting power of the gaze in the child's view of a sibling being nursed by his mother. He relates the gaze to desire and the ubiquity of the evil eye. The powers of the evil eye, according to Lacan, are derived from envy and the concomitant wish to kill, wither, and petrify. *Invidia*, or envy, Lacan observes, is from the Latin *videre*, meaning "to see," and is bound to the *sight* of something.

Lacan distinguishes envy from jealousy, which entails wanting someone else's possessions. True envy, he says, comes about when one encounters an *image* that "makes the subject pale" because it is "a completeness closed upon itself."[18] In other words, the image that arouses envy allows no entry from the outside; it is a complete, self-contained universe. That such is the image confronted by the child watching a sibling at his mother's breast is clear, for example, from the intense concentration of the nursing infants in Henry Moore's 1930 *Suckling Child* [71] and the etching in Figure 72.

In Jan van Eyck's *Lucca Madonna* [78], the mother-child unit is even more apparent, because Mary's gaze meets Christ's. The mutuality of their

78. *Jan van Eyck*, Lucca Madonna, *1435.*
Städelschen Kunstinstituts, Frankfurt.

gaze seems to preclude interruption by a third person, who, in this case, would constitute the proverbial "crowd." The paradox of the exclusionary character of this kind of mother-child unit is its negative, "chilling" impact on the hypothetical envious "watcher" and its beneficent, nourishing, and life-giving effect on the nursing infant.

This paradox is one source of later paranoia. The envious gaze of the sibling can become split off from the experience of the good-enough mother—especially if there wasn't one. In such cases, the envy and its negative associations are projected back onto the mother (or father), who, in turn, is experienced as the dangerous persecutor. Both parent and child, therefore, participate in the ambivalence of the gaze. In Lacan's view, the gaze is *invidious*—"no trace anywhere," he says, "of a good eye."[19] Such is not, however, the case. For if the entourage is good enough and the mother "reflects" the child adequately—as in the *Lucca Madonna*—then the child experiences a positive "eye."

Lacan's "evil eye" logically refers to a developmental phase that follows symbiosis. To be the older child enviously riveted to the sight of a nursing sibling—unless one is a twin or triplet, which presents additional conflicts—one has to be at least nine months of age. Despite Lacan's one-sided insistence on the negative power of the eye, however, his discussion of the "picture" has interesting implications for the positive role of art in transforming and redirecting the invidious gaze.

Lacan defines a picture as "a trap for the gaze."[20] It is by means of the gaze, he says, that one can grasp the "taming, civilizing and fascinating power of the function of the picture."[21] I take this to mean that the "picture"—when it is a work of art—diverts the gaze from a sight that provokes envy and refocuses it. As such, the picture serves a sublimatory function, making the consequent image an aesthetic, rather than an invidious, one.

Lacan's second topic in "What Is a Picture?" concerns the relation between gaze and gesture. The gaze, according to Lacan, "terminates" and "freezes" the gestural movement. What Lacan implies in his distinction between gesture—that is, movement—and arrest can be seen by a comparison of three registers of imagery on the well-known Susa *Painted Beaker* of c. 5000–4000 B.C. [79]. Taking a work of art as an example partly begs the question of the sublimatory character of the picture; nevertheless, it so happens that the sets of pictures on the Susa beaker illustrate Lacan's idea in regard to the perceptual gestalt of arrest versus movement. It is no accident—though perhaps not consciously intended either—that the Susa

79. Painted Beaker, *from Susa, Iran,*
c. 5000–4000 B.C. Louvre, Paris.

beaker was the frontispiece of a book appropriately entitled *Arrest and Movement*, published in 1951, on the representation of narrative in ancient Near Eastern art.[22]

The top two registers of the beaker depict two tempos of movement around its surface. Each corresponds to the natural motion of eye and hand in observing the beaker and rotating it. The uppermost register is covered with repeated, long-necked birds; their diagonal heads and bodies create the impression that they are walking slowly from right to left. Countering their movement are the horizontal animals whose diagonal forelegs and heads in the register below create the illusion of expansive motion from left to right. The observer's response to both registers is the impulse to continue around the body of the beaker—in other words, to move right along with the repeated image.

When the observer encounters the main image—an ibex with long, curving horns contained in a trapezoidal frame—he stops; his gaze is "arrested." This is accomplished by the relatively large size of the ibex and the fact that it is seen as unique rather than part of a pattern. (There are actually three images of the ibex, but only one is visible at a time.) The gaze is further focused—arrested—because the ibex is framed on four sides—instead of two, as the animals in the top two registers are. The ibex, like the viewer's gaze, is "held captive" by the borders of the image. Furthermore, whereas the borders of the top two registers encircle the beaker, carrying the viewer's "eye" around it, the ibex's frame is a trapezoid at formal odds with the beaker's curvilinear surface and therefore stops—or "arrests"—the movement of the eye.

On another level of opposition between "arrest and movement," which goes beyond the purely visual response to an abstract gestalt to the symbolism of content, Lacan cites the popularity of eye iconography in antiquity. He characterizes the phallus as the "homeopathic" eye, whose purpose is to counter the evil eye. The "prophylactic" eye, on the other hand, protects travelers, but only when they are moving; neither the apotropaic phallus, which guarded ancient roadways and entrances, nor the prophylactic eye, according to Lacan, is ever beneficent.

The traveler, in Lacan's formulation, comes closest to being protected, precisely because he is in motion. Since the evil eye has the power to arrest movement, which means to freeze and kill—or petrify, as in the Medusa myth—there is safety in motion. Lacan notes the protective function of gesture and grimace in battle, which explains the popularity of the Gorgonaion (Medusa's head) as an armor and shield device. Medusa's grimacing expression and flashing eyes, as well as her snaky hair, are appropriated by the wearer and turned against the opponent. Whoever goes into battle protected by Medusa's head symbolically "freezes" or "petrifies" the enemies who catch sight of her image. When the enemy stops to look or stops because he has looked, as when Lacan's "child" is stopped by an invidious sight, he is in mortal danger.

The principle of safety in motion and danger in immobility can be seen in children's games as well as in the clinical situation, and it is eternally ambivalent. A game of tag, for example, is won only when the runner is caught—or "tagged"—and has to stand still. The tagged runner then becomes "it" and has to tag someone else. In the game of musical chairs, the players are "safe" as long as they are in motion; the danger occurs when music and motion stop and someone has no chair. Similarly, the child's delight in chasing a butterfly is related to the excitement of motion and an uncertain outcome.

When the butterfly is caught, it may be literally "pinned down," in which case it dies. In verbal pursuit, one tries to "pin down" one's opponent figuratively—which means to make him stop and settle on the "point" of his argument so that it can be "examined" and possibly "pulled apart" (like the butterfly from its wings).

Clinical examples of the relationship between "arrest and movement" are numerous. Anxiety-driven motion often comes from a fear of being seen clearly if one stops. One patient described refusing to be photographed by a friend of his rather seductive mother. The fact that his mother had commissioned a nude photograph of her eight-year-old son barely disguised her wish to "freeze" his image for the purpose of indulging her sexual fantasies. The eight-year-old "solved" his counter-wish not to be the object of his mother's gaze (which, of course, he also did want) by running around the house to elude "capture." It is probably no accident that the word "arrest" denotes capture for illegal acts—associated in the unconscious with the oedipal crimes of incest and murder—and that fugitives from justice are said to be "on the run."

Another patient made paper dolls of his competitors at the office. Each doll was labeled ("tagged") with a name. Since the patient was a high-level executive, he regularly had meetings in which he had to "face down" his colleagues or win his "point" in order to push through a deal. Before each such meeting, the executive would select the paper dolls corresponding to his adversaries and place them in the freezing compartment of his refrigerator. With this modern technological form of voodoo, the executive revised the Medusa myth by turning his enemies to ice (rather than stone).

In terms of the psychoanalytic transference, too, the eye has a defensive significance. Does the patient ward off the analyst's "eye" by sitting up and facing him, or does he lie down and trust the analyst as a benevolent ally? It has become a platitude of the clinical situation that a patient who chooses the former option does so in order to maintain an illusion of control by means of vision. To lie down on the couch and free-associate requires a degree of trust that many people have not established. It is likely that such people have encountered a failure at the earliest levels of mother-child "reflection" and "mirroring." Sometimes this failure can be corrected clinically by a preliminary period in which the patient sits up. If trust is successfully established, the classical analytic procedure can follow. Lacan expresses this analytic dilemma well when he defines positive transference as the patient having a "soft spot" for the analyst and negative transference as "when you have to keep your eye on him."[23]

Giotto's Arena Chapel and
the Arresting Power of the Gaze

The "pictures" on the Susa beaker illustrate the formal differences between arrest and movement. In Giotto's Arena Chapel frescoes, on the other hand, the formal qualities of arrest and movement are synthesized with the content, or iconography, of the scenes. Giotto has always been recognized as a psychological artist, who uses gesture and glance to punctuate narrative sequence and enhance dramatic effect.

Because the Arena Chapel frescoes form narrative cycles—the lives of Mary and her parents (Anna and Joachim) on the top register and the

80. *Giotto,* Nativity, *c. 1305. Arena Chapel,*
Padua.

81. *Giotto,* Presentation of Christ in the Temple,
c. 1305. Arena Chapel, Padua.

life of Christ on the two registers below—there is a flow of movement
from one frame to the next. So unified, in fact, is Giotto's formal construction that the narrative seems to continue uninterrupted, although unseen
by the viewer, behind the borders of each panel.

As Lacan indicates, when gesture predominates, there is a sense of
flowing movement. When two or more figures exchange what is referred
to as Giotto's characteristic "significant glance," the movement stops, held
momentarily by a mutual gaze. On two occasions, Giotto's depiction of the
mutual gaze in the Arena Chapel entails aspects of the mother-child relationship. In the first instance, the *Nativity* [80], a midwife enters the picture
plane from the left and hands the swaddled newborn Christ to the Virgin.

82. *Giotto,* Flight into Egypt, *c. 1305. Arena
Chapel, Padua.*

Mary responds from the opposing direction, reaches out to receive the
infant, and meets his gaze. At that point, the narrative sequence pauses;
mother and child are locked in timeless space. Highlighting their unity,
which corresponds to Lacan's "completeness closed upon itself,"[24] is the
solitary figure of Joseph, whose eyes are closed in sleep. He is depicted as
a solid, volumetric unit, his exclusion from mother and child echoed as he
literally "turns his back" on them. His self-contained solidity emphasizes
the contrasting "created space" between Mary and Christ.

The second instance occurs in the *Presentation of Christ in the Temple*
[81]. In Christ's response to Simeon, the old priest whom God promised
that he would *see* the savior before he died, Giotto has convincingly

depicted "stranger anxiety." There is a rather humorous paradox between the Christian implications of Simeon's sight of Christ and Christ himself, who reacts with apprehension, as a normal infant would. Christ's gaze is driven by fear—like Lacan's hypothetical patient in negative transference, Christ has to "keep his eye on" the object of his distrust. Giotto contrasts the arrested "fixedness" of Christ's eyes with anxiety-driven motion as he twists around to return to the safety of his mother's arms.

If the riveting power of the gaze in the *Nativity* and the *Presentation* is compared with the *Flight into Egypt* [82], the significance of Lacan's distinction between arrest and movement is evident. In the *Flight*, Mary and Christ fit into a triangular shape echoed by the stagelike mountain framing them. Despite their symbiotic unity, however, they do not exchange a glance; instead, they gaze off in opposite directions. As a result, the sequential flow does not stop, nor would it be appropriate, given the narrative requirement of the scene, which is flight, or "being on the run." The figures in Giotto's *Flight* evoke Lacan's ancient "travelers," protected by the "prophylactic eye," here in the guise of the airborne angel, God's emissary, leading them to safety in Egypt.

Saint Augustine Recapitulates Early Child Development

Lacan cites Saint Augustine as a source for his thinking on the death-dealing power of the envious gaze. On reviewing that source, it is apparent that, in Book 1 of the *Confessions*, Saint Augustine recapitulates child development based on memories of his own childhood and observation of others.[25] The point of view of his account shifts from inside the pre-verbal baby to the outside experience of an older child. God, Augustine says, fills the breasts of mothers and nurses with milk, and gradually the baby learns where the milk comes from. But he cannot convey his wishes, which are inside him, to the adults, who are outside. "They had no faculty," Augustine writes, "which could penetrate my mind. So I would toss my arms and legs about and make noises, hoping that such few signs as I could make would show my meaning."[26] In this description, Augustine reiterates Winnicott's formulation of the child's interior/exterior experience.

Whenever his entourage failed to respond, the future saint "would take revenge by bursting into tears."[27] Later, as he learned words, and developed from the gesture symbolism to speech symbolism described by Ferenczi, he found that he could better control his environment and satisfy his wishes by "naming" them.[28] Augustine understood the sexual curiosity of children, their aggressive and jealous natures. He reports a child turning "pale with envy," on seeing his foster brother being nursed.[29] This reaction in Augustine's view—as in Lacan's—was not innocence.

Furthermore, Augustine recalls musing on the origin of life in the manner of sexual research observed by Freud. He sought to discover the role of the womb in creating babies and what preceded it. He asked God for an answer; but none was forthcoming. In this piece of frustrated research, Augustine attempted to fill in one of the gaps in information identified by Freud—namely, the fertilizing role of semen. Finally he learned the answers by watching babies himself and listening to the talk of women.

Saint Augustine was born in North Africa in A.D. 354 to a Christian mother and a pagan father. As Michelangelo would do some eleven hundred years later, Augustine recorded his own family romance. Augustine reports, for example, that God provides food for infants by filling up the mothers' breasts with milk. Such provisioning is the role that Winnicott ascribed to the good-enough father. Augustine has thus unconsciously elevated his father to divine status, while also eliminating his father by giving his job to God. Later, when his mother and father fail to satisfy his infantile sexual curiosity, he again turns to God. In becoming a Christian, Augustine repudiates his father's paganism and worships God. He becomes the bishop of Hippo, "builds" the *City of God*, and expiates his guilt by writing the *Confessions*.

NOTES

1. Freud, S. E. VII, 1905, pp. 123–243.
2. Freud, S. E. XIV, 1914, pp. 67–102.
3. Ibid., p. 88.
4. Ibid., p. 91.
5. Ibid., fn. 1.
6. Ibid.
7. Sandor Ferenczi, "Stages in the Development of Reality," in his *First Contributions to the Theory and Technique of Psychoanalysis*, New York, 1980, pp. 213–39.
8. Winnicott's "good-enough mother" assumes the presence of the good-enough father, who provides a good-enough environment. Otherwise, the mother's tension interferes with her ability to maintain a good-enough relationship to her infant.
9. Steinberg has discussed this condensation in Renaissance art and the temporal condensation of present with future: "The Sexuality of Christ in Renaissance Art and Modern Oblivion," *October* 25 (Summer 1983).
10. Ibid., Figure 136, p. 124: In one painting of c. 1500 by Quentin Massys, which Steinberg illustrates, the infant Christ actually reads a book.

11. In Ferenczi, *Further Contributions to the Theory and Technique of Psychoanalysis*, New York, 1980, pp. 349–50.

12. Susan Deri, *Symbolization and Creativity*, New York, 1984, pp. 247–50.

13. The psychological significance of interior and exterior experience is discussed by Deri, ibid., in relation to preconscious mediating between unconscious and conscious, and by Winnicott as a precursor of creativity. For the application of these concepts to the work of Henry Moore, see Laurie Schneider, "The Theme of Mother and Child in the Art of Henry Moore," *Psychoanalytic Perspectives on Art* 1 (1985): 241–65.

14. Margaret Mahler, Fred Pine, and Anni Bergmann, *The Psychological Birth of the Human Infant*, New York, 1975.

15. The figures in this painting are portraits of Picasso's maid, Inez, and her daughter.

16. Cf. Norman Bryson, *Vision and Painting*, New Haven and London, 1983, especially Chapter 5, "The Gaze and the Glance," and Richard Wollheim, *Painting as an Art*, Princeton, 1987.

17. Jacques Lacan, *The Four Fundamental Concepts of Psychoanalysis*, New York, 1981, Chapter 9, "What is a Picture."

18. Ibid., p. 116.

19. Ibid., p. 115.

20. Ibid., p. 89.

21. Ibid., p. 116.

22. H. A. Groenewegen-Frankfort, *Arrest and Movement*, 1951; reprint, New York, 1978.

23. Lacan, *The Four Fundamental Concepts*, Chapter 10, "Presence of the Analyst," p. 124.

24. Ibid., p. 116.

25. For this reference, I am indebted to Bradley Collins.

26. Saint Augustine, *Confessions*, Book 1, New York, 1961, p. 25.

27. Ibid., Chapter 7, p. 26.

28. Ibid., Chapter 8, p. 29.

29. Ibid., Chapter 7, p. 28.

NINE

Psychoanalytic Readings of Primal-Scene Iconography

I t is the methodological bias of this chapter that certain repeated themes in Western art can be read psychoanalytically without necessarily having recourse to the artist's biography. This approach does not imply that thematic readings are not enriched, or even confirmed by, biographical data—just as they are by other relevant historical, cultural, theological, mythological, or literary associations. The nearest literary version of this methodology is what the French call "explication de texte," or the analysis of a text on its own grounds, independent of the author's life and personality.[1]

Even during the Middle Ages, when artists' individual identities were virtually unknown, certain conventional images, such as the baby king discussed in the previous chapter, can be read psychoanalytically. With Renaissance humanism and the classical revival, a renewed sense of individuality emerged. The very interest in classics encouraged interest in human development and cultural history. One important effect of this intellectual evolution was a more psychological attention to childhood. Vasari's *Lives*, for example, connected childhood events and the family environment of the artist to his later life and work. Like Freud, Vasari recognized the complexity of child development, and both were interested in the factors bearing on issues of creativity.

From the turn of the fourteenth century, with the innovations of Giotto, Italian artists began to reflect the classical revival. Despite setbacks—partly the result of the 1348 plague—there was a change in the direction of psychological depiction that accompanied the shift from the Middle Ages to the Renaissance. From that shift to the present, West-

ern art has been more specifically linked with artistic personality. In ancient Roman, Early Christian, and medieval art, very few *names* of artists,
let alone their biographies, are known. Renaissance writers, therefore,
sought biographical parallels for contemporary artists by turning to ancient Greece, where artists' lives and personalities had been a subject of
historical record. The "cult" of the artist's personality was renewed in the
Renaissance and has continued to interest historians and psychologists in
the modern world.

In this chapter, I take the theme of the primal scene in works of art,
and some related images, as an example of psychoanalytic reading. In
psychoanalysis, the primal scene refers to the child's fantasy of sex between
the parents—whether or not the child has actually witnessed it. The primal
scene is, among other things, related to the gaze, and, like the sight that
produces envy, has the power to rivet the observer.

FREUD AND THE PRIMAL SCENE

In the winter of 1914–15, Freud published "From the History of an Infantile
Neurosis,"[2] also known as "The Wolfman." In that case study, Freud first
calls parental love-making the primal scene, although he had used the term
in a more general way as early as 1897; in *The Interpretation of Dreams*
(1900), Freud had noted the anxiety produced in a child who witnesses
sexual intercourse.[3] In contrast to Freud, Jung insisted that the primal scene
was an adult construction projected back into childhood time. Freud countered that actual events—however perceived by the child—were the origin of primal fantasies.[4]

In the history of the Wolfman, Freud reconstructs what he considers
the basis in reality of his patient's impression of the primal scene. The case
concerned a young Russian man with an obsessional neurosis and a persistent fear of being eaten by a wolf. He suffered from phobias, had a
tendency to masochism related to feminine identification, and was unable
to work. The Wolfman had been a victim of early seduction, which led to
a predominantly negative oedipal constellation and a heightened fear of
castration. In these circumstances—namely, the evidence of exposure to
the primal scene, seduction, and castration fear—the case of the Wolfman
shed light on three of the most significant childhood fantasies.[5]

The Wolfman reported a dream in which he was lying down and
facing the window at the foot of his bed. It was winter. "Suddenly," he told

Freud, "the window opened of its own accord, and I was terrified to see that some white wolves were sitting on the big walnut tree in front of the window. There were six or seven of them." They had big, foxlike tails and ears pricked up as if they were dogs at attention. "In great terror, evidently of being eaten up by the wolves, I screamed and woke up."[6]

The dream first occurred at around three or four years of age; it was the child's earliest anxiety dream, after which he was afraid of pictures of wolves. Freud discovered in the course of the analysis that the wolves represented the boy's fear of being castrated and devoured by his father. The vividness of the dream, according to Freud, indicates its basis in an observed or experienced event—in this case, a primal scene. The fixed stare of the wolves reiterates the child's gaze, riveted on the sight of parental sexual activity. The attentiveness of the wolves likewise reiterates the child's listening to the sounds made by his parents. And the wolves' immobility is a reversal of the parents' movements.

This brief and incomplete summary of the dream's interpretation does not do justice to its complexity or to that of the case as a whole. It does, however, set out certain important elements of the child's primal-scene experience and/or fantasy that are useful in considering works of art. Exposure to the primal scene confronts the child with conflicting information that evokes in him a combination of fear, anxiety, curiosity, and sexual overstimulation. Because the child does not completely understand the mechanics of what he observes, he creates explanations that are either "fantastic," or incomplete, or both. Such explanations are, in effect, attempts to solve the riddle of conception and birth. Derivatives of various fantasies produced to account for the primal fantasies of early childhood can be seen in certain recurring iconographic themes.

THE ANNUNCIATION

The most pervasive and canonical primal-scene image in Christian art is the Annunciation. It depicts Gabriel's announcement of Christ's birth to Mary, and typically refers to impregnation.[7] Certain standard iconographic features of the Annunciation, such as the opened and closed door, denote Mary's receptivity and virginity, respectively. The lilies that are often present, either in a vase or carried by Gabriel, combine Mary's purity with her sexuality (the flower being the reproductive organ of the plant). Gabriel is God's messenger, or go-between, and he, like the Holy Ghost, is winged and therefore phallic. Gabriel imparts God's words to Mary—as the Holy Ghost, specifically identified as Mary's impregnator in the Gospels of Matthew and Luke, imparts his spirit. The popular expression "A little bird told me so," which implies the possession of secret or forbidden knowledge, conveys the sense of a fleeting informant—one that, like Gabriel and the dove of the Holy Ghost, is in transit. It also evokes Leonardo's screen memory (see Chapter 2) and the fantasy of a winged creature dropping in for a temporary visit.

The latter theme figures in Crockett Johnson's 1940s comic strip Barnaby.[8] *Barnaby is the son of relatively well-adjusted, middle-class American parents; occasionally, however, his mother complains that his father doesn't pay enough attention to him. Inspired by bedtime fairy stories, Barnaby longs for a godparent who can grant wishes. One night, a godfather flies through Barnaby's bedroom window. He is a short, square man with pink wings, a green overcoat, and a hat, and he smokes a cigar. His name is Mr. O'Malley.*

Barnaby's parents are distressed at their son's unshakable belief in Mr. O'Malley, and they take him to see a child psychologist. The psychologist draws a map of the mind, which he divides into conscious and unconscious, id, ego, and superego. He asks Barnaby to draw his father, but Mr. O'Malley changes the drawing into a portrait of himself. The psychologist explains that Mr. O'Malley is Barnaby's idealized father, whereupon his real father tries to elevate himself in his son's eyes. He buys him an airplane and a kite; but Mr. O'Malley is always better at such things, especially the flying part.

The fantasy persists, although Barnaby continues to live with his real parents and maintains the illusion of his winged friend. Mr. O'Malley is not a god or a holy spirit; but he is a charming illustration of both the splitting of the ego for purposes of idealization and the family romance. Like the gods and goddesses who interact with mortals, Mr. O'Malley can be read as a projected parental imago expressing the simultaneous disappointment with, and admiration of, Barnaby's real father.

In Jan van Eyck's *Annunciation in a Church* [83] of c. 1434/6, Gabriel's words are in raised gold letters across the picture plane toward Mary's listening ear. Ernest Jones[9] has related this motif to the tradition that Mary was impregnated through her ear—hence the designation, in the Gospel of Luke, of Christ as God's "Word made flesh." Both the visual motif and the biblical image correspond to childhood fantasies of oral impregnation—whether by kissing, whispering, or breathing.

83. Jan van Eyck, Annunciation in a Church, *c. 1434–36. National Gallery of Art, Washington, D.C. Andrew W. Mellon Collection.*

Millard Meiss has analyzed another visual impregnation metaphor inspired by Christian theology, which is illustrated in the van Eyck.[10] He noted Christ's traditional association with light and fire and Mary's with a window. During the ninth century A.D., glass and light were combined in the metaphor "comparing the miraculous conception and birth of Christ with the passage of sunlight through a glass window,"[11] which is precisely the image in van Eyck's *Annunciation.* Just as light could pass through a pane of glass without breaking it, according to the terms of the metaphor, so Mary could be impregnated and give birth without the loss of her virginity.

Around the twelfth century, the development of stained glass inspired a further elaboration of this metaphor.[12] "As light is colored by radiation through stained glass," Meiss wrote, "the Holy Spirit acquired human form by entering the sacred chamber or temple of the Virgin."[13] This makes explicit Mary's role as an architectural enclosure as well as the impregnating function of light. The association of light with fire confirms its phallic role and also refers forward in time to the Pentecost, when, according to Acts 2 : 4, the apostles received the gift of tongues. As a result, the apostles were empowered to spread Christ's word in many languages. Illustrating this connection is Giotto's Arena Chapel fresco of the Pentecost, in which the "gift" is represented as "tongues of flame." At a deep unconscious level, the mechanism of displacement is clearly at work in the dual power of flame and light as tongue and phallus.[14] As we saw in legends accounting for the origins of art, reflections (made by light) and shadows (the absence of light) can function similarly despite being opposites.

In Piero della Francesca's *Annunciation* [32] of c. 1452 in Arezzo, shadow as well as light is used to create the visual metaphor of Mary's impregnation. At the upper left, God sends down rays of light toward Mary, who is simultaneously greeted by Gabriel. Above the portico, to the right of God, stretches a horizontal wooden beam, from which hangs a loop. Because we naturally read paintings from left to right, the shadow cast by the beam appears to enter the loop from the left (that is, from God), turn the corner of the window, and enter the building.[15]

Piero's shadow can be read as an impregnation metaphor; but its meanings are multivalent. Characteristics of the shadow, as described in the Christian literature, include its relation to God's power (Luke 1 : 35 on the Annunciation: "The power of the Highest shall overshadow thee"), its ability to cool the "heats of lust" (see the apocryphal Gospel of the Birth of Mary 7 : 9), and its protective function—whether as God's shadow (Lam. 4 : 20), the shadow of God's hand (Isa. 49 : 2), or of his wings (Ps. 17 : 8). Other biblical references to shadow stress its role as a prefiguration, or fore*shadowing*, of the future. Shadow also has fertilizing power, which accounts for its phallic role and association with strength and sexual potency in cultures throughout the world.[16] In tropical climates, only "mad dogs and Englishmen go out in the midday sun," because at noon one's shadow is shortest.

In addition to light and shadow, Piero's painted architecture can be related to the primal-scene content of his *Annunciation*. The Virgin literally fills the space of the portico. Her voluminous proportions are at once a traditional Christian symbol of her role as the Church building and a projection of the child's view of parents as giants. The contrary character of light and shadow is echoed architecturally in the juxtaposition of the open door behind Mary and the closed door behind Gabriel. Unique to Piero's image is the organic quality of the column, whose shaft bulges at the sides, as if having entasis. Entasis, the Greek word for "stretching," however, is a feature of the Doric order only, whereas this column is a combination of Ionic and Corinthian.[17] Since Mary herself had been compared to a column (by Albertus Magnus),[18] its swelling is an architectural metaphor of her pregnancy.

Piero's *Annunciation* at the top of the Perugia Altarpiece [84] combines light and shadow with perspective in alluding to the primal scene. The Holy Ghost appears in a diagonal of light that hits the row of columns and casts shadows on the colonnade floor. The result is a pattern of alternating light and shadow read as directed toward the Virgin. Echoing the light and shadow architecturally is the configuration of alternating solids (the columns) and voids (the spaces between the columns). The colonnade itself, at the mathematical center of the picture, recedes into space and draws in the viewer's gaze. The orthogonal sides of the colonnade lead to the vanishing point on the solid marble wall at its far end. In the combination of the spatial corridor with the solid wall, Piero repeats architectural opposites—perspectival thrust on the one hand and its obstruction on the other—that allude to Mary's simultaneous receptivity and virginity. Like van Eyck, Piero synthesizes the painter's formal elements—light, dark, and perspective—with established theology and psychology.

In the Annunciation scene, the viewer, like the wolves of the Wolf-man, whose gaze is riveted by a sexual sight, is the outside observer. The Christian mystery of Incarnation is thereby "witnessed" by whoever looks

84. *Piero della Francesca,* Annunciation, *Perugia Altarpiece. Gabinetto Fotografico, Soprintendenza Gallerie, Florence.*

at the picture, although some versions of primal-scene iconography include a viewer as part of the image. In the sixteenth century, Titian painted several primal scenes, which are disguised as mythological seductions or abductions "watched" by a child.[19]

TITIAN'S PRIMAL SCENES

Titian's *Rape of Europa* [85] depicts Zeus in the guise of a white bull as he abducts a mortal girl, Europa. Her pose—as has been noted by several scholars—recalls the traditional reclining nude and thus has an erotic aspect. Although she is on the *back* of the bull, she grasps his horn to avoid falling. She is literally "carried away" by the beautiful bull who has abducted her from her friends. The latter wave excitedly from the distant shore.

The entire picture plane echoes the agitation of Europa's companions. The water is churned and foamy, the sky and mountains a shifting array of lights and darks. Above, two Cupids carrying the arrows of love fly in some disorder toward the amorous couple. Gazing directly at the seduction is the Cupid riding the dolphin; he is the mythological equivalent of the child riveted by the primal scene. His identification with it is clear from his pose, which echoes Europa's; he grasps the dolphin's fin as she grasps the horn. Cupid, too, is caught up in the excitement of the moment, as if "going along for the ride."

Following a pronounced diagonal of sight, Cupid stares at Europa's open legs, accented by the V-shaped arrangement of her drapery. The

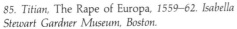

85. *Titian,* The Rape of Europa, *1559–62. Isabella Stewart Gardner Museum, Boston.*

outside observer is drawn into the picture plane by the vista of landscape as well as by the open legs of both Europa and the Cupid watching her. At the same time as the observer's gaze is pulled in by perspective and pose, it is countered by the returned stare of Zeus and the dolphin. Titian humorously evokes the ambivalent looking aroused by the primal scene; we are invited to see while also being seen, to stare and be stared at.

In the Greek myth of Danaë, Zeus, disguised as a shower of gold, seduces the future mother of Perseus. Titian painted three versions of this event, in which a nude Danaë reclines and languidly receives the gold from the sky. The myth conflates the unconscious fantasy that associates money and rain with male potency. Money and gold are literal sources of power, and rain (like the sun's rays) fertilizes the earth. In the unconscious, both money and rain have phallic character—note that in American law firms partners who make big money are called "rainmakers."

In two of Titian's versions of Danaë (in Vienna and Madrid), an old woman, Danaë's nurse, tries to intercept the gold with either a plate or her

86. Titian, Danaë with Cupid, *1545–46.*
Museo Capodimonte, Naples. Brogi 6905.

87. *Titian*, Bacchanal of the Andrians,
c. 1523–25. Prado, Madrid.

apron. In *Danaë with Cupid* of 1545–46 in Naples [86], a Cupid steals off
to the right, as if about to leave. But, expressing the child's ambivalence
in being a witness to the primal scene, he turns back and gazes at the source
of the gold. He looks up and back, and also bends over and starts forward.
In both versions, the old woman who witnesses the descending gold, in
contrast to the young and impressionable Cupid, is not in the least fazed
by the event. Well past her sexual prime, she has to be content with a
substitute for masculine attentions—in this case, gold.[20]

Titian depicted another typical childhood response to encountering
the primal scene in *Bacchanal of the Andrians* of c. 1523–25 [87]. According
to the Greek myth, Theseus deserted Ariadne after she had rescued him

88. *Attributed to Titian and his workshop,* Venus and Adonis, *c. 1560–65. National Gallery of Art, Washington, D.C. Widener Collection.*

from the labyrinth of King Minos on Crete. In Titian's picture, a reclining nude, probably Ariadne, has fallen asleep as Theseus departs by ship in the distance. The picture plane is filled with revelers, engaged in a bacchanalian orgy, which, in and of itself, has primal-scene implications. The dancing and drinking figures, and the presence of Silenus, evoke the sexual excitement sometimes experienced by young observers of the primal scene.

The little intruder in Titian's picture is the nude boy who stands still, raises his drapery, and urinates. In contrast to the rapid movements of the revelers, Ariadne is motionless and the boy nearly so. The latter, therefore, arrest our gaze, as the boy's is arrested by the sight of the nude. In urinating, he conflates excitement with one infantile explanation of the riddle of ejaculation.[21] (In the case of the Wolfman, for example, Freud found that urinating on the floor was an attempt to seduce a girl.[22]) The fact of Theseus's departure means, in the child's mind, that he becomes "the man of the family," taking on the simultaneously desired and dangerous role of the absent father.

A little Cupid hugs a dove in the National Gallery's (Washington, D.C.) *Venus and Adonis* [88] of c. 1560–65, attributed to Titian and his workshop. Cupid cowers under a tree as he watches his mother's efforts to seduce her reluctant younger lover. In this version of the primal scene, Venus is a rotated and assertive variation on the reclining nude. Cupid's anxiety is palpable here, in contrast to his ambivalent counterpart in Titian's *Danaë with Cupid*, or his eager counterpart riding the dolphin in *The Rape of Europa*.

In *Venus and Adonis*, Cupid's castration anxiety is intensified by direct oedipal competition—that is, his mother with a mortal youth, the reverse of Zeus with a mortal woman. In huddling with a dove, whose wing caresses his cheek, Cupid tries to mitigate the fear of castration by contact with the phallic bird. The bird symbolically reassures Cupid against two kinds of loss, that of his own phallus and the loss of his mother to a bigger competitor. The dove also comforts him at a distance from the anxiety-producing scene, and, in that role, the bird (which is an attribute of Venus) functions as a transitional object.

In these examples of primal-scene imagery, the content has an unmistakably oedipal character. In all cases, a god or goddess seduces a mortal; the former unconsciously represent the parents, and the latter, the child. In the Annunciation, God "the Father" impregnates Mary, a mortal descendant of the House of David. In the mythological loves of Zeus, the patriarchal "father of the gods" and ruler of Olympos unfailingly chooses mortal women who are otherwise faithful. As a result, they can be seduced only if their seducer is disguised. The disguise, in this context, serves the manifest narrative of the myth, but its latent content is oedipal; that is, it cloaks the father-daughter seduction in metaphor.

The mother's inevitable jealousy, which is not included in these images, is personified in the myths by the angry Hera. As the goddess of marriage, and Zeus's wife, Hera fights the forces of incestuous adultery to preserve the laws of the family. It is only in the myth of Venus and Adonis that the reverse oedipal situation—symbolically that of mother and son—is expressed. The power of these images, like the medieval motif of Mary as queen and Christ as the baby king, is their fulfillment of unconscious incestuous impulse through aesthetic form.

TO LOOK OR NOT TO LOOK:
TWO PAINTINGS BY ANDREA MANTEGNA

At some point during the 1460s and 1470s, Andrea Mantegna, like Piero and Titian an intensely psychological artist, worked in Mantua (see Chapter 3). He decorated a room, which has been called the ducal bedroom, in the Gonzaga palace.[23] Walls and ceiling are covered with illusionistic scenes of the duke's family, its courtiers, messengers and ambassadors, horses, dogs, and distant landscape. At the center of the ceiling, Mantegna painted a large trompe l'oeil oculus [89], through which one seems to look up, past a round balustrade, to open sky. As those below look up, their gaze is countered by a group of figures—of children and adults—who peer down as if at the inhabitants of the room.[24]

In this picture, Mantegna deals humorously with infantile sexual curiosity. The putti, or small nude boys, are engaged in playful looking. One is about to drop an apple, which, should it land, would certainly interrupt any ongoing sexual activity between the duke and duchess or, indeed, any formal state business being transacted. The apple, of course, alludes to the original primal scene—Adam and Eve's—which is recapitulated in the development of every child. The threat of the falling apple, the flowerpot precariously balanced on a narrow wooden beam, and the putto himself all seem to be spoiling for a fall. In so doing, these images evoke the anxiety of the viewer below and play on the sexual implications of the original Fall.

Although the putto with the apple is in a position to interrupt the implied primal scene below, other putti are not so much in control. Two of them have gotten their heads stuck in the holes at the side of the balustrade. Their expressions of outrage leave the viewer in no doubt about the dangers of sexual curiosity.

The motif of the head caught in a round hole is a witty displacement of castration anxiety. A related image occurs in Botticelli's Mars and Venus *[90], which Barolsky[25] has discussed as a primal scene after the fact. Mars is nude and asleep; Venus is clothed, sitting up, and in control. Botticelli's playful satyrs abscond with Mars's helmet and lance, indicating not the danger of looking, but of succumbing to a woman's charms. The phallic—and childlike— quality of the satyr in mythology reveals the meaning of the "satirical" image at the right. As Mantegna's putti thrust their heads through the holes of the balustrade, so Botticelli's satyr crawls through the circular opening of the war*

89. *Andrea Mantegna, Oculus, 1470s. Camera*
degli Sposi, Ducal Palace, Mantua.

90. Sandro Botticelli, Mars and Venus, *c. 1480.*
National Gallery, London.

god's breastplate, replicating the action of sexual intercourse. Reiterating the
action of his body in microcosm, the satyr sticks out his tongue, simulta-
neously making fun of the whole image and creating a visual metaphor of the
primal scene.

In the oculus, Mantegna depicts the dangers of sexual looking; in
Samson and Delilah [91] of c. 1500, he depicts the dangers of *not* looking.
Samson does not look because he is asleep; but his failure to "see" has
begun much earlier. In Judg. 16, Delilah, at the behest of her fellow
Philistines, persuades Samson to reveal the source of his superhuman
strength. When he does so, she has a man shave his head. Samson is then
captured and blinded by the Philistines. He is imprisoned and grinds a mill,
which, according to the Bible, is woman's work.[26]

In contrast to the playful oculus, Mantegna's *Samson and Delilah* is
based on a biblical text that lies within the tradition of the danger to a man
in being seduced by a woman. This tradition is heightened in the account
of Samson and Delilah by specific details that stand for castration in the
unconscious—namely, haircutting[27] and blinding. But Mantegna has enriched the biblical story with iconographic choices that enhance its psychological subtext.

Samson's pose evokes the motif of the reclining nude female. Delilah
destroys him herself, rather than have someone else do so, as happens in
the biblical account; in keeping with a predominant pictorial tradition, it is
she who administers the haircut. The symbolic castration, echoed visually
in the sawed-off tree branch,[28] is simultaneously denied by the multiplica-

tion of phallic imagery. This is the mechanism described by Freud in his short article "Medusa's Head,"[29] in which he explains the snakes as an upward displacement of the sight of the female genitals. The snaky hair, according to Freud, represents a multiplication of phallic symbols as "compensation" for the fantasy of castration. Likewise, in Mantegna's *Samson and Delilah*, the stream of water pouring from the rock into the basin and out again through a hole at the front of the basin suggests a resurgence of Samson's male potency. The rich foliage and abundant bunches of grapes also imply growth and fertility.

The grapes and the tree have other iconographic meanings as well, including the juxtaposition of life and death, salvation and sin, respectively. Samson is an Old Testament type for Christ, for both have been immacu-

91. *Andrea Mantegna,* Samson and Delilah, *c. 1500. National Gallery, London.*

lately conceived. The tree can be read as a "two-way" type, forward in time to the Cross, and back in time to the Tree of Knowledge. In referring to the Cross, the tree supports the grape vine, with its associations to Christ's blood and the wine of the Eucharist. To the degree that Mantegna's tree is a type for the Tree of Knowledge, the scene itself can be related to the site of the "original" primal scene in the Garden of Eden.

The implication of Mantegna's iconography, that Samson has fallen asleep in a drunken stupor (by reference to the grapes), transforms the grape into Samson's "forbidden fruit." Samson, according to the biblical text, was not allowed to drink wine; this restriction was one of the "payments" for his "divinely ordained role" in delivering the Jews from the Philistines.[30] The snakelike grape vine alludes to the dangerous woman, who is "seduced" by the serpent and then destroys the man, as Eve destroyed Adam. These parallels are confirmed by the Latin inscription on the tree trunk: "A bad woman is three times worse than the devil."

Because Samson failed to look, he misread Delilah and became her victim. He also lacked insight, as did Oedipus, and his impulsive lust "blinded" him to a dangerous reality. Once captured, Samson really *was* blinded—Oedipus blinded himself—and eventually killed himself, along with thousands of Philistines. The association of blindness with lack of insight and castration is as clear in the Samson story as in the Oedipus legend; Mantegna, like Piero, Botticelli, and Titian, understood the ambivalent implications of the narratives they were commissioned, or decided, to depict. Their mastery of the psychological subtexts of their imagery contributed to, and reflected, the humanist intellectual expansion of the Renaissance period.

REMBRANDT'S PRIMAL SCENE:
THE ARTIST AS GOD

Rembrandt's early-eighteenth-century Dutch biographer, Arnold Houbraken, recounts an anecdote in which the artist confronts a derivative of the primal scene, re-enacted by his students.[31] Rembrandt, according to Houbraken, rented a warehouse in Amsterdam to accommodate his many students. Each student had his own room so that he could draw from live models. One warm summer day, when a student took a female model to his room, the others became curious, removed their shoes to avoid being heard, and peered at the unsuspecting pair through a hole in the wall.[32] The art student and his model closed the door to the room, took off their clothes, and told each other jokes. Rembrandt arrived and observed the couple through the hole. He heard them say "Now we are exactly as Adam and Eve in paradise, for we are also naked." At this, Rembrandt knocked his *mahlstick* (painter's stick) against the door and terrified the young couple with " 'But because you are naked you must get out of Paradise.' " Having forced his pupil by threats to open the door, Houbraken says, Rembrandt entered. He "spoilt the Adam and Eve play, transformed comedy into tragedy, and drove away with blows the pretended Adam with his Eve, so that they were only just able, when running down the stairs, to put on part of their clothes, in order not to arrive naked in the street."[33]

In this dramatization of the primal scene, Rembrandt plays a triple role. At first he is like the child who observes, and listens to, a sexually charged encounter. When the couple compare themselves to Adam and Eve, Rembrandt becomes the outraged "God," banging on the door. The *mahlstick* is metaphorically transformed into the sword of the archangel Michael, who drives Adam and Eve from paradise. The dramatic quality of this episode resides in its pictorial character and its evocation of well-known paintings of the Expulsion of Adam and Eve. Houbraken's reference to the "play" of Adam and Eve is at once theatrical and psychological, for "comedy" becomes "tragedy" when adults, who are supposed to be working, play useless sexual games.[34]

Rembrandt recapitulates one line of artistic development in this anecdotal performance. He begins as the sexually curious child, joining his students in watching the couple. At the mention of Adam and Eve, Rembrandt is reminded of the search for knowledge—both sexual and artistic—on the part of the art student and his model. This very combination implies the gaze—also sexual as well as artistic—except that the student is "joking" and not painting. In being a "student," there is a potential for competition with the master, which is explicit in the allusion to Adam. By "joking," both student and model make light of Rembrandt's serious artistic enterprise, which further angers him. The artist is then transformed from the sexual viewer into the creator God and avenging angel.

CÉZANNE, PICASSO, AND THE PRIMAL SCENE

The primal scene and the general subject of sexual looking continue to inform works of art, especially visual images. Children often view the

92. *Paul Cézanne,* The Battle of Love (Bacchanal),
*c. 1880. National Gallery of Art, Washington, D.C.
Gift of the W. Averell Harriman Foundation in
memory of Marie N. Harriman.*

primal scene as an act of violence, imagining the male as the aggressor and
the female as the victim. This particular facet of primal-scene fantasy
appears in *The Battle of Love* [92], also called *Bacchanal*, of c. 1880, by
Cézanne. There is no documentation—which in any case would be extremely unusual—of Cézanne's actual exposure to the primal scene. That
he painted two versions of it (Venturi 379 and 380), however, confirms his
interest in the subject. As his titles suggest, Cézanne thought of the primal
scene as an orgiastic conflict.

Four couples are engaged in a form of hand-to-hand "single combat,"
which a dog observes from the lower right. Schapiro has identified the dog
as Black, a childhood companion of Cézanne and his friends, mentioned by

the artist in his letters.[35] The dog's excitement corresponds to that of the child who watches sexual activity between adults. Cézanne's attraction to the color black, which was predominant in his early pictures, has been associated with the name Black[36]; the dog, therefore, is a multivalent image, standing for Cézanne in the simultaneity of its color and name. Furthermore, young children readily identify with animals; hence their taste for stuffed animals and animal stories.[37] The totemism of childhood informs Cézanne's infantile self-image as the dog Black who views the violent sexual struggles in *The Battle of Love.*

The ambivalence of Cézanne's primal-scene fantasy is evident from his fear that a man risks danger from a woman as well as vice versa. This fear is revealed repeatedly in the artist's paintings and drawings of the Temptation of Saint Anthony. Even more explicit, however, is the poem entitled "Une Terrible Histoire," which Cézanne wrote on December 29, 1859, at the age of twenty.

In the poem, it is a summer night, when couples make love;[38] the author sees Satan and his devils in an approaching storm. Echoing the excitement of sexual passion is the distant sound of galloping horses. They arrive, pulling a carriage, and Cézanne hears a soft voice calling to him from within. He enters the carriage, where a beautiful woman awaits him. He kisses her and she turns into a hollow-eyed skeleton. The artist-poet turns cold and falls as the carriage collapses; probably, he concludes, he has broken his neck.

In this imagery, entering the carriage and confronting a woman who turns into death stands for the castrating dangers of sexual penetration. The woman, like Delilah, is not what she seems. In the Middle Ages, this view of women was exemplified by Frau Welt (Madame World), who was beautiful from the front, but grotesque from the back.[39]

Cézanne's poem takes place at night, in the dark, and therefore when vision is muted. What predominates are sounds and movements, followed by the woman's invitation. Motion is arrested when the artist turns cold, or freezes. At that point, he falls and breaks his neck, a condensation of being feminized (the fallen woman) and castrated (by means of upward displacement).

Picasso's imagery includes numerous versions of primal-scene observation and a wide variety of "watchers."[40] Two of his most powerful examples of primal-scene imagery—namely, the *Minotauromachy* [93] and *Guernica* [94]—were recognized as such by Daniel Schneider in 1950.[41]

93. Pablo Picasso, Minotauromachy, 1935. Art
Institute of Chicago. Gift of Mrs. P. Donnelley,
1947.160.

94. Pablo Picasso, Guernica, 1937. Prado, Madrid.

Scholarly art-historical responses to Schneider's interpretation have been by and large negative.[42] However, in the light of the primal-scene imagery discussed above, it seems that a reconsideration of Schneider's view is called for.

To begin with, *Minotauromachy*. Coming apparently from the water on the right, a powerful Minotaur approaches a staggering, disemboweled horse. A female matador has fallen across the horse's back; her sword is ambiguously depicted so that it is not clear whether she or the Minotaur holds it. The Minotaur extends his other arm as if to block out something, possibly the light carried by the little girl with flowers, or to prevent the two women in the window above from seeing the horse. At the far left, a bearded man climbs a ladder and turns back to look at the scene.

According to Schneider,[43] the girl is Picasso as a child, and the bearded man is Picasso the artist, escaping from the scene and also acknowledging his genius in seeing and depicting. The encounter between Minotaur and horse represents "reduplication symbols portraying aspects of the sexual act as it might be conceived by a child."[44] The sea, Schneider argues, suggests the Rape of Europa, and the tear in the horse's side is a child's sadistic fantasy of birth. *Guernica*, he concludes, is related to the *Minotauromachy* on a political level as the "rape of a nation."

Two discussions of *Guernica*, by Rudolf Arnheim[45] and Otto Brendel,[46] both published in the early 1960s, have bearing on the psychoanalytic reading of its imagery. They also reflect two opposing methodological approaches to works of art. Arnheim criticizes Schneider for "confusing the interpretation of art with speculations about the psychology of the artist and describing the work as a portrait of the artist's private wishes and conflicts."[47] This position recalls the traditional art-historical view that the artist and the work are psychologically unrelated. But Arnheim waffles on this point and turns it into a matter of emphasis. Although admitting that Picasso's imagery may have psychological implications, Arnheim takes a strong stand against giving them too much weight. "They cannot be made to monopolize their meanings without causing total disfigurement," he writes. "Therefore, in choosing the appropriate level of interpretation, we must be guided by the work of art itself."[48]

Arnheim's argument reflects a particularly unpsychological view of art, for the assumption of an "appropriate level of interpretation" downplays the principles of multideterminism and overdetermination. It also tilts in the direction of censorship. One wonders whether historical, theological, or formal readings of art would be pronounced "inappropriate" as readily as the psychological readings.

Brendel's essay on *Guernica,* on the other hand, approaches Picasso's imagery from the vantage point of the classicist aware of complex, dynamic factors that converge in great works of art. From the outset, Brendel recognizes that *Guernica*'s apparently incongruous details and "terrifying imagery" are dreamlike.[49] Their sense, according to Brendel, lies in their relation to one another, in their juxtaposition in space, not in their literal manifest content. He agrees with Schneider that Picasso's horse is associated with the feminine and that the *Minotauromachy* etching has a bearing on *Guernica.* Nevertheless, Brendel does not propose a psychoanalytic reading of *Guernica;* rather, his approach is, first and foremost, that of a classicist, but at the same time is consistent with psychoanalysis.

All the victims in *Guernica,* Brendel notes,[50] are women, the only exception being the fallen warrior. His angular forms and detached limbs, however, suggest a relation to plaster casts, which endows him with a different character from that of the other, more organic, human figures in the painting. Brendel does not elaborate on this observation, but, if he is correct, it is possible that the fallen warrior—a subject of Hellenistic sculpture—represents the death and destruction of tradition in the arts. The association to plaster casts evokes the tradition of academic training that Picasso surely had to topple in order to achieve the full expression of his genius.[51]

Finally, Brendel identifies the woman with the lamp as an onlooker and compares her to the Greek chorus.[52] In a sense, the Greek chorus functions as a transition between the principal characters of a drama and the audience. The members of the chorus comment on, and react to, an unfolding narrative. Likewise, Picasso's woman with the lamp, as well as the little girl in the *Minotauromachy,* forms a transition between the viewer and the object of her own gaze.[53]

The more recent analysis of these works, by Mary Gedo, is biographical; her data, however, are actually quite consistent with a latent primal-scene content. *Guernica,* she points out, was not a fixed conception in advance, because the preparatory drawings show an iconographic evolution.[54] Nevertheless, three elements were included from the first study and retained in the final painting—the bull, the dying horse, and the woman with the lamp.[55] The constant elements, therefore, turn out to be the required cast for a primal scene. The other iconographic features and their varying locations shifted in the course of the drawings; but the constancy of the primal scene and its central position in the finished product reveal its significance for Picasso.

Schneider's view is at once mythical and based on the psychic role of primal fantasy. In that approach, his emphasis differs from Gedo's, whose biographical allusions are to specific events—the earthquake in Málaga and the birth of Picasso's sister when the artist was three, and his relationships with his wife and mistress in 1935–37.[56] Such events may well be linked to Picasso's iconography, and probably are; but they are in the category of "precipitating factors," and do not account for the mythic, primal power of Picasso's images. The Minotaur and the *Guernica* bull combine the artist's self-image as a Minotaur,[57] allusions to Spain and its political perversion by the rule of Franco, with early childhood memories of his father taking him to bullfights. The horse, in the process of being destroyed in both works, is a victim of violence. And in both the *Minotauromachy* and *Guernica*, a female figure with a lamp enters the central space.

Schneider's reference to the Rape of Europa is particularly convincing if one recalls Titian's painting of that event. For, in the *Minotauromachy* as well as in the Titian, a woman reclines on the back of an animal—a horse and a bull, respectively. The darkness made by condensed cross-hatching that pervades the etching and its interruption by the girl's light situates the event at night and places the girl in the role of nocturnal investigator. Her relative stillness highlights the arrest of her gaze, which, like ours, is focused on the energetic movements of horse, matador, and Minotaur. The two women at the window watching the doves, or "love birds," echo those who observe the violent primal scene below. The man climbing the ladder is an expression of ambivalence—rather like the Cupid in Titian's *Danaë* in Naples; both figures are engaged in what is popularly referred to as "coming and going at the same time." Both are looking and running, as if afraid to be caught looking and yet impelled to do so. Arrest and movement thus coexist in the image of a single figure.

The *Minotauromachy* merges personal with classical mythology. In *Guernica*, which was intended as a monumental and international political statement, Picasso has expanded the mythic dimension and subsumed the personal to it. In addition to the three basic primal-scene characters, the painting includes the falling woman on the right with upraised arms, the fallen warrior, the mother with a dead child, and the Minotaur, whose human quality is only faintly suggested by the uncanny flattening of the face. Both the running woman in the foreground and the woman with the lamp are more generalized than the little girl of the etching. None of

95. *Pablo Picasso*, Sixth Sketch of May 1, 1937.
Prado, Madrid.

the *Guernica* figures, in fact, convey any suggestion of portraiture, as do the
girl and the bearded man in the *Minotauromachy*.

As Gedo and others[58] have noted, the preliminary drawings for
Guernica contain several identifiable personal references. One, in particular,
confirms the relation of the wounded horse to the trauma of birth—namely
the sixth sketch of May 1, 1937 [95]. In that image, the horse gives birth
to Pegasus, a baby "flying" horse. Herschel Chipp has related this detail to
the birth of Picasso's illegitimate daughter Maya and his desertion of her
mother, Marie-Thérèse.[59] Gedo generally explains *Guernica* as a reference
to the Málaga earthquake and the birth of Picasso's sister. Picasso's wish
to suppress the meaning of Pegasus, however, is confirmed by its elimina-
tion from subsequent studies and from the finished mural.

If considered in the context of primal-scene investigation, which
Gedo does not discuss, the Pegasus drawing has additional significance.
The child's instinct to solve the riddle of his own origins and birth is

96. Pablo Picasso, Second Sketch of May 1, 1937.
Prado, Madrid.

primary, although it is often set in motion by the birth of a sibling. Despite the sadistic component of Picasso's primal-scene fantasy, in which the father (the bull and/or Minotaur) inflicts damage on the mother (the horse and/or the female matador), in the sixth sketch of May 1, the bull is rather docile. He looks bemused and confused. The horse is in the process of giving birth to Pegasus, who flies (is born) from the opening in her side. (In the only other representation of Pegasus in the *Guernica* drawings, the second sketch of May 1 [96], the little horse is already born and perches on the back of the bull. In the first sketch, an unidentified winged creature, either a bird or a preliminary Pegasus, is drawn on the back of the horse. The sketchy quality of the drawing makes the image ambiguous.)

"Pegasus," given the unconscious tendency to engage in word consonance, could stand for "Picasso." (In Spanish, the second syllable of both "Pegasus" and "Picasso" is accented.) The little Picasso-Pegasus actually has an easy birth, compared with the aggressive imagery of *Guernica* and the other preliminary drawings. The winged horse escapes having to be torn from its mother's body by virtue of its ability to fly. This, then, can be read as Picasso's idealized view of his own entry into the world, with all the attendant ambitious, spiritual, and sexual allusions of flight. It also serves to repair the fantasy of his mother's having suffered physical damage in giving birth. Pegasus is, of course, a boy—so that to the extent that *Guernica* contains birth references, they are primarily his own and only secondarily those of his sister or daughter.

The sequence of the two Pegasus drawings is also significant, for the birth drawing (sixth sketch of May 1) *follows* the version (second sketch of May 1) in which the winged horse is on the back of the bull. In the former drawing, Picasso-Pegasus is already born, and "riding his father's back." He also surpasses him—not in size, but in being "higher up" and winged. The sixth drawing of May 1 answers the riddle of how Picasso-Pegasus arrived at his location in the second drawing. In the sequence of sketches, therefore, Picasso first posed the question and then answered it.

Finally, there is another, mythological aspect to the iconography of Pegasus in Picasso's *Guernica* drawings. The birth of Pegasus identifies the horse as Medusa, which evokes Picasso's psychological detachment from his mother[60] and his avoidance of depicting her frontally (that is, not gazing at her directly).

According to Greek myth, Pegasus and his brother Chrysaor were born from the blood of Medusa's neck when Perseus beheaded her. This event suggests Picasso's unconscious association of birth with castration (represented as decapitation in the death of Medusa). Since "Chrysaor" is Greek for "golden sword," one must wonder whether the dead warrior prominently depicted in this sketch and retained in the mural does not include a reference to Medusa's human son. If so, then he and Pegasus can be read as two aspects of the artist—his human and his "divine" personae. Through his death, the human Chrysaor gives way to divinity and flight, with which, as we have seen, many artists identify. These hidden meanings of the drawings invite further considerations on the iconography and psychological significance of *Guernica*—which I will refrain from pursuing here. Suffice it to say that the dead warrior is a complex, overdetermined motif containing multiple personal, artistic, and mythological significance.

PLATO, LEONARDO, AND DUCHAMP:
THE PRIMAL SCENE AS ANDROGYNE

In Plato's *Symposium* (190–191), the comic poet Aristophanes describes his notion of primeval humans as follows. Instead of two sexes, as there are now, there were originally three—male, female, and the "androgyne," or combination of male and female. The androgyne had a round shape, with four hands and four feet, and one head with two faces. It walked equally well in either direction and rolled over, like an acrobat, when it wanted to go very fast. It was strong and arrogant, and attacked the Olympian gods.

Rather than destroy the androgynes for their hubris, Zeus decided to cut them in half. Once split into male and female, Zeus reasoned, the former androgynes could continue to worship the gods, but they would walk only upright and be more manageable. And, if they persisted in their insolence, Zeus threatened, he would halve them again and they would hop around on a single leg. Ever since, according to Aristophanes, one half of the original androgyne seeks completion by rejoining with the other half and recovering its primal nature.

Aristophanes' identification of three types of humans indicates that individual males and females correspond to the reality of sexual distinction. The androgyne, on the other hand, corresponds to the "canonical" image of sexual intercourse; as such, it is related to Shakespeare's "beast with two backs."[61] A viewer would see the torsos combined, as described by Aristophanes, with four arms and legs. Only the position of the heads would be different. The movements that the viewer sees likewise account for the speed of the androgyne when it wants to go "fast."

Taking an example from the work of Leonardo and Duchamp, both of whom had rich, bisexual fantasy lives, I propose to read two images as reflecting the "androgynous" view of the primal scene. The first is the motif of the near end of the sarcophagus in Leonardo's *Annunciation*[62] of c. 1470 [97]; it faces the picture plane and therefore arrests the viewer's gaze. Theologically, the presence of the sarcophagus alludes to Christ's death at the very moment of his conception, evoking Mary's combined role as womb and tomb described by Saint Augustine. The scallop shell carved in relief on its surface is a traditional reference in Christian art to resurrection and rebirth. In popular folklore, it symbolizes both the vulva, because of its shape,[63] and the *vagina dentata*, because of its perforated edges.[64] These associations, combined with the shell's relation to the sea, led to its metaphorical role as the "uterus of the sea."[65] This, in turn, is consistent with

97. *Leonardo da Vinci,* Annunciation, *c. 1470.
Uffizi, Florence. Gabinetto Fotografico,
Soprintendenza Beni Artistici e Storici di Firenze,
Florence.*

the birth and rebirth iconography of the Annunciation and Mary's designation as "Star of the Sea."

The end of the sarcophagus can be read as a visual metaphor of the lower half of a body, for it stands on lion's feet. They echo the slightly turned-out posture of Mary's feet, and frame the "vaginal" scallop shell. Since the lion—or "Leo"—was Leonardo's name, and the significance of names was a particular feature of Renaissance culture, I read the ensemble as the artist's bisexual self-image. As such it evokes the alchemical androgyne, known in the Renaissance and certainly to Leonardo, who practiced alchemy. Leonardo's female identification with Mary and male identification with the lion is condensed into a disguised metaphor of the primal androgyne.

While Leonardo's sarcophagus juxtaposes male legs with symbolic female genitalia, Duchamp adds male features to a female face in *L.H.O.O.Q.* [63]. Both works are related to the androgyne by their combination of male and female characteristics, and both face the viewer. Duchamp's iconography, like Leonardo's, has alchemical significance, particularly as regards the bisexuality of the creator/artist.[66] The alchemical belief in the androgyne and the search for that divine state is consistent with Jung's view that psychic integration is necessary for the development of a whole self. The self, according to Jung, is achieved by a synthesis of animus and anima, or the male principle in the female and the female principle in the male, respectively.[67]

This notion parallels Freud's conviction that the bedrock of every neurosis resides in bisexual conflict—the man's unconscious wish to be a woman and the woman's to be a man. At the same time, the "archetypal bisexuality of the creator" evokes the child's family-romance view of the parents as gods and endows the ideal resolution of bisexual conflict in the alchemical androgyne with the character of a primal scene.

Duchamp's title, *L.H.O.O.Q.*, quite literally invites comparisons between gazing at a picture and the sight of something sexual. Duchamp instructs the viewer to LOOK at the world's most famous image and to discover its bisexuality. His androgyne, like the original *Mona Lisa*, obligingly returns the viewer's gaze.

NOTES

1. For a methodological discussion of psychoanalytic readings of literary texts, see Francis Baudry, "An Essay on Method in Applied Psychoanalysis," *Psychoanalytic Quarterly* LIII (1984): 551–81.
2. Freud, S. E. XVII, 1918, pp. 3–122.
3. Freud, S. E. V, 1900, p. 585.
4. J. Laplanche and J.-B. Pontalis, *The Language of Psychoanalysis*, New York, 1973, p. 332, note that the primal fantasies consist of the primal scene, castration, and seduction, and that "all are related to origins. Like collective myths, they claim to provide a representation of and a 'solution' to whatever constitutes a major enigma for the child."
5. Ibid.
6. Freud, S. E. XVII, p. 29. For a discussion of this dream in relation to Ingres and Picasso, see Richard Wollheim, *Painting as an Art*, Princeton, 1987, Chapter 5.
7. Cf. Ernest Jones, "The Madonna's Conception through the Ear," in Jones, *Essays in Applied Psychoanalysis*, vol. 2, New York, 1964, pp. 266–357. as above.
8. Crockett Johnson, *Barnaby*, New York, 1975.
9. Jones, "The Madonna's Conception."
10. Millard Meiss, "Light as Form and Symbol in Some Fifteenth-Century Paintings" (1945), in his *The Painter's Choice*, New York, 1976.
11. Ibid., pp. 5–6.
12. Ibid., pp. 6–7.
13. Ibid.
14. Cf. Gaston Bachelard, *La Psychanalyse du feu*, Paris, 1949, and Jacob A. Arlow, "Pyromania and the Primal Scene: a Psychoanalytic Comment on the Work of Yukio Mishima," *Psychoanalytic Quarterly* 47 (1978): 24–51.
15. The motif of the shadow and its allusion to impregnation in this picture has been a staple of Howard McP. Davis's lectures on Italian Renaissance art at Columbia University.
16. For additional references see Laurie Schneider, "Shadow Metaphors and Piero della

Francesca's Arezzo *Annunciation*," Source: *Notes in the History of Art* V, no. 1 (Fall 1985): 18–22.

17. This motif and its meaning were originally noted by Howard McP. Davis.

18. Cited in Eugenio Battisti, *Piero della Francesca*, vol. I, Milan, 1971, p. 83, fn. 112.

19. For a discussion of the literary sources of Titian's mythological paintings for Philip II of Spain, see Jane Clinton Nash, *Titian's "Poésie" for Philip II*, Baltimore, 1986.

20. For the primal-scene significance of gold-as-phallus, see Gregory Stragnell, "The Golden Phallus," *Psychoanalytic Review* XI (1924): 292–323.

21. Freud, S. E. V, 1900, p. 403, fn. 1.

22. Freud, S. E. XVII, p. 93; also pp. 81, 96. Cf. also "A Child Is Being Beaten," S. E. XVII, 1919, pp. 177–204, p. 188.

23. According to Ronald Lightbown, *Mantegna*, Berkeley and London, 1986, p. 99, this room was originally called *camera picta* or *camera depinta*, meaning painted chamber. Such rooms, typical in important fourteenth- and fifteenth-century European palaces, were official state-chambers. As such, they served at once as "a bedroom, a sitting-room where the family met together with its privy courtiers, waiting-women and attendants. . . . To the notions of the age, the presence of a state bed and use as a bedroom in no way precluded these functions." For this reference, I am indebted to Mark Zucker.

24. Cf. Paul Barolsky, *Infinite Jest*, Columbia, S.C. and London, 1978, pp. 24–31.

25. Ibid., pp. 37–50. A more specific comment on Mantegna's oculus is the motif of the urinating boy on the ceiling of the Palazzo del Te, also in Mantua. The psychology of that motif is consistent with the boy raising his drapery in Titian's *Bacchanal of the Andrians* and with Freud's finding that urination is a typical childhood response to the sexual excitement aroused by witnessing a primal scene.

26. See Madlyn Kahr, "Delilah," *Art Bulletin* LIV, no. 3 (September 1972): 282–99.

27. Cf. Freud, S. E. V, 1900, pp. 366–67.

28. Kahr, "Delilah."

29. Freud, S. E. XVIII, 1940, p. 273.

30. Kahr, "Delilah," p. 282.

31. See Tancred Borenius, *Rembrandt: Selected Paintings*, London, 1942, p. 24. For this reference, I am indebted to Richard Leslie.

32. Cf. Karl Abraham, "Restrictions and Transformations of Scopophilia in Psycho-Neurotics; with Remarks on Analogous Phenomena in Folk-Psychology" (1913), in his *Selected Papers on Psychoanalysis*, New York, reprint of 1927 edition, Chapter IX.

33. Houbraken in Borenius, *Rembrandt*, p. 24.

34. On the literal theatricality of this incident, see Svetlana Alpers, *Rembrandt's Enterprise*, Chicago and London, 1988, Chapter 2.

35. Meyer Schapiro, *Modern Art: 19th and 20th Centuries*, New York, 1978, p. 10.

36. Sidney Geist, "What Makes the Black Clock Run?" *Art International* 22, no. 2 (1978): 12.

37. The so-called Blackie Tests are modern psychological projective tests in which children are asked to talk about narratives illustrated with dogs rather than people as the main characters. They have been devised in response to the totemistic nature of childhood identification.

38. For the complete text of the poem see John Rewald, ed., *Paul Cézanne: Letters*, London, 1941, pp. 299–301.

39. Cf. Wolfgang Stammler, *Frau Welt: Eine Mittelalterliche Allegorie*, Freiburg, 1959.

40. Leo Steinberg, "Picasso's Sleepwatchers" (1968), in *Other Criteria*, New York and London, 1972, Chapters 4 and 6.

41. Daniel E. Schneider, *The Psychoanalyst and the Artist*, New York, 1950.

42. For example, Rudolf Arnheim, *Picasso's Guernica: The Genesis of a Painting*, Berkeley, 1962, p. 17, and Mary Gedo, *Picasso: Art as Autobiography*, Chicago and London, 1980. Cf. also Jack Spector, "The State of Psychoanalytic Research in Art History," *Art Bulletin* LXX (March 1988): 56 and fn. 36.

43. Schneider, p. 216.

44. Ibid.

45. Arnheim, *Picasso's Guernica*.

46. Otto J. Brendel, "Classic and Non-Classic Elements in Picasso's *Guernica*," in Whitney J. Oates, ed., *The Present-day Vitality of the Classical Tradition from Sophocles to Picasso*, Bloomington, 1961.

47. Arnheim, *Picasso's Guernica*.

48. Ibid., p. 17.

49. Brendel, "Classic and Non-Classic Elements in Picasso's *Guernica*," pp. 127–28.

50. Ibid., p. 140.

51. For a related view of Picasso and tradition applied to the *Demoiselles d'Avignon*, cf. Ive-Alain Bois, "Painting as Trauma," *Art in America* 76 (June 1988): 138.

52. Brendel, "Classic and Non-Classic Elements in Picasso's *Guernica*," p. 137.

53. In the *Demoiselles d'Avignon*, Picasso eliminated the transitional onlookers, who had been included in preliminary drawings; these were a sailor and a "medical student," who, like the girl and the woman with the lamp, represent Picasso himself. By deleting the two men, Picasso increased the impact of the image, forcing the viewer to confront the brothel directly.

54. Mary Gedo, *Picasso*, p. 177.

55. Ibid. The consistent appearance of these characters had been previously noted by Brendel, "Classic and Non-Classic Elements in Picasso's *Guernica*," p. 129, who also includes the fallen warrior in the original cast.

56. Mary Gedo, *Picasso*, pp. 177–78.

57. Steinberg, "Picasso's Sleepwatchers," p. 100.

58. Cf. Herschel Chipp, "*Guernica*: Love, War and the Bullfight," *Art Journal* 33, no. 2 (Winter 1973–74): 51.

59. Ibid., p. 55.

60. Cf. Gedo, *Picasso*, p. 21 passim on Picasso's detachment from his mother.

61. Cf. *Othello*, Act I, scene i, lines 116–17: ". . . your daughter and the Moor are now making the beast with two backs."

62. Cf. Laurie Schneider and Jack Flam, "Vision Convention, Simile and Metaphor in the *Mona Lisa*," *Storia dell'Arte*, no. 29 (1977): 15–24.

63. A. A. Barb, "Diva Matrix," *Journal of the Warburg and Courtauld Institutes* XVI (1953): 204.

64. Ibid., fn. 184, and *Funk and Wagnalls Standard Dictionary of Folklore*, vol. II, 1950, p. 1152. For further discussion of this motif, see Erich Neumann, *The Great Mother*, New York, 1965, pp. 168–69.

65. Barb, "Diva Matrix," p. 205.

66. Cf. Arturo Schwarz, *The Complete Works of Marcel Duchamp*, New York, 1969, and "The Alchemist Stripped Bare in the Bachelor, Even," in Anne d'Harnoncourt and Kynaston McShine, eds., *Marcel Duchamp*, Philadelphia and New York, 1973, pp. 81–98.

67. Schwarz, "The Alchemist Stripped Bare," in d'Harnoncourt and McShine, eds., *Marcel Duchamp*, p. 83, and Carl G. Jung, *Psychology and Alchemy* (1944), in *Collected Works*, vol. XII, New York, 1953.

TEN

Biography, Autobiography, and Psychobiography

P sychobiography can uncover personal links between artists and their work; it can also provide insights into relationships between individuals and their cultural context that influence their art. This chapter offers some approaches to reading imagery in terms of its biographical significance. To this end, various literary sources, whether anecdotal, archival, biographical, or autobiographical, supplement, or reinforce, visual reading.

In antiquity, biographical references to artists such as Daedalus and Pygmalion are mythic; references to historical artists tend to be anecdotal or fragmentary. From the pre-Christian Roman period through the Middle Ages, artists' biographies are virtually nonexistent. With the Christianization of the West, biographical references to artists seem to have been superseded by the lives and legends of the saints, who took on many qualities formerly attributed to artists. The saints' miracles supplanted artistic "miracles," such as the creation of sculptures that walk and talk, illusionistic paintings, and certain monumental architecture. Similar conventions—both Christ and Michelangelo, for example, were born "under a star"—relate saints as well as gods to artists.

The role of art as a mirror, or "ape," of nature was also incorporated into Early Christian and medieval hagiography. The proliferation of *Speculums*, or *Mirrors*, paralleling aspects of the natural world with the divine world, expressed the view that present reality would have a more perfect counterpart in a future time. The Virgin Mary became a "spotless mirror," an exemplary image held up as an inspiration to "imperfect" real women. Christ became an "example," followed by the saints, most notably by Saint Francis, who consciously led his life "in imitation of Christ."

During the fourteenth century, with the classical revival in Italy, an interest in individual artists begins to emerge in the literary texts.[1] By the sixteenth century, when Vasari wrote the *Lives,* the genre of artists' biography had become well established. As Renaissance artists reclaimed their individuality, autobiography also developed. The literary range of biography and autobiography of artists is, by now, quite extensive. It includes recollections (Leonardo's screen memory), letters (van Gogh), journals (Delacroix), memoirs (Françoise Gilot on Picasso), recorded interviews, films and videos of artists at work, and so forth.

Visual artists, however, express themselves primarily in imagery and only secondarily in words. Their most "truthful" autobiographical statements are their images. To this point, it has been suggested that an individual work of art can be likened to a short story, or a chapter in an artist's life. The oeuvre as a whole then "adds up" to a larger text, comprising the artist's creative biography.[2] Insofar as one can "read," or deconstruct, the artist's imagery, it is possible to arrive at its personal as well as its cultural and historical sources.

In many cases these sources are interrelated. For example, in van Gogh's 1887 *Portrait of Père Tanguy* [98], what the artist says about his subject reveals even more about himself. Julien Tanguy, in whose paint shop in Paris artists liked to congregate, had a rebellious, antisocial nature with which van Gogh identified. Tanguy helped van Gogh by selling him paint on credit and exhibiting his pictures in his shop window. Indeed, van Gogh depicts Tanguy as a benevolent "father"; in contrast to the artist's dour, strict, clerical father, Tanguy is enlivened by bright colors and thick, energetic brush strokes.

Van Gogh refers to the dealer's close association with the Impressionists by surrounding him with Japanese prints. Tanguy's frontality aligns him formally with the prints on the wall, and his pose evokes the contented wisdom of a Buddha, whom van Gogh associated with Christ.[3] This synthesis of East and West in Tanguy's image reflects the influence of Eastern woodblock prints on Impressionism. Van Gogh's own identification with the Far East is evident in the 1888 self-portrait as a Buddhist monk, entitled *Worshiper of the Eternal Buddha,* in the Fogg Museum.

As a sympathetic paternal figure, Tanguy participates in the artist's family romance. By reference to Buddha, van Gogh symbolically elevates Tanguy above his real position as a shopkeeper, associating both Tanguy and his father with divinity. Van Gogh's continual and unsuccessful struggle to identify with his father is reflected in his imagery. He failed in his

98. Vincent van Gogh,
Père Tanguy, 1887.
Rodin Museum, Paris.

attempt to follow his father into the ministry, nor did he marry and have children, as his father did. Père Tanguy is depicted as benevolent and warm, as van Gogh's father was not. Elsewhere, van Gogh represents himself as Christ or Buddha and paints halos of light, sometimes as yellow suns, around figures that can stand singly or simultaneously for himself and his father.

ARTISTS ON ART AND ARTISTS

When artists use visual images to comment on art—especially the art of the past—they are situating themselves within an "artistic" lineage. They are also making autobiographical statements. This offers another method for exploring artists' biographies. Goya, for example, painted the *Family of Charles IV* [99] in 1800 to refer to *Las Meninas* [100] and satirize three generations of Spanish royalty. He is at once identifying with his illustrious seventeenth-century predecessor as the court painter of Spain and also "hiding" his association with a personally unattractive family. Whereas Velázquez proudly occupies the foreground of *Las Meninas,* on the same plane as the infanta, Goya's image is nearly lost in the shadowy background.

In Picasso's August 17, 1957 version of *Las Meninas, After Velázquez* [101], on the other hand, the artist is enlarged, illuminated, and prominently wearing the cross of the aristocratic Order of Santiago. The royal family and its entourage are diminished, either by their smaller size, or minimal delineation. Picasso's relation to Velázquez in this version of *Las Meninas* is more assertive than Goya's; he has literally become a giant painter in

99. *Francisco José de Goya,* Family of Charles IV,
1800. Prado, Madrid.

100. Diego Velázquez, Las Meninas, 1656. Prado, Madrid.

contrast to Goya, who retires into darkness. As autobiographical statements, these images are consistent with the two artists and their intensely psychological iconography. Goya's art reveals inner states of being by subtle formal means—shadow, linear tension, and dramatic contrasts of light, dark, and color. Picasso's psychological intent is not less subtle, but it is bolder in its externalization.

The Mona Lisa, like *Las Meninas,* is an icon of Western art; both have evoked visual commentary from many artists. When Duchamp transformed a reproduction of Mona Lisa into a bearded and mustachioed lady, he was responding to Leonardo's bisexuality and also to his own. Duchamp externalized his alter ego as a woman in the persona of Rrose Sélavy (a pun on "C'est la vie," meaning "That's life"), who embodied the female principle in several forms.

Duchamp, wearing women's clothes, was photographed as Rrose and appeared as such on the label of his Belle Haleine perfume bottle. *Belle*

101. *Pablo Picasso,* Las Meninas, After Velázquez,
August 17, 1957. *Museo Picasso, Barcelona.*

Haleine literally means "Beautiful Breath," but refers by consonance of sound to "Beautiful Helen." The latter evokes Helen of Troy, whose face launched the proverbial "thousand ships," and "destroyed" thousands of men. The latent content of Duchamp's pun thus includes the dangers as well as the sensory pleasures resulting from a man's attraction to female beauty. Although endowed with a beautiful scent, Duchamp implies, Belle Haleine is also a deadly force. An important aspect of Belle Haleine's dangerous potential is her phallic character; she is, in fact, Duchamp in drag.[4]

For the January 1938 International Surrealist Exhibition at the Paris Galerie des Beaux-Arts, Duchamp created a variation on the Readymade-aided, in which he dressed a female mannequin entitled *Rrose Sélavy* in his own hat and coat. In so doing, Duchamp became a Dada version of Pygmalion, and the mannequin, his Dadaist Galatea. (In 1973, the homosexual cult figure of the New York Pop movement, Andy Warhol, contributed to a "Collective Portrait of Marcel Duchamp" by photographing a group of men in drag, which he called *For Rrose Sélavy and Belle Haleine*."[5])

Bisexuality, for Duchamp, had many levels of meaning. It was the archetypal, alchemical androgyne, with the attendant mythical implications of sacred marriage *(hieros gamos)*. It was also consistent with ancient conventions equating artists with gods and the view that the original creator was a bisexual being—a mother and father simultaneously. Psychobiographically, however, Duchamp's preoccupation with the union of male and female revealed in *L.H.O.O.Q.* has been traced to his desire to merge incestuously with his sister Suzanne.[6] The elaborate alchemical associations inherent in his iconography, the implications of the "sacred marriage," and the ideal androgyne can thus be read as metaphors for Duchamp's unconscious incestuous attachment to Suzanne.[7]

VASARI ON PARMIGIANINO

Anecdotes about artists have long been recognized as containing psychological, if not literal, truth. They can also, on occasion, be shown to contain artistic truth. Vasari's *Lives* are particularly rich in anecdotal material that, more often than not, is consistent with an artist's work as well as with his psychology.

Born in Parma, Girolamo Francesco Maria Mazzuoli, called Parmigianino (1503–1540),[8] had so much talent that Raphael's soul was said to have entered his body. Parmigianino's father died early, and the boy was raised by two uncles, who were painters. They soon recognized their nephew's talent and, according to Vasari,[9] "on the one hand they urged him on, and on the other, fearing lest overmuch study might perchance spoil his health, they would sometimes hold him back." This attitude, which might seem to be straightforward avuncular concern for a child prodigy, has a latent content that prefigures the artist's eventual psychotic split.

The ambivalent attitude of Parmigianino's uncles recurs in the artist's ambivalence toward painting. Vasari says that he began to slow down his work on the vault frescoes in Parma's Church of Santa Maria della Steccata. He did so, according to Vasari, because "he had begun to study the problems of alchemy, . . . thinking that he would become rich quicker by congealing mercury."[10] So intense was his obsession that he changed into an "eccentric," "melancholy," "unkempt savage." He died of a fever at the age of thirty-seven, and was buried naked, at his own request, with a cypress cross "upright on his breast."[11]

If these circumstances are considered psychologically, the two uncles correspond to the mental image of a split parent—in this case Parmigianino's dead father, for whom his two uncles were substitutes; Vasari does not mention the artist's mother. In wavering between art and alchemy, Parmigianino repeated the uncles' shift between encouraging and discouraging his artistic activity. Unlike Duchamp, who sublimated his bisexuality by integrating it with his creative wit, Parmigianino *disinte*grated and became obsessed with the unreality of alchemy. The nature of his burial reveals Parmigianino's masochistic feminine identification with Christ's suffering and helpless nakedness. On an even deeper level, it is possible that Parmigianino also identified with his lost, or absent, mother by becoming female himself.[12]

Vasari leaves his readers in no doubt about his disappointment in Parmigianino. The author of the *Lives* had the highest regard for genius and did not like to see it misused. Had he not dishonored his talent, according to Vasari, Parmigianino "would have been without an equal, and truly unique in the art of painting." Instead, however, "by searching for that which he could never find, he wasted his time, wronged his art, and did harm to his own life and fame."[13]

In Vasari's *Life of Parmigianino*, the artistic foreshadowing of the change in his career is implicitly identified in relation to one particular painting—namely, the *Self-Portrait in a Convex Mirror* [102]. The artist, Vasari says, looked at himself in a barber's round mirror and set out to

102. *Parmigianino*, Self-Portrait
in a Convex Mirror, *1524.*
Kunsthistorisches Museum,
Vienna.

replicate its spatial distortions as illusionistically as possible. He curved the
walls and ceilings and enlarged and elongated his right hand in the foreground. Having seen his reflection, according to Vasari, "the idea came to
him to amuse himself by counterfeiting everything."[14] In this notion,
Vasari implies an association between the painter's illusionistic skill and
trickery, which Parmigianino would later split off from his art in unproductive alchemical investigation. That the painting in question represents a
mirror reflection of the artist prefigures the narcissistic character of his
obsession with alchemy. The solitude and social isolation of the alchemist
has been related to its appeal to homosexual men.[15] In Parmigianino's
disintegration, the obsession with alchemy absorbed his energy, as did
Narcissus's obsession with his own image. In both cases, falling prey to
*il*lusions that became *de*lusions ended in *self*-destruction.

HOUBRAKEN ON REMBRANDT

Gold, according to Rembrandt's biographer Arnold Houbraken, had enormous appeal for the artist, who nevertheless did not pursue alchemy. "Such
was his love of money (I will not say craving for money)," Houbraken
writes, "that his pupils who noticed this often for fun would paint on the
floor or elsewhere, where he was bound to pass, pennies, two-penny pieces

and shillings, and so on, after which he frequently stretched out his hand in vain, without letting anything be noticed as he was embarrassed through his mistake."[16]

Rembrandt's relationship to money has been discussed by Alpers,[17] who has analyzed his attraction to selling in the marketplace rather than through patronage. In that way he avoided dealing with patrons, who found him extremely difficult. He made them wait a long time for pictures they commissioned, either because they were unfinished or delivery was delayed. His works were so expensive that, according to Houbraken,[18] "You had to beg of him as well as pay him." It was as if, Alpers writes,[19] "Rembrandt wanted to bring prospective patrons to their knees as part of his payment."

Rembrandt preferred to establish the value of his works in the open market and thereby honor them. This attitude was consistent with seventeenth-century market philosophy, in which a man's value and honor were reflected in his "price."[20] The work of art became a commodity, and its value was a function of the artist who made it—in this case, Rembrandt. Although this view of art accords with our own, Alpers points out,[21] it was new in seventeenth-century Holland and it was essentially Rembrandt's invention. According to Alpers,[22] therefore, Rembrandt "commodified" art. His works were "commodities distinguished from others by being identified as his; and in making them, he in turn commodifies himself."[23] For Rembrandt, the psychological significance of the work of art as a commodity on the open market was freedom from the patronage system.

To Alpers's assertion that "Rembrandt's attraction to paint was akin to his attraction to money,"[24] the psychoanalyst could add the further association to feces. The unconscious equation between gold, money, and feces[25]—in folklore the devil's gold turns to feces (see Chapter 11)—derives from the child's toilet training, which is his earliest "financial transaction." The child is asked to relinquish material produced by his own body "on time" and at certain intervals. In return, he receives praise and approval from his "entourage." Conflicts arising during this period are transformed into such derivatives as stubbornness, hoarding and collecting, excessive preoccupation with money, withholding, stinginess, obsessive thinking, and compulsive behavior.[26]

Although nothing is known of Rembrandt's toilet training, he hoarded and collected, was notably stubborn, and was, in reality, in the position of having to market his paintings for money. To the hoots of skeptics and cries of "reductionism," I hasten to point out that even Rembrandt's own contemporaries referred to his work as "dung,"[27] apparently because of its painterly quality and lack of "finish." Unlike many other northern artists of the seventeenth century, Rembrandt did not paint illusionistic trompe l'oeil works with clear edges and smooth surfaces. Instead, his brushwork is typically "loose," and often literally merges with the object depicted. The very loose quality of Rembrandt's brush strokes indicates his capacity for what the ego psychologists call "conflict-free" creative activity and what Freud calls the ego's synthetic function. Through it, Rembrandt applies paint with greater "freedom" while controlling the image, just as his freedom from patronage placed him in control of his market.

Rembrandt refers to the criticism of his paintings as "dung"—as Alpers suggests[28]—in a drawing entitled *Satire on Art Criticism* [103]. In it, a man with the ears of an ass addresses a group of people, and points with his pipe to a picture. On the right, a man defecates and turns to look at the viewer in a manner characteristic of artists' self-portraits. If the man at the right is, in fact, Rembrandt's self-image, then he defecates on his critics—a "shit for shit" version of the talion law—for comparing his painting to dung. The detail of the ass's ears probably refers to Ovid's (*Meta.* XI) account of King Midas, who judged the mythical music contest between Apollo and Pan. Because Midas had the poor taste to prefer Pan to Apollo, who was the god of music, his ears were changed into those of an ass.

Houbraken, like Rembrandt's critics, implies the fecal quality of the artist's thick brushwork; but he relates it to the necessity of working fast in order to satisfy buyers—that is, to money. Rembrandt's paintings, according to his biographer,[29] "looked like having been daubed with a bricklayer's trowel." When visitors to his studio wanted to examine his paintings closely, they "were frightened away by his saying, 'The smell of the colours will bother you.' "[30]

This account corresponds to the child's experience of his feces, for he who produces them is not offended by their smell. It is, in fact, part of the child's toilet-training process to develop the sense that his feces have an unpleasant, antisocial odor. Earlier on, children typically enjoy their feces, often play with them, and even, to the dismay of their entourage, smear them on walls, furniture, and themselves. In Houbraken's vignette, Rembrandt implicitly takes these dynamics into account, as if warning visitors to beware of

103. *Rembrandt,* Satire on Art Criticism, *17th century. Metropolitan Museum of Art, New York. Robert Lehman Collection, 1975, 1975.1.799.*

the smell of his feces, which he nevertheless enjoys working with—and which he exchanges for money in the real world.

Pursuing the olfactory considerations of Rembrandt's paint, Houbraken reports that the artist "once painted a picture in which the colours were so heavily loaded that you could lift it from the floor by the nose."[31] Which brings us back to Rembrandt's efforts to pick up coins illusionistically painted on the floor by his students.

Rembrandt bypassed the struggle dramatized by his biographer; in the anecdote he is depicted as submitting—lowering himself to the floor—to the gleam of money and doing so before his students. They, in effect, become master of the master, and the master becomes the butt of

104. *Rembrandt,* Danaë, *1636. Hermitage,*
St. Petersburg.

their joke. It is possible that Rembrandt feared his own enslavement to money and to a patron in control of money. Such a hypothesis is supported by Alpers's observation that Rembrandt was "most productive . . . when [for whatever reason] he could not deal with patrons,"[32] because he "was uneasy about admitting to any authority outside of himself."[33] Alpers relates Rembrandt's unease to anxiety about God, fathers, and tradition, and notes his repeated iconographic themes of father-son conflict and conflict between generations.[34] Her observation that paternal figures who sustain bodily injury in Rembrandt's oeuvre tend to be succeeded by a "son"[35] is of psychological significance. That the bodily injuries in question usually involve the loss of the eye illuminates the oedipal cast of Rembrandt's conflicts with patrons.

The relation of the eye and father-son ambivalence to anal conflicts in Rembrandt's mind is reinforced by a specific detail in the Book of Tobit from the Old Testament Apocrypha. Rembrandt illustrates this book "more often than any other biblical text of comparable length."[36] Tobit was a Jew, captured by the Assyrians; although formerly a rich man, he had lost his money and lived piously in exile with his wife, Anna, and his son, Tobias. Tobias shows his father a corpse, which Tobit then buries. He falls asleep next to a wall, whereupon "excrement from a swallow's nest falls on his eyes, covering them with a white film that blinds him."[37]

The theme of blindness pervades Rembrandt's iconography. So does his related preoccupation with the sense of touch, which is evoked also by the particularly tactile quality of his paint. The ambivalence—or juxtaposition—of sight and touch recapitulates the content of Houbraken's anecdote in which Rembrandt "sees" the coins on the floor, reaches for them, and finds that neither sensation is real. When Rembrandt reasserts his position as master, however, it is *he* who paints the gold for which others "reach" by giving him their money in exchange.

Rembrandt's *Danaë* [104] in Saint Petersburg is noteworthy for its absence of money. Alpers proposes that this "might be a case of avoiding the sex-money link."[38] The text of the scene calls for gold coins—compare "pennies from heaven"—which is Zeus's disguise. Titian (see Chapter 9), as we have seen, not only includes the gold, but also an old woman catching it as it falls from the sky. Rather than avoiding the "sex-money link," Rembrandt substitutes light for gold. The psychological implications of that substitution—especially in view of the primal-scene content of the narrative—are many; but they include Rembrandt's association of light with sexual, financial, and intellectual power. In *Danaë*, he specifically links his artistic relation to light—which is both iconographic and formal—to Zeus's disguised sexuality.

As the artist, Rembrandt is also the onlooker, viewing the primal scene. In terms of the family romance, the impregnating father has been elevated to the status of the Olympian "father," and Rembrandt identifies with both the child watcher and Zeus. The artist creating with light and the god procreating with light are thereby conflated.

CELLINI'S TWO SCREEN MEMORIES

Autobiography differs from biography and anecdote in purporting to come from the proverbial horse's mouth. It is the literary equivalent of the artist's self-portrait. When the author of the autobiography is a visual artist, however, the relationship between the verbal statement and the author's artistic imagery becomes a consideration.

In 1557, at the age of fifty-six, the Mannerist sculptor and goldsmith Benvenuto Cellini (1500–1571) dictated his colorful autobiography to a fourteen-year-old male assistant. Cellini was, at the time, under house arrest for sodomy.[39] Actively bisexual, Cellini fathered children, married, was convicted of sodomy, and engaged repeatedly in minor criminal behavior. The bisexual ambivalence at the core of his personality emerges in his autobiographical self-portrait as well as in his art.

The familiar convention of tracing descent from a noble past and its psychological relation to the family romance that we saw in Vasari's life of Michelangelo are present at the outset of Cellini's autobiography. Cellini traces his forebears to a high-ranking captain in the army of Julius Caesar. But his ambivalence asserts itself immediately, for he claims great pride in his humble birth.[40] That Cellini's ambivalence was determined by his bisexuality is seen in the conviction that his parents believed he would be born a girl. He was an "unexpected male child,"[41] declared by his father to be "Benvenuto," meaning "Welcome."

Cellini reports two well-known memories of his early childhood that are clearly screen memories with primal-scene iconography. In the first, Cellini is about three years old, and remembers people "altering a certain conduit pertaining to a cistern, and there issued from it a great scorpion unperceived by them, which crept down from the cistern to the ground, and slunk away beneath a bench."[42] Cellini, however, did notice, ran over to it, and picked it up. "It was so big," he continues, "that when I had it in my little hands, it put out its tail on one side, and on the other thrust forth both its mouths" (that is, open claws).[43] Cellini called to his grandfather, saying, "look at my pretty little crab." His grandfather recognized that it was a scorpion and was terrified. He demanded that Cellini give it to him; but Cellini refused. Cellini's father heard his son's screams and, to prevent the scorpion from killing him, cut off its tail and mouths (claws), while calming and caressing Cellini.

At the outset of the memory, the "male" conduit and the "female" cistern "give birth" to a scorpion, unnoticed by everyone except the three-year-old Cellini, who is impressed by its great size. The scorpion, under whose sign Cellini was born,[44] stands for the artist himself. He reverses the account of his birth in the autobiography, where he is "welcomed" instead of going "unnoticed," as in the memory. When he displays the scorpion, which is an "exhibition" of himself, his father cuts off the tail and claws, symbolically turning his son into the "expected" girl.

The castrative significance of his father's action is obvious, as is the aggressive self-image as a scorpion. Cellini probably knew Alberti's fifteenth-century autobiography, the so-called *Vita anonima*, or *Anonymous Life*, which also contains a vivid scorpion image.[45] Alberti records his passion for reading, but says that "sometimes the letters piled up under his eyes like scorpions."[46] In other words, the sentences began to "deconstruct" and become confused. That this represents an attack on Alberti's eyes and also has latent sexual meaning is consistent with the tradition that the sting of a scorpion could blind its victim and cause syphilis.[47] Alberti's ambivalence is reflected in reading and having his eyes attacked by the words; Cellini's, in a flamboyant bisexual life-style. The scorpion links vision with sexuality in its ability to blind and infect with syphilis. It also has bisexual connotations, because of a tradition associating it with male and female genitalia,[48] which reinforces its role as a self-image in Cellini's screen memory.

Cellini's second memory[49] occurred around the age of five. His father was alone in the basement, where logs were burning; he was playing the viol and singing by the fire. He looked into the flames and saw a lizard "sporting in the core of the intensest coals."[50] He summoned Cellini and his sister, pointed out the lizard, and boxed his son's ears. Cellini cried, and his father pacified him by explaining that he only wanted to make sure he remembered that the lizard was a salamander. "So saying," Cellini concludes, "he kissed me and gave me some pieces of money."[51]

The basement, in dreams, is typically a female sexual image, because it is a dark, lower architectural enclosure. Cellini's father playing music in the "basement" thus connotes sexual activity. When he sees the lizard in the hottest part of the coals, he conflates the sexuality of fire with the lizard as an infant in the mother's womb—that is, in her "bed of coals." He boxes Cellini's ears, while also making him "see" in order to remember, in the belief that trauma, or shock, facilitates memory. In kissing Cellini, his father repeats the action of caressing him while "castrating" the scorpion. In giving him money and kissing him, his father tries to repair the attack on his ears.

These memories are remarkable evidence of Cellini's repeated ambivalence. His father's action of playing the viol corresponds to his persistence in trying to divert Cellini from the goldsmith's art to music. When Cellini was fifteen, according to his autobiography, he finally defied his father and joined a goldsmith, whose trade corresponded with his own natural talents. The struggle with his father over music versus art continued for several years thereafter. Eventually his father admitted that he, too, had been a good draftsman but had chosen music instead (even though he was a professional architect), which suggests an ambivalent oedipal motive on his part.

Cellini and his father continued their ambivalent relationship, with Cellini leaving his father's house and returning again, describing his father as variously loving and unreasonable—all of which presages the artist's "running" from place to place as an adult, whether for political, personal, or legal reasons. The artist's sexual ambivalence is "announced" in the screen memories by the opposing actions of his father—cutting off the scorpion's limbs while caressing Cellini, and boxing his ears and then kissing him and giving him money. Since his father was so intent on Cellini's becoming a musician, it is contradictory that he should box his ears at all. And finally, in the second memory, his father makes him look—a requirement for art—and then hits him because of his *having* looked.

The lizard, like the scorpion, has iconographic associations that contribute to the psychological interpretation of the memory. Lizards were traditionally believed incapable of love and symbolized coldness.[52] Cellini's bisexual ambivalence, though not necessarily "cold," would nevertheless preclude his making a steadfast commitment to one person. The purported coldness of the lizard, furthermore, is in direct opposition to the intense heat of the coals in Cellini's memory.

Both of Cellini's early childhood recollections fulfill the conditions of screen memories as described by Freud; they occurred before the age of seven and are particularly vivid. Their manifest content is unlikely; but, if analyzed according to superimposed layers of latent content, their meaning is consistent with Cellini's adult personality. Both have a primal-scene character that "arrests" attention and focuses the gaze. Both contain castration metaphors, in which Cellini is directly or indirectly punished for having seen or done something. And in both, Cellini's father acts ambivalently. Taken together, the two memories have the quality of an autobiographical "frame." The scorpion refers to the zodiacal sign under which Cellini was born. The identification of the lizard as a salamander refers to his later career, when he worked for Francis I of France, whose emblem was a salamander.

The multifaceted ambivalence of Cellini's life is translated into the form and content of his marble sculpture *Narcissus* [105]. The statue was

105. *Benvenuto Cellini*, Narcissus, 1545–48. *Bargello, Florence.*

106. *Benvenuto Cellini*, Narcissus, *back view of Figure 105.*

not commissioned; its subject was therefore chosen by the artist, and is a reflection of his own taste. It dates from a three-year period (1545–48) during his stay in Florence (1545–57), when he made two other homosexual works in marble, *Ganymede* and *Apollo and Hyacinth.*

Seen from the front, the torso of Narcissus forms a slow curve, carried upward and around the head by the left arm. His implicit invitation to the viewer's gaze is diverted by his down-turned head as he gazes at his own reflection in the pool of water. Narcissus's upraised arm, exposing his armpit, as well as his total nudity, seductively lures the viewer as he lures Echo in the myth, whereas he himself is absorbed by his own seduction.

Seen from the back [106], the boy's feminine quality is even more apparent, both in the graceful curve of the back and in the flowers pressed against the hair. He sits on a brick wall, on which Cellini has carved a tree branch in relief. Under the branch, a small snake evokes the lizard of the artist's screen memory and wriggles through a hole in the brick. It reemerges from another hole a little higher up. The lizard's placement below and behind the seated Narcissus, as well as its action of going in and out of the hole, creates an image of anal penetration, associated with a passive homosexual role.

The detail of the snake is at once hidden and not hidden; the snake goes in and out of the brick, and is at the back of the statue. It is, however, quite visible to whoever looks behind the figure. As such, it reveals Cellini's ambivalence, which, in turn, is revealed by Narcissus himself. An iconographic motif of this kind clearly has personal significance, and in Cellini's case it can be directly related to the screen memory reported in his autobiography. That the lizard in the bed of coals has, in *Narcissus*, become a snake entering and exiting from a hole transforms the childhood primal scene into a metaphor for homosexual *coitus a tergo.*

HENRY MOORE'S PRIMAL-SCENE ANXIETY

Although Cellini describes his life as fraught with bisexual tension, *Narcissus* seems rather languid and free of psychic conflict. Henry Moore had a heterosexual relation to primal-scene material that can be discerned if certain images are combined with statements he made about his work. His particular primal-scene anxiety explains the inhibition he encountered when dealing with the subject of coal miners.

During World War II, Moore did many drawings of mothers and

107. Henry Moore,
Miner at Work, 1942.
Portland (Oregon) Art
Museum. Gift of Dr.
Francis Newton.

children seeking shelter from the Blitz in the London Underground. That experience, according to the artist, inspired the recurrent theme of mother-child protection (see Chapter 8).[53] The success of those drawings led the art critic Herbert Read to recommend that Moore, whose father had been a coal miner, take up that subject.[54] Despite Moore's stated "fascination for the hole,"[55] and his unique iconographic use of literal "holes" in his sculpture and drawing, he was not interested in the mines. He attributed this, in part, to his lack of interest in drawing male figures.[56]

If, however, the mine drawings are considered in relation to the primal scene, both their iconography and their autobiographical significance can be read on a deeper level. In a 1942 drawing, *Miner at Work* [107], for example, a miner drills a small hole into the wall of the mine tunnel. Partially illuminated by a light at the left, the miner reflects Moore's interest in the illusion of form emerging from darkness. Moore was also struck by the impression of "something half-hidden" created by the contrast between the dark tunnel and the light that the miners carried into the mines.[57]

The primal-scene character of the drawing [107] is barely disguised. Earth, mining, and ores have ancient maternal associations that have been traced back to pre-antiquity.[58] Caves and mines were compared with the womb of Mother Earth, while ores and metals were her embryos. Henry Moore's miner boring into the Earth Mother can be seen in this context as the fertilizing agent, which is male. Moore's reference to these forms as "half-hidden" evokes the child's nocturnal primal-scene experience and the mystery that accompanies it.

Henry Moore, in contrast to Picasso in *Guernica*, did not synthesize his childhood experience with classical mythology. Instead, although otherwise an enormously prolific artist, when it came to coal miners in the mines, Moore became inhibited. For Moore, in contrast to Picasso, there was a real threat to his father's life from explosions in the mines. Thus, Moore's oedipal feelings toward his father were in a continual state of tension from the daily possibility of death. The further content of explosion, drowning, being burned, or being smothered to death by the earth itself can evoke unconscious fears of sexual danger. That these conflicts are at least partly responsible for Moore's inhibition toward miners comes from their connection with oedipal conflicts. For the closer the iconography comes to the apparent fulfillment of the taboo oedipal wish—here, the father's death—the greater the likelihood of an inhibition.

By the artist's own assertion, he did not have the same problem with depictions of the female figure, or of mothers and children. Moore has related rubbing his mother's back as a child to the prominence of women's backs in his sculptures.[59] Whatever ambivalence he might have had in regard to seductive closeness with his mother, he solved it by literally opening up sculptural spaces so that the viewer sees the work simultaneously as solid form and open space.[60] Open space would likewise counter the claustrophobic atmosphere of the mines, and also provide the air that would save the miner's life in case of danger.

Both Moore and Picasso dealt with themes of bombing (the Blitz and the town of Guernica), and merged them with themes of explosion (the coal mines and the Málaga earthquake). Destruction from above thus combines with upheaval from the ground below. Autobiography becomes iconography as both artists synthesize their personal primal-scene fantasies[61] with powerful events in reality.

VELÁZQUEZ'S *LAS MENINAS* AS AUTOBIOGRAPHY

In the above discussion of Cellini and Moore, the psychobiographical exploration of imagery is reinforced by the artists' own statements. Such documentation is not always available, however, in which case different methodology is called for. The life of Velázquez (1599–1660) is fairly well documented by contemporary and near-contemporary accounts;[62] but there are no extant writings by Velázquez himself—no personal records or letters of any kind. His father-in-law and teacher, Pacheco, has described Velázquez's early career as court painter to Philip IV of Spain, and Palomino, court painter to Charles II, published a biography of Velázquez in 1724. Palomino's sources include recollections of people who had known the artist, a lost biography by one of Velázquez's students, and the Spanish royal archives.

Velázquez's major autobiographical statement is *Las Meninas* [100], painted in 1656 when the artist was fifty-seven. At the manifest level of autobiography, *Las Meninas* is a picture of the artist's position vis-à-vis the royal family. Velázquez has placed himself in the same space as the infanta and her servants. In the background, the queen's chamberlain is framed by an illuminated doorway next to a mirror reflection of the king and queen. The intentional ambiguity of the king and queen leaves open the question whether they are reflected from Velázquez's canvas, which is seen only from the back, or from a position in front of the infanta.[63]

In either case, Velázquez has placed himself in medias res; although to the left of center, he is between his canvas and the mirror. The autobiographical character of this painting operates iconographically on many levels; one is Velázquez's position as a member of the family's inner circle, while also being an employee. In his role as court painter, Velázquez had to achieve and maintain a high artistic status; he was also a kind of visual scribe, whether recording the royal family or creating other images for its collection. He is represented in that role in *Las Meninas*, where he stands in front of a large canvas, paintbrush and palette in hand, and looks out of the picture plane at the viewer, and possibly also at the king and queen. His interest in status is evident in the red cross of the noble Order of Santiago on his vest; he was not awarded membership in the order until 1659, and therefore must have added the emblem three years after the painting had been completed.

Not only did Velázquez want to elevate his own social position, he also wanted painting raised from the status of a handicraft to that of a

Liberal Art, which it enjoyed in Italy. This ambition for his art mirrored his personal ambition—since those who practiced crafts did not receive the Order of Santiago. In 1659, at the age of sixty, Velázquez succeeded in being acknowledged a member of the nobility.

A review of Velázquez's biography indicates a synthesis of genius with oedipal integration that fueled and propelled the artist's professional success. Born in 1599 in Seville, he was the first of seven children in a middle-class family of the lesser nobility. His father ensured that he would receive a good education at a time when only twenty percent of Spain was literate. When Velázquez was eleven, in 1610, his father apprenticed him to Pacheco, a mediocre painter and the author of a treatise calling for the unification of Arts with Letters, the latter being a Liberal Art in Spain. Pacheco held an important position in a humanist academy based on those in fifteenth-century Florence, and he introduced Velázquez to the leading Spanish humanists, who studied Renaissance culture and the classics. In 1618, Velázquez married Pacheco's daughter, with whom he had two daughters, born in 1619 and 1621.

Pacheco provided Velázquez with access to a highly cultivated, intellectual circle. From there, Velázquez's entry into Philip's court was the next logical step. Philip IV, called the Planet King—because the sun was fourth in the planet hierarchy—admired literature and music, and was an avid art collector. His grandfather, Philip II, also a collector, had been particularly drawn to Flemish painting and the works of Titian.

Once Velázquez entered Philip's court, competition intensified. In 1627, a contest was held among the Spanish court painters because Velázquez had been accused of knowing only how to depict heads. Velázquez's victory was mainly due to the avant-garde tastes of the judges, and his prize was the Office of the Usher of the Privy Chamber. Stiffer competition, however, came from Rubens, then in Spain on a diplomatic mission. In 1628, for example, Rubens's portrait of Philip IV on horseback replaced that by Velázquez in the Alcazar gallery. Rubens had also mastered Italian Renaissance art, especially that of Titian, which Velázquez had yet to do. Two months after Rubens left Spain, Velázquez departed for an eighteen-month stay in Italy, where he succeeded in his ambition to absorb Italian Renaissance art in general and Titian in particular. By 1640, at the age of forty-one, Velázquez was receiving an annual stipend from Philip, and his position at court was secure.

Velázquez's biography, if considered psychologically, exemplifies a successful oedipal outcome that is reflected in his work. Whereas Michelangelo's father reportedly beat him for his ambition to become a sculptor, Velázquez's paved the way for his son's success. Like Raphael, Velázquez was apprenticed to an appropriate master at an early age. All three artists spent important years of their adolescence in classically oriented, humanist environments—Michelangelo in the household of Lorenzo de' Medici, Raphael at the court of Urbino, and Velázquez at Pacheco's academy. That Velázquez went on to marry Pacheco's daughter and proceed from the academy to the court indicates the determined focus of his career. When Velázquez ran into obstacles in the form of competition with Titian, his predecessor, or Rubens, his contemporary, he overcame them by applying his genius to study and work.

Velázquez did not write about any of this himself; it is known only from secondary sources and the evolution of his style. What Velázquez did do, however, is *paint* about himself. How consciously or unconsciously he did so is impossible to reconstruct. Nevertheless, if we take the theme of competition, which had enormous biographical significance for Velázquez, we can read it as a subtext of *Las Meninas* and a not so *sub*text elsewhere.

One route to the latent meaning of *Las Meninas* is through the content of the two pictures on the back wall. Their mythological subjects— Athena's weaving contest with Arachne on the left and Marsyas's musical challenge to Apollo on the right—are well established, even though the images are no longer very clear. Several other paintings on the right wall are virtually impossible to see. Two have been identified as *Prometheus Stealing Fire* and *Vulcan Forging Thunderbolts*.[64] The theme of competition, however, is most apparent in the mythological contests of creative challenge depicted on the back wall. Both myths contain latent oedipal and pre-oedipal significance and, as such, constitute an autobiographical subtext.

Two Myths of Creative Challenge

The myths of Marsyas, who challenged Apollo to a musical contest, and of Arachne, who challenged Minerva (the Roman equivalent of Athena) to a weaving contest, illustrate oedipal failure resulting from unresolved pre-oedipal grandiosity. The former dramatizes the boy's conflicts with his father, and the latter, the girl's with her mother. In each case, the parental figure is represented as a god and the challenger as a lesser being— Marsyas a satyr, and Arachne a mortal.[65]

In Ovid's account of Marsyas (*Meta.* VI), the satyr retrieves pipes discarded by Minerva because playing them made her cheeks puff up.

Marsyas boasted that he could play better than Apollo, the god of music as well as the sun god. Apollo won the contest, punished Marsyas for his presumption by flaying him alive, and then hung the flayed skin in his temple as an example to other would-be challengers. The spectacle of the skin, like the "pitture infamanti" hanging from buildings in medieval and Renaissance Italy (see Chapter 7) and the gallows in Lorenzetti's *Allegory of Good and Bad Government* (see Chapter 3), was intended as a warning, an image of the consequences of defying an established order.

Arachne was the most renowned weaver in Lydia; but she refused to acknowledge Minerva, the goddess of weaving, as the source of her talent. Being also a goddess of wisdom, Minerva tried to show the mortal girl the error of her ways. But Arachne, like Marsyas, persisted, and the contest proceeded. Adding insult to injury, Arachne wove scenes of the male gods' infidelities, especially with mortal women. In so doing, she forced Minerva to confront (to "see") the oedipal desires of the male gods, including those of her own father, and dared her to accept the daughter's symbolic defeat of the mother in the oedipal contest for the father (the "god"). Minerva wove scenes of an exemplary nature; they depicted the punishments inflicted on those who defy the gods. So angered was Minerva by the high quality of Arachne's scenes that she hit her three times with the spindle. The underlying grandiosity of Arachne's challenge, despite her talent, is evident in its fragile character—for no sooner did Minerva vent her rage than Arachne tried to hang herself. Even that, however, was not to be within the girl's control, for Minerva lifted her up and saved her life. Then the goddess changed Arachne into a spider, to "hang and weave forever." As a spider, Arachne was no longer a threat to Minerva. Without her human brain and hands, Arachne could weave only a spider's web, programmed by virtue of her species, rather than a creative human product.

In both the Marsyas and Arachne myths, the challengers had real talent, which they misused. Their transgression was not in the display of their abilities, but in their confrontation with the gods. In being gods, Apollo and Minerva were destined to win, making the respective challenges of Marsyas and Minerva impossible. With regard to the oedipal implications of their challenge, it is clear that Apollo—particularly as sun god—represents the father's authority. Minerva, on the other hand, combines the phallic character of the pre-oedipal mother with oedipal envy, which is consistent with Freud's finding that, for the girl, the pre-oedipal stage plays a greater role in subsequent development than for the boy.

The punishments meted out by Apollo and Minerva, like God's

"Babel of tongues," serve to "reduce" the competitors—or "cut them down to size"—in more or less severe ways. All, however, are powerful attacks on the narcissistic exhibitionism of the challenger.

VELÁZQUEZ'S MYTHOLOGICAL AND ICONOGRAPHIC SUBTEXTS

Competition and the role of the artist vis-à-vis society, nobility, and the gods is a recurrent theme of Velázquez's life and art. In *Las Meninas*, tension between generations informs the iconography of the queen watching the five-year-old infanta. The queen herself was Austrian, and her daughter was engaged from birth to a Viennese cousin. The infanta, thus slated to become queen in her mother's native land, was simultaneously her oedipal rival and royal successor.

The myth of Minerva and Arachne echoes the mother-daughter conflict that is manifest in the Austrian queen of Spain's "keeping an eye on" the infanta. Likewise, the father-son conflict is manifest in the musical contest between Apollo and Marsyas, in which the satyr's flaying is symbolic castration for oedipal transgression. More complex, however, are the creative implications of these contests for Velázquez and their relation to his social and artistic ambitions. That the one contest is a weaving competition and the other a musical one juxtaposes a handicraft with an art having higher status. Throughout the Renaissance in Italy, the mathematical character of music had been related to the motion of the heavens, especially by humanist thinkers. In this juxtaposition, Velázquez refers to his ambition that painting, a manual pursuit like weaving, be elevated to a Liberal Art.

He does so, however, by implication only; the art of painting does not figure in the mythical contests of *Las Meninas*, although they have pictorial features. Both Arachne and Minerva weave scenes that are exemplary images, but from opposing sides of oedipal rivalry. Apollo makes an example of Marsyas's flayed skin, which is the symbolic limp phallus of the defeated rival and also the god's trophy. The exemplary sense of these two myths is their caution against grandiosity. Like Raphael, who informed Castiglione that he hoped his desire to re-create the forms of antiquity would not be the flight of Icarus (see Chapter 4), Velázquez's two pictures on the back wall of *Las Meninas* indicate his insight into the dangers of unrealistic ambition.

Danger can also be related to autobiographical subtexts in other paintings. Two works by Velázquez first documented when they were sold in 1634 were, according to Palomino, painted during the artist's 1629 trip to Rome. That both were uncommissioned increases their personal significance for Velázquez.[66] *Joseph's Bloodied Coat Presented to Jacob* (El Escorial, Nuevos Museos) mirrors the theme of competition at the Spanish court. Like the artists who envied Velázquez and accused him of being unable to paint full figures, Joseph's brothers envied the "coat of many colors" that exemplified their father's favoritism. It would seem that Joseph's colorful coat became a metaphor for the artist's genius with paint, which, like Minerva and Arachne with their threads, he "weaves" into pictorial images. Jacob is likewise a metaphor for those paternal figures—the artist's father, Pacheco, Philip IV, even the judges in the artistic contest held at court— who recognized Velázquez's talents and singled him out because of them. The dangers of recognition were as clear to Velázquez as the dangers of hubris, for they exposed him—like the biblical Joseph—to the anger of those less successful than himself.

The other painting assigned by Palomino to Velázquez's Roman trip is *The Forge of Vulcan* [108], in which Apollo informs Vulcan of his wife's infidelity. In the Roman pantheon, Vulcan was married to Venus, goddess of love and beauty, who committed adultery with the war god, Mars. According to Ovid (*Meta.* IV, 173 ff.), after Vulcan learns of the betrayal, he makes a bronze net, throws it over the sleeping pair, and invites the other gods to witness the crime. Ovid's assertion that the net of bronze was so finely woven that it surpassed even the spider's web evokes the fate of Arachne in her weaving contest with Minerva.

Athena (the Greek Minerva) and Vulcan's Greek counterpart, Hephaestos, have an ancient mythological history that infiltrates the latent content of Velázquez's iconography. In the Greek texts, the very existence of Athena and Hephaestos was derived from divine competition. Both were born of a single parent. The Homeric hymn *To Pythian Apollo* (311 ff.)[67] describes Hera's anger when Zeus fathers Athena without her participation. In Hesiod (*Theogony*, 927 ff.),[68] Hera retaliates by giving birth to Hephaestos without Zeus. Athena and Hephaestos are the offspring of brother (Zeus) and sister (Hera) gods, step siblings without a parent of the same sex. As such, their oedipal configuration shifts in a way that virtually eliminates competition for the parent of the opposite sex—in this case, the only parent. In that light, it is surely significant that both Athena and Hephaestos are associated with creativity and that they are credited with

108. *Diego Velázquez,* The Forge of Vulcan, *before 1634. Prado, Madrid.*

having taught people crafts. Those crafts, according to the Homeric hymn *To Hephaestos,*[69] made it possible for people to stop living like beasts and take up peaceful residence in houses.

Although Athena is not present in Velázquez's *Forge of Vulcan,* she is related to him mythologically in her manner of birth and in the impact of her creativity on human civilization. Her juxtaposition as Minerva with Apollo on the back wall of *Las Meninas* also provides a link with Apollo's presence in *The Forge of Vulcan.* Vulcan, like Hephaestos, was the smith god, who made Apollo's chariot (Ovid, *Meta.* II, 106). In Velázquez's painting, Vulcan and Apollo are juxtaposed in their confrontation with each other. Both have a relation to creativity, as do Athena as Minerva and Vulcan as Hephaestos; but Vulcan and Apollo are male gods, and in the hierarchy of the arts of a different order than Athena's weaving. For although Vulcan as Hephaestos is a craftsman in the Homeric hymn, his role as the smith has a special, even magical, significance that transcends *craft*.

An iconographic detail in *The Forge of Vulcan* that seems to refer to Velázquez's dual identification with Apollo and Vulcan is the large V formed by the placement of two hammers to the left of the forge. Each diagonal of the V rises toward one of the gods, linking them by reference to the first letter of the artist's name. The coincidence of the V in Vulcan's name reinforces the reading of the hammers as a kind of "hidden" image, connecting the human artist with the artistic god. (In Ovid's account of the musical contest between Apollo and Marsyas, the god's regal demeanor is emphasized.)

Just as Vulcan/Hephaestos was smith to the classical gods and heroes (he forged the arms of Achilles and the shield of Heracles), so Velázquez was Philip IV's court painter. His lower social status allies him with Vulcan, and his ambitions to become noble, with Apollo. Philip's association to Apollo is contained in his designation as Planet King[70] and in his representation in the mirror of *Las Meninas*. Velázquez has painted a circular red form glowing above his head that has been related to Philip's identification with Apollo as the sun god.[71]

As a smith, Vulcan controls fire, which he uses to smelt metals. In that function, he is allied with the alchemical implications of the forge. The creative aspect of forming natural material that belongs to Vulcan is related to depicting form with paint. Vulcan, like the biblical Joseph, and Velázquez himself, uses his talents to "win" in the end. His craft—compare "crafty" and "craftiness"—permits him to trap Venus and Mars; Joseph's ability to interpret the pharaoh's dreams results in his prosperity; and Velázquez attains noble status. It is no coincidence that Velázquez depicted Vulcan's forge and the story of Joseph and his brothers during his Italian trip. The style of these works reflects the assimilation of Italian Renaissance painting that permitted Velázquez to compete with Rubens and to become the undisputed master of Spanish Baroque.

Fire, and its control,[72] has been identified as the theme of a picture on the side wall of *Las Meninas*.[73] The picture's mythological subject, Prometheus Stealing Fire, combines hubris against the gods with artistry. Prometheus, described by Hesiod as "crafty" and "cunning,"[74] steals fire from Zeus. He does so in order to breathe life into his statues, thereby making living figures. (It is no coincidence that Mary Shelley refers to Frankenstein as the "Modern Prometheus.") In creating life, Prometheus rivals the gods, who punish him with eternal torture. The myth underscores the oedipal nature of his crime by his punishment—a vulture eats his liver, which is a displacement from the phallus; the gods thus retaliate by symbolic castration. The control of fire, which the gods had jealously guarded, made life possible and also contributed, as did crafts, to the development of human civilization.

In the other subject identified on the side wall of *Las Meninas*, Vulcan forges thunderbolts. These belong to Zeus in the Greek pantheon, and to Jupiter in the Roman. With them, the ruler of Olympos counters the sunlight of Apollo and roars his displeasure. He controls the sky, as Vulcan, at work in his cave, controls the forge. Together these subjects can be read as metaphors of Velázquez's ambition: that is, the father's authority associated with Jupiter and King Philip on the one hand and, on the other, the creative activity of the smith, who necessarily withdraws from soci-

109. Diego Velázquez, The Spinners, *c. 1656.*
Prado, Madrid.

ety—here into a cave—in order to work. In becoming a knight of the Order of Santiago, as well as the greatest Baroque artist in Spain, Velázquez synthesized the ambitions embodied by Jupiter and Vulcan.

One other painting by Velázquez related to the mythological subtext of *Las Meninas* is *The Spinners*, also called *The Fable of Arachne* [109]. In that work, Velázquez juxtaposes three levels of time and place. Five contemporary Spanish women weave in the foreground, while in the background, raised up as if on a stage, Minerva and Arachne pursue their contest. Arachne's tapestry depicting the Rape of Europa hangs on the far wall. Exemplifying Zeus's lust for mortal women, the scene forces Minerva to "see" the symbolic oedipal crime of incest. She is thus doubly challenged— as an artist and as a goddess. The seventeenth-century viewer knew that Arachne was about to become a spider for her grandiosity and also recognized that her woven scene replicates Titian's painting. His *Rape of Europa* [85], purchased by Philip IV's grandfather, Philip II, was then in the Spanish royal collection. In *The Spinners*, therefore, Velázquez proclaims his assimilation of Titian, acknowledges the distinctions between human and mythological time by spatial arrangement, and warns of the dangers of hubris.

These myth pictures—by no means all that Velázquez painted—and his *Joseph*, if taken together, constitute latent themes that run through the artist's life. In them, he has painted the tensions between gods and mortals as metaphors for those between creators and rulers, parents and children, artistic competitors, and siblings. *Las Meninas* is a summation of these autobiographical themes and an expression of the family romance, through which Velázquez aligns himself socially with the royal family of Spain and artistically with mythological creators.

NOTES

1. Cf. Paul Watson, "The Cement of Fiction: Giovanni Boccaccio and the Painters of Florence," *Modern Language Notes* 99, no. 1 (January 1984): 43–64.
2. Suggested by Muriel Oxenberg Murphy in a personal communication.
3. H. R. Graetz, *The Symbolic Language of Vincent van Gogh*, London, 1963, p. 212.
4. For this observation I am indebted to Bradley Collins.
5. Illustrated in Anne d'Harnoncourt and Kynaston McShine, eds., *Marcel Duchamp*, Philadelphia and New York, 1973. p. 227.
6. Arturo Schwarz, in d'Harnoncourt and McShine, eds., *Marcel Duchamp*, p. 84.
7. Ibid.
8. Giorgio Vasari, *Lives of the Most Eminent Painters, Sculptors, and Architects*, trans. Gaston du Vere, vol. 2, New York, 1979, pp. 1138–49.

9. Ibid., p. 1138.
10. Ibid., p. 1146.
11. Ibid., p. 1147.
12. Proposed by Bradley Collins.
13. Vasari, *Lives*, vol. 2, p. 1138.
14. Ibid., p. 1140.
15. Gaston Bachelard, *La Psychanalyse du feu*, Paris, 1949.
16. Houbraken in Tancred Borenius, *Rembrandt: Selected Paintings*, London, 1942, p. 28.
17. Svetlana Alpers, *Rembrandt's Enterprise*, Chicago and London, 1988. See especially Chapter 4.
18. Houbraken, p. 26.
19. Alpers, p. 91.
20. Ibid., p. 106.
21. Ibid., p. 102.
22. Ibid., p. 110.
23. Ibid., p. 118.
24. Ibid., p. 110.
25. See Freud, "Character and Anal Erotism," S. E. IX, 1908, pp. 173–74.
26. Ibid., p. 171.
27. Alpers, *Rembrandt's Enterprise*, p. 92.
28. Ibid.
29. Houbraken in Borenius, *Rembrandt*, p. 26.
30. Ibid.
31. Ibid., p. 27.
32. Alpers, *Rembrandt's Enterprise*, p. 91, fn. 6, cites Gary Schwartz here and elsewhere for a different interpretation of the same circumstances, in Schwartz's *Rembrandt: His Life, His Paintings*, New York, 1985.
33. Ibid., p. 118.
34. Ibid., pp. 118–19.
35. Ibid., pp. 118–19.
36. Julius S. Held, *Rembrandt's "Aristotle,"* Princeton, 1969, p. 104.
37. Ibid., p. 105.
38. Alpers, *Rembrandt's Enterprise*, p. 112.
39. The following is from *The Autobiography of Benvenuto Cellini*, trans. John Addington Symonds, New York, 1937.
40. Ibid., pp. 3–4.
41. Ibid., p. 6.
42. Ibid., p. 7.
43. Ibid.
44. John Pope-Hennessy, *Cellini*, New York, 1985, p. 23.
45. Leon Battista Alberti, *Vita anonima*, in R. Fubini and A. M. Gallorini, "L'autobiografia de Leon Battista Alberti. Studio e edizione," *Rinasimento XXII* (December 1971): 69 ff.
46. Laurie Schneider, "Leon Battista Alberti: Some Biographical Implications of the Winged Eye," *Art Bulletin LXXII*, no. 2 (June 1990): p. 264.
47. L. Aurigemma, *Il segno zodiacale dello scorpione nelle tradizioni occidentali*, Turin, 1976, pp. 78, 108, 110, 166.
48. Ibid.
49. Cellini, *The Autobiography of Benvenuto Cellini*, pp. 7–8.
50. Ibid., p. 7.
51. Ibid., p. 8.

52. Donald Posner, "Caravaggio's Homo-Erotic Early Works," *Art Quarterly*, Autumn 1971, p. 305.
53. Kenneth Clark, *Henry Moore on Drawing*, London, 1974, pp. 155, 249. Cf. also Anna Freud and Dorothy T. Burlingham, *War and Children*, New York, 1945.
54. Brewster Ghiselin, *The Creative Process*, Los Angeles, 1952, p. 216.
55. Henry Moore and J. Hedgecoe, *Henry Moore*, New York, 1968, p. xli.
56. Ghiselin, *The Creative Process*, p. 216.
57. Kenneth Clark, *Henry Moore on Drawing*, p. 291.
58. Mircea Eliade, *The Forge and the Crucible*, New York and Evanston, 1971, Chapters 1–5.
59. Henry Moore, *Henry Moore*, London, 1944, p. 328.
60. Cf. Rudolph Arnheim, "The Holes of Henry Moore," *Journal of Esthetics and Art Criticism* 7, no. 1 (1948): 29–38.
61. Cf. the expression denoting successful sexual intercourse—"The earth moved."
62. The following account of Velázquez's life is based on Jonathan Brown, *Velázquez*, New Haven and London, 1986.
63. Leo Steinberg, "Velázquez's *Las Meninas*," *October* 19 (1981): 45–54.
64. Steven Orso, "A Lesson Learned: *Las Meninas* and the State Portraits of Juan Carreño de Miranda," *Record of The Art Museum of Princeton University* 41 (1982): 24–34.
65. For psychoanalytic discussions of the Marsyas and Arachne myths, see Laurie Adams, "Apollo and Marsyas: A Metaphor of Creative Conflict," *The Psychoanalytic Review* 75, no. 2 (Summer 1988): 319–38 and "The Myth of Athena and Arachne: Some Oedipal and Pre-Oedipal Aspects of Creative Challenge in Women and their Implications for the Interpretation of *Las Meninas* by Velázquez," *International Journal of Psychoanalysis* 71 (1990): 597–609.
66. Brown, op. cit., p. 71.
67. In Hesiod, *The Homeric Hymns and Homerica*, Loeb Library edition, trans. H. G. Evelyn White, Cambridge, Mass., and London, 1982, p. 374.
68. Ibid., p. 149.
69. Ibid., p. 447.
70. Brown, *Velázquez*, p. 43.
71. See J. A. Emmens, "Las Ménines de Velázquez. Miroir des princes pour Philippe IV," *Nederlands Kunsthistorisch Jaarboek* 12 (1961): 77, and M. C. Volk, "On Velázquez and the Liberal Arts," *Art Bulletin* LX (1978): 74.
72. Freud, "The Acquisition and Control of Fire," S. E. XXII, 1932, pp. 187–93.
73. Orso, "A Lesson Learned."
74. Hesiod, *Works and Days*, pp. 48 ff., in *Homeric Hymns and Homerica*, Cambridge, Mass., and London, 1982, pp. 4–7.

ELEVEN

Psychobiography:
Caravaggio, Artemisia, Brancusi

B rancusi has been quoted as having said, "Art is committed—created or performed—only in austerity and in drama, like a perfect crime."[1] In that statement, the artist refers to the sublimatory character of creativity. He echoes Freud's discovery that the two oedipal crimes of the unconscious, incest and murder, are hidden and transformed in the arts.

In this chapter I propose to consider the issue of crime and art as it relates to three different artists: first, Caravaggio—the artist as criminal; second, Artemisia Gentileschi—the victim of a crime; and third, Brancusi, for whom art disguised "crime." In contrast to Caravaggio, whose criminal themes were as overt in his lifestyle as in his art, Brancusi's life and art were "secretive" and hidden. Artemisia, as the victim of a real crime, had to work out the trauma in order to pursue her art successfully.

CARAVAGGIO (1571–1610)

Caravaggio stands out in the history of Western art as one of the rare examples of a significant artist whose criminal acts included murder. In 1604, the Dutch biographer Carel Van Mander published the following description of his Italian contemporary: ". . . he [Caravaggio] does not study his art constantly, so that after two weeks of work he will sally forth for two months together with his rapier at his side and his servant-boy after him, going from one tennis court to another, always ready to argue or fight, so that he is impossible to get along with. This is totally foreign to art: for Mars and Minerva have never been good friends."[2]

Van Mander has captured Caravaggio's shifts from artist to criminal, which expressed his internal conflicts. On the one hand, Caravaggio created the most innovative paintings of his generation in Italy, and, on the other, he repeatedly committed minor infractions of the law. His criminal activity escalated until, in 1606, he killed a man in an argument over a tennis match. Caravaggio fled to the island of Malta, where, because of his abilities as a painter, he became a knight. There, too, he ran into trouble, and was jailed in the secure Maltese prison. His remarkable escape to the Italian mainland, at least one encounter with unknown attackers, and a fever, led to his death at the age of thirty-eight.

Very few clues to Caravaggio's character are provided by the scanty evidence of his childhood and family.[3] He was born in 1571 and lived in Milan until 1576, when his family moved back to their native town of Caravaggio. His father, Fermo di Bernardino Merisi, was either an architect or a mason who admired Michelangelo Buonarroti and named his son after him. A brother, Giovanni Battista, born a year after Caravaggio and the only sibling to live past childhood, became a priest. Fermo died in 1577, when Caravaggio was six, and his mother died thirteen years later, in 1590. At the age of twelve, Caravaggio was apprenticed to a painter from Bergamo who had been a student of Titian's.

According to G. P. Bellori (writing in the second half of the seventeenth century),[4] Caravaggio's volatile nature is first recorded in 1599, when he left Milan as a result of some quarrels. Other sources place him in Rome, at the age of twenty, where an uncle, who was a priest, lived. His brother Giovanni was in Rome in 1596–99, but Caravaggio is reported to have denied him.

Caravaggio's criminal activity, as documented by seventeenth-century police records, includes minor infractions involving personal offenses and libel, inflicting wounds with weapons, other physical violence, and finally murder.[5] His hostile behavior, as evidenced in denying his brother, emerged most clearly at the beginning of his move to Rome. He nicknamed his first Roman patron "Monsignor Insalata," allegedly because he fed the artist only salad. Later, in April 1604, Caravaggio insulted a waiter and threw artichokes at him. On September 1, 1605, Caravaggio's landlady sued him for breaking a window shutter. He was six months behind in his rent, and she had seized his furniture.

These incidents, revolving around themes of food and lodging, reflect the artist's basic conflicts over entitlement. Their origin in early childhood is suggested by Caravaggio's rage at not being properly fed or housed free of charge. A transformation of that rage appears in *Boy with a Basket of Fruit*

[66], in which the deliciously painted fruit complements the attraction of the boy himself. Both, Caravaggio seems to say, are edible. On the one hand, the boy solicits the viewer with his gaze, open mouth, and exposed shoulder, and, on the other, he holds the fruit close. This painting dates from Caravaggio's stay in the household of the homosexual Cardinal del Monte, through whom Caravaggio met other important patrons and received his first commission from the Church. Nevertheless, his bellicose nature continued to result in conflicts with the law.

From 1600 to 1606, Caravaggio's work on major commissions was punctuated by criminal activity. On November 19, 1600, he was accused of assault; on February 21, 1601, he wounded a sergeant while illegally carrying a sword restricted to the upper classes. He also dressed in velvet, which was reserved for the nobility. In 1603, he was sued for libel by three artists, and in 1604 he was in prison twice—for throwing stones and insulting an officer. In May 1605, he was arrested for bearing arms without a license, and a sword and a dagger were confiscated from him. In July of that year, he was jailed for offending a woman; he later assaulted a notary and left Rome for a month.

Caravaggio's impulsive, aggressive outbursts reveal his conflicts with authority. The iconography of certain paintings suggests that such infractions of the law were derived from the artist's experience of his father. The murderous impulse on the part of Abraham toward Isaac, discussed in Chapter 5, is a direct expression of a father's rage toward his son. A more veiled instance occurs in the *Rest on the Flight* [110], in which the father—in this case, Joseph—is seduced by the sight of the androgynous, nude, music-making angel in front of him. Joseph's "capture" by, and submission to, the angel is reinforced by his subservient position: he sits, and the angel stands; he holds up the music that the angel plays.

Joseph's sexual excitement is revealed by his feet as he rubs one big toe over the other. Echoing his erotic anticipation is the phallic detail of the wine cask, whose neck, and the cloth stuffed inside it, seems to poke out of its covering. Likewise, the large, staring eyes of the donkey echo Joseph's riveted gaze. The psychic violence hidden in this deceptively peaceful scene is increased by the strong vertical of the angel's wing, which divides the sleeping Virgin and Christ from the homosexual seduction between Joseph and the angel.

The latent psychological message of the *Rest* does not seem to have created conflicts with the Church. On other occasions, however, Caravaggio did offend ecclesiastic sensibilities. The reasons given for the of-

110. *Michelangelo da Caravaggio,* Rest on the
Flight to Egypt, *1594–95. Palazzo Doria, Rome.*

fenses never quite correspond to the subtext, or latent content, of the
imagery in question.

The *Death of the Virgin* [111] of 1605–6, now in the Louvre, was
allegedly rejected by the Church because of Mary's unseemly bare feet and
swollen body. This depiction defied Counter-Reformation ideology, according to which Mary died without pain or physical disfigurement. One
of Caravaggio's biographers, G. Mancini, has reported that the model for
the Virgin was a prostitute.[6] Whatever the actual reasons for the rejection
were, the *Death of the Virgin,* like Caravaggio's *Amor,* [52] was purchased
by a secular collector who recognized its originality.

In another painting, rejected a month before Caravaggio committed
murder, *Madonna and Child with Saint Anne* [112], c. 1605, Caravaggio's

hostility assumes an oedipal cast. The work was commissioned for Saint Peter's altar of papal grooms, or *palafrenieri*, and therefore marked a significant advance in his career. Mary and Christ together step on a serpent's neck while Saint Anne looks on. The theological meaning of the iconography is the triumph of the New Dispensation—Mary and Christ—over the Fall of Man, and the redemption of Eve's original sin. Even though the image was consistent with a Counter-Reformation papal bull issued in 1560,[7] it offended the Church.

The unconscious meaning of Caravaggio's iconography is the oedipal victory of the son over the father. Mother and son join forces to destroy the father, symbolized by the phallic snake. That they do so by stepping

111. *Michelangelo da Caravaggio,* Death of the Virgin, *1605–6. Louvre, Paris.*

112. *Michelangelo da Caravaggio,* Madonna and Child with Saint Anne, *Palafrenieri Altarpiece, 1605. Galleria Borghese, Rome.*

on his neck resonates with the biblical "it [the seed of woman] shall bruise thy head, and thou shalt bruise his heel" (Gen. 3 : 15), as well as with the prevalence of decapitation imagery in Caravaggio's oeuvre. The reasons for the rejection of this work are not documented; several explanations have been suggested, including the focus on Christ's nudity.[8] It is true that Christ's phallus points directly at Mary's toe pressing on the serpent's neck and that this emphasizes the phallic competition between them.

Even more problematic than his nudity, however, is Christ's age, for he is no longer an infant. He has the body and head of an adolescent, but he is held forward by his mother, as a younger child might be. This odd juxtaposition of age is also characteristic of the *Amor,* whose body belongs to an older, more physically developed man and is not consistent with the youthful, adolescent face. It is possible that the maturity of Christ's body highlights the oedipal, and therefore incestuous, meaning of the image and that, in sensing this, the patrons decided against displaying the work.

The instance in which the reasons for rejection are clearest is the *Inspiration of Saint Matthew* for the Contarelli Chapel in Rome's Church of San Luigi dei Francesi. In this case, both the original, rejected image [113] and the second, accepted version [114] are known. The ostensible cause for the rejection was the visibility of the bottom of the saint's foot. But from a comparison of the rejected (destroyed in World War II) with the accepted version (in the Church), it is evident that what has changed is the degree to which homosexuality is more or less manifest.

In the rejected picture, the angel's mouth is slightly open, as in *Boy with a Basket of Fruit.* He leans toward the saint, so that their heads seem to touch, and the wing frames and caresses the saint's head. The curve of the angel's body is so arranged that the diagonal of his right leg flows into the saint's. Arms and hands move around the book so that in all the limbs there is a seductive play on merging form and softness of touch. The homosexual appeal of this work at the time of its execution is suggested by the fact that, on its rejection, it was purchased by the same patron who owned *Amor.* In the accepted *Inspiration of Saint Matthew,* Caravaggio has mitigated—though not eliminated—the homosexual relationship of Matthew with the angel. Instead of physical contact, they are held by a mutual gaze; and, as the angel enumerates his message on his fingers, a piece of his drapery reaches out, as if beckoning the saint.

The social, political, and legal issue of homosexuality is a complex one. Liberal factions of the Church and licentious members of the clergy notwithstanding, homosexuality had been considered a crime against nature since the fourth century A.D., and, by the sixth century, homosexuality was being blamed for arousing the wrath of God and causing the destruction of entire cities. The example of Sodom and Gomorrah led to cries of pestilence, which, in Greek myth, had been the punishment inflicted on Thebes for Oedipus's incest and parricide.

In the Middle Ages and in the Renaissance, the statutory punishment for homosexuality in Italy, Spain, and France included castration, dismemberment, and burning. Punishment was by example, for purposes of creating a deterrent, which corresponds to the pictorial character of oedipal fantasy. That sexual inversion, such as sodomy, was treated as parallel to revolution as an inversion of the established order is evident from their parallel punishments. Perpetrators of both crimes could be publicly hanged upside down.

113. *Michelangelo da Caravaggio*, Inspiration of Saint Matthew *(rejected), c. 1597–98, destroyed 1945. Formerly Kaiser Friedrich Museum, Berlin.*

In addition to many paintings with a criminal subtext, Caravaggio painted several pictures of manifest criminal activity. In the *Cardsharps*, he portrays cheating at cards, and in the *Fortune-teller* (Louvre), a Gypsy girl seduces an unsuspecting youth with her gaze while slipping a ring from his finger. Both works illustrate genre conventions to which Caravaggio was attracted. In the *Calling of Saint Matthew* for the Contarelli Chapel, Caravaggio combines genre with theology. He depicts the saint with a gold coin tucked into the brim of his hat, gambling among unsavory street characters with an illicit interest in money.

Caravaggio's attraction to criminal subjects is consistent with his predilection for violence. His most pervasive violent theme is decapitation, and it is clear that he projected himself into such decapitated heads as that of Goliath in [11]. In *Judith and Holofernes* [115], the man is beheaded by a duplicitous woman, just as the fortune-teller robs the unsuspecting youth. *The Head of Medusa* [116], painted at the end of the early series of transvestite boys (compare *Boy with a Basket of Fruit*), is a masterful image of gender confusion. The physiognomy, which is not clearly male or female, is probably the artist's self-image.

In a later portrait, of the Grand Master of the Knights of Malta, Alof de Wigancourt [117], Caravaggio disguises these themes and mitigates the violence by displacing from head to helmet. A young page holds de Wigancourt's plumed helmet and gazes wistfully at the viewer. Except for his helmet, de Wigancourt, in contrast to the page, is fully armed. Here, as in the Borghese *David* [11], albeit symbolically, Caravaggio has given a young boy control of an older man's "head."

In creating art, as Van Mander writes, Caravaggio followed Minerva; but in his propensity for violence and lawlessness, he followed Mars. In life,

114. Michelangelo da Caravaggio, Inspiration of Saint Matthew (accepted), 1602. Contarelli Chapel, San Luigi dei Francesi, Rome.

115. *Michelangelo da
Caravaggio*, Judith and
Holofernes, *1598–99.
Palazzo Barbarini, Rome.*

116. *Michelangelo da
Caravaggio*, The Head of
Medusa, *c. 1596–98 (?).
Uffizi, Florence.*

he could not integrate art and criminal activity, but shifted between them, and died as a result of the crime. A latent subtext of the alternation between the creativity implied by the female goddess Minerva and the destructive character of the bellicose Mars is the bisexual shift between feminine and masculine identification.

In the art itself, however, Caravaggio integrated, but in a unique way. Although he offended the Church on several occasions, for the most part he sublimated his hostility and kept his most outrageously perverse imagery for private patrons. Caravaggio's detached heads represent his self-image as a castrated victim; but some also protest their fate. This psychological shift between victimization and protest echoes the criminal behavior in which the artist incites the anger of others and then objects to

117. Michelangelo da Caravaggio, Alof de Wigancourt, *1608. Louvre, Paris.*

118. *Michelangelo da Caravaggio,* Beheading of
John the Baptist, *1608. Valletta Cathedral, Malta.*

it. Likewise, the decapitated heads, which are simultaneously alive and
dead, echo the transitional sexuality of the transvestites and *Medusa.*

Caravaggio's only signed painting, the *Beheading of John the Baptist* of
1608 [118], has a powerful biographical subtext. In contrast to some of
Caravaggio's other heads, John's is dead (as it is in *Salome Receiving the Head
of John the Baptist,* now in London). In the *Beheading,* Salome holds out a
platter to receive John's head. The executioner leans over, grasps John by
the hair, and prepares to finish the job with his knife. When the painting
was cleaned in the 1950s, it was discovered that the blood flowing from
John's neck contained the artist's signature: F Michel A. . . . According to
Howard Hibbard,[9] the signature probably read Fra Michel Angelo: "meaning that he was already a Knight of Malta."

But another, more psychological reading is possible, if Hibbard's
reconstruction of the signature is correct. "Fra" means "brother," and
though it designates "brother" in the religious sense of "friar," there can be
no doubt of its association with a biological brother, or "fratello." Caravaggio had already denied his younger brother, the priest Giovanni Battista, or *John the Baptist.* In other paintings, the artist kills Giovanni symbolically in making the heads of John the Baptist dead, whereas those with

which he himself identifies (Medusa and Goliath) are still alive. In this light, the signature connotes a brother killing a brother, and indicates that the painting is the work of John's brother, Michelangelo Merisi da Caravaggio.[10]

ARTEMISIA GENTILESCHI (1593–AFTER 1651)

Artemisia Gentileschi, daughter of the painter Orazio, was a follower of Caravaggio, whom she may have known personally. Born in Rome in 1593, she was Orazio's only daughter and first child; her mother died when she was twelve, leaving her and her brothers in the care of her father. Artemisia was trained as an artist by Orazio and, despite the many difficulties facing women artists, she became one of the leading painters of her generation. She married, had two daughters of whom little is known, and separated from her husband.

Artemisia is of particular interest as a woman in the art world, which, in the sixteenth and seventeenth centuries, was more dominated by men than it is today. Because she was the victim of a rape, made notorious by the suit her father brought against the rapist, Artemisia's iconography has been seen in the light of her victimization.[11]

In March 1612, Orazio sued Agostino Tassi, a painter whom he had hired to teach his daughter perspective, for raping her. In the ensuing trial, Artemisia testified that in May of 1611 Agostino forced her into her bedroom and locked the door.[12] He threw her on the bed, stuffed a cloth in her mouth to prevent her from crying out, and raped her. When he had finished, she said, she grabbed a knife and threw it at him, managing only to spill a few drops of blood. Tassi calmed her by promising to marry her and, as a result of the promise, she continued to yield to him for several months. Eventually, however, she realized that he was leading her on; she learned that he was previously married and had been accused of killing his wife. He had also been jailed for incest with his sister-in-law, who was the mother of his children.

In contrast to the early childhood memories that shed light on the psychosexual development of such artists as Leonardo, Michelangelo, and Cellini, Artemisia's biographical trauma has traditionally been billed as her rape. Its relatively late occurrence—at the age of eighteen—puts it in a different psychological category from screen memories and childhood fantasies. At eighteen, Artemisia was in an advanced stage of her training and well on her way to becoming a prominent artist. For the circumstances surrounding the rape and the supporting cast, the best original source is the trial itself. Unfortunately, it is clear that several witnesses, notably the accused and his defenders, were unreliable. Although Tassi was convicted, he spent only eight months in jail and was released when the case was subsequently dismissed. Artemisia was thus doubly "raped"—in the act itself and again at the trial, where she was betrayed by certain witnesses and tortured by her questioners.

From the point of view of art and psychoanalysis, the significance of the rape and its aftermath lie in their dynamic relationship to Artemisia's past and the ways in which both influenced her painting. After Artemisia's mother died, she developed a friendship with an older woman, one Tuzia, and her daughter, who were tenants of her father. At the trial, in true *Rashomon* fashion, Artemisia testified that Tuzia had functioned as a "procuress"[13] for Agostino Tassi, and Tuzia testified that Artemisia had behaved seductively toward Tassi. In short, Artemisia felt betrayed by an older woman to whom she had become attached as a kind of substitute mother.

Also, one might wonder about the possible ambivalence of Artemisia's father. On the one hand, he recognized her talent and taught her painting; on the other, he hired Tassi—allegedly to teach her perspective—despite his bad reputation and criminal sexual history. Nor does Orazio seem to have been particularly vigilant in matters of his daughter's chastity. Even more curious from a modern perspective, it seems that both Orazio and Artemisia would have let bygones be bygones if Tassi had come through on his promise of marriage. Breach of promise, it would appear, was a worse offense than rape. The argument that no one would marry a "used" woman loses force in the light of Artemisia's marriage shortly after the trial.

However one views the attitudes of Artemisia's time, she had good reason to feel outraged at her treatment, from several quarters. That she projected her feelings into her paintings is a psychoanalytic given; how she did so is open to discussion. In general, Artemisia painted powerful heroines, and it is likely that she identified with them, especially as one who had to overcome formidable professional obstacles. The evidence of the extant work indicates that she painted more pictures of Judith and Holofernes—five autograph—than of any other subject. In view of its repetition, from c. 1612–c. 1625, Artemisia might have been "working through" (see Chapter 7) her traumatic rape over a period of some fourteen years.

*Working through, in Artemisia's case, as in the clinical situation, is to be
distinguished from repetition, which Freud discovered in the shell-shock victims of World War I. At first he was puzzled to find that soldiers kept returning
in nightmares to relive their traumatic circumstances. In* Beyond the Pleasure
Principle *(1920), Freud revised his view of the pleasure principle and explained
the greater force of the repetition compulsion, which he attributed to the death
instinct. In working through, therefore, one gains control of the trauma and
is freed from the compulsion to repeat.*

Artemisia's Judith: Psychoanalysis and Feminism

In the apocryphal Book of Judith, the Assyrian general Holofernes is about
to conquer the Israelite city of Bethulia. Judith, a Hebrew widow, accompanied by her maid, Abra, sets out for Holofernes' tent with the intention of
saving her people. She pretends to help her enemy with false information
about the Israelites. Holofernes invites her to dinner and is sexually aroused
by her beauty. He gets drunk, however, and falls asleep. Judith decapitates
him with his own sword, gives his head to Abra, who places it in her bag
of food, and the two women return home. Judith presents Holofernes' head
to the Israelites and tells them to display it from the city walls. The
Assyrians scatter at the news of their leader's death, Judith is now a
heroine, famous and honored by her people; she is courted by many men,
whom she rejects; and she lives to the ripe old age of one hundred and five.

Mary D. Garrard's recent monograph on Artemisia is an extremely
useful scholarly study of the artist and her themes. Her interpretations,
however, highlight the methodological differences between a scholarly
feminist approach to imagery and a psychoanalytic one. Garrard objects to
reading Artemisia's portrayal of Judith as merely a revenge on Agostino
Tassi, seeing this as an oversimplification. It is "not so much the male
character who is acted upon," she writes, "but the female character who
acts."[14] In place of the "prevailing and almost obsessive interpretations of
the painting as savage revenge," Garrard calls for the recognition of the
"positive and healthy elements of [Artemisia's] identification with her
character."[15] To the suggestions by several scholars that Artemisia painted
herself as Judith, Garrard points out, rightly, that it was a Renaissance
tradition for artists to project themselves into their imagery and to identify
with certain figures.

The caveat that artists project their own images into their work,
however, in no way diminishes the validity of the reading in a specific

instance (providing, of course, that the reading is correct). A review of the apocryphal text does, in fact, suggest several parallels between Artemisia's personal experience and Judith's. Artemisia's betrayal by the woman Tuzia, regardless of whose account one believes, can be linked with the role of Abra, Judith's maid. Garrard's suggestion that the relationship of the two women is a transformation of Artemisia and Tuzia makes psychological sense. For the real unity of purpose shared by Judith and Abra is in sharp contrast to Tuzia's duplicity. In this regard, the apocryphal narrative could have served a reparative purpose—two women joined together in their opposition to a dangerous man.

Whereas Judith and Abra are a kind of foil for Artemisia and Tuzia, Holofernes can be seen as a psychological parallel to Agostino Tassi. In the ancient Near East, the Assyrian armies were known for their barbarism; yet some of the most bloodthirsty Assyrian leaders were profoundly interested in education, art, and literature. The same paradoxical combination of violence and art coexisted—on a lesser scale—in Artemisia's rapist and art teacher. To call Holofernes "Everyman," as Garrard does,[16] is to risk blurring the specificity of his associative power for Artemisia. Likewise, Garrard's view that Judith is a metaphor for "female defiance of male power"[17] tends to "reduce" her actions to the level of protest rather than allowing for the force of independent thought. It also detracts from the "positive and healthy" qualities that Garrard recognizes in interpreting Artemisia's identification with Judith.

From a psychoanalytic point of view, it is the mutual *abuse* of power by Holofernes and Tassi that connects them in Artemisia's mind, and not their role as "Everyman" or as abstract symbols of "patriarchal" injustice. It is not so much revenge, per se, that determines Artemisia's choice of the Judith theme, as the avenues for identification provided by the apocryphal narrative. By her decapitation of Holofernes, Artemisia as Judith reverses passive into active, which is one of the ego's defense mechanisms. Holofernes' sexual desire for Judith evokes the motive for Tassi's rape, which Artemisia could not prevent in reality, but which she reversed, and worked through, in the paintings. She also surpassed Tassi as an artist and, like Judith, who was honored in her own country, fulfilled the heroic wishes Freud attributed to the creative daydreamer.

Artemisia's *Judith* in Naples' Capodimonte Museum [119] is dated c. 1612–13 by Garrard (that is, soon after the trial). Both the violence to the man and the unified purpose of the two women are unmistakable. Compared with Caravaggio's *Judith and Holofernes* of 1598–99 [115], Artemisia's

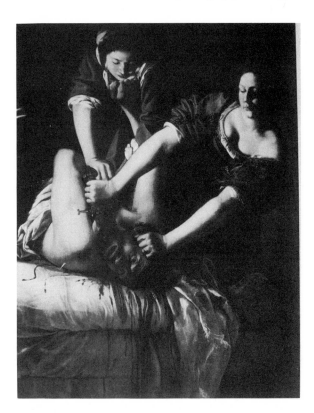

119. Artemisia
Gentileschi, Judith,
c. 1612–13. Museo
Capodimonte, Naples.

painting is more of a close-up and thus, although both are extremely violent, has a more direct impact. The women, especially Abra, push down with greater vertical force against Holofernes, who, in turn, resists more vigorously than he does in Caravaggio's image. Caravaggio's heroine holds the sword at a horizontal angle and seems to be gingerly sawing across her victim's neck. The intermingling of arms in Artemisia's version evokes the actual, desperate physical struggle of a rape, whereas Caravaggio's Judith remains at arm's length, and his Holofernes, taken by surprise from behind, grasps the bedclothes.

Two specific details reported by Artemisia in her testimony can be noted in relation to the Naples Judith. One is Holofernes' open mouth, which is also a feature of Caravaggio's picture. Artemisia testified that Tassi had stuffed a cloth into her mouth, which she counters by adopting the characteristic open mouth of Caravaggio's decapitated victims, who scream in protest. The other detail is the amount of blood. According to Artemisia, she threw a knife at Tassi, only to spill a few drops of his blood. In this

120. *Artemisia Gentileschi,*
Judith and Her
Maidservant, *c. 1613–14.*
Pitti Palace, Florence.
Brogi 2919.

painting, however (and in the Uffizi version), Holofernes' blood pours from
his neck and streams down the sheets. In the former detail, Artemisia
permits Holofernes to do what she wished to do during her own rape—
that is, to cry out—and in the latter, she does to Holofernes what she tried
unsuccessfully to do to her attacker.

A year or so later, c. 1613–14, Artemisia painted a more restrained
work, *Judith and Her Maidservant* [120], in which the unity of the two
women is even more pronounced. Abra, seen from the rear, holds the
basket containing Holofernes' head, and Judith, seen from the front, rests
the sword on her shoulder. Both women turn sharply to the right, as if
something has caught their attention. Adorning the pommel of Judith's
sword is a Medusa head [121]. As Judith and Abra turn away, Medusa's
head screams down at the decapitated head of Holofernes. There is thus an
iconographic play on paired heads, each pair in a diagonal plane reinforced
by gesture and drapery.

Garrard's feminist reading of this Medusa is at odds with its psychological significance.[18] According to Garrard, the Medusa head is a "talisman . . . that complements and extends her [Artemisia's] own identity."[19] Because there are no snakes in Medusa's hair, Garrard asserts, she is a "benevolent," "positive Medusa type," a "mother image," and a "personal female emblem."[20] Garrard calls this a "sea-change" in Medusa's iconography and attributes it to the "reversal of sex roles," because Judith confronts a male, in contrast to Perseus and Odysseus, who confronted the female Medusa.[21]

This reading highlights the difference between feminist and psychoanalytic interpretation—for, if Artemisia's Medusa is a "talisman" complementing and extending Judith's identity, which seems a reasonable conclusion, then Judith must be related to Athena. As the Greek goddess of war and wisdom, she counseled Perseus in his pursuit of Medusa and took the head for her aegis. An identification with Athena, as indicated by the Gorgoneion on the pommel, would be consistent with Judith's heroic and quasi-military role in saving the Israelites from the Assyrian army. Athena's aspect as a virgin goddess would also resonate with Artemisia's wish to have prevented her rape and to remain a virgin until marriage.

Nor is there any "sea-change" reflected by the iconography of this particular Medusa, and, even if there were, there is no "reversal of sex roles" in any case. The absence of the snakes, which Freud identified as

121. Detail of Figure 120: Medusa on the pommel of Judith's sword.

upwardly displaced phalli intended to ward off and deny the possibility of castration,[22] does not make Artemisia's Medusa "benevolent," "positive," or maternal. Medusa is rarely, if ever, benevolent, although her visual image undergoes many transformations. From the Hellenistic period, Medusa could be beautiful and idealized—as in the marble *Rondanini Medusa* in Munich. In the nineteenth century, the Romantics simultaneously adored and dreaded her;[23] she represented the deadly—because aloof, distant, and cold—mother actually experienced by certain poets. She is exemplified as such in Keats's "La Belle Dame Sans Merci," and as the siren of Cézanne's "Une Terrible Histoire" (see Chapter 9). Above all, Shelley's poem, inspired by the Uffizi *Medusa*, which literally crawls with images of snakes, bats, lizards, and other phallic creatures, has been called almost a manifesto of the Romantic conception of beauty. Shelley describes this unappealing picture according to the ambivalence of the nineteenth-century Medusean aesthetic—"Its horror and its beauty are divine."[24]

Medusa is first referred to in Homer (*Iliad* XI, 36), as *the* Gorgon, or Gorgo, which was a detached head. It was set like a crown on the shield of Agamemnon, had a terrifying glare and shaggy hair, and was flanked by Fear and Terror. Homer describes the Gorgon on Athena's shield as noisy, and compares her gaze with the eyes of Hector in battle as "man-destroying" (*Iliad* VIII, 349). In the *Odyssey*, the Gorgon head is associated with the dangers of Mother Earth, in which aspect she threatens Odysseus in the underworld (*Odyssey* XI, 633–35). In Hesiod, all three Gorgons wear snaky belts, and cause fear and panic (*Shield of Heracles*, 220–339, and *Theogony*, 270–295).

In ancient art and literature, as well as in the Renaissance, the attributes of Medusa vary. Although there is usually an abundance of phallic symbols, they can be in the form of bulging eyes, fangs, prominent teeth, and serpentine hair or belts. Sometimes wings replace the snaky hair, and sometimes both are present. Artemisia's Medusa conforms to the Homeric description of a detached head and armor device. Her eyes bulge and she cries out noisily, as in the *Iliad*. Her snaky hair, though not explicit, is alluded to in the surrounding scroll designs. The absence of snakes in Artemisia's iconography, therefore, in no way signifies a radical departure ("sea-change") from traditional Medusa images.

It is interesting that Artemisia's Medusa seems to be glaring down at Holofernes' decapitated head. Symbolically and psychologically, Judith's assumption of the Gorgoneion on her sword is a kind of talion image—a head for a head—in a painting designed as a play on four heads. Its role as a talion is reinforced by its location on Judith's sword—rather than on a shield or breastplate, which is the more usual location—for it is by the sword that Holofernes dies. Finally, the traditional apotropaic character of Medusa's head resonates both with Artemisia's wish to have warded off her rapist and with Judith's recommendation that the Israelites hang Holofernes' head from the city walls. In the Apocrypha, therefore, his decapitated head serves a combined apotropaic and exemplary purpose, and warns against laying siege to Judith's town.

BRANCUSI (1876–1957)

Brancusi not only equated art with crime, he also related the work of art with its maker when he asserted with disapproval that "aesthetes have an aversion to biography."[25] That statement affirms the biographical connection between artists and their art, even when form seems to prevail over content. Despite the quasi-geometric qualities of Brancusi's sculptures, they are modeled on recognizable natural forms. The significance of their forms nevertheless remains ambiguous in most cases. This ambiguity is somewhat relieved by a poetic title, which creates a verbal link to content and iconography. To this point, Brancusi declared "They are imbeciles who call my work abstract!" By this he meant that his sculptures were "real" in the sense of being Platonic "essences." In pursuing the titles of his works, however, it is possible to discover biographical subtexts in Brancusi's art.

Constantin Brancusi was born in a Romanian farming village, on February 19, 1876. His parents were peasants; he had three older half-brothers, two full brothers, and one sister. He was attached only to his mother and sister; his father beat him and put "horse dung" under his nose. "He wanted a daughter," according to the artist.[26] By the age of nine, Brancusi had tried to run away from home on two occasions, and at eleven he succeeded. In 1894, an employer recognized his talent and arranged for him to enter a trade school in Craiova.

Brancusi later studied at the Bucharest School of Fine Arts and the Paris Ecole des Beaux-Arts. He worked briefly for Rodin in 1907, but broke away from him when he received an independent commission. In 1913, he exhibited five works in the Armory Show and, like Duchamp, was criticized in the American press for his avant-garde imagery. Brancusi's work tends to draw the viewer's attention to the formal tour de force of his polished surfaces and reduction of detail to what he liked to call an "essence."

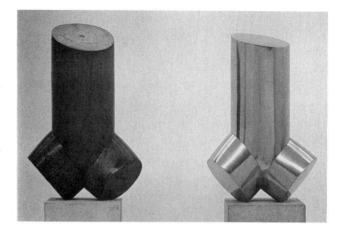

122. *Constantin Brancusi*, Torso.
Left: 1917–22.
Arensberg Collection, Philadelphia Museum of Art.
Right: 1917.
Cleveland Museum of Art.

His earliest sculptures were relatively naturalistic portraits; but in a 1906 bust of a boy modeled on a child who was blind (Geist #22),[27] the right shoulder is cut off. Despite this violence to the body, the effect is not shocking, which is a tribute to Brancusi's formal skill. It also prefigures the partial character of the artist's later human subjects. With only two exceptions, Brancusi's human figures are part figures, whereas his animals (except for the penguins) are complete.[28] *Torment*, the title of two sculptures of boys made in 1906 and 1907, represents a state of mind and, as such, can be related to late-nineteenth-century Symbolism. This title also, however, echoes Brancusi's own suffering and damaged self-image, brought about, at least in part, by his father's beatings.

The *Torso* [122], which is phallic in shape but without a genital, is psychologically an image of the artist's ambivalent relation to his masculinity. It is a phallus deprived of a phallus, just as Brancusi was a boy whose father wanted him to be a girl. The idea of a detached phallus displaced upward recurs in Brancusi's numerous sculptures of detached heads. The heads are the descendants of his early portraits, but they have become "modern," "abstract," and polished to such a degree that the "violence" to the body is hidden by the elegant form.

Brancusi and the Primal Scene

Several images created by Brancusi can be read as having primal-scene content. His marble *Leda* [123] of 1920 (Geist #131), for example, is a mythological version of the primal scene in which Zeus, disguised as a

123. *Constantin Brancusi,* Leda,
1920. Chicago Art Institute.

swan, seduces Leda. In the sculpture, Zeus and Leda merge, and Leda literally "becomes the swan."[29] Brancusi later said of this work, "It is Leda, not Jupiter, changing into a swan. A man is as ugly as a frog; a swan has exquisite curves like those of a woman's body."[30]

In that statement, the artist expressed his dislike of the male form, psychologically his masculine self-image. The traditional fairy-tale motif in which the frog becomes a prince, or the ugly duckling becomes a swan, is transformed into the woman becoming the swan/prince. Brancusi thus replicates the child's primal-scene confusion, the uncertainty about who does what to whom, and expresses his confused body image.

One of Brancusi's "most disquieting" creations, according to Sidney Geist,[31] is the wooden *Nocturnal Animal* (Geist #178) of c. 1930 [124]. But why "disquieting"? It lies in a horizontal plane, its rounded surface and absence of differentiation suggest a bloated slug. Less elegant than the artist's other animals, this has a slightly repellent quality. *Nocturnal Animal* is closed in on itself, without the sleek extension of Brancusi's fishes, turtles, and birds. It seems to hug the ground, as if trying to elude notice. It is perhaps the most "hidden" of his works in a narrative sense and the most minimal in a formal sense. Thus, I would propose reading *Nocturnal Animal* as Brancusi himself—the artist of the hidden and the child who lurks in darkness, seeking the answer to the riddle of birth.

In the repeated versions of *The Kiss* [125], Brancusi worked out the primal scene most completely. Geist[32] has identified the autobiographical subtext of this theme. Preceding the first *Kiss*, of 1907–8, is *Pride*, 1905, in which a girl repels the advances of an unattractive man. Geist notes that the male figure in the 1907–8 *Kiss* resembles Brancusi himself, suggesting that it attempts to "repair" the earlier rebuff. Years later, Brancusi would draw a *Kiss* on his calling card, indicating that it had become a "personal emblem."[33] In the meantime, he reworked the theme of the kiss many times. It reached its culmination in the 1938 *Gate of the Kiss* [126], in the public park of Tîrgu Jiu, in Romania.

As Brancusi developed the theme of the kiss, the embracing figures merged into the geometry of the rectangular block. The sense of oneness, as if a fulfillment of the Platonic androgynous union, increased. Referring to the *Gate of the Kiss*, Geist[34] describes the embracing couple constituting the column in terms that evoke the primal scene: "The circular motifs on the columns join the tall curved planes immediately below to make a magical image of merged male and female genitals. The inward curve of the planes and the outward bulge of the split circle above may be seen to rehearse the movement of the sexual act."

Also increasingly merged from the first *Kiss* to the *Gate* are the two eyes whose two profile views resemble a single frontal eye. The motif of the lovers is repeated forty times in the *Gate of the Kiss*, sixteen on the long sides of the lintel and four on each short side. The large single eye, created by the combined profile eyes, and situated on either side of the column, seems to look at whoever approaches the gateway. The "eye" thus has a double function; as a profile, it participates in the lovers' embrace, and as a frontal image, it watches those who enter and leave by the gate. As such, the "eyes" of the columns act like Janus, the Roman god of gateways, whose double face allowed him to see in two directions at once.

Brancusi's sculptures reveal a preoccupation with beginnings and with the origin of life. Their relationship to primal-scene curiosity is evident from their titles. As a kiss begins the physical relationship between lovers,

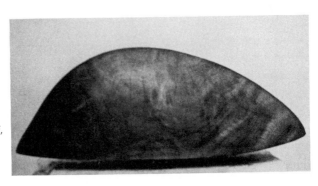

124. *Constantin Brancusi, Nocturnal Animal, c. 1930. Musée d'Art Moderne, Paris.*

125. *Constantin Brancusi,*
The Kiss, *1907–8.*
Craiova Museum of Art,
Romania.

126. *Constantin Brancusi,*
Gate of the Kiss, *1937–38.*
Tîrgu Jiu, Romania.

Brancusi seems to say, so the egg is the beginning of life. Hence the ovoid shape of many of his sculptures of "beginnings": *Beginning of the World, The Newborn,* and *The First Cry.* The artist brought these notions together in his undated version of the "Readymade-aided" when he painted the *Kiss* four times on an egg.[35]

Brancusi and the Eye-Phallus Equation

Brancusi's preoccupation with the motif of the eye, as well as with beginnings, also has autobiographical significance. When he met the Hungarian artist Margit Pogany, he sculpted her head (Geist #60) and endowed all the versions of it with particularly large eyes [127]. The fact that Brancusi made several versions of the Pogany heads from 1912 to 1935 points to his experience of her as a source of inspiration. At the same time, however, the detachment of the head, combined with the huge eyes, suggests a latent image of the woman as dangerous; symbolically, she is both castrated (beheaded) and phallic (the large eyes). This reading is reinforced by the fact that the first marble version of Mlle Pogany was exhibited as a Danaïd, a daughter of Danaüs in Greek mythology. The Danaïds were fifty in number, and all were ordered to kill their husbands on their wedding night.

127. *Constantin Brancusi,*
Mlle Pogany, *1912.*
Philadelphia Museum of Art.

128. *Constantin Brancusi,*
Narcissus Fountain, *1910.*
Musée d'Art Moderne, Paris.

129. Constantin Brancusi, Princess X,
1916. Philadelphia Museum of Art.

It would appear from the conflation of Margit Pogany with the Danaïds that the dangerous phallic woman persisted in Brancusi's fantasy, as it had in Leonardo's and Michelangelo's. In Brancusi's iconography, the fantasy is explicit in the formal relationship between the *Narcissus Fountain* [128] (Geist #82) of 1910 and *Princess X* [129], executed in marble and bronze in 1916 (Geist #96 and 97). Both are unmistakably phallic, and *Princess X* was withdrawn from the Salon des Artistes Indépendants in 1920 for that very reason.[36] The figure in *Narcissus*, who leans over as if to gaze at himself in a pool of water, is, like the *Torso*, a body-as-phallus.

These particular sculptures can be related to the psychoanalytic "phallic character," of which "phallic narcissism" is the most prominent feature. This has been explained theoretically as a narcissistic confusion of self and body with phallus, generally as a compensation for the castration complex. The clinical picture of the phallic narcissist includes exaggerated vanity, oversensitivity, and reckless behavior, which is often mistaken for courage. Such behavior is a defensive-reaction formation against fear of narcissistic dependence. Phallic narcissism is expressed in the so-called Don Juan character; because such men have not worked out their oedipal attachment to their mothers, they go from woman to woman rather than become committed to one woman.[37]

This is not to suggest that Brancusi was a phallic narcissist. But he never married and, despite his attraction to Margit Pogany, portrayed her as a figure from Greek myth who kills her husband on their wedding night. Brancusi's repeated iconography of the woman-as-phallus reveals his ambivalent relation to women. The same can be said of his "eyes," which range from relatively naturalistic in size to very large, and from open to closed. Several figures (usually heads) are asleep, and some have no eyes at all. *Sculpture for the Blind* (Geist #98), which is also ovoid, "speaks" to the eyes of the viewer, presumes them to be unseeing, and invites a literal tactile, rather than a visual, response. In the final resolution of *The Kiss*, Brancusi seems to have "solved" the dangers of the eye by the combined frontal and profile views. The lovers are free to merge with each other and, by so doing, also "keep an eye on" the observer watching them.

130. *Constantin Brancusi*, Pasarea Maiastra, *1912. John Cowles Collection, Minneapolis.*

Brancusi's Birds

Among Brancusi's best-known works are his *Birds*, which must be seen as self-images. They began not as the slender verticals of *Bird in Space* [58], but as *Pasarea Maiastra* [130], Romanian for "Master Bird" and "Magical Bird."[38] According to Brancusi, Pasarea Maiastra was a character from Romanian folklore who led Prince Charming to his beloved. In fact, however, there is no such Romanian tale; it is the artist's fiction. That this motif appears in Brancusi's oeuvre about the time of his first encounter with Margit Pogany, who was for him a muse, raises the likelihood of its connection with a "real" romantic aspiration. He reworked *Pasarea Maiastra* in bronze and marble through 1915, and gradually transformed it into the more minimal *Birds in Space*.

131. Constantin Brancusi, The Cock, 1924.
Museum of Modern Art, New York.

132. *Constantin Brancusi,*
Endless Column, *1937.*
Tîrgu Jiu, Romania.

In addition to the larger *Birds,* Brancusi also made *Little Birds* and *Cocks.* Both the *Birds,* which become progressively "abstract," and the *Cocks,* of which there are six in all, start out small [131] and become larger.[39] The last cock, made of plaster in 1949 (Geist #204), is 191 inches high. Shades of Flaubert and Emma Bovary—Brancusi declared, "I am the Cock!"[40] Possibly the ultimate transformation of Brancusi's phallic self-image as one who reaches toward the sky is the *Endless Column* at Tîrgu Jiu [132]; it suggests the paradox of an Icarus with his "feet on the ground."

Brancusi's Alchemy

Geist wrote that Brancusi "miraculously avoids the appearance of a severed head" and endows the object with "independent existence."[41] In his partial and cut-off features of the body, which were influenced by Rodin, Brancusi hid the violence of dismemberment. He cloaked historical sources—African, Greek, Egyptian, Southeast Asian—in a kind of minimalism *avant la lettre*, especially *Endless Column*. He accomplished this by drastic reductionism, formal elegance, and unprecedented smooth, dazzling finish; his surfaces become content and mask the underlying narrative.

The hidden alchemical meaning of such material transformation was probably not unconscious on Brancusi's part. In 1915, he made a watercolor based on a photograph of himself, titled *Brancusi at the Anvil* [133]. The

133. Constantin Brancusi, Brancusi at the Anvil, *1915. Collection Samuel Staempfli, Bern.*

picture shows the artist as a smith. In that role, he is related to Hephaestos and Vulcan. Like the alchemist, the smith changes the ores of the Earth Mother into craft and, in Brancusi's case, into art.

The alchemist-smith is a "master of fire"; he works for the gods, but he also has a civilizing influence on mankind as the bearer of fire.[42] Brancusi's heads, entitled *Prometheus*, who angered the gods by stealing fire and was himself a sculptor, further reveal the artist's identification with mythological artists.

An artist who ran away from home as a child, Brancusi was unable to identify with his abusive father. His *Prodigal Son* [Geist #91] of 1915 (the same year as the watercolor) reveals a continuing ambivalent relation to his father. Among the gods of classical antiquity, Brancusi found alternate "fathers," and from Mother Earth he took the materials he transformed into "gold." The thievery of Prometheus, combined with the civilizing benefits of his theft, reflects Brancusi's ambivalent position vis-à-vis gods. His resolution of these conflicts resides in the sublimatory character of art, which is an alchemical operation of mind and spirit.

NOTES

1. Petre Pandrea, *Brancusi, Amintira Si Exegeze*, Bucharest, 1967, p. 241.
2. Cited in Howard Hibbard, *Caravaggio*, New York, 1983, p. 344.
3. Cf. "Michelangelo Merisi da Caravaggio: A Documentary Survey of His Life," in *The Age of Caravaggio*, Metropolitan Museum Catalogue, New York, 1985, pp. 198–200. Dates given for Caravaggio in the text are from this source.
4. G. P. Bellori, *Le vite de' pittore, scultori et architetti moderni* (1672) ed. E. Borea, Rome and Turin, 1976, p. 202.
5. In *The Age of Caravaggio*, pp. 198–200.
6. In Hibbard, *Caravaggio*, p. 202.
7. Ibid., p. 197.
8. Ibid., pp. 197–98.
9. Ibid., p. 231.
10. John Gedo, *Portraits of the Artist*, New York and London, 1983, pp. 184–85, also notes Caravaggio's murderous intent toward his brother and the repetition of John the Baptist in his iconography.
11. The following account of Artemisia is based on Mary D. Garrard, *Artemisia Gentileschi*, Princeton, 1989, and dates cited are from this source.
12. For the trial transcript, see Garrard, *Artemisia Gentileschi*, Appendix B, p. 416.
13. Ibid., p. 21.
14. Ibid., p. 279.
15. Ibid.
16. Ibid.
17. Ibid., p. 280.

18. Cf. Freud, "Medusa's Head" (1922), S. E. XVIII, 1940, pp. 273–74; Sandor Ferenczi, "On the Symbolism of the Head of Medusa," in his *Further Contributions to the Theory and Technique of Psychoanalysis,* London, 1926; and Laurie Schneider, "Ms. Medusa: Transformations of a Bisexual Image," *Psychoanalytic Study of Society* 9 (1981): 105–53.

19. Garrard, *Artemisia Gentileschi,* p. 319.

20. Ibid.

21. Ibid.

22. Cf. Freud, S. E. XVIII, pp. 273–74.

23. Mario Praz, *The Romantic Agony,* Oxford and New York, 1983, p. 25.

24. Ibid.

25. Sidney Geist, *Brancusi: A Study of the Sculpture,* New York, 1968, p. 156.

26. Cited in Sidney Geist, "Brancusi's *Bird in Space:* A Psychological Reading," *Source: Notes in the History of Art* III, no. 3 (Spring 1984): 30.

27. Geist number references are to works illustrated in Geist, *Brancusi: A Study of the Sculpture,* 1968.

28. Sidney Geist, *Brancusi: The Sculpture and Drawings,* 1975, p. 17; penguins for Brancusi stood for humans by association to Anatole France, *L'Ile des pingouins,* a parody on human history and psychology.

29. Geist, *Brancusi,* 1968, p. 26.

30. Cited in Geist, *Brancusi,* 1968, p. 153.

31. Geist, *Brancusi,* 1968, p. 108.

32. Geist, *Brancusi: The Kiss,* New York, 1978, pp. 42–44.

33. Ibid., p. 69.

34. Ibid., p. 76.

35. Ibid., p. 81, Fig. 63.

36. Geist, *Brancusi,* 1968, p. 4.

37. Otto Fenichel, *The Psychoanalytic Theory of Neurosis,* New York, 1945, pp. 495–96.

38. Geist, *Brancusi,* 1968, pp. 37 ff.

39. Geist, *Brancusi,* 1975, p. 15.

40. Geist, *Brancusi,* 1968, p. 137.

41. Ibid., p. 35.

42. Cf. Mircea Eliade, *The Forge and the Crucible,* New York and Evanston, 1971, p. 79.

TWELVE

Aesthetics on Trial:
Whistler vs. Ruskin

B rancusi's assertion that "aesthetes have an aversion to biography" notwithstanding, the fact is that aesthetic response can be just as psychologically determined as an artist's choice of iconography, theme, or medium. The libel trial between the great Victorian art critic John Ruskin and James McNeill Whistler, the American painter living in London, is a case in point. It illustrates, in dramatic form, the aesthetic quarrel between "realism" and Impressionism that raged in Europe during the second half of the nineteenth century. Ruskin, the older and more established figure, took a strict, "academic" stance, while Whistler, who was fifteen years younger, championed the Impressionist cause. The absurdity of trying to "legislate taste" is nowhere more evident than in the Whistler-Ruskin trial, which, as a result, highlights the psychological factors influencing aesthetic response.

On June 18, 1877, Ruskin published the following statement in *Fors Clavigera,* or *The Hammer of Fate,* subtitled "Letters to the Workmen and Labourers of Great Britain":

> For Mr. Whistler's own sake, no less than for the protection of the purchaser, Sir Coutts ought not to have admitted works into the gallery in which the ill-educated conceit of the artist so nearly approached the aspect of wilfull imposture. I have seen, and heard, much of Cockney impudence before now; but never expected to hear a coxcomb ask two hundred guineas for flinging a pot of paint in the public's face."[1]

Ruskin was referring to Whistler's impressionistic painting of fireworks on the Thames, entitled *Nocturne in Black and Gold: The Falling Rocket* [134]. Whistler was outraged, and sued for libel; for two days, November 25 and 26, 1878, aesthetic arguments filled the courtroom. Even though a psychotic episode prevented Ruskin from appearing, the style and spirit of his lawyer's arguments and the aesthetic stance of his witnesses were Ruskin's. For Whistler, the proceedings were a performance, during which he proclaimed his philosophy of art and reenacted his favorite social roles.

In its manifest aspect, the trial between Whistler and Ruskin was a libel trial and therefore a war of words; but the real battle was about pictures and truth in art. Whistler felt personally attacked, and retaliated with a public display of wounded narcissism. He tried to repair his wounds, while Ruskin asserted his divine right to criticize. At the same time, each man was unconsciously attacking an unacceptable and latent aspect of himself in his opponent.

In "Psychoanalysis and Legal Evidence,"[2] Freud notes that the difference between a criminal and a neurotic is that the former intentionally hides a secret, whereas in the latter, the secret is hidden from consciousness. Both Whistler and Ruskin had unconscious "secrets" that continually threatened to erupt into consciousness and occasionally did. When their unconscious "secrets" emerged, they interfered with creative pursuits, whether Whistler's painting or Ruskin's art criticism. Ruskin's published objection to Whistler focused on the artist's manifest, flamboyant narcissism; but Ruskin's dour, puritanical style matched the style of Whistler's mother, thereby arousing the artist's latent feminine identification. Whistler's flagrant dandyism also matched the hidden, and forbidden, feminine identification of Ruskin, who condemned it in Whistler and denied it in himself.

Before we consider some of the latent meanings of the aesthetic argument between Whistler and Ruskin, highlights of their personal histories, including some of their significant imagery, need to be established.

WHISTLER (1834–1903)

James Abbott Whistler was born in Lowell, Massachusetts, on July 11, 1834.[3] His father, Major George Washington Whistler, was a railway engineer with a contradictory nature—he was at once a dandy and a military man. He graduated from West Point, where he won first prize in drawing. He was also musical; his proficiency as a flutist earned him the nickname "Pipes." In becoming an engineer, Pipes Whistler found a satisfactory and lucrative combination of his talents as a designer and a scientist. He had three children by his first wife before her death; James was his oldest child by Anna McNeill, his second wife.

134. *James McNeill Whistler*, Nocturne in Black
and Gold: The Falling Rocket, *c. 1875. Detroit
Institute of Arts. Gift of Dexter M. Ferry, Jr.*

To the casual observer, Anna must have seemed the very opposite of her husband. She was a strict puritan of Scottish and American southern descent and felt very much at home in the Calvinist atmosphere of nineteenth-century New England. Her religious devotions included daily family Bible reading before breakfast. One of Whistler's English friends later said that she "liked being up in her bedroom because there she felt nearer her Maker."[4] On Saturday afternoon, the toys in the Whistler household were put away in order to prepare for the pieties of Sunday. Playing was not allowed again until Monday.

In 1843, at the age of nine, Whistler accompanied his family to Saint Petersburg, Russia, where his father advised the czar on the new railway line to Moscow. Despite the professional success of Major George Whistler, however, his family suffered a high incidence of death among its children. By the time James was eight, two half-brothers had died. On the boat to Russia the following year, his fourteen-month-old brother Charles died, leaving only James and William. William, two years younger than James, would become a doctor. Their half-sister Deborah later married an English surgeon, Seymour Haden, and lived in London.

In Russia, Anna had a fourth son, who died in infancy. One of Whistler's earliest traumas was thus the repeated loss of his siblings. He, himself, was often sick with rheumatic fever, which eventually affected his heart. It is possible that William chose a medical career in response to the deaths of his brothers and half-sister. James was more overtly conflicted; he made paintings, and when he sold them, he acted as if, like children, they were still his. His two biological children, on the other hand, were discarded and disowned.

As a child, Whistler was exposed to several languages, and to life in Russia and in England, where, like his half-sister, he finally settled. As an adult, Whistler was a restless, even compulsive, traveler, possibly repeating his childhood moves and his father's constant business travel. The family's biggest move was the trip to Russia, where Major George Washington died in 1846, shortly before James's twelfth birthday.

Whistler's interest in art began early; he drew avidly from the age of three. His parents encouraged his talent and allowed him to study art while in Russia; but his mother advised him to become either an architect or an engineer like his father. Nevertheless, Whistler persisted in his wish to paint, and was finally sent to Paris to study art.

The confused and confusing nature of Whistler's identifications began to emerge most clearly when, like his father, he attended West Point. There he rebelled against the discipline and, also like his father, grew his hair long. In contrast to his father, however, Whistler was expelled. Around 1851, at the age of seventeen, Whistler changed his middle name from Abbott, which had been his father's name, to his mother's name, McNeill. In so doing, he intended to assume her more aristocratic heritage and reject his father's lower-class Irish background. This alteration corresponded to Whistler's self-image as a pure-bred southern gentleman, attired in a white duck suit and virulent in his dislike of Blacks and Jews.

Later, Whistler would add the exotic mantle of Russian birth and perjure himself by testifying in court that he had been born in Saint Petersburg rather than in Lowell, Massachusetts. Choosing to be born in the land of his father's death and shedding his father's name points to a continuing oedipal ambivalence. At the same time, Whistler would always refer to himself as a "West Point Man," thereby insisting on a military identification with his father that, in view of his expulsion, was false. He modeled his mustache and beard on the style of a colonel and was continually involved in brawls.

The ambivalence of Whistler's military persona is illuminated by his sudden departure from London in 1866 at the age of thirty-two. Though established as a painter, with his mother living in his house and his mistress, Jo Heffernen, installed elsewhere, Whistler went to Chile, which was at war with Spain. No sooner had he arrived at the port of Valparaiso than he distinguished himself as a coward by running from the Spanish guns. That this was a failed attempt to compete with his brother William is certain; William had fought heroically and served as a surgeon for the Confederate Army in the American Civil War. In 1865, he arrived in London. It appears that William's real military courage and arrival in London highlighted the pretense of James's military facade. Flight, in the face of anxiety, was one of Whistler's characteristic reactions.

Whistler's military pose was only one manifestation of his "false self."[5] When, at the age of twenty-one, he went to Paris to become an artist, he donned the character of a Bohemian dandy. In addition to his white duck suit, he wore wide-brimmed hats and tight, patent-leather shoes. Later, in London, he elaborated the outfit, carrying around one black and one white umbrella as a comment on the inclement English weather. He wore a monocle for his right eye, which was an affectation as well as a remedy for his nearsightedness. Later still, he added a long, thin cane, accenting his short stature, and tied pink ribbons on his shoes.

For Whistler, dandyism was not merely an affectation; it was an integral part of his character and corresponded to a prevailing nineteenth-century aesthetic. In France, dandyism had been elevated to a philosophy of life by such writers as Baudelaire and Barbey d'Aurevilly, with whom Whistler was quite familiar. In England, furthermore, Whistler would have found prominent models for his "double self." Distinguished "split personalities" included Yeats and Lewis Carroll[6] and, in literature, the theme achieved immortality in the characters of Dorian Gray, and Dr. Jekyll and Mr. Hyde.

The nineteenth-century aesthetic of "art for art's sake" reflected the view that art was above the mundane concerns of social utility, ethics, and morality. Similarly, Whistler was his own work of art, a self-created masterpiece, unconcerned with social, financial, or moral responsibilities. In separating art from its social context, therefore, Whistler reenacted his self-proclaimed separateness from the facts of his own biography. In his continually evolving roles, Whistler took charge of his own creation, in part denying his father's role in his birth and ensuring his *re*-birth as an aristocrat. He was irresponsible with money, which he was forever borrowing. He spent extravagantly, and was known, on occasion, to have stolen paint from other artists. By living an expatriate's life, he submerged his American roots and developed a new identity. At London parties, he played different roles, including those of female French cabaret singers.

Whistler's roles point to a lifelong confusion of identity, which was constantly shifting within the framework of the dandy. He tried to incorporate this confusion into a philosophy of art by insisting, for example, that his paintings look effortless when, in fact, he struggled painfully over each one. He wanted to *appear* capable of creating art by means equivalent to the child's "magic gesture" described by Ferenczi.[7]

The infantile character of this attitude suggests a childhood derivation, but is difficult to pinpoint. It is complicated by the fact that, though an exhibitionist and a grandiose narcissist with a flair for "magic gesture," Whistler really did work hard. It was the *impression* of not working that he wanted to create. It is possible that the deaths of his younger siblings seemed to fulfill the natural death wishes of older children toward their younger brothers and sisters. As is evident from his military posturing, Whistler the adult continued the competition with William in his search for a positive oedipal identification with his father. Since Whistler's brothers were all born at home, he would have been aware of his mother's real work in bearing them. Later, when Whistler made paintings, he disguised the effort necessary to their creation, possibly attempting to repair his mother's suffering in giving birth to, and then burying, her children.

Whistler's father, in contrast to his mother, was flamboyant and expressive, characteristics that were enhanced by real abilities in art and music. Whistler identified with his father's dandyism, combined it with a wish to be God-like and irresponsible, and also took his artistic efforts very seriously.

Whistler's Ten O'Clock lecture,[8] discussed in Chapter 4, in which he introduced himself as "The Preacher" and dressed accordingly, reveals an aspect of his identification with his mother. At her death, Whistler berated himself for not becoming a parson, as she had wished. In the Ten O'Clock, Whistler's fantasy of the first artist as staying "by the tents with the women" (see Chapter 4) confirms his association of creating art with female pursuits. Whistler did, in fact, make a feminine impression on several contemporaries. He had a high-pitched falsetto laugh, and, in 1881, Edmond de Goncourt referred to "his way of looking like a weird and macabre pederast."[9] Ten years later, Huysmans said of the artist, "There is something of a meticulous old maid about him."[10]

Whistler's view of artists as a breed apart, "chosen by the gods," is consistent with his self-creation as an aristocrat. Also consistent with being "chosen" is the fact of having survived the deaths of several younger children. It is no doubt of considerable significance that Whistler named his first child Charles, the name of the brother who died en route to Russia. He threw his daughter out of his house, along with his mistress of fifteen years.

Still another important element in Whistler's "creation fantasy" is its relation to his family romance. He "renounced" an aspect of his biological father—his name—and assumed a more "divine" origin. At the same time, his adoption of musical titles can be seen as an identification with "Pipes." This particular inclination on Whistler's part coincided with the suggestion of his most important patron, Sir Frederick Leyland, that he give the title *Nocturne* to a night scene. Whistler took the suggestion and found, to his delight, that critics disliked musical titles: "You have no idea," he told Sir Frederick, "what an irritant it proves to the critics, and consequent pleasure to me."[11]

Also exemplifying Whistler's contradictory nature was his studio. For despite his dandyism and his pretense of not having to work hard, Whistler's studio was austere and reflected the seriousness with which he regarded his work; it also mirrored the puritanical style of his mother rather than the elegant flamboyance of his father.

Most clearly indicating the latent bisexual character of his contradictions was Whistler's butterfly signature.[12] The popular term "social butterfly" applies well to Whistler and, as symbols go, the butterfly seems more female than male. Whistler's butterfly has been called his "totem and heraldic symbol"; it appeared on his "cards, letters, brochures, and linen, at his exhibitions, and in every situation in which he went forth to joust with his enemies."[13]

The psychoanalyst Karl Abraham has discussed the butterfly in two ways that can be applied to Whistler's personality. On the one hand, because of the motion of the wings, the butterfly is a dream image signifying the opening and closing of the female genital.[14] As a totem animal, on the other hand, the butterfly has "the character of making a sudden appearance." It represents "the father who surprises the child by suddenly appearing near it or by alarming it with a threatening voice. . . . Thus these small flying animals indicate . . . the dangerous power of the father, but serve . . . as an expression for the child's ideas of getting rid of him."[15] In this context, it is clear that the butterfly synthesized Whistler's female identification with an unresolved oedipal ambivalence toward his father. In addition, the butterfly's sudden appearances recapitulate the action of Whistler's father in returning home from frequent business trips.

Whistler's identification with the butterfly is further complicated by the fact that when he wrote letters, many of which were published in the press, he attached a scorpion's tail. Whistler himself later collected and reprinted the letters in a work whose very title reveals his penchant for transforming conflict into wit: *The Gentle Art of Making Enemies.* When he wrote letters, Whistler signed himself as a butterfly with a sting. The drawings themselves resemble posing, bowing females, rather like flitting, mannered versions of Peter Pan's Tinkerbell.

The ambivalent character of the stinging butterfly emerges in Whistler's bisexual, sadomasochistic conflicts—for, in writing letters, Whistler exposed himself to ridicule as often as he symbolically stung his adversaries. In his dress, too, Whistler shifted between sadism and masochism. He suffered exhibitionistically by wearing tight narrow shoes and complaining loudly of sore feet. He used his walking stick to poke at animals and, on one occasion, in Venice in 1880, he impaled a scorpion on an etching needle and watched it flail.[16]

Whistler's reservation of the butterfly for his pictures and combined butterfly/scorpion for his letters evokes the conflict between line and color, which had been a subject of aesthetic controversy since the seventeenth century. Whistler made the issue a personal, even sexual, matter. In 1867, he wrote, "Drawing, by God! Color is vice, although it can be one of the finest virtues. When controlled by a firm hand, well-guided by her master, Drawing, Color is then like a splendid woman with a mate worthy of her—her lover but also her master—the most magnificent mistress possible. But when united with uncertainty, with a weak drawing, timid, deficient, easily satisfied, Color becomes a bold whore, makes fun of her little fellow, isn't it so?"[17]

This statement, made after his return from Chile, reflects Whistler's change in taste from Courbet (the colorist) to Ingres, who championed line. It also followed his rupture with his mistress, Jo, who had posed for Courbet during Whistler's absence from London. Whistler's change of taste in art coincides with increased combativeness, mounting financial problems, and violent family arguments.

In subsequent years, Whistler's artistic activity was fervent but unproductive. He resumed his social life; but, instead of a female companion, Whistler was most often accompanied by his brother William. In 1869, he had a new mistress, who was the mother of the son named for his dead brother. During the turmoil of 1867–70, from the age of thirty-three to thirty-six, Whistler experienced creative block. He worked hard, but finished no pictures. In 1871, he painted the portrait of his mother entitled *Arrangement in Grey and Black No. 1*. This seems to have resolved his block, for he soon entered a period of renewed productivity. It is interesting, whether by coincidence or overdetermination, that his mother's picture was painted on the back of a canvas; on the front was a picture of a child. The oedipal implications of this circumstance are inescapable, and they evoke Whistler's oedipally tinged adoption of his mother's name. In the light of pre-oedipal significance, it would appear that painting his mother freed and fueled his creativity. Having completed her portrait, he was able once again to produce the only children that were of any consequence to him, his paintings.

Whistler's mistresses have been described as motherly, possessive, and jealous. His wife was obese. He did not marry until the age of fifty-four, after his mother's death.

RUSKIN (1819–1900)

John Ruskin[18] was born in London on February 8, 1819. His hereditary predisposition to madness, combined with an emotionally disturbed upbringing, resulted in a character structure that, like Whistler's, was severely split between male and female.[19] Ruskin's Scottish paternal grandfather slit his own throat and then walked into the drawing room, where his niece, Margaret, held together the skin as the doctor stitched it up. He died a few days later. Margaret married his son, her first cousin, after a nine-year engagement. John Ruskin was their only child.

Ruskin shared many of Whistler's bisexual conflicts. Diagnosed as the victim of cyclothymic depression,[20] Ruskin suffered several psychotic episodes and spent the last ten years of his life in total insanity. He describes his childhood in his autobiography, *Praeterita*, as dismal and severely restricted, despite his family's wealth. By his own account, he had few toys and no playmates of his own age; on Sundays he was not allowed to look at the paintings by Turner that his father collected.

Ruskin's father was a successful sherry trader who, like Whistler's father, was often away on business and let his wife dominate his son's education. He himself joined her in an intrusive approach to their son, as he later read all Ruskin's mail, including love letters. Ruskin's mother, a devout puritan, dedicated her son to God, hoping he would enter the church, as Whistler's mother had. Margaret Ruskin thought of her husband's sherry business as "dirty" and low class, thereby discouraging Ruskin's estimation of his father from the outset.

Nor was Ruskin permitted a boy's usual sublimatory sports or games, because his mother worried about his health. At the same time, however, her contradictory nature expressed itself in alternating seductiveness and sadism. She beat Ruskin if he tripped on the stairs, but was oversolicitous when he had a cold. When he was two years old, his mother instructed his nurse to let him burn his hand on a hot tea kettle so he would learn the meaning of obedience. When Ruskin went to Oxford, his mother went too. His father joined them on weekends. Later, Ruskin would say that he was raised with nothing to love.

Ruskin's life and thought were a tangled web of contradictions. He was equally contradictory in describing himself. In *Praeterita*, he says he is a Communist and a Tory. He inherited his father's wealth, but identified with Saint Francis, who renounced his father's goods, and supported Utopian working-class projects. He praised the simple life, but did not travel without a cook. For Ruskin, money, like sex, was an evil manifestation of Satan.

Ruskin's fundamental gender confusion emerged in his unresolved male-female identifications. Similar to Whistler's, though far more disturbed, was Ruskin's association of painting and color with female quality, and writing (or line) with masculinity. These associations became attached to Ruskin's confusion of art and literature, which he tried to synthesize by his unique literary style of "painting with words." Quentin Bell has noted Ruskin's creation of "a form of art criticism which is neither descriptive nor explanatory; not so much an account as the poetical equivalent of a painting."[21] As an example, Bell cites Ruskin's discussion of Turner's *Slave Ship*:

> It is a sunset on the Atlantic, after a prolonged storm; but the storm is partially lulled, and the torn and streaming rain-clouds are moving in scarlet lines to lose themselves in the hollow of the night . . . the fire of the sunset falls along the trough of the sea, dyeing it with an awful but glorious light, the intense and lurid splendour which burns like gold, and bathes like blood.[22]

In Ruskin's more self-related imagery, he is quite specific about his gender confusion. When he describes showing his prose to his parents, for example, he compares himself to a girl showing "her sampler."[23] As an adult, he would refer to the mothers of little girls with whom he made friends as "mama." Such imagery suggests an unconscious transsexual fantasy of being a woman in a man's body—or even a little girl inside a man. Ruskin exhibited none of Whistler's dandyism, nor is there any evidence of overt homosexual behavior. His dress, except for a light blue scarf, was traditionally masculine. Nevertheless, he liked the company of little girls, became for a time a mascot at a girls' school, and, toward the end of his life, delighted in playing games and cooking with neighborhood children. In these activities, Ruskin virtually became a little girl himself. His female character, like Whistler's, was evident to several of his contemporaries. To this point, John Ludlow wrote that he "had a woman's soul lodged in a man's body."[24]

Ruskin's adult relationships reflected his continuing struggle with his internal split between male and female. He fell in love with a fifteen-year-old French girl and had a physical breakdown when she married someone else. He coughed blood and left Oxford to travel with his parents. Ruskin's psychosomatic tendencies, along with morbid hypochondria and an obsessive, delusional fear of blindness, continued throughout his life. After his first romantic disappointment, Ruskin fell in love with his first cousin Euphemia Gray, who was also fifteen. He courted her ardently until they finally married.

An enormous amount of biographical ink has flowed over this marriage, which was annulled after six years on grounds of nonconsummation. Ever since, descendants and scholars alike have taken a position favoring Ruskin or Effie. A cryptic remark in one of Effie's letters has been interpreted as a reference to Ruskin's disgust at the sight of her pubic hair. In 1854, in the last year of their marriage, she wrote as follows:

> He [Ruskin] alleged various reasons, hatred to children, religious motives, a desire to preserve my beauty, and finally this last year told me his true reason (and this to me is as villainous as all the rest) that he had imagined women were quite different from what he saw I was, and that the reason he did not make me his wife was because he was disgusted with my person the first evening."[25]

Ruskin's dislike of children and his references to babies as "lumps of putty" reveal the anal conflicts one might expect from a childhood such as his. Indeed, many years later, Ruskin would attempt to sublimate his anal concerns in projects to clean up the environment. He purified a spring, which he called "Margaret's Well" after his mother. When this and similar projects failed because the wells and rivers became polluted again, Ruskin compared them to dirty children who had to be continually looked after.[26]

One needs only moderate familiarity with Ruskin's imagery in his ardent love letters to Effie to recognize the intensity of his *vagina dentata* fear and his florid castration fantasies. In a letter of December 15, 1847, he referred to Effie as Medusa and described her as a "wrecker on a rocky coast, luring vessels to their fate." She was, he said, a pleasant forest with a "cold and impenetrable" center. Her smiles were a "false light lighted on the misty coast of a merciless gulph." Beneath her "soft-swelling lovely fields . . . are winding clefts and dark places in its cold—cold ice—where men fall and rise not again." They were married the following year.

Effie was outgoing and sociable; Ruskin was a recluse. Toward the end of their marriage, tension and bitterness reached a crescendo as each accused the other of insanity. Ruskin's alleged aversion to Effie's pubic hair seems confirmed by his delusion about Medusa and his obsession with snakes. They populated his fantasies, nightmares, hallucinations, and his famous stormcloud delusion that England was being destroyed by Industrial Revolution smog. For Ruskin, the storm cloud was Medusa, and

Nature was the more benign, phallic goddess Athena. As a personification of Nature, Athena was the phallic mother, who nevertheless had her dangerous side, the left, where she wore her Gorgoneion aegis. Athena and Medusa stood for Ruskin's split image of the good and bad mother, respectively. In view of such delusions, Ruskin's refusal to consummate his marriage can be read as a defensive form of self-preservation.

Following the rupture, Effie married the painter John Millais, with whom she had six children. Ruskin's erotic attachment to young, prepubescent girls now became more overt. His most serious involvement, with Rose La Touche, lasted until she died at the age of seventeen. By "putting girls to sleep," as it were, or choosing those who were too young to reproduce, Ruskin avoided the dangers of his castration fantasy. These sexual predilections colored his aesthetic judgment, sometimes adversely. Although there are actually some great works of art praised by Ruskin that depict sleeping or dead girls—Quercia's *Ilaria del Caretto* and Carpaccio's *Dream of Saint Ursula*—his critical faculties were sometimes completely invaded by his sexual confusion. His praise of Kate Greenaway's "coloring book" little girls, for example, cannot be taken seriously except as an expression of approaching psychosis.

Ruskin was disturbed by many erotic works of art, and sanctioned only those in which he discerned redeeming spiritual quality.[27] On one occasion, in 1853, he cut up manuscripts in his collection because evil spirits were "throwing them into disorder."[28] Despite his approval of Titian in principle—as his witnesses would testify—Ruskin referred to the sensual Pitti Palace *Mary Magdalen* as "disgusting." Ruskin's fear of looking at the nude body is evident in his extraordinary belief that art students should learn drawing from nature and avoid the human form. His aversion to Michelangelo, for whom the human figure was paramount, was particularly virulent; he called the artist "the chief captain in evil"[29] and attributed to his corrupt influence the decline of Italian art. Michelangelo's homosexuality was also an affront to Ruskin, whose own masculine identification was on shaky ground.

Ruskin's aesthetic contradictions derived in part from his split maternal image, his incestuous attraction to his mother on the one hand and his terror of her castrating nature on the other. His conflicted identification with his father appears in his negative attitude toward money, which he nevertheless held onto, and his aversion to becoming a father himself. The five-volume *Modern Painters*, written originally as a tribute to Turner, the artist most admired and collected by Ruskin's father, was directly responsible for Turner's high reputation. Like all of his writing, however, *Modern Painters* reflects Ruskin's mental condition.

Despite its promising beginning, *Modern Painters* became grandiose, increasingly incoherent, and finally delusional. Ruskin himself described the work in confused, mixed metaphors that mirror his growing psychosis. Having started out, he said, to write "a small pamphlet defending Turner . . . the thing swelled under my hands; before the volume was half-way dealt with it hydra-ized into three heads, and each head became a volume. . . . Finding that nothing could be done except on such enormous scale I determined to take the hydra by the horns and produce a complete treatise on landscape art."[30]

The fantasies that illustrate Ruskin's castration fear most vividly, like his description of *Modern Painters*, involve snake phobias. Related to the latent meaning of his snake imagery was his pathological conviction, in spite of perfect eyesight, that he was going blind. In this he identified with his mother, who, like Whistler, was nearsighted and had a squint. In his autobiography, Ruskin alludes to one of the childhood derivations of these fears in his accounts of visual and tactile deprivation. He was not allowed toys, but could play with a set of keys. His mother took away a *Punch and Judy* given to him by an aunt. In not being allowed to look at paintings on Sundays even though they hung on the walls, he was forced to avert his eyes.

Early in *Praeterita*, Ruskin describes what appears to have been a screen memory of the primal scene.[31] In this, too, snakes play a prominent role. He reports staring with fascination from his window—an arrested gaze—at a pipe as water dripped slowly from it into the trapdoors of a water cart. By his own account, he watched in rapturous excitement[32] and never tired of "contemplating that mystery." The pipes, he said, were "like boa-constrictors."[33] Since boa constrictors kill by strangulation, Ruskin's aversion to consummating his marriage takes on a new coloring—for, in addition to fearing his own destruction from the dangers of a woman (compare the "*trap*doors"), he must have feared his own aggressive impulse to squeeze the life out of his sexual partner (which, though figuratively, he very nearly did in Effie's case). Just as *Modern Painters* got "out of hand" and "hydra-ized," so Ruskin felt he could not control his sexual aggression in relation to an adult woman. His defense against these fears took the form of choosing girls whose youth, death, or sleeping state precluded adult sexuality.

At the end of his life, when he retired to Brantwood and complete insanity, Ruskin furnished his house with his parents' belongings. He even used their decorator, as if trying one last time to repair the damage wrought by his childhood. He began writing *Praeterita* on the centennial of his father's birth; there is no reference to his marriage in it. According to his guardian, Ruskin wandered about the house repeating "Everything black, everything white,"[34] the final and most definitive expression of his psychotic split.

Up to this point, the most important reparative strength of Ruskin's character was his genius. Despite his mad fantasies and outlandish behavior—while giving a lecture at Oxford, he suddenly began flapping his gown and crowing like a rooster—Ruskin was indisputably the greatest English art critic of the nineteenth century. Were it not for his genius and Whistler's prominence as an artist, the notorious and slightly ridiculous libel trial would have long since been forgotten. The manifest issues in the courtroom were art, style, and money; the latent issues were the psychic conflicts of Whistler and Ruskin.

THE TRIAL

The trial[35] took place in London's Court of the Exchequer, Westminster. From the point of view of the history of art, the trial reflected the conflict between the established Pre-Raphaelite style, sanctioned by the British Royal Academy, and the newer Impressionist style. Impressionism had begun in the 1860s, in Paris, where taste was dictated by the conservative French Academy. Ruskin had championed the Pre-Raphaelites, and it was largely through his efforts that they had become the established artists of their generation in England. Whistler, in contrast, had studied with the younger generation of Impressionists in Paris and, in choosing to live in London, was partly responsible for Impressionist inroads across the Channel.

The inevitable oedipal dynamics in the rivalry between establishment and innovation were exemplified by Ruskin's defensive, authoritarian stance and Whistler's infantile sado-masochistic narcissism. These differences of personality in the protagonists were mirrored by their witnesses. Despite his madness, for example, Ruskin succeeded in mustering distinguished witnesses to back up his unwavering position. Whistler's witnesses, like the artist himself, were overtly ambivalent. They were also less prominent than those who testified for Ruskin.

The opening statement for Whistler was weak. His counsel, Serjeant Parry, asserted that the artist was a tireless worker, well known for his paintings and etchings. He had been personally injured by Ruskin's unjust and ungentlemanly remarks. The critic, according to Parry, had treated the artist with "contempt and ridicule." Whistler, he said, was entitled to damages.

Ruskin's counsel was Sir John Holker, the Attorney General. He opened with an impassioned, sermonizing defense of the critic's high standards and his distinction as Oxford's Slade Professor. Ruskin, asserted the Attorney General, revered, indeed idolized, artistic genius. He denounced the crass materialism of modern society in general and modern art in particular. "An artist's fame should be built upon not what he received but upon what he gave," thundered Ruskin's lawyer. He further objected to Whistler's musical titles as "fantastic conceits" (an attack on the artist's already conflicted identification with his musical father and on the narcissism of both).

Ruskin's counsel did not mention the "Cockney" in his client's original remarks. But, in view of Whistler's attempts to present himself to the world as a Southern Cavalier, a Russian aristocrat, a witty socialite, and a great artist "chosen by the gods," his outrage at being called a "Cockney" is predictable. In testifying that he had been born in Russia, the land of his father's death, Whistler simultaneously renounced his father and his country. The coincidence of his father's name, George Washington, with the "father of his country" illustrates the overdetermined character of Whistler's decision to testify as he did and to live as an expatriate.

Although ignoring the "Cockney" in Ruskin's original criticism of Whistler, the Attorney General had a lot to say about the meaning of "coxcomb." It was, he pointed out, a licensed jester, wearing a cap with bells and a cock's comb in it, who performed for a master and his family. In this image, Ruskin evoked Whistler's colorful performances as a dandy, together with his realistic necessity as an artist, especially a portraitist, to please his patrons. Ruskin, on the other hand, had inherited his wealth and, as a critic, judged the artistic performance of others. Since Whistler's relationships with his patrons were fraught with continual conflict and paranoia, Ruskin had struck a very sensitive nerve. The assertion by Ruskin's counsel that Whistler's pictures were themselves a jest, and thus not worth the prices asked, added insult to injury.

Ruskin's counsel concluded that, if the verdict went against his client, it would be "an evil day" for the art of England and would "paralyze" the hands of that country's leading critic. He appealed to the jury's xenophobia, implying that Whistler might contribute to the downfall of English art (as Ruskin believed Michelangelo had caused the decline of Renaissance art in Italy). Whistler's position as an expatriate, together with his aesthetic preference for Impressionism, made him a permanent outsider and repeated his childhood moves and lack of enduring social ties.

As for the "paralysis" of Ruskin's hands, the castrative significance of a critic deprived of his pen is obvious. Ruskin's assertion that a guilty verdict would force him to lay down the tools of his trade and renounce his exalted position in the world of art sounds very much like a threat of oedipal abdication. This imagery evokes Ruskin's self-appointed, godlike role and the fact that his mother had dedicated him to God. Since Whistler, who felt that *his* mother had wanted him to be a parson, thought of himself as chosen by the gods, Ruskin's attitude was a frontal attack. But the defensive nature of Ruskin's belief in his paternal, regal, even divine right to his position is highlighted by the paradox of his refusal to become a father and his phobic dislike of small children.

Whistler's stance appeared more childish than Ruskin's, for the critic was better able to hide the "secret" of his regressive nature. As a dandy and a wit, Whistler's pose required the overt display of his narcissism. Likewise, his wish to create the impression that his pictures were effortless worked against him during the trial. In fact, the opposite of Whistler's facade was true; he worked long and hard both as a painter and as a dandy. His sitters often gave up before their portraits were finished. When Ruskin granted Whistler's pose, criticized him for not working, and accused him of flinging pots of paint at the art-loving public, Whistler did an about-face and protested.

At the trial, Whistler was his own first witness. He defended his musical titles and his antagonism to critics, and elaborated the more general nineteenth-century conflicts between form and content. He argued in favor of the Impressionist view that formal arrangements and atmospheric effects were more important in a picture than narrative content (story *line*) and clear edges. Whistler's pictures, unlike the linear Pre-Raphaelite and Neo-classical works, are impressionistic in their softened, blurred outlines. His musical titles—"Arrangements," "Nocturnes," and "Symphonies" in color—echo his aesthetic choices.

For Whistler and Ruskin, the larger aesthetic quarrels of the contemporary art world were personal as well. Whistler suffered a personal conflict between line and color. In his letter of 1867, he had explained that line represented masculine control, which was threatened by the "bold whore" that was color. Even though Whistler was a superb etcher, capable of great precision in drawing, his originality lay in his color and atmosphere. His internal struggle with this issue manifested itself not only in his statements, but also in his erratic working procedure, his periods of creative block and inhibition, and the fact that his self-portraits and the portrait of his mother are among his least colorful works.

Ruskin, on the other hand, had his own internal conflicts that were aroused by the spectacle of Whistler's dandyism and atmospheric pictures. Whistler's choice of the Thames, for example, though a favorite Impressionist subject, and his atmospheric depiction of its foggy, polluted skies, aroused Ruskin's environmental concerns. It is likely, given the characteristic invasion of Ruskin's taste and social philosophy by his fantasy life, that his response to Whistler's pictures of fireworks at night resulted from the anxiety created by his storm-cloud delusion. Whistler's blurred images must have seemed the fulfillment of Ruskin's worst fears of the effects of industrialization. They probably also evoked Ruskin's pathological fear of blindness.

In court, Ruskin's objections to Whistler's style were vigorously reinforced by his witnesses. The more ambivalent nature of Whistler's witnesses was consistent with the artist's own ambivalence. Ruskin's ambivalence was more hidden; so threatening was his identity confusion that he erected an austere and rigid facade as a bastion against psychosis. Whistler's greater flexibility permitted him to indulge a more overt display of his feminine nature. And it was this very aspect of Whistler that Ruskin's lawyer attacked; he asked about "eccentricity," which Whistler's witnesses defended as "originality." In fact, however, Whistler *was* eccentric, and his arrogant freedom of expression was a direct threat to Ruskin. Conflicted as Whistler was, it is possible that his psychic flexibility defended him against the complete psychotic breakdown suffered by Ruskin.

Edward Burne-Jones, the prominent Pre-Raphaelite painter, confirmed Ruskin's aesthetic position. He testified that Whistler's paintings were unfinished; they lacked composition and detail, and they were "bewildering in form." Here, again, the aesthetic issue of "finish" and "detail" seems to echo Ruskin's awareness of his own deteriorating ego boundaries as his psychosis approached. Reiterating the critic's patriotic appeal to national morality, Burne-Jones asserted that too many "unfinished" pictures would lead to a degeneration of artistic standards. Likewise, Ruskin's fear of psychosis is reflected in the conviction that relaxing aesthetic standards would result in artistic chaos.

The editor of *Punch*, Tom Taylor, said that Whistler's painting of fireworks on the Thames was not serious; it was no better than wallpaper. William Power Frith, the Royal Academician, said Whistler's only asset as a painter was his use of pretty color. These arguments reflect the nineteenth-century objections to Impressionism and seem to prefigure twentieth-century criticisms of Abstract Expressionism, in some of which all reference to recognizable form is eliminated.

In the allusions to wallpaper and pretty color, Ruskin's witnesses degraded Whistler by lowering his status from artist to decorator, thereby wounding his narcissism and attacking his self-image. Untrue though history has proved such criticisms to be, the fact is that Whistler *was* a professional interior decorator. Indeed, one of his most lavish displays of eccentricity occurred when he painted the Peacock Room, now in the Freer Gallery in Washington, for Sir Frederick Leyland. Whistler soon got carried away, painting over leather and wood furniture; he sent out notices inviting the public to witness his performance. One journalist described the scene as follows:

> Mr. Whistler, dressed wholly in black velvet, with knickerbocker pantaloons stopping just below the knees, black silk stockings, and low pointed shoes, with black silk ties more than six inches wide and diamond buckles, was flat on his back, fishing-rod in hand and an enormous eyeglass in one eye, diligently putting some finishing touches on the ceiling, his brush being on the other end of the fishpole.[36]

The result was a rupture with Leyland, an important patron who would become a target of some of Whistler's most virulent attacks. In this behavior, which was part of a repeated pattern, the artist exhibited a narcissistic rage against a symbolic father figure in the person of a rich and influential patron. Similarly, the trial was Whistler's attempt to dethrone Ruskin publicly and get some of his money.

Under cross-examination, Whistler was questioned on the relationship between time and money. Though Ruskin did not have to work for *his* money, he liked to see evidence of others having done so. Whistler, on the other hand, believed that if he had had money, he would have been a better painter. Ruskin's attorney accused Whistler of overcharging in relation to time spent painting. Whistler countered by saying that he charged for the experience of a lifetime.

In regard to time and money, both men were severely conflicted. Whistler was overtly irresponsible with money, while Ruskin made a pretense of responsibility he never had. As Whistler grew older, he fought against time like a woman, by wearing makeup and primping before the mirror while keeping people waiting for him. He also lied about his age. Ruskin's response to time and age was to become more openly attached to little girls, or to pictures, statues, and stories of little girls. Ruskin strived to maintain a bourgeois facade by seeking to marry the unlikely, prepubescent objects of his affections. Whistler flagrantly challenged bourgeois morality. He went ruthlessly from mistress to mistress until his marriage at fifty-four to an obese, motherly, and possessive woman. Ruskin avoided children by refusing to consummate his marriage, Whistler by ignoring and disowning those he had.

In his summation, Whistler's counsel accused Ruskin of sitting on a "throne of art," arbitrarily wielding ridicule through personal criticism. The summation for Ruskin emphasized his august position as a critic; the trial ended on an oedipal note, with Ruskin, the king of taste, in power, and Whistler, an upstart in search of financial compensation for wounded narcissism.

The judge instructed the jury to find Ruskin guilty of libel and to award Whistler a farthing in damages. The jury obliged. Both artist and critic were thus degraded; Ruskin's inviolable right to arbitrate taste was called into question, and Whistler failed to get his money.

The very fact of the trial was symptomatic of Whistler's litigious paranoia and narcissistic rage. The obscurity of Ruskin's pamphlet, in which he published his remarks, meant that they would have gone unnoticed had Whistler not brought them to the attention of the public. In suing for libel, Whistler set the stage for an exhibitionistic and masochistic display of himself as the injured party. Ruskin relished the opportunity to reinforce his unassailable seat on the throne of English art. Before the trial, Ruskin had boasted that it was "nuts and nectar . . . the notion of having to answer for myself in court, and the whole thing will enable me to assert some principles of art economy."

Typical of one of Whistler's most consistent behavior patterns, he reversed the masochistic display of himself into sadistic revenge against those he blamed for his defeat. He published an account of the trial, accompanied by witty attacks against the opposing side; for Whistler, wit was expressed in words, its purpose being to demolish his adversaries. He would later call the trial a conflict between "the brush and the pen"—between painter and critic. But the very same conflict raged within the protagonists. Whistler painted and wrote, painted and etched; for him brush and pen were equivalent to paint and words, color and line, masochism and sadism, female and male identifications, respectively.

For Ruskin, the conflict was similar, but in reverse. He required that the brush be contained by the pen, the form and content bordered by a clear edge. He covered his female self with a masculine exterior, and his sexual delusions with an ecclesiastic style. In the hallucinations that kept him out of court, Ruskin imagined Satan in the form of a black cat, jumping at him from behind a mirror and compelling him to commit licentious acts. Ruskin, like Whistler, was an excellent draftsman, but painted only watercolors. Instead of serious painting with color, Ruskin painted with words. As Quentin Bell wrote, Ruskin "was the first art critic to create one masterpiece in praising another."[37]

The trial was a landmark and a failure in the lives of both men. It left Whistler owing court costs and bankrupt. He suffered a nearly permanent creative block, and his litigiousness and paranoia increased. Ruskin resigned his Slade Professorship at Oxford and accelerated his steady decline toward complete madness.

Despite Whistler's characteristic reservation of the butterfly for pictures and the butterfly/scorpion for letters, there is one extant painting that he signed with the latter emblem. By 1879, a year after the trial, Whistler had shifted his paranoia from Ruskin to Leyland. Whistler owed his former patron money and blamed him for his bankruptcy. In that mood, he painted three pictures that savagely criticized Leyland. Two are lost; but their titles reveal their sadistic intent—*The Loves of the Lobsters: An Arrangement in Rats* and *Mount Ararat* (with emphasis on the *rat*).

The extant painting, *The Gold Scab: Eruption in Frilthy Lucre* [135], is an exercise in visual sadism. Leyland is depicted playing the piano; he is characterized as a combination of Satan, a serpent, and a peacock—a reference to the Peacock Room. His body is covered with coins—the gold scabs. *Frilthy* condenses *frill*, referring to his ostentatious costume, and *filthy*, which denotes the unconscious connection of gold and feces.[38] The notion of an eruption of gold and filth indicates the parallel between the scabs and the emergence from repression of evil unconscious impulses.

135. *James McNeill Whistler,* The Gold Scab:
Eruption in Frilthy Lucre, *1879. Fine Arts
Museum of San Francisco. Gift of Mrs. Alma de
Bretteville Spreckels through the Patrons of Art and
Music.*

Leyland is shown sitting on Whistler's London home, the White House, which the artist was forced to sell because of financial hardship. His relationship in Whistler's mind to "Pipes" is likely in view of their real similarities. Both men were musical, and financially successful. Leyland's semitic physiognomy, besides evoking Whistler's hatred of Jews, associates him with the devil, whose gold, in European folklore, turns to feces (filthy lucre). Whistler's Leyland is Satan as the negative father, indifferent to his son's welfare, a modern Nero playing while Rome burns. Whistler identified with this aspect of the negative father, treating *his* children far worse than Leyland *or* his own father had treated him.

This painting is a good example of the unproductive effects of narcissistic rage. Signed as it is with both the butterfly and the scorpion's sting, it is a kind of cartoon picture. Its satire resides in its literary character, which is atypical of Whistler and runs counter to the nature of his talent. It has the clear outlines, narrative content, and "finish" that Ruskin's aesthetic demanded, and none of the atmosphere for which Whistler is rightly esteemed. Just as the gold scabs erupt on Leyland, so Whistler's penchant for self-destruction erupted in the very conception and execution of this unsatisfactory picture.

CONCLUSION

An important lesson of the clash between Whistler and Ruskin is the degree to which mental disturbance interferes with, and inhibits, creative work. Countering the "romantic" notion that neurosis and madness enhance creativity are their demonstrable negative effects on Whistler and Ruskin. Whistler's efforts in suing Ruskin indulged his neurosis and absorbed time, energy, and money that would have been better spent on his art. When he vented his rage on Leyland in painting three "literary" satires, he produced work that was far below his potential. Ruskin, for his part, was endowed with a remarkable genius for "painting with words." His psychosis, however, one episode of which he referred to as a "Long Dream," wreaked havoc on his life and work. Just as he could not appear in court during such an episode, so he was unable to write art criticism.

The trial is an example of one of the ways in which neurosis and psychosis disrupt creativity. In reviewing the biographies of Western artists, this becomes ever more clear. Van Gogh could not work while hospitalized for a condition whose diagnosis is still in dispute. The causes of Michelangelo's *non finito* are still moot; but that they are psychological is certain. Neither Caravaggio nor Cellini could work while running from the law, a life-style that killed Caravaggio prematurely.

The artists who are least conflicted in their art are freer and more productive than those who are blocked by mental disturbance. How to achieve maximal freedom is the question. Artists' biographies indicate that the response to a child's talent—whether by a parent or another significant person—is a crucial factor. The wider social and cultural context is also important, which is reflected in the tendency of artists to congregate in facilitating environments—for example, Rome in the sixteenth century, Paris in the nineteenth, New York from the Second World War. Sometimes artists go to great lengths to find the right environment; Gauguin went to Tahiti, Brancusi set out on foot from Romania for Paris, and the Abstract Expressionists traveled from the American Far West and Eastern Europe to settle and work in New York City.

The cultural environment, however, is preceded by the family. Together with Alberti, therefore, the psychoanalyst would argue the advantages of recognition, encouragement, and reflection as early as possible in the child's life. Taking a leaf from Alberti's metaphor, one must conclude that childhood is the foundation of life, and the parents its architects. Whatever the raw material, whether genius or not, development benefits from enlightened attention. Without it, even genius can become inhibited and misdirected into unreality.

Despite Leonardo's genius, his art was drastically curtailed by his obsessional character, which led him into unrealistic alchemical investigations. Parmigianino gave up painting altogether in order to pursue the delusion that gold can be made from base metal. Brueghel, who had more insight than Parmigianino, painted many warnings against delusional folly. His 1558 drawing *The Alchemist* bitterly satirizes alchemy as destructive to the stability of the family. In the seventeenth century, when Rubens—as prolific an artist as one could hope to find—was offered an alchemical partnership, he declined. He had already found his philosopher's stone, he said, in his paints and brushes. Duchamp, working in the twentieth century, said, "If I have ever practiced alchemy, it was in the only way it can be done now, that is to say, without knowing it"[39]—that is, unconsciously.

NOTES

1. John Ruskin, Letter 79, in his *Fors Clavigera*, vol. IV, New York, 1968, p. 73.
2. Freud, S. E. IX, 1906, p. 111.
3. The literature on Whistler is vast. The main biographical sources are Joseph and Elizabeth Pennell, *The Life of James McNeill Whistler*, Philadelphia, 1908, and *The Whistler Journal*, Philadelphia, 1921.
4. In Roy McMullen, *Victorian Outsider*, New York, 1973, p. 119.
5. Cf. D. W. Winnicott, "True and False Self," in his *Playing and Reality*, New York, 1971, and Greenacre, "The Relation of the Impostor to the Artist" (1958), in *Emotional Growth*, vol. 2, New York, 1971, Chapter 26.
6. Phyllis Greenacre, *Swift and Carroll*, New York, 1977.
7. Cf. Sandor Ferenczi, "Stages in the Development of Reality" (1913), in his *First Contributions to the Theory and Technique of Psychoanalysis*, New York, 1980, p. 196.
8. London, February 20, 1885, published in *The Gentle Art of Making Enemies*, London, 1892, pp. 139 ff.
9. McMullen, *Victorian Outsider*, p. 220.
10. Ibid., p. 249.
11. Ibid., p. 161.
12. Rossetti had suggested an initial like the PRB designating the Pre-Raphaelite Brotherhood. Whistler then signed paintings JMW and in the 1870s changed to a butterfly. Cf. Laurie Schneider, "Butterfly or Scorpion: A Note on the Iconography of Whistler's Signatures," *Source: Notes in the History of Art* II, no. 2 (Winter 1983): 26–29.
13. McMullen, *Victorian Outsider*, p. 156.
14. In Karl Abraham, *Selected Papers on Psychoanalysis*, New York, reprint of 1927 edition, p. 245.
15. Ibid., pp. 228–29.
16. Stanley Weintraub, *Whistler*, New York, 1974, p. 245.
17. Ibid., p. 124.
18. As with Whistler, there is an enormous literature on Ruskin. A good selected bibliography appears in Joan Abse, *John Ruskin: The Passionate Moralist*, London, 1980, pp. 344 ff.
19. Cf. Laurie Schneider, "Everything Black, Everything White," *Art History* 5, no. 2 (June 1982): 166–79.
20. R. H. Wilenski, *John Ruskin*, London, 1933; Louis J. Braagman, "The Case of John Ruskin: A Study in Cyclothymia," *American Journal of Psychiatry* XCL (1935): 1137–59; John Ruskin, "The Late John Ruskin's Illness Described by Himself," *British Medical Journal*, vol. 1, January 27, 1900, pp. 225–26.
21. Quentin Bell, *John Ruskin*, New York, 1978, p. 29.
22. Ibid.
23. E. T. Cook and Alexander Wedderburn, eds., *The Works of John Ruskin*, London, 1903–12, vol. 35, pp. 367–68.
24. In Abse, *John Ruskin*, p. 165.
25. W. M. James, *The Order of Release*, London, 1947, p. 220.
26. John Rosenberg, *The Darkening Glass*, New York and London, 1961, p. 189 and fn. 4.
27. Bell, *John Ruskin*, p. 328.
28. Peter Quennell, *John Ruskin*, London, 1949, pp. 106–7.
29. Bell, *John Ruskin*, p. 101.
30. Wilenski, *John Ruskin*, p. 201.

31. John Ruskin, *Praeterita*, London, 1949, p. 7.
32. Ibid., pp. 7–8.
33. Note the identical sound of Ruskin's "pipes" and the nickname of Whistler's father, "Pipes."
34. Abse, *John Ruskin*, p. 328.
35. The original trial transcripts are no longer completely extant. What remains of them can be found in Laurie Adams, *Art on Trial*, New York, 1976; Whistler, *The Gentle Art*; H. Montgomery Hyde, *Their Good Names*, London, 1970; and Weintraub, op cit.
36. McMullen, *Victorian Outsider*, p. 179.
37. Bell, *John Ruskin*, p. 148.
38. Cf. Freud, "Character and Anal Erotism," S. E. IX, 1908, pp. 169–75.
39. Arturo Schwarz, "The Alchemist Stripped Bare in the Bachelor, Even," p. 81 and note 1, in Anne d'Harnoncourt and Kynaston McShine, *Marcel Duchamp*, New York and Philadelphia, 1973.

Bibliography

WORKS CITED

Books

Abse, Joan. *John Ruskin: The Passionate Moralist.* London, 1980.

Adams, Laurie. *Art on Trial.* New York, 1976.

Aelian. *On the Characteristics of Animals,* 3 vols., trans. A. T. Scholfield. Loeb Library Edition, Cambridge, Mass., and London, 1958–59.

Alberti, Leon Battista. *The Family in Renaissance Florence.* trans. Renée Neu Watkins, Columbia, S.C., 1969.

———. *Vita anonima.* in R. Fubini and A. M. Gallorini, "L'autobiografia de Leon Battista Alberti. Studio e edizione," *Rinasimento* XXII (December 1971): 69 ff.

———. *On Painting,* trans. John R. Spencer. New Haven and London, 1966.

———. *On the Art of Building in Ten Books,* trans. J. Rykwert, N. Leach, and R. Tavernor. Cambridge, Mass., and London, 1988.

Alpers, Svetlana. *Rembrandt's Enterprise.* Chicago and London, 1988.

Anzieu, Didier. *Freud's Self-Analysis.* Madison, Conn., 1986.

Arnheim, Rudolf. *Picasso's Guernica: The Genesis of a Painting.* Berkeley, 1962.

Augustine. *Confessions.* New York, 1961.

Aurigemma, L. *Il segno zodiacale dello scorpione nelle tradizioni occidentali.* Turin, 1976.

Bachelard, Gaston. *La Psychanalyse du feu.* Paris, 1949.

Barolsky, Paul. *Infinite Jest.* Columbia, S.C. and London, 1978.

———. *Michelangelo's Nose.* University Park and London, 1990.

———. *Why Mona Lisa Smiles and Other Tales by Vasari.* University Park and London, 1991.

———. *Giotto's Father and the Family of Vasari's Lives.* University Park and London, 1992.

Battisti, Eugenio. *Piero della Francesca,* 2 vols. Milan, 1971.

Bell, Quentin. *John Ruskin.* New York, 1978.

Bellori, G. P. *Le vite de' pittore, scultori et architetti moderni* (1672). Rome and Turin, 1976.

Bloom, Harold. *The Anxiety of Influence.* New York and London, 1973.

Borenius, Tancred. *Rembrandt: Selected Paintings.* London, 1942.

Brown, Jonathan. *Velázquez.* New Haven and London, 1986.

Bryson, Norman. *Vision and Painting.* New Haven and London, 1983.

Cellini, Benvenuto. *The Autobiography of Benvenuto Cellini*, trans. John Addington Symonds. New York, 1937.

Chipp, Herschel B. *Theories of Modern Art*. Berkeley and London, 1968.

Clark, Kenneth. *Leonardo da Vinci*. Harmondsworth, 1963.

——. *Henry Moore on Drawing*. London, 1974.

Deri, Susan. *Symbolization and Creativity*. New York, 1984.

Edgerton, Samuel Y., Jr. *Pictures and Punishment*. Ithaca and London, 1985.

Ehrenzweig, Anton. *The Hidden Order of Art*. Berkeley and Los Angeles, 1967.

Eissler, Kurt. *Leonardo da Vinci: Psychoanalytic Notes on the Enigma*. New York, 1961.

Eliade, Mircea. *The Forge and the Crucible*. New York and Evanston, 1971.

——. *A History of Religious Ideas*, 2 vols. Chicago, 1978.

Fenichel, Otto. *The Psychoanalytic Theory of Neurosis*. New York, 1945.

Freedberg, David. *The Power of Images*. Chicago, 1989.

Freud, Anna. *The Ego and the Mechanisms of Defense*. New York, 1966.

Freud, Anna, and Burlingham, Dorothy T. *War and Children*. New York, 1945.

Freud, Sigmund. *The Complete Psychological Works of Sigmund Freud*, 24 vols. London, 1953–73.

Fuller, Peter. *Art and Psychoanalysis*. London, 1980.

Funk and Wagnalls Standard Dictionary of Folklore, Mythology, and Legend. New York, 1950.

Garrard, Mary D. *Artemisia Gentileschi*. Princeton, 1989.

Gedo, John. *Portraits of the Artist*. New York and London, 1983.

Gedo, Mary. *Picasso: Art as Autobiography*. Chicago, 1980.

Geist, Sidney. *Brancusi: A Study of the Sculpture*. New York, 1968.

——. *Brancusi: The Sculpture and Drawings*. New York, 1975.

——. *Brancusi: The Kiss*. New York, 1978.

Ghiselin, Brewster. *The Creative Process*. Los Angeles, 1952.

Ghiberti, Lorenzo. *Commentari*. Naples, 1947.

Golzio, Vincenzo. *Raffaello ne documenti, nelle testimonianze dei contemporanei e nella letteratura del suo secolo*. Vatican, 1936.

Graetz, H. R. *The Symbolic Language of Vincent van Gogh*. London, 1963.

Greenacre, Phyllis. *Swift and Carroll*. New York, 1977.

Groenewegen-Frankfort, H. A. *Arrest and Movement*. New York, 1978 (first published London, 1951).

Grolnick, Simon A., and W. Muensterberger, eds. *Between Reality and Fantasy*. New York and London, 1978.

Held, Julius S. *Rembrandt's "Aristotle."* Princeton, 1969.

Hesiod. *The Homeric Hymns and Homerica*. trans. H. G. Evelyn-White, Loeb Library Edition, Cambridge, Mass., and London, 1982.

Hibbard, Howard. *Michelangelo*. New York, 1974.

——. *Caravaggio*. New York, 1983.

Hobbs, R. *Robert Smithson: Sculpture*. Ithaca and London, 1981.

Homer. *The Iliad*, 2 vols., trans. A. T. Murray. Loeb Library Edition, Cambridge, Mass., and London, 1978–85.

——. *The Odyssey*, 2 vols., trans. A. T. Murray. Loeb Library Edition, Cambridge, Mass., and London, 1980–84.

Hyde, Montgomery H. *Their Good Names*. London, 1970.

James, W. M. *The Order of Release*. London, 1947.

Johns, Catherine. *Sex or Symbol*. Austin, 1982.

Johnson, Crockett. *Barnaby*. New York, 1975.

Jones, Ernest. *Essays in Applied Psychoanalysis*, 2 vols. New York, 1964.

————. *The Life and Work of Sigmund Freud,* 3 vols. New York, 1953–57.

Jung, Carl G. *Psychology and Alchemy* (1944), in *Collected Works,* vol. II. New York, 1953.

Kemp, Martin, ed. *Leonardo on Painting.* New Haven and London, 1989.

Kohut, Heinz. *The Restoration of the Self.* New York, 1977.

Kramer, Samuel Noah. *The Sumerians.* Chicago and London, 1963.

Kris, Ernst. *Psychoanalytic Explorations in Art.* New York, 1952.

Kris, Ernst, and Otto Kurz. *Legend, Myth, and Magic in the Image of the Artist* (1934). New Haven and London, 1979.

Kristeva, Julia. *Desire in Language.* New York, 1980.

Lacan, Jacques. *Ecrits.* Paris, 1949.

————. *Speech and Language in Psychoanalysis.* Baltimore, 1968.

————. *The Four Fundamental Concepts of Psychoanalysis.* New York, 1981.

Laplanche, J., and J.-B. Pontalis. *The Language of Psychoanalysis.* New York, 1973.

Lavin, Marilyn Aronberg, *The Place of Narrative.* Chicago and London, 1990.

Liebert, Robert, M.D. *Michelangelo: A Psychoanalytic Study of His Life and Images.* New Haven and London, 1983.

Lightbown, Ronald. *Mantegna.* Berkeley and London, 1986.

————. *Piero della Francesca,* New York, 1992.

Lubin, Albert J. *Stranger on the Earth.* New York, 1972.

MacCurdy, E., ed. *The Notebooks of Leonardo da Vinci.* New York, 1956.

Mahler, Margaret, Fred Pine. and Anni Bergmann, *The Psychological Birth of the Human Infant.* New York, 1975.

McMullen, Roy. *Victorian Outsider.* New York, 1973.

Meiss, Millard. *Painting in Florence and Siena After the Black Death.* Princeton, 1951.

Melville, Robert. *Henry Moore.* New York, n.d.

Merejkowksi, Dimitri. *The Romance of Leonardo da Vinci.* New York, 1928.

Metropolitan Museum of Art, New York. *The Age of Caravaggio.* New York, 1985.

Moore, Henry. *Henry Moore.* London, 1944.

Moore, Henry and J. Hedgecoe. *Henry Moore.* New York, 1968.

Nash, Jane Clinton. *Titian's "Poésie" for Philip II.* Baltimore, 1986.

Neumann, Erich. *The Great Mother.* New York, 1965.

Niederland, William G. *The Schreber Case.* New York, 1974.

Nunberg, Herman, and Ernst Federn, eds., *Minutes of the Vienna Psychoanalytic Society,* vol. 1, 1906–8. New York, 1962.

Ovid. *Metamorphoses,* 2 vols., trans. Frank Justus Miller. Loeb Library Edition, Cambridge, Mass., and London, 1984.

Pandrea, Petre. *Brancusi, Amintira Si Exegeze.* Bucharest, 1967.

Panofsky, Erwin. *Studies in Iconology.* New York, 1962.

Pater, Walter. *The Renaissance.* Berkeley and Los Angeles, 1980.

Pennell, Joseph and Elizabeth. *The Life of James McNeill Whistler.* Philadelphia, 1908.

————. *The Whistler Journal.* Philadelphia, 1921.

Pliny. *Natural History,* 10 vols., trans. H. Rackham, W. H. S. Jones, and D. E. Eichholz. Loeb Library Edition, Cambridge, Mass., and London, 1971–84.

Pope-Hennessy, John. *Cellini.* New York, 1985.

Praz, Mario. *The Romantic Agony.* Oxford and New York, 1983.

Proust, Marcel. *What Art Is,* publication commemorating the twentieth anniversary of the Proust Group, New York, 1991.

Quennell, Peter. *John Ruskin.* London, 1949.

Quintilian. *De institutione oratoriae,* 4 vols., trans. H. E. Butler. Loeb Library Edition, Cambridge, Mass., and London, 1979.

Rank, Otto. *The Double*. Chapel Hill, 1971.

Rewald, John, ed. *Paul Cézanne: Letters*. London, 1941.

Richter, Hans. *Dada*. New York and Toronto, 1978.

Rose, Gilbert. *The Power of Form*. New York, 1980.

Rosenberg, John. *The Darkening Glass*. New York and London, 1961.

Roskill, Mark W. *Dolce's "Aretino" and Venetian Art Theory of the Cinquecento*. New York, 1968.

Ruskin, John. *Praeterita*. London, 1949.

———. *Fors Clavigera*. 4 vols., New York, 1968.

———. *Works*, 35 vols. E. T. Cook and A. Wedderburn, eds. London, 1903–12.

Saslow, James. *Ganymede in the Renaissance*. New Haven and London, 1986.

Saussure, Ferdinand de. *Course in General Linguistics*, trans. Wade Baskin. New York, 1966.

Schapiro, Meyer. *Modern Art: 19th and 20th Centuries*. New York, 1978.

Schneider, Daniel E. *The Psychoanalyst and the Artist*. New York, 1950.

Schwartz, Gary. *Rembrandt: His Life, His Paintings*. New York, 1985.

Schwarz, Arturo. *The Complete Works of Marcel Duchamp*. New York, 1969.

Stammler, Wolfgang. *Frau Welt: Eine mittelalterliche Allegorie*. Freiburg, 1959.

Stechow, Wolfgang. *Bruegel*. New York, 1990.

Steinberg, Leo. *Other Criteria*. New York and London, 1972.

———. *Michelangelo's Last Paintings*. New York, 1975.

Tolnay, Charles de. *Michelangelo*, 5 vols. Princeton, 1943–60.

Vasari, Giorgio. *Lives of the Most Eminent Painters, Sculptors, and Architects*, 3 vols., trans. Gaston du Vere. New York, 1979.

Virgil. *Aeneid*, 2 vols., trans. H. R. Fairclough. Loeb Library Edition, Cambridge, Mass., and London, 1986.

Weintraub, Stanley. *Whistler*. New York, 1974.

Whistler, James McNeill. *The Gentle Art of Making Enemies*. London, 1892.

Wilenski, R. H. *John Ruskin*. London, 1933.

Winnicott, D. W. *Playing and Reality*. New York, 1971.

———. *The Maturational Processes and the Facilitating Environment*. New York, 1965.

———. *Therapeutic Consultations in Child Psychiatry*. New York, 1971.

Wittkower, Rudolf and Margot. *Born Under Saturn*. New York, 1963.

Wollheim, Richard. *Painting as an Art*. Princeton, 1987.

Articles

Abraham, Karl. "Restrictions and Transformations of Scopophilia in Psycho-Neurotics; with Remarks on Analogous Phenomena in Folk-Psychology" (1913), in his *Selected Papers on Psychoanalysis*, New York, reprint of 1927 edition.

Adams, Laurie. "Les Sanson: An Oedipal Footnote to the History of France," *Psychoanalytic Study of Society* 10 (1984): 227–48.

———. "Apollo and Marsyas: A Metaphor of Creative Conflict," *The Psychoanalytic Review* 75, no. 2 (Summer 1988): 319–38.

———. "The Myth of Athena and Arachne: Some Oedipal and Pre-Oedipal Aspects of Creative Challenge in Women and Their Implications for the Interpretation of *Las Meninas* by Velázquez," *International Journal of Psychoanalysis* 71 (1990): 597–609.

Almansi, Renato. "The Breast-Face Equation," *Journal of the American Psychoanalytic Association* 8 (1951): 43–70.

Arlow, Jacob A. "Pyromania and the Primal Scene: A Psychoanalytic Comment on the Work of Yukio Mishima," *Psychoanalytic Quarterly* 47 (1978): 24–51.

Arnheim, Rudolf. "The Holes of Henry Moore," *Journal of Aesthetics and Art Criticism* 7, no. 1 (1948): 29–38.

Barb, A. A. "Diva Matrix," *Journal of the Warburg and Courtauld Institutes* XVI (1953): 193–238.

Barolsky, Paul and Andrew Ladis. "The 'Pleasurable Deceits' of Bronzino's So-called London *Allegory*," *Source* X, no. 3 (Spring 1991): 32–36.

Baudry, Francis. "An Essay on Method in Applied Psychoanalysis," *Psychoanalytic Quarterly* LIII (1984): 551–81.

Beck, James. "Ser Piero da Vinci and his Son Leonardo," *Source: Notes in the History of Art* V, no. 1 (Fall 1985): 29–32.

Beckson, Karl. "Oscar Wilde and the Masks of Narcissus," *Psychoanalytic Study of Society* 10 (1984): 249–67.

Bernfeld, Suzanne Cassirer. "Freud and Archeology," *American Imago* (1951): 107–21.

Bois, Ive-Alain. "Painting as Trauma," *Art in America* 76 (June 1988): 131–73.

Braagman, Louis J. "The Case of John Ruskin: A Study in Cyclothymia," *American Journal of Psychiatry* XCL (1935): 1137–59.

Brendel, Otto J. "Classic and Non-Classic Elements in Picasso's *Guernica*," in Whitney J. Oates, ed., *The Present-day Vitality of the Classical Tradition from Sophocles to Picasso*, Bloomington, 1961.

Chipp, Herschel. "*Guernica:* Love, War and the Bullfight," *Art Journal* 33, no. 2 (Winter 1973–74): 100–15.

Davis, Howard McP. "Gravity in the Paintings of Giotto" (1971), in Laurie Schneider, ed., *Giotto in Perspective*, Englewood Cliffs, 1974, pp. 142–59.

Devereux, George. "The Self-Blinding of Oidipous in Sophokles: *Oidipous Tyrannos*," *Journal of Hellenic Studies* XCIII (1973): 36–49.

Emmens, J. A. "Las Ménines de Velázquez. Miroir des princes pour Philippe IV," *Nederlands Kunsthistorisch Jaarboek* 12 (1961): 51–79.

Ferenczi, Sandor. "Symbolism" (1912), in his *First Contributions to the Theory and Technique of Psychoanalysis*, New York, 1980.

———. "Stages in the Development of Reality" (1913), in his *First Contributions to the Theory and Technique of Psychoanalysis*, New York, 1980.

———. "On the Symbolism of the Head of Medusa" (1923), in Ferenczi, *Further Contributions to the Theory and Technique of Psychoanalysis*, London, 1926.

———. "The Dream of the Clever Baby" (1923), in Ferenczi, *Further Contributions to the Theory and Technique of Psychoanalysis*, London, 1926, pp. 349–50.

Geist, Sidney. "What Makes the Black Clock Run?" *Art International* 22, no. 2 (1978): 8–14.

———. "Brancusi's *Bird in Space:* A Psychological Reading," *Source: Notes in the History of Art* III, no. 3 (Spring 1984): 30.

Gottlieb, Carla. "Picasso's *Girl Before a Mirror*," *Journal of Aesthetics and Art Criticism* 24 (1966): 509–18.

Greenacre, Phyllis. "The Family Romance of the Artist" (1958), in Greenacre, *Emotional Growth*, vol. 2, New York, 1971, pp. 479–504.

———. "The Childhood of the Artist" (1957), in Greenacre, *Emotional Growth*, vol. 2, New York, 1971, pp. 505–32.

———. "The Relation of the Impostor to the Artist (1958), in Greenacre, *Emotional Growth*, vol. 2, New York, 1971, Chapter 26.

———. "Play in Relation to Creative Imagination" (1959), in Greenacre, *Emotional Growth*, vol. 2, New York, 1971, Chapter 27.

Guinan, Ann. "The Perils of High Living: Divinatory Rhetoric in Summa Alu," in Hermann Behrens, Darlene Loding, and Martha T. Roth, eds., *DUMU-E.-DUB-BA-A: Studies in*

Honor of Ake W. Sjöberg, Occasional Publications of the Samuel Noah Kramer Fund, vol. 11, Philadelphia, 1989, pp. 227–35.

Guinan, Ann Kessler. "The Human Behavioral Omens: On the Threshold of Psychological Inquiry," *BCSMS,* (Bulletin of the Canadian Society for Mesopotamian Studies) 19, Toronto, 1990, pp. 9–13.

Jones, Ernest. "The Theory of Symbolism," in Jones, *Papers on Psycho-Analysis,* London, 1950.

Kahr, Madlyn. "Delilah," *Art Bulletin* LIV, no. 3 (September 1972): 282–99.

Kulturmann, U. "William Holman Hunt's *The Lady of Shallott,*" *Pantheon* 38 (1980): 386–92.

Kuspit, Donald. "A Mighty Metaphor: The Analogy of Archaeology and Psychoanalysis," in *Sigmund Freud and Art,* London, 1989, pp. 133–51.

Lewin, Bertram D. "The Body as Phallus," *Psychoanalytic Quarterly* II (1933): 24–47.

Meiss, Millard. "Light as Form and Symbol in Some Fifteenth-Century Paintings" (1945), in Meiss, *The Painter's Choice,* New York, 1976.

Mohacsy, Ildiko. "The Many Faces of Love," *Contemporary Psychoanalysis* 2, no. 1 (1992): 89–96.

Muller, John. "Lacan's Mirror Stage," *Psychoanalytic Inquiry* 5, no. 2 (1985): 233–52.

Niederland, William. "Clinical Aspects of Creativity," *American Imago* 24 (1967): 6–34.

———. "Psychoanalytic Approaches to Artistic Creativity," *Psychoanalytic Quarterly* 45 (1976): 185–212.

Noy, Pinchas. "A Theory of Art and Aesthetic Experience," *Psychoanalytic Review* 55 (1968): 623–45.

———. "About Art and Artistic Talent," *International Journal of Psychoanalysis* 53 (1972): 243–48.

Orso, Steven. "A Lesson Learned: *Las Méninas* and the State Portraits of Juan Carreno de Miranda," *Record of The Art Museum of Princeton University* 41 (1982): 24–34.

Poseq, Avigdor W. "Bernini's Self-Portraits as David," *Source: Notes in the History of Art* IX, no. 4 (Summer 1990): 14–22.

———. "Soutine's Paraphrases of Rembrandt's *Slaughtered Ox,*" *Konsthistorisk Tidskrift* LX, Hafte 3–4 (1991): 210–22.

Posner, Donald. "Caravaggio's Homo-Erotic Early Works," *Art Quarterly,* Autumn 1971, pp. 301–24.

Rosenblum, Robert. "The Origin of Painting: A Problem in the Iconography of Romantic Classicism," *Art Bulletin* 39, no. 4 (December 1957): 279–90.

Ruskin, John. "The Late John Ruskin's Illness Described by Himself," *British Medical Journal* 1, January 27, 1900, pp. 225–26.

Schapiro, Meyer. "Two Slips of Leonardo and a Slip of Freud," *Psychoanalysis* 2 (1955): 3–8.

———. "Leonardo and Freud: An Art-Historical Study," *Journal of the History of Ideas* XVII, no. 2 (April 1956): 147–78.

Schneider, Laurie. "The Iconography of Piero della Francesca's Frescoes Illustrating the Legend of the True Cross in the Church of San Francesco in Arezzo," *Art Quarterly* 32, no. 1 (1969): 22–48.

———. "Ms. Medusa: Transformations of a Bisexual Image," *Psychoanalytic Study of Society* 9 (1981): 105–53.

———. "Everything Black, Everything White," *Art History* 5, no. 2 (June 1982): 166–79.

———. "Butterfly or Scorpion: A Note on the Iconography of Whistler's Signatures," *Source: Notes in the History of Art* II, no. 2 (Winter 1983): 26–29.

———. "A Note on the Iconography of Henry Moore's *King and Queen,*" *Source: Notes in the History of Art* II, no. 4 (Summer 1983): 29–32.

———. "The Theme of Mother and Child in the Art of Henry Moore," *Psychoanalytic*

Perspectives on Art 1 (1985): 241–65.

———. "Shadow Metaphors and Piero della Francesca's Arezzo *Annunciation*," *Source: Notes in the History of Art* V, no. 1 (Fall 1985): 18–22.

———. "Leon Battista Alberti: Some Biographical Implications of the Winged Eye," *Art Bulletin* LXXII, no. 2 (June 1990): 261–70.

Schneider, Laurie, and Jack Flam. "Visual Convention, Simile and Metaphor in the *Mona Lisa*," *Storia dell'Arte*, no. 29 (1977): 15–24.

Schwarz, Arturo. "The Alchemist Stripped Bare in the Bachelor, Even," in Anne d'Harnoncourt and Kynaston McShine, eds., *Marcel Duchamp*, Philadelphia and New York, 1973, pp. 81–98.

Spector, Jack. "The State of Psychoanalytic Research in Art History," *Art Bulletin* LXX (March 1988): 47–76.

Steinberg, Leo. "Michelangelo's *Last Judgment* as Merciful Heresy," *Art in America*, November–December 1975, pp. 48–63.

———. "The Line of Fate in Michelangelo's Painting," *Critical Inquiry* 6, no. 3 (Spring 1980): 411–54.

———. "A Corner of the *Last Judgment*," *Daedalus* 109, no. 2 (Spring 1980): 207–73.

———. "Velázquez's *Las Meninas*," *October* 19 (1981): 45–54.

———. "The Sexuality of Christ in Renaissance Art and Modern Oblivion," *October* 25 (Summer 1983).

———. "Shrinking Michelangelo," *New York Review of Books*, June 28, 1984, pp. 41–46.

Sterba, R. and E. "The Anxieties of Michelangelo Buonarroti" *International Journal of Psychoanalysis* 37 (1956): 7–11.

———. "The Personality of Michelangelo Buonarroti: Some Reflections," *American Imago* 35 (1978): 156–77.

Stragnell, Gregory. "The Golden Phallus," *Psychoanalytic Review* XI (1924): 292–323.

Szaluta, Jacques. "Freud's Ego Ideals: A Study of Admired Historical and Political Personages," *Journal of the American Psychoanalytic Association* 31, no. 1, (1983) pp. 157–85.

Volk, M. C. "On Velázquez and the Liberal Arts," *Art Bulletin* LX (1978): 69–86.

Waelder, Robert. "The Principle of Multiple Function: Observations on Overdetermination," *Psychoanalytic Quarterly* 5 (1936): 45–62.

Walsh, Maurice N. "Notes on the Neurosis of Leonardo da Vinci," *Psychoanalytic Quarterly* 30 (1961): 232–42.

Watkins, Renée Neu. "L. B. Alberti's Emblem, the Winged Eye, and His Name, Leo," *Mitteilungen des kunsthistorischen Instituts in Florenz* IX (1960): 256–58.

Watson, Paul. "The Cement of Fiction: Giovanni Boccaccio and the Painters of Florence," *Modern Language Notes* 99, no. 1 (January 1984): 43–64.

Whistler, James McNeill. "Whistler's Ten O'Clock" (1885), in Robin Spencer, ed., *Whistler: A Retrospective*, New York, 1989, pp. 212–27.

Zucker, Mark. "Raphael and the Beard of Pope Julius II," *Art Bulletin* LIX (1977): 524–33.

SUGGESTIONS FOR FURTHER READING

Books

Barolsky, Paul. *Walter Pater's Renaissance*, University Park and London, 1987.

Bergmann, Martin S. *In the Shadow of Moloch*. New York, 1992.

Bersani, Leo. *The Freudian Body: Psychoanalysis and Art*. New York, 1986.

Bonaparte, Marie. *Female Sexuality*. New York, 1953.

Bowie, T., and C. V. Christensen, eds. *Studies in Erotic Art.* New York, 1970.

Broude, Norma, and Mary D. Garrard. *The Expanding Discourse.* New York, 1992.

Chasseguet-Smirgel, Janine. *Creativity and Perversion.* New York and London, 1985.

Chipp, Herschel B. *Picasso's "Guernica,"* Berkeley and London, 1988.

Cohen, Kathleen. *Metamorphosis of a Death Symbol: The Transi Tomb in the Late Middle Ages and Renaissance.* Berkeley and London, 1973.

Colterra, Joseph T., ed. *Lives, Events and Other Players.* New York and London, 1981.

Coudert, Allison. *Alchemy.* Boulder, 1980.

Devereux, George. *Dreams in Greek Tragedy.* Berkeley and Los Angeles, 1976.

Elworthy, Fredrick Thomas. *The Evil Eye.* New York, 1958.

Fine, Elsa Honig. *Women and Art.* New York, 1978.

Finegan, Jack. *Light from the Ancient Past,* vol. I. Princeton, 1959.

Foucault, Michel. *This Is Not a Pipe.* Berkeley and London, 1982.

Gedo, Mary, ed. *Psychoanalytic Perspectives on Art,* 3 vols. Hillsdale, N.J., 1985–88.

Geist, Sidney. *Interpreting Cézanne.* Cambridge, Mass., 1988.

Heyd, Milly. *Aubrey Beardsley.* New York and Bern, 1986.

Hirn, Yrjo. *The Sacred Shrine.* London, 1912.

Kuhns, Richard. *Psychoanalytic Theory of Art.* New York, 1983.

Legge, Elizabeth. *Max Ernst: The Psychoanalytic Sources.* Ann Arbor, 1981.

Metz, Christian. *The Imaginary Signifier.* Bloomington, 1977.

Murdoch, Iris. *The Fire and the Sun: Why Plato Banished the Artists.* Harmondsworth, 1990.

Neumann, Erich. *The Archetypal World of Henry Moore.* Princeton, 1959.

———. *Art and the Creative Unconscious.* Princeton, 1974.

Pollock, G., and J. M. Ross, eds. *The Oedipus Papers.* Madison, Conn., 1988.

Scully, Vincent. *The Earth, the Temple and the Gods.* New Haven and London, 1962.

Sharpe, Ella Freeman. *Collected Papers on Psychoanalysis.* New York, 1978.

Smith, E. Baldwin. *The Dome.* Princeton, 1950.

Wind, Edgar. *Pagan Mysteries in the Renaissance.* New Haven, 1958.

Articles

Barb, A. A. "Antaura: The Mermaid and the Devil's Grandmother," *Journal of the Warburg and Courtauld Institutes* 29 (1966): 1–23.

Beres, David. "The Contribution of Psycho-Analysis to the Biography of the Artist: A Commentary on Methodology," *International Journal of Psychoanalysis,* vol. 40, pp. 26–37.

Bergmann, Martin. "Limitations of Method in Psychoanalytic Biography," *Journal of the American Psychoanalytic Association* 21 (1973): 833–50.

Bonaparte, Marie. "Notes on the Analytic Discovery of a Primal Scene," *Psychoanalytic Study of the Child* I (1945): 119–25.

Bonfante, Larissa. "Nudity as a Costume in Classical Art," *American Journal of Archaeology* 93, no. 4 (October 1989): 543–70.

Eager, Gerald. "Born Under Mars: Caravaggio's Self-Portraits and the Dada Spirit in Art," *Source: Notes in the History of Art* V, no. 2 (Winter 1986): 22–27.

Geist, Sidney. "The Secret Life of Paul Cézanne," *Art International* 19 (1975): 7–16.

Greenacre, Phyllis. "Vision, Headache, and the Halo," in Greenacre, *Trauma, Growth and Personality,* New York, 1952, Chapter 6.

———. "A Contribution to the Study of Screen Memories," *Trauma, Growth and Personality,* New York, 1952, Chapter 9.

———. "Play in Relation to Creative Imagination," in *The Psychoanalytic Study of the Child*

14 (1959): 61–80.

Havelock, Christine. "Plato and Winckelmann: Ideological Bias in the History of Greek Art," *Source: Notes in the History of Art* V, no. 2 (Winter 1986): 1–6.

Klein, Melanie. "Infantile Anxiety-Situations in a Work of Art and in the Creative Impulse," in Klein, *Contributions to Psycho-Analysis,* London, 1929.

Kohen, Max. "The Venus of Willendorf," *American Imago* 3 (1942–46): 49–60.

Mohacsy, Ildiko. "Fusion and Anxiety: Children's Drawings and Renaissance Art," *Journal of the American Academy of Psychoanalysis* 4 (1976): 501–14.

Oremland, J. "Michelangelo's *Pietas,*" *The Psychoanalytic Study of the Child* 33 (1978): 563–91.

———. "Mourning and Its Effect on Michelangelo's Art," *Annual of Psychoanalysis* 8 (1980): 317–51.

Pfister, Oskar. "Kryptolalie, Kryptographie und unbewusstes Vexierbild bei Normalen," *Jahrbuch für psychoanalytische und psychopathologische Forschungen* 5 (1913): 117–56.

Reff, Theodore. "The Bather with Outstretched Arms," *Gazette des Beaux-Arts,* March 1962, pp. 173–90.

———. "Cézanne, Flaubert, St. Anthony and the Queen of Sheba," *Art Bulletin* 44 (1962): 113–25.

———. "Cézanne's Dream of Hannibal," *Art Bulletin* 45 (1963): 148–52.

———. "Cézanne and Hercules," *Art Bulletin* 48 (1966): 35–44.

Riess, Anneliese. "The Mother's Eye: For Better and for Worse," *The Psychoanalytic Study of the Child* 33 (1978): 381–409.

———. "The Power of the Eye in Nature, Nurture, and Culture: A Developmental View of the Mutual Gaze," *The Psychoanalytic Study of the Child* 43 (1988): 399–421.

Rose, Gilbert. "Body Ego and the Creative Imagination," *Journal of the American Psychoanalytic Association* 11 (1963): 775–89.

Schapiro, Meyer. "Muscipula Diaboli: An Art Historical Study," *Journal of the History of Ideas* 17 (1956): 147–78.

Schneider, Laurie. "Donatello and Caravaggio: The Iconography of Decapitation," *American Imago* 33, no. 1 (Spring 1976): 76–91.

———. "Raphael's Personality," *Source: Notes in the History of Art* III, no. 2 (Winter 1984): 2–22.

———. "Mirrors in Art," *Psychoanalytic Inquiry* V, no. 2 (1985): 293–324.

Szaluta, Jacques. "Freud on Bismarck: Hanns Sachs' *Interpretation of a Dream,*" *American Imago* 37, no. 2 (Summer 1980): 215–44.

Trosman, Harry. "Freud's Cultural Background," *Psychological Issues* IX, nos. 2/3 (1976): 46–70.

Wilson, Laurie. "Louise Nevelson: Personal History and Art," *American Journal of Art Therapy* 20, no. 3 (1981): 79–97.

Wolf, Ernest S. "Saxa Loquuntur: Artistic Aspects of Freud's 'The Aetiology of Hysteria,'" *Psychological Issues* IX, nos. 2/3 (1976): 208–28.

Index

NOTE: Page numbers in italics refer to illustrations.

DATE DUE

MAR 25 1994	